A Research Agenda for Place Branding

T0327383

Elgar Research Agendas outline the future of research in a given area. Leading scholars are given the space to explore their subject in provocative ways, and map out the potential directions of travel. They are relevant but also visionary.

Forward-looking and innovative, Elgar Research Agendas are an essential resource for PhD students, scholars and anybody who wants to be at the forefront of research.

Titles in the series include:

A Research Agenda for Knowledge Management and Analytics
Edited by Jay Liebowitz

A Research Agenda for Heritage Tourism
Edited by Maria Gravari-Barbas

A Research Agenda for Border Studies
Edited by James W. Scott

A Research Agenda for Sales
Edited by Fernando Jaramillo and Jay Prakash Mulki

A Research Agenda for Employee Engagement in a Changing World of Work
Edited by John P. Meyer and Benjamin Schneider

A Research Agenda for the Entrepreneurial University
Edited by Ulla Hytti

A Research Agenda for Place Branding
Edited by Dominic Medway, Gary Warnaby and John Byrom

A Research Agenda for Place Branding

Edited by

DOMINIC MEDWAY
Manchester Metropolitan University, UK

GARY WARNABY
Manchester Metropolitan University, UK

JOHN BYROM
University of Liverpool, UK

Elgar Research Agendas

Cheltenham, UK • Northampton, MA, USA

Published by
Edward Elgar Publishing Limited
The Lypiatts
15 Lansdown Road
Cheltenham
Glos GL50 2JA
UK

Edward Elgar Publishing, Inc.
William Pratt House
9 Dewey Court
Northampton
Massachusetts 01060
USA

Paperback edition 2022

A catalogue record for this book
is available from the British Library

Library of Congress Control Number: 2021932422

This book is available electronically in the **Elgar**online
Geography, Planning and Tourism subject collection
http://dx.doi.org/10.4337/9781839102851

MIX
Paper from
responsible sources
FSC   FSC® C013604
www.fsc.org

ISBN 978 1 83910 284 4 (cased)
ISBN 978 1 83910 285 1 (eBook)
ISBN 978 1 0353 0679 4 (paperback)

Printed and bound by CPI Group (UK) Ltd, Croydon, CR0 4YY

Contents

Figures

Tables

Contributors

Raoul Beunen is Associate Professor of Environmental Governance at the Open University, the Netherlands. His research explores the potentials and limitations of environmental policy and planning from the perspective of adaptive governance and sustainability. It focuses on innovation and evolution in governance, paying attention to the dynamics of policy implementation and integration, multi-level governance, stakeholder involvement, and the performance of institutional structures.

Stephen Brown is lost. He can be found wandering the condemned corridors of Ulster University's Jordanstown campus, wondering where it all went wrong. Empty, eerie, impossible to escape, the management school maze is slowly driving him mad. Some compare him to Jack Nicholson in *The Shining* – 'Heeere's Stevie!' – others say he's harmless, let him be. With his *Rough Guide to Rough Guides* in hand, he'd really rather not be disturbed.

John Byrom is Senior Lecturer in Marketing at the University of Liverpool Management School. His research interests include place management, retail marketing, and consumer behaviour. His research has been published in *Sociology, European Journal of Marketing, Journal of Business Research, Marketing Theory,* and *Cities,* amongst others. He is Co-Editor of *Case Studies in Food Retailing and Distribution* (2019) and has also authored chapters in edited books covering various aspects of marketing.

Adriana Campelo is Director of Resilience for the City of Salvador, Brazil, and Chief Resilience Officer as part of the Global Resilient Cities Network. She led the Salvador Resilience Strategy and the Climate Action Adaptation and Mitigation Plan. She holds a PhD in Marketing Management from the University of Otago in New Zealand. Her work and research includes place making and branding, urban resilience and sustainability, and sustainable development.

Cecilia Cassinger is Associate Professor of Strategic Communication at Lund University, Sweden. Her research currently concerns the transformative potential of place branding and communication strategies to mitigate conflicts in places. She has published articles in journals such as *Place Branding and Public Diplomacy*, *Journal of Place Management and Development*, *International Journal of Tourism Cities*, and *European Journal of Cultural Studies*; and she co-edited *The Nordic Wave in Place Branding* and *The Routledge Companion to Media and Tourism*.

Jack Coffin is Lecturer in Marketing at the University of Manchester. His research interests include the unconscious, spatiality, and posthumanism. Indeed, the overlap between these three areas of inquiry might be described as Dr Coffin's academic USP.

Simon Cryer completed a Master's by Research in the field of human geography and place management in 2017, where he investigated mitigation of the barriers preventing routinised engagement with urban green spaces. He is concluding a PhD at Manchester Metropolitan University, conducting research into the consumption of place through the non-visual senses and the potentialities for place marketing and place management practices. Simon is a lecturer and tutor in marketing and brand management.

Tim Edensor is Professor of Human Geography at the Institute of Place Management, Manchester Metropolitan University. He has written about tourism, national identity, industrial ruins, rhythmanalysis, walking, urban theory, creativity, and football. More recently, he has authored *From Light to Dark: Daylight, Illumination and Gloom* (2017) and *Stone: Stories of Urban Materiality* (2020). He is also Co-Editor of *The Routledge Handbook of Place* (2020), *Rethinking Darkness: Cultures, Histories, Practices* (2020), and *Weather: Spaces, Mobilities and Affects* (2020).

Aram Eisenschitz is Senior Lecturer in the Department of Marketing, Branding and Tourism at Middlesex University Business School. He currently teaches on the tourism programme and has published widely in the fields of urban regeneration, social exclusion, and the political economy of tourism and place marketing. Before joining Middlesex University he was previously Planning Advisor at the London Chamber of Commerce.

Szilvia Gyimóthy is Associate Professor in Tourism Marketing at Copenhagen Business School. Her research is focused on how tourism is shaping places and place-making practices in the wake of global mobility and mediatised travel. Szilvia's research projects bridge the fields of market communication and branding, tourism geography, and consumer culture studies; exploring, among others, the Nordic terroir, adventure sports, Bollywood films, and the marketisation of social relationships in communitarian businesses.

Henrik Halkier is Professor of Tourism and Regional Development, and Dean of the Faculty of Humanities, at Aalborg University, Denmark.

Sonya Hanna is Lecturer in Marketing at Bangor Business School. Her research interests are focused on the marketing and branding of places and the process of strategic place brand management. Her more recent publications look in greater detail at the components of the strategic process, including place brand personality, place brand communications and their co-creation in the digital arena, and the alignment of stakeholder objectives and brand architecture.

Andrea Insch is Associate Professor at the University of Otago, New Zealand. Before undertaking her doctorate at Griffith University in Brisbane, Andrea worked at Queensland's Department of State Development. In 2005 Andrea moved to New Zealand to join the Marketing Department at the Otago Business School. Andrea's research expertise is interdisciplinary, connecting marketing, urban studies, and tourism. Andrea is the Book Review Editor and Regional Editor (Australia and New Zealand) for *Place Branding and Public Diplomacy*.

Laura James is Associate Professor of Tourism and Regional Change at Aalborg University, Denmark. Her research interests include destination development, tourism policy, and sustainability issues in tourism. She has previously written about 'green' place branding and policy tourism.

Mihalis Kavaratzis is Associate Professor of Marketing at the University of Leicester School of Business and holds a PhD on City Marketing. Mihalis is Co-Founder of the International Place Branding Association and a Senior Fellow of the Institute of Place Management. He has published some of the most cited work in the field and has co-edited (amongst others) *Inclusive Place Branding* (with M. Giovanardi and M. Lichrou, 2017) and *Rethinking Place Branding* (with G. Warnaby and G.J. Ashworth, 2015).

Brendan James Keegan is Senior Lecturer in Digital Marketing at Manchester Metropolitan University. Interested in digital place making, digital and social media analytics, and agency–client relationships, his research has been published in various journals including *European Journal of Marketing, European*

Management Review, and *Management Decision.* Brendan is the principal investigator for the GOGREEN ROUTES Horizon 2020 project, investigating the role of digital place making and its relationship with the psychology of wellbeing through interconnected green corridors in public spaces.

Nicole Koenig-Lewis is Associate Professor in Marketing at Cardiff University's Business School. Her research interests include drivers and barriers to sustainable consumer behaviour, festivals, and visitor experiences with a focus on engagement, emotions, and attitudes. Her work has been published in journals such as *Annals of Tourism Research, Tourism Management, Journal of Services Marketing,* and *Journal of Business Research.* She is Co-Editor of *Public Value: Deepening, Enriching, and Broadening the Theory and Practice* (2019).

Maria Lichrou is Lecturer in Marketing at the University of Limerick Kemmy Business School. Her research builds on critical marketing and consumer research perspectives, with a focus on tourism, place, and consumption. Recent publications include work in *Tourism Management, European Journal of Marketing, Journal of Place Management and Development,* and the *Journal of Macromarketing.*

Andrea Lucarelli is Associate Professor at Stockholm Business School, Stockholm University. Andrea's main research interests are related to the geographical, political, and historical dimensions of consumption, advertising, and marketing, the politics of marketing, and the role of techno-digital culture in the construction of market and sport-related phenomena.

Dominic Medway is Professor of Marketing in the Institute of Place Management at Manchester Metropolitan University. Dominic's work is primarily concerned with the complex interactions between places, spaces, and those who manage and consume them, reflecting his academic training as a geographer. He is extensively published in a variety of leading academic journals, including: *Environment and Planning A, European Journal of Marketing, Journal of Environmental Psychology, Marketing Theory, Mobilities, Space and Culture, Tourism Management,* and *Urban Geography.*

Steve Millington is a Reader in Place Management at the Manchester Metropolitan University Business School, and Director of the Institute of Place Management. He has previously written about branding Manchester City Football Club in papers published in *Global Networks* and *Marketing Theory.* In addition, he has written about the disruption to match-day routines resulting from Manchester City's stadium relocation, published as a book chapter in *Stadium Worlds: Football, Space and the Built Environment* (2010).

Eduardo Oliveira is a Researcher at the University of Kiel, Germany. He is interested in place branding and spatial planning, and the embedding of both in strategic governance systems. His research explores the effectiveness of strategic spatial planning processes in supporting the social and economic development of urban regions, whilst assessing their effect on environmental sustainability.

Lisa O'Malley is Professor and critical marketing scholar at the University of Limerick. Her research interests encompass consumer research, relationship marketing, sustainability, place, and tourism. Recent publications include work in *Marketing Theory, European Journal of Marketing, Journal of Business Ethics, Consumption, Markets and Culture*, and *Technology in Society*. She is Deputy Chair of the Academy of Marketing and a member of the editorial boards of *Marketing Theory* and *Journal of Marketing Management*.

Laura Reynolds is a Postdoctoral Researcher at Cardiff University, currently working with the Welsh Economy Research Unit and starting a Economic and Social Research Council Postdoctoral Fellowship in January 2020. Her research interests include place branding governance, cultural heritage, stakeholder engagement, sensemaking, and critical theory. She is Co-Editor of *Cultural Heritage* (2018) and has presented her research at a number of international conferences, including the Institute of Place Management's International Biennial Conference where she won Best Paper in 2017.

Gareth Roberts is Projects and Operations Manager at the Institute of Place Management (IPM) and Associate Editor of the *Journal of Place Management and Development*. Gareth is currently programme managing the United Kingdom Government's High Streets Task Force initiative, alongside multiple IPM contract and funded research projects working in partnership with place organisations in Europe. Gareth holds an MSc in Place Branding, and is currently studying for a PhD on the impact of cultural events on places.

Jenny Rowley is Professor in the Faculty of Business and Law at Manchester Metropolitan University. She is an interdisciplinary scholar with recent publications in scholarly communication, trust in information seeking, and higher education and learning, as well as an established profile of contributions on various aspects of place and destination branding. These include brand personality and the place brand web. She is currently working on developing understanding of the concept of the co-branding of places and destinations, and the role of social media in place branding.

Efe Sevin is Assistant Professor of Public Relations at the Department of Mass Communication at Towson University, Maryland. His current research focuses on identifying and measuring the impacts of social networks on place branding and public diplomacy campaigns. His works have been published in several academic journals and books including *American Behavioral Scientist*, *Public Relations Review*, and *Cities*. His most recent co-edited volume, *City Diplomacy: Current Trends and Future Prospects*, was published in 2020.

Chloe Steadman is Lecturer in Marketing at Manchester Metropolitan University, with a background in consumer research. She is also a Researcher at the Institute of Place Management and High Streets Task Force. Her academic research is interdisciplinary in nature, but largely revolves around using a range of qualitative methodologies to explore consumer culture, embodiment, temporality, experiences of places, and vulnerability. Research contexts have included the consumption of tattoos, football, and, most recently, craft beer festivals.

Anette Therkelsen is Associate Professor of Tourism and Market Communication at Aalborg University, Denmark. Her research interests focus on place branding at different geographical scales and various aspects of tourism-related consumer studies, and she has published internationally on both of these topics. She is currently working on a project on sustainable tourism development.

Kristof Van Assche is Professor of Planning, Governance and Development at the University of Alberta, and Senior Fellow at the German Institute of Development Research, ZEF/Bonn University. He is interested in evolution and innovation in governance, with special emphasis on environmental, planning, and development policy.

Aleks Vladimirov is a PhD researcher at Manchester Metropolitan University's Institute of Place Management. His experience includes working in brand management, place management, and digital user experience research. Aleks focuses his PhD research on decision making related to place. Contrasting emerging insights from behavioural economics with more traditional notions of standard rationality, Aleks looks to add to the understanding of how graduates choose where to live.

Gary Warnaby is Professor of Retailing and Marketing, based in the Institute of Place Management at Manchester Metropolitan University. His research interests focus on the marketing of places (particularly in an urban context) and retailing. Results of this research have been published in various academic journals in both the management and geography disciplines. He is Co-Editor of *Rethinking Place Branding: Comprehensive Brand Development for Cities and Regions* (2015) and *Designing With Smell: Practices, Techniques and Challenges* (2017).

1 Place branding's present and past realities, and future research agendas

Dominic Medway, Gary Warnaby and John Byrom

How and why we arrived here

Around two years ago, the publisher Edward Elgar approached us and asked if we were interested in editing a new collected volume for their Research Agendas series on 'place branding'. It was a surprise, as our track record on this subject is one in which we have been critical of the concept. The arguments in this regard are well rehearsed. In essence, we have at various times suggested that place branding, and wider place marketing, emerges far too often as a top-down management activity, which largely sidesteps citizens' viewpoints, rather than a bottom-up approach which includes them (Warnaby and Medway, 2013). This accords with other ongoing dialogues amongst scholars regarding the level of inclusiveness of the place branding process, particularly in terms of residents' involvement (see, for example, Braun et al., 2013).

The criticisms of place branding do not end here. For example, whilst on the one hand place branding might be viewed as a purely rational management act fuelled by market forces around supposed place competitiveness, some have argued that place branding 'is not as innocent as some like to think of it and observations on the current state of the discipline make any critical researcher engage in serious wonderings around place brands and their effects on places and the people that live in them' (Lichrou et al., 2018: 1). In this regard, actions undertaken to supposedly enhance the place brand, such as altering the place name itself (Medway and Warnaby, 2014), are likely to have significant political repercussions. Linked to this, others, such as Oliveira and Ashworth (2017), have indicated that place branding remains overly embedded in the mindsets of management and marketing, whilst lacking sensitivity and openness to multiple disciplinary viewpoints like planning, architecture, social policy, transport development and sustainability.

Elsewhere, we have been particularly reproving of much of the literature on place branding for its obsession with measurement (see Medway and Warnaby, 2017), such as assessing supposed place brand 'personality' through the numeric values people attach to places in relation to various identified human characteristics – e.g. stylishness, creativity, optimism and tolerance (see, for example, Kaplan et al., 2010). Of course, as soon as you start to measure things in this manner, then a logical next step is to compare the results of this process, irrespective of whether they make much sense – it is an approach that delivers outcomes such as the Anholt Ipsos Nation Brand Index, which ranks nations according to a brand score made up of key measures across six dimensions.[1] We have argued that such mindless metricisation represents the very worst of place branding and presents a reductive view of place,[2] in which:

> the views of those engaged with the places in question are boiled down to mere numbers relating to attributes, which have typically been pre-determined in closed survey questions. A glaring omission in such enquiry is that it ignores the fact that places are experienced at a multisensory level by those within them, be they tourists, residents, visitors, or other place stakeholders. This phenomenological understanding of place interaction is absent in a positivist world of scale developments that are used to objectively further our 'understanding' of place brands and place branding activity. (Medway and Warnaby, 2017: 151)

All of the above critiques of place branding, in which we have clearly been active and willing participants, provides some background on the manner in which we have arrived to the point of editing this book (or the 'how'), but it does not explain the 'why'. Specifically, why as authors with an evident critical perspective on place branding were we asked by the publishers if we would compile a volume on its future research agendas; and, perhaps even more perplexing for some readers, why did we agree to do it? The answer to the first of these questions probably comes down to the mordant reality that others had already been asked and refused, but we, after some consideration, didn't – the publisher was honest enough to intimate as much, but we feel our academic egos can cope with being the last (and only) men (three of them in this case) standing… you take what you can get, etc. If you are reading this and thinking (à la Brando[3]) that 'I was asked first and I coulda' been a contender', then we can only apologise for acquiescing so readily to the publisher's request to edit this book; which brings us right back to that second question of why we actually did. It is certainly something we thought carefully about, and on which we came to the following conclusion and justification. It appears we have spent several years, probably a decade or so in fact, looking in from time to time on the practice of place branding, and the enthusiastic scholarship that surrounds it, and, like some other scholars highlighted above, assuming a rather externalised and disparaging viewpoint upon such activity. The opportunity to edit this book, therefore, was a chance to enter into the place branding fold and shake things up a bit; the rationale being if you don't like something very much then it is best to question it from within if you wish to shift perspectives and understanding. Put otherwise, and to paraphrase former United States President Lyndon Johnson, we thought we should accept the challenge of working inside the place branding 'tent' for a change, rather than standing outside it and 'pissing in'.[4]

With this approach in mind, the original brief for the book which we circulated to potential authors invited them to explore ideas and debates they thought could inform the future of research in place branding. In so doing, we encouraged the interplay of oppositional perspectives, ranging from those who see place branding as a potential means of improving the economic vitality and viability of places, to others who might consider much existing place branding activity as exclusionary to certain sectors of society and, thereby, politically divisive. Capturing such a diversity of standpoints emphasised a need to open contributions out to the widest possible range of subject areas. We therefore welcomed authorship from a range of discipline areas, including (but not limited to): marketing, geography, planning, management and tourism. Sifting through the contributor biographies at the start of this book, one can see that we were lucky and privileged enough to attain this breadth of scholarship. And, with chapter authors and subjects finalised by the early autumn of 2019, the wind was set fair for a seamless delivery of first drafts in the early spring of 2020 – and then Covid-19 struck…

Present and past realities

It is surely a truism that there are few aspects of human endeavour that are not in some way affected by the current Covid-19 pandemic; and there is no obvious reason why place branding would be an exception to that. As draft chapters started to ping into our email inbox in April 2020, as editors we had already started to question whether a book on place branding had much relevance anymore. In short order, one of the principal reasons to enact place branding is to attract potential income streams to the place in question, whether this is in the form of tourist visits and their associated spend, or inward investment and development by organisations, institutions and other bodies outwith the place. Covid-19 has radically changed both these worlds.

Regarding tourism, for example, a recent report by McKinsey (Constantin et al., 2020) has suggested that international tourist arrivals could plunge by 60 to 80 per cent in 2020 across the globe, and that tourism spending is not likely to return to pre-Covid-19 levels until 2024, putting up to 120 million jobs at risk. The challenges of overtourism in popular and previously crowded locations like Venice have seemingly evaporated, only to be replaced by concerns from governments, those who live in tourist destinations, and even potential tourists themselves, about the risks that tourism brings for an accelerated spread of the virus. Tourist attractions (art galleries, museums, theatres, historic buildings and sites, etc.) remain closed or under tight restrictions on visitor numbers to ensure social distancing. And, in some instances, the welcome given to visitors by local communities living in tourist hotspots has even turned to hostility with, for example, the UK press reporting how visitors to Cornwall in July 2020 were greeted with a handmade banner on the A30, one of the main roads into the county, telling them to 'Turn around and fuck off'. This is the kind of reputational 'stink bomb' that no place manager needs when trying to nurture their destination's positive image, and it explains why the chief executive of Visit Cornwall, Malcolm Bell, called the sign 'offensive and unforgivable' (Mathers, 2020). In terms of tourism, then, place branding has lost some of its *raison d'être*; if tourists do not want to visit, and in cases of Covid-19 restrictions and lockdowns may not even be allowed to do so, then perhaps part of the notion of a place brand becomes a little redundant.

Turning to inward investment, a key driver of this is large organisations tapping into new customer bases and labour forces, but certainly where the service sector is concerned, Covid-19 has exposed the fact that the necessity for these fixed ties to place has reduced in importance – at least for now. White-collar workers have learnt to rapidly adapt to virtual and footloose modes of working, and have embraced a whole host of video conferencing technologies and networking platforms to achieve this (e.g. MS Teams, Zoom, Adobe Connect, etc.). This is not a disappearance of those industrial agglomerations or spatial clusterings of like-minded firms and service providers which economic geographers have long talked about as a means by which collaborative, creative and productive synergies emerge to create 'local buzz' (see, for example, Bathelt et al., 2004; Pinch et al., 2003); rather it is a migration of those clusterings towards a mode of spatiality where the relational assumes greater importance than the Cartesian, and where an employee's position in (virtual) industrial networks of human interaction holds greater influence than the location from which they work. However, this does not bode well for the place branding of the world's major service centres, where the financial and legal sectors dominate. Indeed, one only has to look at the challenges London is facing, with empty streets and unused ancillary services (sandwich and coffee shops, taxi drivers, dry cleaners) now that much of the work on which the city's economy is built is being conducted from home offices and kitchen tables around the UK and Europe (see, for example, Partridge, 2020), and with many employees seemingly reluctant to venture back into their former workplace geographies, mobilities and routines (Nikolic, 2020).

Whilst the above challenges make the future for place branding look potentially bleak, there are perhaps two fundamental considerations to bear in mind that make the activity itself, as well as a forward-facing research agenda on the topic, worthy of discussion in a book such as this. The first observation is that nothing lasts forever, and it is as inevitable as sunrise that we will eventually emerge from Covid-19 to a future in which tourism will once again thrive, and where inward investment will again be important; it is simply that the basis on which these things occur may look very different to how it has been previously. In this regard, it is often helpful to take lessons from history, and we would like to take readers back to the 1937 *Exposition Internationale des Arts et Techniques dans la Vie Moderne* (International Exposition of Art and Technology in Modern Life) held in Paris, France from 25 May to 25 November 1937 (see Figure 1.1).

In many ways the 1937 Paris Exposition was a place or nation branding exercise writ large: a host of countries from across the globe exhibited impressive, purpose-built pavilions displaying their nation's achievements and prowess in art and technology. But the event was dominated by the large Soviet and German pavilions, which faced each other in front of the Eiffel Tower. The former was topped by a massive statue of a male worker and a female peasant (*Worker and Kolkhoz Woman* by Vera Mukhina), their hands aloft holding a hammer and a sickle. Directly opposite, the imposing tower of the German pavilion had been designed by Hitler's architect Albert Speer to be slightly higher, so that the Nazi symbols of the eagle and swastika looked down on this monument to communism (see Figure 1.1). The event arguably symbolised how thin the line between nation branding and unfettered nationalism can become, and was a clear harbinger of the imminence and devastation of World War II. Yet from that war, for all its misery, death and destruction, a new world order emerged in which the globalised flow and integration of financial and human capital (workers, tourists, etc.), and associated wealth, grew for many nations. In such a climate, place branding has had an important and largely positive role to play, far removed from the sinister nationalistic sabre rattling of the 1937 Paris Exposition.

Source: Images kindly loaned from the 'museum_of_stuff' on Instagram.

Figure 1.1   Images of the official plan for the 1937 International Exposition of Art and Technology in Modern Life, Paris

Rather like World War II, Covid-19 appears to have again brought humanity to another critical point in history at which the 'reset buttons' for all different forms of public diplomacy (place branding included) are activated, and from which such activities are likely to emerge in a different form to how they were before – a so-called 'new normal'. In discussing a research agenda for place branding, which is by necessity future oriented, it is reassuring to see, therefore, that three of the chapters in this book mention and consider the impact of Covid-19 (Campelo, Keegan and Oliveira et al.), albeit very briefly in the latter two instances. This is especially impressive as the virus was not even on the radar when these authors agreed to write these chapters. Beyond this, many of the topics discussed throughout this book as part of a future research agenda for place branding have the potential for a high level of relevance in a post-Covid-19 world.

This brings us to our second point, which is that place branding in a post-Covid-19 context has the potential to be as important as it ever was; it is simply that the audience for its execution and effort may need major reconsideration. In the past, it is perhaps fair to say that much place branding has had an external focus, working across national or regional boundaries to attract attention, reputation and the inflow of human and financial capital. But in a world where international movement and associated air travel is falling away as people 'stay local' for work and tourism, we perhaps need to think about the potential to switch place branding efforts closer to home. As noted above, previous research has considered the importance of place branding campaigns having the involvement of residents in terms of determining how a place is defined and represented, but perhaps such local populations now need to be the principal focus of those campaigns too. In the UK, for example, the news media is awash with stories of people (re)discovering 'hidden gems' and the attraction, beauty and excitement of where they live under lockdown (Ivey, 2020), as well as embracing the benefits of a 'staycation' (Monk, 2020). It feels as if place branding has an important role to play in helping us to 'mainline' this resurgence of topophilia (Tuan, 1974) and 'bring dwelling to the fullness of its nature' (Heidegger, 2001: 159). Put more simply, this is about humanity learning to better appreciate and (re)connect with where we live. Home, after all, is where the heart is, and that is just as well as it looks as if we will all be spending much more time there in a post-Covid-19 future. Place branding, it seems, could have an important role to play in helping citizens nurture their feelings of local embeddedness, place attachment, care and associated safety and security. Accordingly, it seems timely and appropriate that scholars might use the unwelcome opportunity of this significant episode in history (a global health crisis with a geographical scope and impact not seen since the 1918 flu pandemic, and before that probably the Black Death of 1346 to 1353) to step back and survey the academic landscape of place branding to this point in time, before turning to (re)consider the direction(s) place branding practice might now take and the future research agendas this establishes. This is exactly what this book hopes to achieve.

Future research agendas

Deciding how an edited book should be structured, and how the various contributions could hang together, is always an interesting challenge, and especially so as we encouraged our contributors to write about pretty much anything they felt had relevance to a future research agenda for place branding. Nevertheless, the initial abstracts potential contributors submitted revealed some broad, albeit porous, boundaries that could be drawn between the various proposed chapter topics. From this stage onwards four parts of the book started to emerge: the first on issues of place branding 'governance', the second covering different place branding 'contexts', the third concerned with matters of 'experience' and place branding and the fourth and final part addressing place branding and 'creativity'.

Transitioning between the abstract submission stage of the editorial process to the receipt and review of the final draft chapters, our view on titles and order of parts did not really change. This was largely because of the rigorous manner in which contributors stuck to their original chapter proposals. This reassured us of the potential coherence of the book, and that sense of positivity was further reinforced by the excellent quality of writing in the first drafts of the chapters we received. In this regard, overseeing and nurturing the development of an edited academic volume can often be a fairly thankless task, with contributions of very variable (and sometime dubious) scholarly and narrative quality being a common challenge. We can honestly say this was never the case with this book, and from start to finish it was a pleasure to work with the contributing authors, all of whom are well established or up-and-coming scholars in their fields.

Governance

In Part I, the order of play sets off with Aram Eisenschitz's chapter (Chapter 2), 'Place branding and the neoliberal class settlement'. This takes a politically oriented and overtly critical approach to place branding, arguing that it is not just a means of helping cities become more competitive, but is also an aspect of the class settlement in which neoliberalism displaced social democracy. Thus, he argues that place branding does not just sell places by changing their image, but actively engages in the political transformation of cities as well as displaying many of the assumptions of that settlement which help to legitimate it. Incorporating vignettes of place branding, including London's South Bank and Canary Wharf, Glasgow, New York and the Great Exhibition, Aram argues that we should evaluate the impacts of place branding policies by looking not at places but at people; thus, rather than trying to encourage tourism, for instance, we should be asking what tourism can do for the inhabitants.

Efe Sevin's chapter (Chapter 3) proposes a research agenda for computational approaches in place branding, highlighting two different domains for future enquiry. The first refers to changes in practice, arguing that as algorithm-based thinking in place development (evident in the concept of smart cities/ destinations) is increasingly adopted by city managers/marketers, then as a practice-driven field, place branding scholarship should also incorporate those changes into its research agendas. The second domain relates to consequent changes in the availability of data/analysis methods for researchers, as they increasingly gain access to larger and more diverse datasets on individual attitudes and behaviours, which may potentially replace traditional data-gathering methods or enable identification of previously undiscovered patterns across datasets. Nevertheless, Efe sounds a cautionary note that large datasets are not a substitute for a sound theoretical framework, and these computational approaches should be led by theory.

Andrea Insch's chapter (Chapter 4) aims to examine and clarify the concepts of participation and engagement in urban branding and to identify the forms that this can take for members of the local community. The chapter analyses previous research into this important aspect of place branding practice to dissect forms of participation and engagement and the mechanisms that can act as enablers and barriers to participation and engagement. Andrea concludes by arguing that the evolution of participatory approaches to the process of urban branding must move beyond a one-dimensional view, which is focused principally on including a wide range of participants, to a two-dimensional view that also enables their deep engagement in these ongoing and dynamic processes. It follows that future research on the governance of place branding, which is typically played out in multistakeholder environments, should embrace this perspective.

The final chapter of Part I (Chapter 5), by Eduardo Oliveira, Kristof Van Assche and Raoul Beunen, discusses the relationship between spatial planning and place branding, in terms of guiding the location of development and physical infrastructure and for promoting social, economic and ecologically sustainable development. They argue that planning and branding have the potential to work together in contributing to the integrated socioeconomic development and environmental sustainability of places, and that this contribution can only be effective if they are not isolated from the broader realms of decision making, and from each other. The chapter highlights the multidisciplinary roots of place branding research, and the need to draw from and synthesise these different disciplinary approaches if we are to obtain the fullest understanding of the concept.

Contexts

Part II brings together chapters that cover place branding and concomitant research agendas from a broad variety of contexts – e.g. academic, political, geographical, sporting, environmental and digital.

Chapter 6, by Aleks Vladimirov and Gary Warnaby examines place branding through the ever popular lens of behavioural economics. Specifically, they examine the potential of this academic discipline to explain the locational choices made by individuals (acting for their own ends, or on behalf of organisations they are part of) in response to the associated marketing/branding activities that are used to enhance the attractiveness of places by those responsible for their management. The focus here is on heuristics and biases – or the 'cognitive shortcuts' – that may influence decision making in terms of choosing where, for example, to live, work and invest. This is in contrast to neoclassical economists' view of 'homo economicus', making optimally rational decisions which deliver maximum personal utility. They conclude by indicating the potential for behavioural economics to influence how we research place branding in the future. In particular, it is a perspective that can help us understand how humans can make locational decisions that are not solely rooted in the rational pursuit of maximising financial opportunity, but can also be influenced by other perceived benefits inherent in the familiarity of our surroundings, including our social relationships and sense of belonging to places.

In Chapter 7, Adriana Campelo explores the role of cities in taking leadership on global agendas such as sustainability and climate change, and how this impacts on city branding. The chapter starts with discussion of the Resilient Cities programme, which is concerned with urban resilience and place making. Concepts relating to social-ecological systems theory are considered, and cities' initiatives in terms of climate change are examined. Adriana concludes by proposing how issues such as sustainability, resilience and carbon neutrality are an important new avenue for future research in place branding; this is especially salient in the light of Covid-19. How cities and countries are acting to deal with these ongoing challenges will affect their images and reputations for a long time into the future. This raises important and fundamental questions, such as how city branding can effectively foster resilience and embrace climate emergency action.

Cecilia Cassinger, Andrea Lucarelli and Szilvia Gyimóthy consider the specifics of Nordic approaches to place branding in Chapter 8. They emphasise how 'the Nordic wave' provides not only a geographical context for work on place branding, but also a particular ideological mindset that can fashion distinctive approaches to concepts, strategies and tactics. They argue for a Nordic approach to place branding that sits between 'management' and 'critical' standpoints, and go on to articulate what this means in terms of global reflexivity and responsibility, legitimisation of place branding practices, and shifting geopolitical boundaries. In doing so, they invite us to question commonly held stereotypes of the Nordic, with their emphases on social welfare and peaceable coexistence, and instead highlight how such countries have their own troubled histories and ongoing issues relating to marginalisation in various forms.

In Chapter 9, Steve Millington, Chloe Steadman, Gareth Roberts and Dominic Medway turn to consider different scales as they relate to place branding literature and practice. Specifically, they explore 'the relative neglect of scalar tensions between the local and global, and the glocal and grobal'. They do this by analysing longitudinally the branding practices of one of the UK's leading football (soccer) teams, Manchester City, alongside the activities of its 'parent' organisation City Football Group, and the City of Manchester. They discuss the often complex interplay of factors that underpin the operation of a football club with global ambitions; drawing out how the local operations of the club are intertwined with the activities of its United Arab Emirates-based parent and the ambitions of the city's political elite to reframe Manchester as a future global city.

Switching back to the sustainability context raised, in part, in Chapter 7, Anette Therkelsen, Laura James and Henrik Halkier further examine the role of the United Nations Sustainable Development Goals (SDGs) in Chapter 10. They identify that the SDGs have left a mark on the rhetorical strategies of cities and countries, but that it remains to be seen how they will influence place development practices across the world in future. Areas for researchers to examine will be a balance of quick wins against long-term solutions, along with the challenge of aligning the SDGs with the multiple and often conflicting market interests of place branding. For example, the altruistic engagement of residents with sustainability issues may clash with the more competitive mindsets of other private and public stakeholders, who may favour short-term solutions to ensure a better position for a given town, city, region or nation in the enduring competition between places.

In Chapter 11, Brendan James Keegan considers aspects of digital transformation in relation to place. Adopting a systematic literature review, he approaches this through a tripartite categorisation – or what he terms the 'trifecta' of place marketing, place making and place maintenance. Relevant examples that illustrate the potential of digital applications are mooted, including technologies that can alert residents to neighbourhood crime. While recognising the nascent status of much of the research in this area, Brendan points out that long-term studies into the role of digital applications in places are lacking. He proposes that future research considering the digitalisation of place should centre on three key areas: artificial intelligence, automation processes and social media sentiment analysis.

Experience

Part III draws together chapters concerned with how places are experienced and the implications of this for a place branding research agenda. Experience here covers concepts such as co-creation, authenticity, sensemaking and non-representational theory. However, in the first contribution to this part (Chapter 12) Jack Coffin moves away from a principally human focus to consider what places are like for nonhumans, and the implications of this for place branding research. As Jack notes, 'most scholars focus exclusively on the *human* experience of place'; but following a posthuman approach, this chapter challenges us to ask how animals, smart objects and other nonhumans might also experience places. This raises other important questions; not just how humans might affect nonhuman experiences of place(s), but also how nonhuman actors and actants can impact on human experiences in turn. Jack concludes the chapter by indicating how a posthuman research agenda may help engender a more ecological and equitable approach to place branding theory and, potentially, practice in the future.

In recent decades, the concept of co-creation has featured increasingly in marketing and other cognate disciplines, recognising as it does the significant role that consumers can play in the design of products and services. In Chapter 13, Jenny Rowley and Sonya Hanna consider the phenomenon as it relates to place branding. They highlight the different stakeholders that can be involved in the development of place brands, as well as the various ways in which this can take place. The significant potential for co-creation via social media and other online platforms is also highlighted, although Jenny and Sonya illustrate the importance of ensuring that user-generated content aligns with how the destination marketing organisation wishes to project the place. They conclude by presenting a number of foci for future research, including, perhaps most pertinently, further theoretical development of the distinction between a place stakeholder and customer and the consequences of this for the co-creation of place brands.

In Chapter 14, Maria Lichrou and Lisa O'Malley consider first how place branding practices with their all too common focus on the commodification of formulas for supposed success, including the serial reproduction of cultural attractions, can have a homogenising effect on places, whilst at the same time fuelling a touristic desire for greater place authenticity. They explore how more recent marketing thinking opens up new possibilities for action, facilitating experience co-creation, the realisation of value and the potential for existential authenticity. Such an approach suggests that the marketing strategy of tourism places cannot simply be determined in advance of the tourist's lived place experience. This suggests that future research and practice would do well to consider how tourism places might produce the resources out of which value can be created. From this, the place brand is likely to emerge as a symbolic resource that serves to more effectively mediate and integrate marketing activities.

Chapter 15 by Laura Reynolds and Nicole Koenig-Lewis discusses how place brand meanings are developed and transferred across different stakeholder groups through stakeholder engagement. This is at the heart of the participatory and collaborative place branding processes that have been an important theme in recent place branding research. Using a case study based on stakeholder interviews, Laura and Nicole utilise the notions of sensemaking and sensegiving to examine how people form and convey meanings assigned to the places they live, work and invest in; and by adding a sensefiltering layer, consider how influence can be shaped by stakeholders' possession of resources and leadership. In this regard, they offer an explanation for managing complexity, transition and change which is at the heart of a participatory approach to place branding.

In Chapter 16, Simon Cryer argues for an approach to place branding that captures more fully the range of our senses and our experience in place. He considers how a non-representational approach can be drawn on to investigate 'the relationships between place, space, the senses, and life'. Simon invites us to reflect on how place branding might be approached from alternative angles, or from the perspective of those elements of place that might frequently be overlooked. There is perhaps a signal here to think not only about how place branding can take better account of the ways in which people might experience place in non-representational or more-than-representational ways, but also how the activity of place branding itself might engage more effectively with its audiences by using multisensory approaches that move beyond the visual media on which it appears so heavily reliant.

Creativity

Part IV, focused on creativity, is the shortest part, containing as it does only three chapters. However, it was clear from the outset that these three contributions were very distinct from the rest of the submissions and therefore deserved their own separate billing in the running order. The first two chapters herein focus on human creativity in the visual forms of light and art, and consider the implications of this for place branding research and practice. And, aside from its subject content, the final chapter by Stephen Brown belongs in this part as much for its creative approach to academic writing. It is also a natural and fitting sign off to this book.

Chapter 17 by Tim Edensor builds on his already extensive work on light festivals, and considers whether they homogenise or enhance place. He presents two opposing and, to a certain extent, scalar perspectives. On the one hand there are the typically larger light displays that critics assert can be bland, environmentally unsustainable and lacking in place specificity. On the other hand, our attention is directed to increasingly popular smaller, local light festivals that are being used to undergird place identity. Overall, a clear message emerging from Tim's chapter is that place branding research would do well to examine further how the creative, collaborative and sometimes experimental uses of illumination can be a powerful tool for generating exciting place potentialities.

Mihalis Kavaratzis and Gary Warnaby consider in Chapter 18 how to engage creatively in place branding research. They recognise the increasing attention being paid to the affective associations that places hold, and link these to more artistic modes of enquiry. Drawing on their own experiences of exhibiting creative work relating to their own research into place (Mihalis's visual art and poetry, and Gary's photo-essays), they argue for an approach to place branding research which can facilitate arts-based practices. For this to work, they emphasise the importance of having a clear justification for the approach taken, a relevant agenda of themes that can be tackled and a clear sense of the different methods that can be adopted.

As noted above, in the final chapter of Part IV (Chapter 19), and of the book, Stephen Brown takes a creative and 'almost-autobiographical' approach in considering place marketing and place branding and what the future might hold. The conclusion is that such activity has 'peaked', and that less place marketing is needed rather than more. Stephen's approach is undoubtedly pitched as deliberately provocative, or as he terms it 'irreverent and ridiculous by turns', yet beneath its welcome humour his chapter does pose some important and uncomfortable questions for place branding research and practice as we move forward – What and who are we doing it for? Who benefits and who loses from such activity? And ultimately, echoing a challenge from Medway et al. (2015), 'Are we wasting our time'?

What this book reveals throughout its chapters is that it is not yet time to shut up shop and to give up entirely on place branding. However, reprising ideas discussed above, we are perhaps at a point in time where a logical and sensible step is to push the 'reset button' on such activity and fully (re)consider its purpose and goals. We believe the following chapters serve as an excellent start to this rebooted journey, providing a wealth of creative and innovative suggestions from our contributors on how place branding might be done, thought about and researched differently in the future.

Notes

1. See for example: www.ipsos.com/sites/default/files/20-03-60_anholt-ipsos_place branding.pdf.
2. See for example: www.ipsos.com/en-us/news-polls/Germany-Retains-Top.
3. Those unfamiliar with this reference should watch Marlon Brando's performance as Terry Malloy in the 1954 film *On the Waterfront*.
4. The full quote, as reported in *The New York Times* (31 October 1971), and attributed to Lyndon Johnson's comments regarding FBI Director J. Edgar Hoover, is: 'It's probably better to have him inside the tent pissing out, than outside the tent pissing in'.

References

Bathelt, H., Malmberg, A. and P. Maskell (2004), 'Clusters and knowledge: Local buzz, global pipelines and the process of knowledge creation', *Progress in Human Geography*, **28** (1), 31–56.

Braun, E., Kavaratzis, M. and S. Zenker (2013), 'My city – my brand: The different roles of residents in place branding', *Journal of Place Management and Development*, **6** (1), 18–28.

Constantin, M., Saxon, S. and J. Yu (2020), 'Reimagining the $9 trillion tourism economy – what will it take?', McKinsey and Company, accessed 21 August 2020 at: www.mckinsey.com/industries/travel-logistics-and-transport-infrastructure/our -insights/reimagining-the-9-trillion-tourism-economy-what-will-it-take.

Heidegger, M. (2001), 'Building, dwelling, thinking', in M. Heidegger (trans. Albert Hofstadter), *Poetry, Language, Thought*, New York: Perennial, pp. 141–59.

Ivey, P. (2020), 'London in lockdown: Hidden gems we've discovered during quarantine', *ES Homes and Property*, 28 May, accessed 28 August 2020 at: www.homesandproperty.co.uk/property-news/london-hidden-gems-lockdown-a138581.html.

Kaplan, M. D., Yurt, O., Guneri, B. and K. Kurtulus (2010), 'Branding places: Applying brand personality concept to cities', *European Journal of Marketing*, **44** (9/10), 1286–304.

Lichrou, M., Kavaratzis, M. and M. Giovanardi (2018), 'Introduction', in M. Kavaratzis, M. Giovanardi and M. Lichrou (eds), *Inclusive Place Branding: Critical Perspectives on Theory and Practice*, Abingdon: Routledge, pp. 1–10.

Mathers, M. (2020), 'Cornwall tourist chief condemns sign telling visitors to "f**k off"', *The Independent*, 6 July, accessed 21 August 2020 at: www.independent.co.uk/news/uk/home-news/cornwall-tourism-sign-a30-bodmin-seaside-lockdown-a9603961.html.

Medway, D., Swanson, K., Neirotti, L. D., Pasquinelli, C. and S. Zenker (2015), 'Place branding: Are we wasting our time? Report of an AMA special session', *Journal of Place Management and Development*, **8** (1), 63–8.

Medway, D. and G. Warnaby (2014), 'What's in a name? Place branding and toponymic commodification', *Environment and Planning A*, **46** (1), 153–67.

Medway, D. and G. Warnaby (2017), 'Multisensory place branding: A manifesto for research', in A. Campelo (ed.), *Handbook on Place Branding and Marketing*, Cheltenham, UK and Northampton, MA, USA: Edward Elgar Publishing, pp. 147–59.

Monk, Z. (2020), 'UK staycation boom looks set to continue into 2021, new research finds', *Boutique Hotelier*, 14 August, accessed 28 August 2020 at: www.boutiquehotelier.com/uk-staycation-boom-looks-set-to-continue-into-2021-new-research-finds/.

Nikolic, I. (2020), 'British workers are the most reluctant in Europe to come back to the office because of second wave fears, says study as Business Secretary Alok Sharma calls for return to the workplace', *Mail Online*, 25 August, accessed August 28 at: www.dailymail.co.uk/news/article-8661463/UK-workers-reluctant-return-office-second-wave-fears-says-study.html.

Oliveira, E. and G. Ashworth (2017), 'A strategic spatial planning approach to regional branding: Challenges and opportunities', in A. Campelo (ed.), *Handbook on Place Branding and Marketing*, Cheltenham, UK and Northampton, MA, USA: Edward Elgar Publishing, pp. 22–40.

Partridge, J. (2020), 'UK office workers slower to return to their desk after Covid', *The Guardian*, 5 August, accessed 27 August 2020 at: www.theguardian.com/business/2020/aug/05/uk-office-workers-slower-to-return-to-their-desk-after-covid.

Pinch, S., Henry, N., Jenkins, M. and S. Tallman (2003), 'From "industrial districts" to "knowledge clusters": A model of knowledge dissemination and competitive advantage in industrial agglomerations', *Journal of Economic Geography*, **3** (4), 373–88.

Tuan, Y.-F. (1974), *Topophilia: A Study of Environmental Perception, Attitudes, and Values*, Englewood Cliffs, NJ: Prentice Hall.

Warnaby, G. and D. Medway (2013), 'What about the "place" in place marketing?', *Marketing Theory*, **13** (3), 345–63.

PART I

Governance

2 Place branding and the neoliberal class settlement

Aram Eisenschitz

Introduction

London is one of the most high-profile cities in the world and one that is heavily branded, yet in the borough of Westminster, where tourists spend well over £6 billion per annum, the official rate of child poverty is 46 per cent, the sixth highest in the country (Greater London Authority, 2011; Stone and Hirsch, 2019). What does this say about place branding?

The principal criterion for selecting an aspect of this activity for further research should be whether one can use it to say something meaningful. In their analysis of how to inject meaning into the social sciences – 'so much noise, so little to say' – Alvesson et al. (2017: 3) argue that systems of meaning are constituted by the prevailing relations of power. Research should address society's political, economic and social relations and it should run counter to the fragmentation of knowledge in which we know more and more about less and less. We should therefore not forget Weber's assertion that social science's central question is 'what shall we do and how shall we live' (Alvesson et al., 2017: 24). In the light of these exhortations, this chapter argues that research should address a more substantial aspect of place branding, namely its contribution to the construction, reproduction and legitimation of the class settlement that emerged out of the transition from social democracy to neoliberalism, a transition that is still ongoing, and which has had such an impact on people's lives everywhere.

Place branding does not sell places; it sells political transformation to investors, visitors and residents. It has been involved in this political transition by helping to change the way we conceptualise class relations in order to more easily facilitate the restructuring of the international division of labour. Place branding is part of a process of making places more competitive in the global market by developing narratives that build on a place's uniqueness and authenticity in order to attract inward investment, tourists, students, residents and government funding. On the contrary, the approach adopted in this chapter argues that what makes a place competitive is not changing imagery, but what underlies such change, the shift in class relations that allows finance and the owners of property to reshape cities (Harvey, 2006: 89). Only by changing class relations is it possible to remove barriers to the profitable accumulation of capital. Place branding is the final stage of a wider sequence of renewal, the aim of which is to change class relations and the perception of them, in order to stimulate the process of accumulation. This sequence starts with introducing entrepreneurial forms of governance and follows with strategies for regeneration.

This shift in perspective means that gentrification, for instance, is more than a welcome inflow of an entrepreneurial middle class that hopefully will improve a city's growth. It is symptomatic of deregulated housing and finance markets that demonstrate the abrogation of the right to democratically control our own lives and abandon the century-old politics of subsidised and secure housing for workers. Exponents of place branding should therefore think carefully before celebrating gentrification. The fashioning of a new image has less to do with attracting certain sectors than with facilitating a class settlement that shifts the balance of power between labour and capital. Many symptoms of place branding, such as urban tourism, therefore, actively help to encourage and develop these new class relations.

The starting point of this analysis is the fall in the rate of profit and its share of value added in the Organisation for Economic Co-operation and Development countries, which reached a nadir in the early 1980s (Glyn, 2006; Kliman, 2012). Neoliberalism is the logical response to that crisis (Das, 2017; Mandel, 1975), developing policies over every aspect of society in order to remove the impediments to profitable accumulation that stem from a working-class social and political infrastructure (Gough et al., 2006). This left cities free to recapitalise, free from the radicalism associated with the large workforces that characterised industrial cities.

As cities started to de-industrialise in the late 1960s, the resulting social dislocation led to ever increasing political demands for the state to meet the needs of the abandoned populations. That in turn generated fiscal crises that social democracy was unable to stem (O'Connor, 1973). Neoliberalism, however, by jettisoning social democracy, has developed an urban economy focussing on experiential and intangible goods, with social and political implications that would not have been previously countenanced such as the low wages in the hospitality sector. The class nature of this politics, such as deregulating land and labour markets, dismantling democratic local government and reducing local governments' financial and political autonomy, attracts investors and knowledge workers. Place branding changes selected city images to demonstrate that they can provide the new middle classes with the services and environment they require. It also introduces various ideological concepts such as the culture of entrepreneurialism, that legitimates the new politics by contrasting it with welfare's alleged culture of dependency.

In this reading, place branding assumes a much greater significance than in conventional analyses because it becomes an active element in changing the balance of institutional class power. Class not imagery explains its rationale. The image, epitomised by the spectacle, is, as Debord (1995) explained, a class relation. The built environment, architecture, aesthetics, design and urban planning express class domination in stone, or as McGuirk (2014: 31) expresses it, 'urbanism is frozen politics'. The spectacle demonstrates how class power is exercised in entrepreneurial cities (Cronin and Hetherington, 2008), by associating it with the values of the political settlement and its particular interpretation of society. Since class politics has a low profile, people accept the new social order on the strength of these physical changes – East London's transformation that started with Canary Wharf, for instance, has without doubt helped to create a consensus around neoliberalism (Gough et al., 2006).

Place branding is important because it helps solve neoliberalism's dilemma of how to gain legitimacy. Class settlements in a democracy must be consensual rather than imposed, yet how is this possible for a settlement that has created such injustice? This is a question for the politics of knowledge to which place branding contributes – why are social phenomena interpreted in certain ways and not in others? To Rex (1974) social knowledge is distorted so as to mystify power and class relations and hide their negative impacts. Neoliberal society interprets itself in ways that socialise populations into believing in its consensual and universal nature. By viewing society through the lens of the built environment, place branding tends to obscure neoliberalism's political agenda, and that in turn may accommodate an intensification of class relations without provoking a political reaction. Place branding's concern with consent reflects the turbulent politics that underlies urban regeneration. Baltimore's Harbor Place, for instance, a spectacle of leisure, was explicitly developed to recreate feelings of inclusion in the face of the civic unrest in the 1960s that had been stimulated by the redevelopment of the city centre (Harvey, 1989). Yet that redevelopment, heavily branded, was part of the politics that has effectively juxtaposed a first and fourth world city, two worlds with nothing in common except a class relation.

Place branding has been criticised for its socially regressive impacts and its link to the dominant economic interests (Kavaratzis et al., 2018). The argument here is that not only does it represent these interests, but it also grapples with capitalism's central dilemma, how to preserve the class relations of appropriation while simultaneously meeting popular demands for liberty, democracy and an improved quality of life. One and a half centuries of reform was working towards these demands and had contained radical pressure without diminishing those relations of appropriation, but that contradiction could no longer be contained during the 1970s and 1980s as capital broke the social contract implicit in the Keynesian welfare state (Streeck, 2014). The effect of that action is that capitalism lost its most important means of legitimation, namely democracy. How does one gain mass consent for a class settlement when the dominant politics is primarily concerned with increasing capital's share of gross national product and when the democratic deficit is clearly visible? The battle for hearts and minds is now central to the future of many developed countries as the deep fissures in society become increasingly visible.

This is the context for situating place branding – it is part of the revival of economic liberalism yet it is also an activity that encourages consent. It therefore pulls in two directions at once. It makes promises about the possibilities of renewing poorly performing cities, yet it achieves this in ways that remove the protections that shielded residents and workers from the market. It contributes to the revival of disciplinary class relations through what Graham (2011) terms military urbanism, yet it successfully diverts people's attention from this resurgent class politics. Spectacles such as the Olympics embody this double-edged sword, their popularity facilitating more oppressive changes such as surveillance, that may encourage further capital inflows into the city. These entanglements make the subject worthy of further research.

The next section examines how place branding legitimates changes in class relations by its influence over our perceptions; and that in turn makes it possible to expand the sphere of accumulation. Subsequently, examples are provided of place branding's contribution to the new class settlement.

Place branding and the reproduction of neoliberal values

The origin of contemporary place marketing is the profits crisis of the 1970s, when capital felt as if its very survival was at stake (Glyn, 2006). The response was a range of class-driven strategies – globalisation, privatisation and deregulation – aimed at breaking the collective thinking of social democracy and re-establishing capital's hegemony. Place branding not only restructured society's social and political landscape by its actions on class relations, it also changed the ideas we use to explain everyday life. The doctrine of the entrepreneurial city dismisses globalisation as inevitable, but nothing could be further from the truth – its origins lie with pressures to loosen democratic control by the nation state over private property (Slobodian, 2018). Maintaining that control was central to social democratic politics, but neoliberalism's aim to return control to the owners of capital explains its antipathy to democracy. The political difficulties this involves also explain the chasm between the reality and the rhetoric around neoliberalism's policies, and why its defence tends to be couched in abstract rhetorical language (Slobodian, 2018). Place branding similarly justifies its actions in general terms – improving competitiveness – because of the political difficulty of admitting to, or even recognising, neoliberalism's own class analysis.

This attitude explains why the profession does not offer evidence for the impact of branded cities on quality-of-life indicators such as income and wealth distribution, social mobility or life chances. The practitioners' agenda is concerned primarily with effectiveness of its own aims – how can we best market the cities and improve their competitive position? Place branding aims to attract money to the city, yet one cannot assume that this will improve people's lives. For that reason we should be asking more questions. Which groups should benefit? Where do the additional revenues go? How much money leaks away to other locations, how much goes to property owners in higher rents, how much to shop assistants? Who benefits from tourism and who pays? Do the post-industrial sectors benefit the vulnerable? How could cities illustrate the social and political alternatives that have been experimented with in the last four decades of urban policy in Britain, such as the social economy (Amin, 2009)? These are questions for further research.

Ironically, while the argument here is for prioritising a class analysis, place branding's narrative depoliticises the last five decades of urban history by omitting a political analysis of urban problems. De-industrialisation is presented as a fact of nature rather than an explicit political choice that was designed to reduce both production costs and the power of the unions. Capital's return to the city is also presented in a consensus framework as beneficial to its populations. Yet underlying place branding's appearances is a highly political model that demonises social democracy for its economic naivety, that asserts the effectiveness of markets in restoring cities to their former wealth, yet which offers no protection to those facing housing problems and that creates a class of rentiers that live off the enhanced land values that branding creates (Harvey, 2012).

Place branding's conventional narrative projects neoliberalism's key assumptions and presents a provocative model of politics as common sense so as to change how populations are socialised. The regeneration agenda articulates the values of this class settlement so that the built environment projects a particular interpretation of social reality which is read and accepted. Place branding accordingly projects neoliberal assumptions and confirms the dominant narrative of a knowledge-based globalisation (Thomson, 2013) in which the cities must be restructured for the professionals associated with the post-industrial and consumer service economy. Cities obscure the class realities of this politics.

The combination of entrepreneurialism, regeneration and place marketing makes a powerful narrative because it introduces politics in a non-threatening way. It uses keywords such as creative cities, business-friendly politics, gentrification, culture, competitiveness, trickle-down and civil society to portray a new start for problem cities. These keywords are presented as a linked set of assumptions that reconceptualises relations between state, individual, civil society, markets and class in order to justify the new class settlement. Hence growth depends on low taxes, the economy is to be prioritised over welfare, welfare is a cost to society, subsistence goods should be supplied privately not collectively, trade unions should be excluded from participation in governance and enterprise and self-help are beneficial values for people and places. The practice of place branding repeats these fundamental neoliberal ideas and, by combining them with the spectacle's visual stimulus, demonstrates their truth (Eisenschitz, 2018).

The spectacle gives neoliberalism a benign image because it overshadows class. Dubai, for instance, owes everything to class relations: the semi-slaves that build it, the absence of citizenship among most of the population and its existence as the ruling family's private fiefdom (Davis, 2006). It illustrates a simple truth about place branding, that it is most effective in places where key markets – land, property, labour and finance – are unregulated and where it can present the spectacle of tourist utopias with no hint of the political relationships underpinning it. Dubai, Glasgow, Prague and even London's Docklands are presented as free from the restrictive politics of the past and as islands of consumption, freedom and consent. Yet they rest upon a divisive and invisible, neoliberal politics. As Monbiot (2016) notes, neoliberalism is almost invisible in Britain despite being the ruling politics – place marketing demonstrates the truth of that statement in supporting an interpretation of a convincingly apolitical world.

Place branding in practice

Place branding refracts the abstractions of neoliberalism through the lens of the physical so that physical symbols overshadow and obscure its class politics. Glasgow's time as European City of Culture in 1990 transformed its image from razor gangs, unemployment and alcoholism to a celebration of design, architecture, culture and retail (Garcia, 2004). The event was, however, more significant for the defeat of the traditional socialist establishment (McLay, 1990), a defeat that saw local and central government subsequently ignore the severe structural issues that make it Britain's most deprived locality (Mooney, 2004) in their aim to facilitate Glasgow's post-industrial path as a leisure destination. While the image helps to construct political consent, one must not forget the iron fist that preceded this velvet glove, the human costs of its economic collapse and the political marginalisation of those affected. Glasgow's heavily subsidised development of the leisure economy was the result of deliberate class politics: new investment targeted to the surrounding areas, a democratic deficit, a poor physical environment, the transfer of the Council's housing stock to the housing associations and the encouragement of a tourism sector with a low-wage, non-unionised workforce. The result is a premature mortality rate 30 per cent higher than cities in England and Wales with similar levels of deprivation (Walsh et al., 2016). Old industrial cities that have found a future in tourism have discovered that not only do the new jobs not compensate for those that were lost, but that they tend to have a polarised income distribution and a declining middle class (Guilluy, 2019).

Canary Wharf provides another example of the power of the spectacle in changing class politics through its impact upon perceptions. It was the centrepiece of Margaret Thatcher's claims that markets could overcome socialism's stifling impact upon human potential and economic development, audaciously built in the heartland of British socialism. Place branding depends upon the proposition that the real is rational; a building's physical presence tends to reinforce the politics that it embodies. The Enterprise Zone in which Canary Wharf was located was designed to show how Hong Kong-style liberalisation could transform Britain's poorest areas, while simultaneously making a statement about the failure of political democracy, welfare, local government and the public ownership of land. Regeneration simply required the liberation of the market. Canary Wharf's very existence demonstrates the truth of these statements. Yet this is rhetoric. London Docklands' success depended on a moment of raw political power, in which central government transferred public land and planning policy to the private sector by stripping local government of its democratic powers and spending billions on business-supporting infrastructure. Place branding is essential to making the cities attractive to capital and influencing public perceptions of that process (Bird, 2000).

Neoliberal politics helped clear the cities of manufacturing by facilitating the movement of capital overseas and opening them to the production of experiential goods that are less prone to unionisation. To attract visitors cities must capture and market a place's symbolic capital, which as Harvey (2012) points out is collective and an externality. The art of place branding is to ensure that these externalities – a place's unique culture, history, art, architecture, atmosphere, people – are transformed into private gain. This is the equivalent of privatising the commons. Creating imagery around the location lets it be priced into the goods that are sold there, whether that is retail, tourism or property, with the ultimate aim of raising land values and rents.

This material – Glasgow's cultural assets and working-class history, Birmingham's canals, Liverpool's music and cobbles, London's domestic Georgian houses, its Cockney culture – is sanitised, packaged and interpreted in ways that maximise rents. The beneficiaries are developers, housebuilders, landlords, hotels, tourist attractions, business services and retailers, all of whom extract that rent from their customers. These newly commodified externalities are sold to those able to afford them, this is the process of gentrification. Positive externalities are portrayed as universally good for everyone, overlooking the impact on vulnerable groups that are often forced to relocate in what is sometimes termed social cleansing. All this may occur only once neoliberal class relations have restructured the institutions that organise the urban environment. For example, the recent public investment and community building undertaken by London's great estates such as Howard de Walden in Marylebone or the Cadogan in Chelsea are successful instances of branding (NLA, 2013) as a means of increasing the rent roll.

Place branding advertises consensus by asserting that its strategies provide universal benefits. New Orleans uses ethnic diversity to proclaim such universality. Afro-American New Orleans is a commercialised, branded spectacle open to all and constructed around the cultural externalities of food, music and history (Gotham, 2007). Yet the universal promises displayed to tourists contrasts with the deep-seated exclusion endemic to Afro-Americans. This group, already marginalised in the tourism economy, was prevented from returning to the city after Hurricane Katrina as investment was directed to the central area and the white suburbs (Boyer, 2014).

By stressing universality, spectacles dampen social instability. That grandfather of place marketing, the Great Exhibition in Hyde Park, successfully obscured the turbulence of 1848, the first global resistance to the capitalist order (Saville, 1987). It was visited by one third of the country's population, becoming an enduring signifier of modernity, the capitalist social order, economic liberalism and the freedoms of empire. Spectacles like that symbolically articulate ideas of a consensual future by breaking down feelings of 'them and us'. The 2012 Olympics illustrated an entrepreneurial city engaging with the politics of city branding to promise to raise local residents' socio-economic wellbeing to the London average. Yet like all mega-events implemented within a neoliberal polity, its spatial, social, economic and political impacts rarely impact positively on vulnerable communities (Weber-Newth et al., 2017). Not only do they encourage the process of accumulation by dispossession, they are part of a narrative around the regulation and management of 'problem' people and 'problem' places, presenting a normative model of consumer-citizenship that has become an updated variant of blaming the poor for their condition (Paton et al., 2014). As these authors argue, this interpretation curtails a more collective interpretation of the causes of and possibilities that have arisen out of de-industrialisation. Mega-events must therefore be seen as powerful agents for the socialisation of working-class populations

The spectacle is a means used by all political interests to legitimate themselves. London's South Bank illustrates how conflict over land use is ultimately a conflict over class. Part of the area had been the site of the Festival of Britain in 1951, a spectacle aimed at consolidating the Labour government's politics, but its symbolic impact had been so powerful that Churchill's first action as incoming prime minister was to tear the site down. Land use determination in the area remained highly political. Further commercial development had been resisted by an alliance of unions, the community and local government, as illustrated in the 1980s by a community group gaining a major site, Coin Street, after a lengthy court battle. That victory, however, could not be consolidated. Central government intervention had so impoverished the local authorities that the group was forced to join the local regeneration partnerships in order to finance its development plan and that meant suppressing its more radical aims. These partnerships are power brokers representing major interest groups such as the London Tourist Board, Transport for London and local employers, and have access to finance as well as the ear of central government.

Such private–public partnerships at arms length to the state, classically use place branding to facilitate commercial regeneration and prevent more prime sites falling into working-class hands (Baeten, 2000). Yet they also depoliticise the development process by normalising the primacy of market forces in the land market. This consensus, however, has been imposed by force since it involved central government's victory over local governments' ability to raise money and the abolition of the first tier of London Government in 1986. In order to symbolise abolition, its headquarters, County Hall, was sold and developed for the tourist industry. Yet as neoliberalism's political power consolidated, place branding managed to hide a class-based interpretation of urban change and presents a political consensus that shows how it has contributed to the creation of an inclusive festival area, a mix of culture and entertainment illustrated by the London Eye and Tate Britain.

These examples illustrate how an interpretation around class relations differs from the conventional approach to understanding place branding. A final instance sees New York's place branding campaign as central to its economic renewal since the dark days of the early 1970s (Bendel, 2011). Harvey (2005) on the other hand takes a class perspective in which he attributes the revival of the city's fortunes to the coup staged by the banks to push the city into bankruptcy. They used their financial leverage to pay off the bondholders and slash the living standards of its working-class residents, stripping the city government and the unions of much of their powers. The elite subsequently restructured the institutions of governance, replacing democracy with entrepreneurialism, subsidising an infrastructure for business, renewing the economy around finance, law, media and cultural production, and encouraging a consumer economy, gentrification and neighbourhood revival. The famous place branding campaign was just one aspect of this process but ideologically it was significant because it obscured this wider political context. If, as these vignettes demonstrate, a symbolic urban politics helps construct the new class settlement, then this opens new areas of research for place branding.

Conclusion

We may draw four conclusions to inform further research. First if ever there was an activity requiring an interdisciplinary approach it is place branding. Its origins and impacts relate to so many aspects of society – socialisation and political legitimation, the development of class relations and political action, attitudes to production and consumption, interpretations of social inclusion and exclusion and the legitimation of gentrification and tourism – that one cannot treat it as an activity that simply attracts economic activity to a locality. Second, the distinction between academics and practitioners should be upheld, since the former are not constrained by the job and are therefore able to explore frameworks that transcend the activity's common-sense assumptions and assertions. However, much academic work is to support practitioners in being more effective in their limited aims. Third, academics should be aware of and test these hidden assertions. What are the implications of developing regeneration policy for, rather than with, the politically powerless? Is place branding really apolitical? What is the latent politics associated with the notion of the creative city (Peck, 2005)? Does improving a local economy improve the quality of life of local populations? Questioning place branding's assumptions will encourage the development of more criteria to assess it other than job creation or economic growth. Fourth, one must develop the range of explanations and interpretations of place branding in various paradigms rather than accepting the dominant one.

A typical comment summarises the profession's dilemmas. Hospers (2004) argues that Glasgow's strategy for arts and culture failed to recognise that the residents' history was rooted in class struggle and municipal socialism. His solution is to seek a consensus between people, the political and economic institutions, the local economy, cultural bodies and education. Yet by assuming that consensus is possible, he avoids confronting the possibility that this failure is not a mistake, but instead reflects real power relations. If that is so then the expectation of finding consensus should be critically examined – is consent possible, or is it part of neoliberal rhetoric that distracts from urban and social conflict? One should instead investigate why that strategy took the form it did and relate it to Glasgow's urban politics. An interdisciplinary framework would show how the organisation of urban space expresses political argument and that the reasons for image manipulation lie in the connections between material, symbolic and political conflicts. Rather than simply finding solutions within a narrow paradigm, research into place branding should be reflexive in order to develop critical interpretations of its own practice and ultimately to inform its future.

References

Alvesson, M., Yiannis, G. and R. Paulsen (2017), *Return to Meaning: A Social Science with Something to Say*, Oxford: Oxford University Press.

Amin, A. (ed.) (2009), *The Social Economy*, London: Zed.

Baeten, G. (2000), 'From community planning to partnership planning: Urban regeneration and shifting power geometries on the South Bank, London', *Geojournal*, 51 (4), 293–300.

Bendel, P. (2011), 'Branding New York City – the saga of "I love New York"', in K. Dinnie (ed.), *City Branding: Theory and Cases*, Basingstoke: Palgrave Macmillan, pp. 179–83.

Bird, J. (2000), 'Dystopia on the Thames', in M. Miles, T. Hall and I. Borden (eds), *The City Cultures Reader*, London: Routledge, pp. 305–9.

Boyer, C. (2014), 'Reconstructing New Orleans and the right to the city', in I. Stanek, C. Schmid and A. Moravanszky (eds), *Urban Revolution Now*, Farnham: Ashgate, pp. 173–90.

Cronin, A. and K. Hetherington (2008), 'Introduction', in A. Cronin and K. Hetherington (eds), *Consuming the Entrepreneurial City: Image, Memory, Spectacle*, New York: Routledge, pp. 1–17.

Das, R. (2017), *Marxist Class Theory for a Skeptical World*, Leiden: Brill.

Davis, M. (2006), 'Fear and money in Dubai', *New Left Review*, **41**, 47–68.

Debord, G. (1995), *The Society of the Spectacle*, New York: Zone Books.

Eisenschitz, A. (2018), 'Place marketing for social inclusion', in M. Kavaratzis, M. Giovanardi and M. Lichrou (eds), *Inclusive Place Branding*, Abingdon: Routledge, pp. 37–50.

Garcia, B. (2004), 'Urban regeneration, arts programming and major events', *International Journal of Cultural Policy*, **10** (1), 103–18.

Glyn, A. (2006), *Capitalism Unleashed*, Oxford: Oxford University Press.

Gotham, K. (2007), 'Ethnic heritage tourism and global–local connections in New Orleans', in J. Rath (ed.), *Tourism, Ethnic Diversity and the City*, Abingdon: Routledge, pp. 125–41.

Gough, J., Eisenschitz, A. and A. McCullogh (2006), *Spaces of Social Exclusion*, Abingdon: Routledge.

Graham, S. (2011), *Cities under Siege*, London: Verso.

Greater London Authority (2011), *The Local Area Tourism Impact Model Results for 2008 and 2009*, London: GLA.

Guilluy, C. (2019), *Twilight of the Elites*, New Haven, CT: Yale University Press.

Harvey, D. (1989), *The Condition of Postmodernity*, Oxford: Blackwell.

Harvey, D. (2005), *A Brief History of Neoliberalism*, Oxford: Oxford University Press.

Harvey, D. (2006), *Spaces of Global Capitalism*, London: Verso.

Harvey, D. (2012), *Rebel Cities*, London: Verso.

Hospers, G. (2004), 'Place marketing in Europe: The branding of the Oresund Region', *Intereconomics*, **39** (5), 271–9.

Kavaratzis, M., Giovanardi, M. and M. Lichrou (2018), 'Introduction', in M. Kavaratzis, M. Giovanardi and M. Lichrou (eds), *Inclusive Place Branding*, Abingdon: Routledge, pp. 1–10.

Kliman, A. (2012), *The Failure of Capitalist Production*, London: Pluto.

Mandel, E. (1975), *Late Capitalism*, London: Verso.

McGuirk, J. (2014), *Radical Cities*, London: Verso.

McLay, F. (1990), *The Reckoning*, Glasgow: Workers City.

Monbiot, G. (2016), 'Neoliberalism – the ideology at the root of all our problems', *The Guardian*, 15 April, p. 16.

Mooney, G. (2004), 'Cultural politics as urban transformation? Critical reflection on Glasgow, European City of Culture 1990', *Local Economy*, **19** (4), 327–40.

NLA (2013), *Great Estates: How London's Landowners Shape the City*, London: NLA.

O'Connor, J. (1973), *The Fiscal Crisis of the State*, London: St Martin's Press.

Paton, K., Mooney, G. and K. McKee (2014), 'Class, citizenship and regeneration: Glasgow and the Commonwealth Games', *Antipode*, **44** (4), 1470–89.

Peck, J. (2005), 'Struggling with the creative class', *International Journal of Urban and Regional Research*, **29** (4), 740–70.

Rex, J. (1974), *Sociology and the Demystification of the Modern World*, London: Routledge and Kegan Paul.

Saville, J. (1987), *1848: The British State and the Chartist Movement*, Cambridge: Cambridge University Press.

Slobodian, S. (2018), *Globalists: The End of Empire and the Birth of Neoliberalism*, Cambridge, MA: Harvard University Press.

Stone, J. and D. Hirsch (2019), *Local Indicators of Child Poverty, 2017/18*, Loughborough: Loughborough University.

Streeck, W. (2014), *Buying Time: The Delayed Crisis of Democratic Capitalism*, London: Verso.

Thomson, P. (2013), 'Romancing the market: Narrativising equity in globalising times', *Discourse: Studies in the Cultural Politics of Education*, **34** (2), 1–15.

Walsh, D., McCartney, G., Collins, C., Taulbut, M. and M. Batty (2016), *History, Politics and Vulnerability: Explaining Excess Mortality in Scotland and Glasgow*, Glasgow: Glasgow Centre for Population Health.

Weber-Newth, F., Schluter, S. and I. Helbrecht (2017), 'London 2012: "Legacy" as a Trojan horse', *Acme*, **16** (4), 713–39.

3 Computational approaches to place branding: A call for a theory-driven research agenda

Efe Sevin

Introduction

There is an abundance of 'data', especially thanks to our reliance on digital communication technologies to fulfill various functions in our lives. Consider your personal use: from the social media posts you created to the ride-sharing trips you took, from your financial transactions to movies you streamed, from your exercise routines to your search engine history; you consistently leave digital traces about your life and habits. The quest to gather – and, of course, analyze – data is not necessarily new. Marketing professionals have been working for decades to predict customer habits and changes in their lives. Indeed, a prominent retail store in the United States was able to tell that a customer was pregnant and started sending her maternity-relevant coupons before the individual was able to share the news with her parents around a decade ago (Duhigg, 2012). What is new, though, is the relative ease of access to data and analysis tools. The retail store had access to a large dataset and the individual's purchase history thanks to its size and loyalty programs. Moreover, it was able to employ an entire division of predictive statisticians. A similar analysis can be carried out based on 'found data' – datasets that are generated almost organically as a result of our new usage patterns and reliance on digital technologies (Groves, 2011). Google's now defunct Flu Trends, for instance, was such an attempt to aggregate web search queries to forecast the spread of the influenza virus based on specific keywords and search volumes (Dugas et al., 2013). The project is credited with forecasting the 2009 influenza spread patterns sooner and more accurately than the Center for Disease

Control and Prevention's system that was based on reporting by health-care providers (Cook et al., 2011).

Within this background, I propose a research agenda for place branding that is based on computational approaches. I use this particular label to bind our discussions within the field of place branding with larger discussions in social sciences (see Ünver, 2018 for a detailed discussion on the history and trajectory of computational social sciences), and to ensure the proposed research agenda is led by the new data sources and analyses capabilities, and not by new technologies per se. Place branding studies should not let specific platforms and functions present research questions, but rather should focus on how this new age of data is changing the relationship between places and individuals. Computational approaches 'exploit the advanced and increasingly powerful instruments of computation to see beyond the visible spectrum available through the traditional disciplines' (Cioffi-Revilla, 2010: 267). In the subsequent sections, I highlight two different domains that are affected by these instruments in place branding: changes in practice and changes in the availability of data/analysis methods for researchers.

First, computational approaches have been adopted by the practice as we have indeed welcomed algorithm-based thinking to place development through the concept of smart cities (see Albino et al., 2015; Caragliu et al., 2011 for examples), where cities have made use of information and communication technologies to deliver services ranging from mobility (Benevolo et al., 2016) to tourism promotion (Buhalis and Amaranggana, 2013). We have even seen that there is enough data, accompanied by relevant analysis powers, to start designing 'neighborhood(s) built from the internet up' as Google has proposed to do in Toronto (Scola, 2018). The chapter highlights main areas that are likely to change in the field of place branding and posits new research areas.

Second, researchers have more access to larger datasets – ranging from social media posts (e.g. Andéhn et al., 2014; Kassens-Noor et al., 2019) to ride-sharing movements (e.g. Uber, 2019) – and accompanying analysis methods. Matei and Kee (2019) argue for two strains of research based on these new datasets. Initially, a deductive research strain is possible. In other words, we can replace our traditional data resources with found data to explain place branding-relevant phenomena. New datasets and analysis methods will make it possible to contribute to existing research domains. Thanks to the sizes and diversity of these new datasets, it is also possible to observe new patterns and inductively explain the impacts of place branding campaigns on places and societies. Big data might be used to discover patterns in human behavior that were previously not observed.

The rest of the chapter is presented in four parts. First, I provide succinct working definitions for the concepts I use across the chapter. Second, I discuss how the ability to analyze larger datasets is likely to change the practice of place branding and open up new avenues for research. Third, I introduce ways scholars can access found data to amplify their research agendas. I conclude the chapter by delineating major future research areas in place branding and highlighting the shortcomings of overreliance on data.

Working definitions

Despite – or perhaps thanks to – the advancements in the field, we still observe a more solid consensus on what place branding is not rather than what it is (Kavaratzis and Ashworth, 2008). Within this conceptual richness (see Lucarelli and Berg, 2011 for a longer discussion), it is important to state explicit working definitions of terms. A place brand, in its essence, is a network of associations in the minds of individuals about a given place (Zenker and Braun, 2017). These associations 'are constructed from… various contributory elements' (Warnaby et al., 2015: 243), including what a place has to offer (e.g. its landscape, architecture, goods, services), what it communicates with the outside world (e.g. its advertisement campaigns), and what others communicate about the place (e.g. chatter on social media, reviews on websites, conversations among friends) (Kavaratzis, 2004).

Place branding is a practice based on the observation that the associations in the minds of individuals can be influenced (Sevin, 2014) through communication as well as policy making (Ashworth and Kavaratzis, 2010). For the sake of parsimony, it is possible to posit that place branding practice includes two major functions. On the communication side, places have used available marketing and advertising tools to disseminate their messages as well as to monitor the chatter about themselves (Braun et al., 2014). On the policy side, practitioners have supported 'policies that aimed at improving the place to the benefit of residents, businesses and visitors' (Boisen et al., 2018: 4), such as restructuring city centers (Peel and Parker, 2017), influencing spatial planning (Oliveira, 2015), and even changing overall policy priorities (Andersson, 2016).

Computational research refers to the availability of both datasets and the tools to carry out analyses. We, our devices, and our transactions keep generating new datasets. Within this context, I differentiate between two main types of data: found and big. The former refers to by-products of our digital interactions. These datasets are not necessarily created for our specific research questions but can be helpful in answering them. Users do not tweet about cities to help place branding researchers; however, their tweets can be analyzed to measure place brands (Sevin, 2014). The latter refers to the size and complexity of datasets (Harford, 2014). Within the context of this chapter, I use big data to refer to diverse and high-volume data available about individuals as well as our ability to merge different datasets, such as tweets and ride-share trips, to search for new patterns in individual behavior.

Practicing place branding in the age of data

Place branding is a predominantly practice-driven field of study (Lucarelli and Berg, 2011), therefore, it is not unexpected to start contemplating a research agenda by discussing how practice is going to change as a result of computational approaches. Places enjoy relatively easier and cheaper access to larger datasets to analyze their target audiences, and these target audiences can use multiple platforms and resources to learn more about those places. This dual increase in information is likely to affect the way place branding is practiced.

We have already started to observe such changes, for instance, via social media. As more and more potential travelers use web searches in their decision-making process (Molinillo et al., 2018), places have been exponentially increasing their online activity. When Sweden became the first country to have an official Twitter account and hand its control to its citizens in 2011, it was seen as a ground-breaking innovation (Curators of Sweden, 2018). Yet, in the last decade, at least '25 other countries, as well as numerous regional and city accounts' followed the country's lead (Christensen, 2013: 32). Social media graduated from being a stunt and became a staple component of place branding campaigns. A new genre of web-based communities, ranging from industry-specific ones such as TripAdvisor to generic ones such as YouTube, have changed the market conditions for place branding practitioners (The Place Brand Observer, 2019 para. Eduardo Oliveira). Electronic word of mouth established itself as an area to be controlled (Litvin et al., 2008). Places monitored the digital chatter to assess the perception of the audiences and to guide their branding campaigns (Andéhn et al., 2014). The arguments and examples presented here do not attempt to position social media as a new means to disseminate messages. From a computational approach perspective, these platforms are repositories of user-generated content (Li et al., 2018). These new practices encouraged scholars to pay further attention to how places were utilizing user-generated content to inform their policies and campaigns (see Ketter and Avraham, 2012, for a longer discussion on the issue).

Hyper-personalization is another outcome of big data that is likely to affect place branding in the future. As companies have more data points about a single individual in a cost-efficient manner, they can go beyond simple psychographic audience groups or other traditional groups in their interactions with target audiences. For instance, the consumer goods industry can produce vitamins or facial serums that are uniquely created for an individual's needs (Rosenbaum et al., 2019). Airlines and hotel groups are already investing in data infrastructure to better track the preferences and predict the needs of individual travelers (Whitby, 2019). And, in terms of the place product, the city of Lyon, France created a common database of customer-related information of around 2 million individuals and sends individuals customized messages to 'enhanc[e] the customers' experience and enable them to truly enjoy all aspects of the city' (Scholz and Friends, 2019: 39).

Another relevant practice is real-time marketing, that depends on dynamic data-mining processes combining and contextualizing a variety of internal (e.g. purchasing behavior, social media sentiment, and demographic information) and external (e.g. weather, traffic, and events) points of information to generate customized experiences for individuals (Buhalis and Sinarta, 2019). Actimel, a health supplement brand, made use of real-time marketing in the British market by incorporating weather forecasting, television programming, and social media data to target individuals having bad days (TVTY, 2016). Consequently, their outreach would increase on days with rain, television shows about healthy living, or increased complaints about train delays on Twitter (TVTY, 2016). In another case, Marriott's monitoring of social media and mass media data helped them generate an ad hoc advertising campaign when a house was sold for $65 million in Hong Kong (Hudson and Hudson, 2017). A regional newspaper included the particular house in a news article on the most expensive apartments and the article gained further traction on social media (Hudson and Hudson, 2017). Marriott realized one of its properties had the same harbor view as the house and decided to use side-by-side photos of the hotel room and the house in a digital advertising campaign (Hudson and Hudson, 2017). It is likely that we will observe the inclusion of various other real-time data points, such as tourist flows in specific places (Wei et al., 2017), and mobility (Benevolo et al., 2016) to craft time- and individual-specific messages in place branding.

Last but not least, we should expect to see vanity projects testing the boundaries of access to data. Washington, DC is one such city that employs a self-driving bus that relies on data coming from light detection, radars, and GPS (Aaron, 2019). Melbourne ran a 'remote control tourist' campaign in which an individual with helmet cameras live-streamed their walking tour of the city (MacLeod, 2013). The team behind the idea relied on social media data to crowdsource the route for the walking tour, Google Maps data to create real-time tracking information, and a notification system (MacLeod, 2013). It is probably too soon to label these projects as stunts or trailblazers, but it is not unimaginable that place branding campaigns might invest in using data for creative purposes.

Researching place branding in the age of data

The research into place branding predominantly asks three questions: how are brands produced, how do audiences interact with and react to brands, and what are the social outcomes of branding (Lucarelli and Berg, 2011)? Across all three, scholars rely, or rather relied, on data mainly coming from place branding campaigns gathered through qualitative methods (Lucarelli and Berg, 2011). As discussed in the previous section, the increasing interest of practitioners in social media encourages scholars to study these platforms. But the value of social media in research goes beyond the opportunity to observe place branding practice as user-generated content can be seen as found data, replacing traditional data-gathering methods.

Within a contemporary communication context, the utility of found data is two-fold. On the one hand, social media data includes unprompted reactions of users (Groves, 2011) that might be used to better capture the honest associations in people's minds (Sevin, 2014). Hjalager and Nordin (2011), for instance, recommend blog mining as a method to gather uncensored user comments. Equally, Shafranskaya (2016) used Instagram data to measure city happiness in Perm, Russia. Instead of relying on traditional data-gathering methods – in her case survey results or combining other statistical measures – Shafranskaya scraped geo-tagged photos from Instagram, overlaid them on a map of Perm, and used software to evaluate people's emotions. Beyond using found data to examine the production of brands, her work is also crucial in reconceptualizing what data should look like. In measuring place brands, scholars rely on textual data (Lucarelli and Berg, 2011), with minor exceptions looking at behavioral (e.g. decision to visit, study) outcomes (Tam and Kim, 2019). Utilizing an individual's facial expression by incorporating multimedia data is an important contribution to the literature. Oliver (2016), similarly, used cameras mounted on researchers to augment narrative data with video in her attempt to operationalize place identity in the city of Wollongong. Place identity was not necessarily only the words uttered but also the imagery captured by the researchers. In both Shafranskaya's and Oliver's research, multimedia data was further plotted onto maps, with the former using the entire city while the latter focused on walking tours. Tourism and hospitality research have already incorporated geo-tagged data primarily through file information gathered from digital photos (Wong et al., 2017). Place branding can also use the geographic information coming from social media data to better explain the relationship between spaces and associations in audiences' minds.

On the other hand, found data is also a by-product of how individuals interact with places. As these interactions become mediated by digital devices, it is easier to generate information about such experiences (Tussyadiah et al., 2018). Portable and wearable devices currently have the potential to act as tour guides. When users opt in to use their personal devices instead of another guide (e.g. human, guidebook, audio guides), their interactions with the places can be followed more closely. Such devices can be used to record and analyze patterns. Google Glass, a frame of glasses with a camera and heads-up display, was used to observe individual behavior in art galleries (Leue et al., 2015). Moreover, these devices gather information about overall physical movement and environmental variables, making it possible to explore the context in which individuals are found (Choe and Fesenmaier, 2017). In other words, portable and wearable technologies generate data that both can replace traditional methods of data gathering and pave the way for big data.

Yet, big data has been seen, by social scientists, as a 'world [that] is dominated by computer scientists' (Foster et al., 2017: 1). By definition, computational problems and challenges accompany big data as the datasets that can be classified as such are large and complex. There is indeed a methodological push in the social sciences to incorporate fundamental computer skills, such as programming languages and relational database management (Foster et al., 2017; Ünver, 2018). A meta literature review on the use of big data in tourism studies shows that scholars utilize three types of data: transaction, device, and user-generated content (Li et al., 2018). Transaction data includes resources such as web searches, online bookings, loyalty cards, and even highway traffic patterns. Device data relies on the network, location, and wireless connection details provided by connected devices. The last type, user-generated content, covers all textual and visual content disseminated by ordinary internet users. These datasets are invaluable resources that can be used to provide new explanations for individual behavior (Li et al., 2018).

Conclusion: Need for theory

In this chapter, I pointed out what possible research areas can be opened by computational approaches for place branding researchers. The chapter was intentionally limited to data sources and analysis tools. Even though these topics go hand in hand with the implementation of digital technologies, a focus was kept on the abundance of datasets and our ability to make better sense of these pieces of information. Technology, even without data per se, has already introduced a variety of new concepts to place branding practice and study, from gamification (Xu et al., 2017) to augmented and virtual reality (Govers, 2015), and to smart tourism (Gretzel et al., 2015). Yet, such changes were beyond the scope of the chapter.

The premise of the chapter is built on the concepts of found and big data. With the increasing adoption of digital communication technologies, individuals are leaving behind larger footprints for both place branding practitioners and scholars. The future research agenda should incorporate the new practices that are made possible by these new datasets as well as the new questions that can be answered by using them in research. More specifically, I posit that computational approaches enable practitioners to engage with audiences at a more individualized level. Social media monitoring and customized interactions on such platforms are already well established. As practitioners get more comfortable with computational approaches, the customization is likely to get even more focused. Hyper-personalization and real-time marketing are two tactics that have been observed in corporate branding and the hospitality industry, for example. Their applications in place branding can be a viable research area.

Found data has been instrumental in expanding the definition of 'data'. Moving beyond solely texts, scholars have already incorporated visuals and locations into their studies. This move should come as no surprise given the fact that place branding is basically a relationship between individuals and geographic spaces (Boisen et al., 2018). Multimedia data better captures human experiences, whereas location data contextualizes these in spatial terms. With the increasing adoption of wearable devices, users will generate even higher and more diverse volumes of data. Although big data has presented logistical challenges for social scientists, ignoring the existence of large-scale observations on different aspects of social life limits our ability to explore and explain social phenomena. Incorporating such datasets into place branding research and pushing the interdisciplinarity of place branding to include computer sciences can be another viable research area.

Although the chapter presents an enthusiastically supportive case for found and big data in social science research, it should be noted that these concepts are not without their problems and challenges. Privacy and security of data are paramount concerns (see Cuzzocrea, 2014, for a longer discussion). Individuals are not necessarily aware of the extent of digital surveillance. Similarly, academia has been slow in adapting its regulations on human subject research to catch up with the latest changes. Second, the excitement over big data makes the mistake of exaggerating the role of observation. Tim Harford (2014), in his lecture at the Royal Statistical Society International Conference, warns the audience of these tendencies by quoting an article published in *Wired*, a popular technology magazine, where the author claims that the 'hypothesize-model-test' approach to science is becoming obsolete as the volume of observations ensures correlation is enough (Anderson, 2008).

Big and found data are solely research tools created by technology and should be used as such. They do not replace insights or inference (Harford, 2014) provided by analytical and theoretical frameworks. Scholars should be careful in incorporating such resources into their research agenda to make sure they do not repeat the mistakes of place branding practitioners. Technology has been used in lieu of place branding 'as an end in itself [reflecting] commodit[z]ed virtual brand values of modernity, openness and innovation, as opposed to being a tool to reflect meaningful... brand values' (Govers, 2015: 73). Succinctly stated, even though computational approaches pave the way to exciting research using datasets of unprecedented sizes and ranges, works presenting theory-led methods are likely to have continued influence in the future.

References

Aaron, J. (2019), 'WATCH: Self-driving shuttle bus coming to National Harbor, Arlington', *WTOPnews*, 5 June, accessed 13 July 2020 at: https://wtop.com/dc-transit/2019/06/watch-self-driving-shuttle-bus-coming-to-national-harbor-arlington/.

Albino, V., Berardi, U., and R. M. Dangelico (2015), 'Smart cities: Definitions, dimensions, performance, and initiatives', *Journal of Urban Technology*, **22** (1), 3–21.

Andéhn, M., Kazeminia, A., Lucarelli, A., and E. Sevin (2014), 'User-generated place brand equity on Twitter: The dynamics of brand associations in social media', *Place Branding and Public Diplomacy*, **10**, 132–44.

Anderson, C. (2008), 'The end of theory: The data deluge makes the scientific method obsolete', *Wired*, 23 June, accessed 13 July 2020 at: www.wired.com/2008/06/pb-theory/.

Andersson, I. (2016), "Green cities" going greener? Local environmental policy-making and place branding in the "Greenest City in Europe"', *European Planning Studies*, **24** (6), 1197–215.

Ashworth, G. and M. Kavaratzis (2010), 'Conclusion', in G. Ashworth and M. Kavaratzis (eds), *Towards Effective Place Brand Management: Branding European Cities and Regions*, Cheltenham, UK and Northampton, MA, USA: Edward Elgar Publishing, pp. 234–9.

Benevolo, C., Dameri, R. P., and B. D'Auria (2016), 'Smart mobility in smart city', in T. Torre, A. M. Braccini and R. Spinelli (eds), *Empowering Organizations: Lecture Notes in Information Systems and Organisation*, Vol. 11, Cham: Springer International Publishing, pp. 13–28, https://doi.org/10.1007/978-3-319-23784-8_2.

Boisen, M., Terlouw, K., Groote, P., and O. Couwenberg (2018), 'Reframing place promotion, place marketing, and place branding: Moving beyond conceptual confusion', *Cities*, **80**, 4–11.

Braun, E., Eshuis, J., and E.-H. Klijn (2014), 'The effectiveness of place brand communication', *Cities*, **41**, 64–70.

Buhalis, D. and A. Amaranggana (2013), 'Smart tourism destinations', in Z. Xiang and I. Tussyadiah (eds), *Information and Communication Technologies in Tourism 2014*, Cham: Springer International Publishing, pp. 553–64, https://doi.org/10.1007/978-3-319-03973-2_40.

Buhalis, D. and Y. Sinarta (2019), 'Real-time co-creation and nowness service: Lessons from tourism and hospitality', *Journal of Travel and Tourism Marketing*, **36** (5), 563–82.

Caragliu, A., Del Bo, C., and P. Nijkamp (2011), 'Smart cities in Europe', *Journal of Urban Technology*, **18** (2), 65–82.

Choe, Y. and D. R. Fesenmaier (2017), 'The quantified traveler: Implications for smart tourism development', in Z. Xiang and D. R. Fesenmaier (eds), *Analytics in Smart Tourism Design: Tourism on the Verge*, Cham: Springer International Publishing, pp. 65–77, https://doi.org/10.1007/978-3-319-44263-1_5.

Christensen, C. (2013), '@Sweden: Curating a nation on Twitter', *Popular Communication*, **11** (1), 30–46.

Cioffi-Revilla, C. (2010), 'Computational social science', *Wiley Interdisciplinary Reviews: Computational Statistics*, **2** (3), 259–71.

Cook, S., Conrad, C., Fowlkes, A. L., and M. H. Mohebbi (2011), 'Assessing Google Flu Trends performance in the United States during the 2009 influenza virus A (H1N1) pandemic', *PLoS ONE*, **6** (8), e23610, https://doi.org/10.1371/journal.pone.0023610.

Curators of Sweden (2018), *Thank You, Curators of Sweden!*, https://curatorsofsweden.com/.

Cuzzocrea, A. (2014), 'Privacy and security of big data: Current challenges and future research perspectives', *Proceedings of the First International Workshop on Privacy and Security of Big Data - PSBD '14*, Shanghai.

Dugas, A. F., Jalalpour, M., Gel, Y., Levin, S., Torcaso, F., Igusa, T., and R. E. Rothman (2013), 'Influenza forecasting with Google Flu Trends', *PLoS ONE*, **8** (2), e56176, https://doi.org/10.1371/journal.pone.0056176.

Duhigg, C. (2012), 'How companies learn your secrets', *New York Times Magazine*, 16 February, accessed 13 July 2020 at: www.nytimes.com/2012/02/19/magazine/shopping-habits.html?pagewanted=1&_r=1&hp.

Foster, I., Ghani, R., Jarmin, R. S., Kreuter, F., and J. Lane (eds) (2017), *Big Data and Social Science: A Practical Guide to Methods and Tools*, Boca Raton, FL: CRC Press.

Govers, R. (2015), 'Rethinking virtual and online place branding', in M. Kavaratzis, G. Warnaby, and G. J. Ashworth (eds), *Rethinking Place Branding: Comprehensive Brand Development for Cities and Regions*, Cham: Springer International Publishing, pp. 73–83.

Gretzel, U., Sigala, M., Xiang, Z., and C. Koo (2015), 'Smart tourism: Foundations and developments', *Electronic Markets*, **25** (3), 179–88.

Groves, R. M. (2011), 'Three eras of survey research', *Public Opinion Quarterly*, **75** (5), 861–71.

Harford, T. (2014), 'Big data: A big mistake?', *Significance*, **11** (5), 14–19.

Hjalager, A.-M. and S. Nordin (2011), 'User-driven innovation in tourism: A review of methodologies', *Journal of Quality Assurance in Hospitality and Tourism*, **12** (4), 289–315.

Hudson, S. and L. Hudson (2017), *Marketing for Tourism, Hospitality and Events: A Global and Digital Approach* (1st edition), London: Sage.

Kassens-Noor, E., Vertalka, J., and M. Wilson (2019), 'Good games, bad host? Using big data to measure public attention and imagery of the Olympic Games', *Cities*, **90**, 229–36.

Kavaratzis, M. (2004), 'From city marketing to city branding: Towards a theoretical framework for developing city brands', *Place Branding and Public Diplomacy*, **1** (1), 58–73.

Kavaratzis, M. and G. Ashworth (2008), 'Place marketing: How did we get here and where are we going?', *Journal of Place Management and Development*, **1** (2), 150–65.

Ketter, E. and E. Avraham (2012), 'The social revolution of place marketing: The growing power of users in social media campaigns', *Place Branding and Public Diplomacy*, **8** (4), 285–94.

Leue, M. C., Jung, T., and D. tom Dieck (2015), 'Google Glass augmented reality: Generic learning outcomes for art galleries', in I. Tussyadiah and A. Inversini (eds), *Information and Communication Technologies in Tourism*, Cham: Springer International Publishing, pp. 463–76.

Li, J., Xu, L., Tang, L., Wang, S., and L. Li (2018), 'Big data in tourism research: A literature review', *Tourism Management*, **68**, 301–23.

Litvin, S. W., Goldsmith, R. E., and B. Pan (2008), 'Electronic word-of-mouth in hospitality and tourism management', *Tourism Management*, **29** (3), 458–68.

Lucarelli, A. and P. O. Berg (2011), 'City branding: A state-of-the-art review of the research domain', *Journal of Place Management and Development*, **4** (1), 9–27.

MacLeod, D. (2013), 'Melbourne remote control tourist', *Inspiration Room*, 11 October, accessed 13 July 2020 at: http://theinspirationroom.com/daily/2013/melbourne-remote-control-tourist/.

Matei, S. A. and K. F. Kee (2019), 'Computational communication research', *Wiley Interdisciplinary Reviews: Data Mining and Knowledge Discovery*, **9** (4), e1304, https://doi.org/10.1002/widm.1304.

Molinillo, S., Liébana-Cabanillas, F., Anaya-Sánchez, R., and D. Buhalis (2018), 'DMO online platforms: Image and intention to visit', *Tourism Management*, **65**, 116–30.

Oliveira, E. H. da S. (2015), 'Place branding in strategic spatial planning: A content analysis of development plans, strategic initiatives and policy documents for Portugal 2014–2020', *Journal of Place Management and Development*, **8** (1), 23–50.

Oliver, J. L. (2016), *Researching Place Identity: Developing a Systemic Semiotic Multi-Modal Participative Framework*, PhD, Wollongong: University of Wollongong, https://ro.uow.edu.au/theses/4788.

Peel, D. and C. Parker (2017), Planning and governance issues in the restructuring of the high street', *Journal of Place Management and Development*, **10** (4), 404–18.

Rosenbaum, M. S., Ramirez, G. C., Campbell, J., and P. Klaus (2019), 'The product is me: Hyper-personalized consumer goods as unconventional luxury', *Journal of Business Research*, S0148296319303297, https://doi.org/10.1016/j.jbusres.2019.05 .017.

Scholz and Friends (2019), *Compendium of Best Practices*, 2019 European Capital of Smart Tourism competition, European Commission, accessed 14 July 2020 at: https://smarttourismcapital.eu/best-practices/.

Scola, N. (2018), 'Google is building a city of the future in Toronto. Would anyone want to live there?', *PoliticoMagazine*, accessed 14 July 2020 at: https://politi.co/ 2ICaQGW.

Sevin, E. (2014), 'Understanding cities through city brands: City branding as a social and semantic network', *Cities*, **38**, 47–56.

Shafranskaya, I. (2016), 'Using data from geo-tagging to map the Happy City', *Institute of Place Management Blog*, 11 July, accessed 14 July 2020 at: http://blog .placemanagement.org/2016/07/11/happy-city/.

Tam, L. and J.-N. Kim (2019), 'Who are publics in public diplomacy? Proposing a taxonomy of foreign publics as an intersection between symbolic environment and behavioral experiences', *Place Branding and Public Diplomacy*, **15** (1), 28–37.

The Place Brand Observer (2019), *How Do Social Media Affect Place Brands? Opportunities and Risks*, 13 August, accessed 14 July 2020 at: https://placebrandobserver.com/how -social-media-affect-place-brands/.

Tussyadiah, I., Jung, T. H., and M. C. tom Dieck (2018), 'Embodiment of wearable augmented reality technology in tourism experiences', *Journal of Travel Research*, **57** (5), 597–611. https://doi.org/10.1177/0047287517709090.

TVTY (2016), *Mastering Moment Marketing: An Analysis of Moment Marketing Adoption and Best Practice Strategy*, accessed 14 July 2020 at: www.iabuk.com/sites/ default/files/public_files/Mastering_Moment_Marketing.pdf.

Uber (2019), *Uber Movement: Let's Find Smarter Ways Forward, Together*, accessed 14 July 2020 at: https://movement.uber.com/explore/washington_DC/travel-times/ query?lang=en-US&si=186&ti=&ag=censustracts&dt[tpb]=ALL_DAY&dt[dr][sd] =2018-12-01&dt[dr][ed]=2018-12-31&dt[wd;]=1,2,3,4,5,6,7&cd=&sa;=&sdn.

Ünver, H. A. (2018), 'Computational international relations: What can programming, coding and internet research do for the discipline?', *All Azimuth*, **8** (2), 157–82.

Warnaby, G., Ashworth, G. J., and M. Kavaratzis (2015), 'Sketching futures for place branding', in M. Kavaratzis, G. Warnaby, and G. J. Ashworth (eds), *Rethinking Place Branding: Comprehensive Brand Development for Cities and Regions*, Cham: Springer International Publishing, pp. 241–8.

Wei, J., Ma, L., and Z. Zhang (2017), 'A research on smart tourism-oriented big data real-time processing technology', *2017 29th Chinese Control and Decision Conference*, 1848–51, https://doi.org/10.1109/CCDC.2017.7978817.

Whitby, P. (2019), 'Japan Airlines, RCI and Allegiant: The journey to hyper-personalization with a human touch', White Paper in conjunction with *Analytics and AI in Travel North America*, 14–15 March, accessed 15 July 2020 at: www.eyefortravel .com/social-media-and-marketing/japan-airlines-rci-and-allegiant-journey-hyper -personalization-human-0.

Wong, E., Law, R., and G. Li (2017), 'Reviewing geotagging research in tourism', in R. Schegg and B. Stangl (eds), *Information and Communication Technologies in*

Tourism 2017: Proceedings of the International Conference in Rome, Italy, January 24–26, 2017, Cham: Springer International Publishing, pp. 43–58.

Xu, F., Buhalis, D., and J. Weber (2017), 'Serious games and the gamification of tourism', *Tourism Management*, **60**, 244–56.

Zenker, S. and E. Braun (2017), 'Questioning a "one size fits all" city brand: Developing a branded house strategy for place brand management', *Journal of Place Management and Development*, **10** (3), 270–87.

4 Demystifying participation and engagement in the branding of urban places

Andrea Insch

Introduction

As place branding has moved into the realm of urban policy portfolios, interest in ways of fostering greater involvement from community members has garnered increasing attention. Importantly, over the past decade a growing number of studies document collaborative and participatory place branding to inform best practice and in turn bring about greater benefits of place branding for all. Despite such good intentions, the conceptual underpinnings and philosophical basis for participatory place branding have not been given sufficient consideration. The aim of this chapter is, therefore, to examine the foundations of inclusive place branding and to identify the different forms that this may take in the urban branding process. After defining the conceptual boundaries of the urban branding domain, a systematic literature review is applied to answer the following questions: 1) What forms of participation and engagement in urban branding are evident? and 2) How do members of local communities become actively involved or excluded in this process?

In answering these questions this chapter aims to contribute to the intersecting disciplines of urban studies, place branding and governance by clarifying understanding of the participation and engagement of local community members in the process of branding urban places, elucidating how this process could be more inclusive to capture and represent the multiplicity of identities in towns and cities (Dinnie, 2018). This research also responds to calls for scholars to develop a critical understanding of urban branding practices, with a focus on the representation of place identity and how the process of urban branding privileges some groups over others (Mayes, 2008; Vallaster et al., 2018).

The chapter begins by considering the participants in the urban branding process. Next, the concepts of participation and engagement are defined before examining the scope of community participation. To understand the varieties of participation and engagement in urban branding, previous research is analysed to identify the forms of participation and what mechanisms can act as enablers and barriers to participation and engagement. Throughout this discussion, the chapter aims to show that the evolution of participatory approaches to urban branding must move beyond a one-dimensional view that is focused principally on including a wide range of participants, to a two-dimensional view that also enables their deep engagement in various aspects of the ongoing and dynamic process of urban branding.

Participants in branding urban places

Place branding is a process of creating, reinforcing and re-creating place identity and selectively communicating elements of this identity to intended and unintended audiences. This selective representation (Boisen et al., 2011) of different aspects of a place can be undertaken in a highly structured and organised way, such as in the case of a territorial authority's city branding campaign to inform groups such as potential visitors, migrants and investors about the city's unique cityscape, assortment of attractions, events and hospitality options. Applying sophisticated marketing tools and techniques, this can occur in a highly targeted manner adopting the latest digital technologies (Florek, 2011; Strekalova, 2018) alongside more traditional ways of communicating to chosen audiences (Florek et al., 2006; Janiszewska and Insch, 2012). Depending on the communication platforms employed by the marketing professionals, insider audiences including residents, business operators and former locals who are still highly connected to the place may become aware of the efforts to raise awareness of the place brand among outsider (external) audiences (Insch and Stuart, 2015; Sherman, 2010). Whether or not community members are content with the representation of their place will influence their attitude towards place branding as a policy and practice of the local governing authority (Insch and Stuart, 2015), the strength of their connection to the place brand (Kemp et al., 2012a) and their likelihood to promote it to others (Kemp et al., 2012b). As established by Zenker and Seigis (2012), citizens also value being respected by public officials responsible for place marketing; it may influence their inclination to become involved in the place branding process in a more or less collaborative fashion.

At the heart of the debate on collaborative and participatory forms of place branding is the assumption that participation and engagement in its many forms and manifestations is a good thing for places of differing scales (i.e. national, regional, city, town, neighbourhood and street levels).[1] This is predicated on the basis that the various members of the community with an interest and stake in the city have the right to contribute to decisions about how the place in which they live, work and play – which in turn is part of their self-identity – should be represented within the community and to various out(side) groups. This argument is one that has been strongly embraced in the place branding literature, particularly to make the case for why those with institutional responsibility for governing and managing the place brand should gain the support and buy-in of members of the place brand community in its widest possible sense.

Individuals on their own, and collectively within organisations, need motivation to engage with the place brand. This can be intrinsically through a sense of pride that they feel for a given place. For example, Andersson and Ekman's (2009) study demonstrated that individuals who choose to become place brand ambassadors were motivated by the chance to 'help create a positive momentum for the place' and their curiosity about what the role would entail (2009: 50). Members of the network were also motivated by the opportunity to gain first-hand information about what was happening in the place and to assist with its marketing. There might also be external motivation such as the desire to benefit from the place gaining wider recognition and attracting additional resources that might ultimately benefit the individual directly or an organisation of which they are a member (e.g. their employer). Alternatively, some forms of governance that dictate compliance with the ruling regime and prevailing social norms may serve as an extrinsic motivation for community members to support the place brand.

A number of researchers report instances of protest and resistance to authorities' attempts at place branding (Maiello and Pasquinelli, 2015). Here, there is a clear mismatch of values and ideas about a place and the way that it should be represented (Walters and Insch, 2018). Some individuals and groups have taken their disagreement further and created an alternative representation of the place brand, or have directly attacked the official expressions of the place brand using an anti-branding campaign (with differing impact, uptake and effect) (Vallaster et al., 2018). Lack of support by residents for place branding can also take passive forms, including apathy and disengagement from authorities' official expressions and attempts at branding. This is driven by residents' lack of brand awareness/knowledge, lack of brand identification, disapproval of local government actions and cynical attitudes towards involvement (Insch and Stuart, 2015). There is also evidence that disengaged residents may perceive the goals of city branding as threatening their place identity and thus are resistant to this urban governance strategy (Insch and Walters, 2018). These represent formidable, but not unsurmountable, barriers to stakeholder participation and engagement in city branding.

The terms participation and engagement have gained increasing currency in the attention economy as individuals face information overload (Lichrou et al., 2017) and can become overstimulated (Kane, 2019). These concepts also apply to the context of a civic community where individuals live in two spheres (i.e. digital and physical), which are becoming increasingly intertwined. Determining the difference between participation and engagement is thus necessary for examining participatory approaches to urban branding which take place in this intersecting context. Fundamentally, the concept of participation involves the act of taking part or sharing with others, whereas engagement can be conceived as 'occupying the attention or efforts of' others (Anon, 2009). Engagement can be viewed as a 'step beyond participation' whereby an individual adds to the effort or activity in which they are a participant by making a valuable investment of their resources. Increasing participation in place branding tends to focus more on raising the number of stakeholders involved in the process, rather than improving the quality of their contribution, which is the domain of engagement. There are a number of ways to enhance the engagement of those interested in participating. Previous research shows that individuals who participated in brand ambassador networks demonstrated greater commitment to the network over time when the network's purpose was focused and expectations of their role were clear and concise (Andersson and Ekman, 2009). Further, individuals indicated greater likelihood of being engaged if they were given concrete tasks to perform. This is consistent with research in organisational psychology which indicates that individuals are more likely to be engaged when given actionable things to do (Squires, 2015).

Participation and engagement of a wide range of community members in collaborative decision making can bring benefits such as increasing legitimacy, transparency and accountability in the governance of urban brands (Eshuis and Edwards, 2013; Sevin, 2011). As is the case with other urban policy contexts, urban branding is 'an ongoing process… where the focal "organization" is a constellation of different groups rather than a more monolithic business organization. Such processes are, of course, driven by interactions' (Le Feuvre et al., 2016: 59). However, too little is known about the dynamics of branding urban places and why some community members participate and others are excluded (Insch and Walters, 2018). This is a global problem requiring further research: how can urban branding enable wider participation and deeper engagement of community members (Kavaratzis and Hatch, 2013; Lichrou et al., 2017; Reynolds, 2018)?

What does participation in branding urban places look like?

Due to the complexities of constructing urban brand identities that capture the diversity within communities, governance of urban brands is usually top down with limited involvement of local community members (Casais and Monteiro, 2019; Kavaratzis and Kalandides, 2015), despite the need for collaboration between all relevant stakeholders (Lichrou et al., 2017). There have been a number of concerted efforts over the past decade to involve diverse and disparate groups of stakeholders in different aspects of place branding (Eugenio-Vela et al., 2019; Kavaratzis and Kalandides, 2015; Reynolds, 2018). However, the adoption of collaborative and inclusive forms of place branding is far from universal, in spite of the purported benefits (Eshuis and Edwards, 2013). Similarly, the forms of participation differ considerably and the emergence of a standardised approach does not appear to be possible, or advisable, given the diversity of urban contexts. Yet, it is possible to delineate different perspectives on participation by examining who is involved, how they are involved and what their influence is on the place branding process.

First, addressing the question of who is involved, it is possible to apply traditional marketing and strategic management frameworks such as stakeholder analysis to sort individuals, groups and organisations into those with a stake in the process (Helmi et al., 2019; Reynolds, 2018; Ripoll Gonzalez and Lester, 2018). Such approaches focus on classifying stakeholders into groups, based on their interests, characteristics or sectoral affiliations in relation to a focal firm, with less attention given to more complex networks of stakeholder relationships characterised by dynamic interactions among a 'very diffuse and amorphous agglomeration of groups from public, private and voluntary sectors, with different ethea, mindsets, perspectives, modus operandi etc.' (Le Feuvre et al., 2016: 56).

Alternatively, place branding scholars and practitioners can borrow from the social science disciplines of social and cultural geography to understand how members of society may be permitted or barred from being involved through the concepts of exclusion, segregation, integration and inclusion. An exclusive approach to selecting participants may be taken by those responsible for managing a city's brand when certain criteria are employed, such as position in the community, profession or celebrity status (Andersson and Ekman, 2009). Participants are typically invited to participate and numbers tend to be restricted. This strategic inclusion of specific target groups demonstrates a clear agenda to purposefully exclude others (Boisen et al., 2011: 143).

Members of the community can also be excluded from participating in an otherwise open invitation due to certain barriers that may restrict them from joining in. This notion of exclusion incorporates those lacking the economic and social means to participate effectively. Duffy (1995: 5) explains this concept of exclusion as 'low material means and the inability to participate effectively in economic, social, political, and cultural life, and, in some characterisations, alienation and distance from the mainstream society'. In this definition, social differences are inherent in processes of exclusion where mechanisms for encouraging participation are designed for mainstream society. Figure 4.1 shows how members of a community have differential rights and abilities to participate in civic processes, in this case, urban branding. For example, in a conceptual study of participatory place branding, Kavaratzis and Kalandides (2015) recognise that a limitation of a place branding project in Bogotá, Colombia (Kalandides, 2011) was the inclusion of only educated middle-class participants, 'mostly for reasons of access'; thereby excluding 'a large section of the city's residents' (Kavaratzis and Kalandides, 2015: 1378). There are several other examples in empirical studies that acknowledge the lack of diversity of participants in place branding campaigns and the exclusion of members from different groups in the wider community (Eshuis and Edwards, 2013).

Diversity is an inherent characteristic of cities. Cities and other urban places by their very nature are concentrations of people who exhibit various social differences (e.g. ethnicity, age, occupation, social class, gender and disability). To make the urban brand meaningful for diverse social and cultural groups, the processes of urban branding must endeavour to give voice to the multiplicity of identities therein. This can be accomplished in part by cultivating a sense of belonging and place attachment. For example, the 'Be Berlin' campaign launched in 2008 sought to invite a wide representation of Berliners to tell their story via the campaign's website. Citizens of Berlin, including those from ethnic minorities that did not feature in previous campaigns, were able to tell their story (Colomb and Kalandides, 2010).

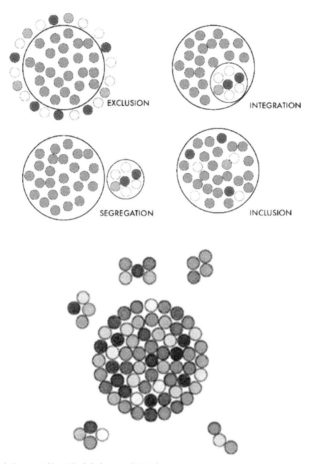

Source: (a) Gendel (2019); (b) Carter (2020).

Figure 4.1   Differing approaches to participation in urban branding

In contrast, there are examples of place branding initiatives that endorse a segregation or integration approach. Aligned with a segregation approach, members of the community that are identified as outside the mainstream may be given the right to access specialised roles, such as the case of volunteer roles which require participants to be available during the day to assist visitors to the city. Thus, a role may be crafted for a specific group – such as retirees – enabling them to take part in the city's branding process. Whereas, place branding that takes an integrative approach creates policies and mechanisms that enable members of a group identified as outside the mainstream to be able to access the same roles as those within the mainstream. Through fostering a sense of belonging to a community, members of that community are more likely to feel that they are in a position to participate and have their voices heard like everyone else. According to Fosslien and Duffy (cited in Hoenigman Meyer, 2019: 1), 'diversity is having a seat at the table, inclusion is having a voice, and belonging is having that voice be heard'. To counter barriers to inclusion and encourage community members to engage, individuals with responsibility for driving and governing the brand 'need organizational and discursive strategies that are designed to build voice, to foster a sense of common benefit, to develop confidence among disempowered groups, and to arbitrate when disputes arise' (Friedmann, 2010: 161).

Forms of participation in branding urban places

Over the past decade over two dozen studies have been published examining the nature of participation and collaboration within the place branding activities of different urban authorities and amongst place branding practitioners (see Table 4.1). The majority of these studies are empirical, with a few focused on developing conceptual frameworks to depict the process. Most of the empirical studies select European cities as their research setting, with studies also set in South America, Australia, the United States and South Korea. In some cases, there is an overlap between place branding and place making, and urban planning and development (Van Assche and Lo, 2011; Zenker and Seigis, 2012). This is unsurprising given the blurred lines and interdependencies between each of these domains (Eshuis and Edwards, 2013).

Arguably, it is difficult to depict any identity-driven process as a linear one, yet many identity-shaping processes are drawn in this way to simplify their management. This applies to managerial approaches to place branding, which have dominated theory and practice in this field. However, as the complexities and contradictions of place branding are increasingly recognised, there have been several contributions that conceptualise it as a dynamic process of a more fluid nature, rather than a collection of discrete stages (Kavaratzis and Hatch, 2013; Kavaratzis and Kalandides, 2015). Juxtaposed to these conceptual advances, many of the studies of participatory place branding examine only one aspect of the dynamic process. Typically, studies focus on the preliminary stages of a place branding campaign or strategy, that is the identity-defining or redefining component, to contribute ideas towards the concept, values and visual identity (Sarabia-Sanchez and Cerda-Bertomeu, 2017).

Table 4.1   Main studies on participatory approaches to branding urban places

Authors	Paper type (setting)	Participants	Stage and form of participation
Andersson and Ekman (2009)	Empirical (Sweden, Finland, Norway, Denmark and the United Kingdom, Scotland)	Members of brand ambassador networks	Promoting the place brand, contributing ideas for place development through meetings and events.
Colomb and Kalandides (2010)	Empirical (Berlin, Germany)	Residents	Contributing their stories for the 'Be Berlin' campaign.
Zenker and Seigis (2012)	Empirical (Hamburg, Germany)	Residents	Varying types of participation in place development projects (resident participation in place marketing, binding character of participation, open question type and repeated participation).
Kempet al. (2012 b)	Empirical (Austin, Texas, United States)	Residents	Brand advocacy.
Eshuis and Edwards (2013)	Empirical (Rotterdam, the Netherlands)	Residents	Contributing to the content of the brand campaign. Limited direct citizen participation.
Kavaratzis and Hatch (2013)	Theoretical	Advocates for a wide scope of stakeholder participation, in particular residents	Dialogue, debate and contestation.
Zenker and Erfgen (2014)	Conceptual	Residents	Ambassadors and advocates controlling their own branding projects.
Kavaratzis and Kalandides (2015)	Conceptual and empirical (Bogotá, Colombia)	Tourism officials, architects, historians, planners, business representatives and residents	In-depth interviews with different stakeholders. Focus groups of educated middle-class participants.

Authors	Paper type (setting)	Participants	Stage and form of participation
Monteiro (2016)	Empirical (Porto, Portugal)	Residents	Residents' participation in the creation of the brand.
Sarabia-Sanchez and Cerda-Bertomeu (2017)	Empirical (Latin America and Spain)	Experts (politicians, scholars, public managers and consultants)	The strategic design stage (mission, vision, long-term objectives).
Hereźniak (2017)	Conceptual with empirical examples	Residents as citizens	City branding process.
Braun et al. (2018)	Empirical (Germany and the Netherlands)	Professionals in place marketing and branding	Stakeholder opportunities to contribute to open debate and discussion in the process of developing and implementing a place brand. Potential for brand ambassadorial/ advocacy roles.
Hereźniak and Florek (2018)	Empirical (Lisbon, Zaragoza, Milan, Wrocław and Łodz)	Citizens and representatives of expos held in various European cities	Importance of stakeholder involvement during the event and to a lesser extent before the event.
Ripoll Gonzalez and Lester (2018)	Empirical (Tasmania, Australia)	Government, industry, non-governmental and not-for-profit organisations and civil society (residents)	Place identity formation. Consultative engagement, residents traditionally paying lip service.
Joo and Seo (2018)	Empirical (Seoul, South Korea)	Residents	Consultation and input into various city branding projects.
Reynolds (2018)	Empirical (Bath and Bristol, United Kingdom)	Salient stakeholders from the business community, local authority, local community and visitor economy	City branding process (ownership, construction and consumption).

Authors	Paper type (setting)	Participants	Stage and form of participation
Vallaster et al. (2018)	Empirical (Munich, Germany)	Residents	Residents' collective actions and dynamic social construction of the city brand.
Hudak (2019)	Conceptual framework with empirical examples	Residents	Interactive stakeholder conversations concerning the place brand and collaborative place branding projects.
Casais and Monteiro (2019)	Empirical (Porto, Portugal)	Residents	Top-down approach, public discussion with citizens (contributing to the development of the logo created).
Eugenio-Vela et al. (2019)	Empirical (Spain, northern Catalan region Empordà)	A wide range of local stakeholder groups and opinion leaders	Development and implementation of the place branding strategy.
Rebelo et al. (2020)	Empirical (Carvalhal de Vermilhas, Portugal)	Residents	Hypothetical place branding strategy (shaping and conveying the place brand and acting as informal brand ambassadors).

Note: Where the explicit focus of the study was on a destination brand or for destination branding purposes, these have been excluded from the list.

There is less research on the implementation of a crafted place brand identity and its execution (Hudak, 2019). Other aspects of the place branding process which have also received attention include participants' role in advocating the place brand, both as formal and informal brand ambassadors in face-to-face meetings and through digital platforms (Andersson and Ekman, 2009; Braun et al., 2018; Rebelo et al., 2020). However, overall, research has not been designed to examine ongoing participation as part of the dynamic process of urban branding, despite its potential importance (Hereźniak and Florek, 2018). This may be due to restrictions and limitations of research funding and/ or the challenges of maintaining ongoing access to research settings, including the participants themselves.

In many urban policy contexts, there is a presumption that stakeholders enjoy ease of access and have an interest in contributing to shaping their urban environment and community. On this premise, the mechanisms established for members of the community to participate can be quite rudimentary and egalitarian. For example, city authorities may offer the opportunity for residents to express their opinions and feedback about a retail precinct upgrade, designed to modernise the identity of the city and support its brand experience, by placing a box in a central public space (see Figure 4.2).

Figure 4.2   'Have Your Say' feedback box

This mechanism, while in a prominent place, may not be otherwise communicated and may not be accessible to all residents. It could also be viewed negatively by some residents who did not have the opportunity to contribute their ideas initially and may consider the method of feedback as easily dismissed and non-binding.

Being offered the chance to contribute ideas and feedback 'after the fact', following the decision of an elite group of decision makers, is reported as commonplace in existing research (Casais and Monteiro, 2019; Kavaratzis, 2008; Ripoll Gonzalez and Lester, 2018). This form of participation is viewed as a tokenistic form of engagement to consulting with residents and the wider community and is predictably rejected as genuine. When vital aspects of the place branding process have occurred independently from residents and other key stakeholders and the focus of a campaign has been afforded to outside target groups, such as tourists, the wider community may be suspicious and hesitant to offer support, especially when their input and local or insider perspective is requested (Houghton and Stevens, 2011; Insch and Stuart, 2015). Some residents may be reluctant to support a place brand that targets potential tourists as they perceive that there are already too many tourists in some parts of the city. Likewise, local businesses such as cafés and restaurants, and even tourism operators, may be reluctant to get behind the city brand alongside promoting their organisation's brand (Bregoli, 2013; Casidy et al., 2019).

Different types of governance regimes will permit differing levels of input from residents and other groups. For example, in the case of Beijing's rebranding prior to the 2008 Olympics, the city's '"top down" defined, intangible values of culture were not well understood and were not widely acceptable' by residents and visitors surveyed about their perceptions of the city (Zhang and Zhao, 2009: 250). Yet, in the majority of studies examining inclusiveness and participation, power (i.e. ownership and governance) over urban brands is still concentrated in the hands of urban elites (Lichrou et al., 2017). This agency may be extended to a variety of institutions and/or individuals. Design and branding agencies are often given the task of crafting an urban identity on behalf of a city and its constituents. Such arrangements usually disconnect the community from the branding process, with a new brand identity later being unveiled to the community and causing resentment and disengagement (North, 2014). In contrast, some participatory arrangements may be purposefully built to encourage deep engagement, particularly where participants are given well-defined roles, but also given autonomy and the necessary resources to achieve their ambitions (Zenker and Erfgen, 2014). Residents, and other stakeholders, may also be given a say in how their city's budget for place branding is allocated to projects in the local community (Hereźniak, 2017). A transfer of agency into the hands of those that make up the community and are passionate about their place and its urban identity may be conducive to building and communicating the associated brand values to interested audiences. Ambassadorial roles are clear examples where this type of engagement in the branding process can work effectively given the right conditions (Andersson and Ekman, 2009). Residents often take on these roles in an informal capacity, when they are inspired and enriched by their city and want to promote and recommend it to others. Alternatively, but a less preferable option, there are a range of commercial situations whereby individuals can be directed or (financially) supported by city marketing organisations to actively endorse the city and its offerings. Unfortunately, this is often the option chosen by governing authorities to promote their place brand experiences.

In extant research and in practice, a variety of different platforms are available for participants to be part of the place brand: digital and online forms of participation that allow co-creation of the place brand, alongside more traditional face-to-face forms of interaction that are more or less orchestrated and organised by brand governors or guardians (Hereźniak, 2017). For instance, as part of the 'Brand New Helsinki 2020' project, the city of Helsinki, Finland, aimed to engage city stakeholders through different social media platforms. Thus, to facilitate a continuous dialogue between the city and its residents an online platform (MyHelsinki.fi) has been established to allow people to share their best local experiences and to offer trustworthy recommendations to all those with an interest in Helsinki (Florek and Insch, 2020). City officials are also viewed as city brand ambassadors, and many participate in excursions such as seashore yoga sessions and nature trail walks, followed by discussions and reflection to identify ways to link these activities and experiences in communicating the city's brand (Jokela, 2020).

Implications for research and practice

This chapter responds to calls in urban studies and place branding for scholars to develop a critical understanding of urban branding practices, with a focus on the representation of place identity, and how the daily production of urban brands privileges some groups, especially private-sector actors (Sadler, 1993), while marginalising others (Lichrou et al., 2017). Fundamentally, inclusivity and engagement are at the core of demystifying collaborative and participatory approaches to urban place branding and considerable progress has been made empirically to understand the forms that such participation has taken in a variety of urban contexts around the world. Considerably less scholarly work has focused on envisioning the structures and mechanisms underlying effective and deep engagement of members of diverse urban communities in place branding.

Research into the dynamics of stakeholder interactions in urban partnerships offers useful insights for place branding. In a study of stakeholders in a partnership in the Greater Manchester region of the United Kingdom, Le Feuvre et al. (2016) emphasise the need to minimise several inhibitors – insularity, goal misalignment, apathy, role ambiguity and bureaucracy – to improve the interactions between stakeholders. Importantly, the study also demonstrated that research on urban stakeholders should shift from stakeholders as a unit of analysis and focus more on the nature of their interactions to enhance the quality of their engagement and ways to encourage meaningful communication. This aligns with the notion of place brands as constantly evolving through social interaction (Kavaratzis and Hatch, 2013; Kavaratzis and Kalandides, 2015). A clearer understanding of the processual mechanisms for enabling genuine participation and engagement in urban branding is thus needed.

Some researchers (Zenker and Seigis, 2012) argue that the methods of participation in place branding are not as important as the right to be included and to be respected. Other researchers do not evaluate the effectiveness of various methods. A potential limitation with viewing all methods as equal is to ignore their fallibility in offering a platform for inclusiveness. Part of their limitation may derive from an assumption that anyone can participate in place branding effort, if invited. However, there appears to be a bias towards the participation of particular socio-economic groups, especially the middle classes and dominant ethnic groups (Colomb and Kalandides, 2010; Kavaratzis and Kalandides, 2015). This may be a reflection of the membership of those governing bodies, authorities and institutions that have jurisdictional control over places. Taken to the extreme, the purposeful selection and control of those members of the public that participate in a place branding process can be seen as a way to exclude certain members of the community from this, such as immigrants. This question, amongst others, represents a key aspect to be developed for future research in this field, and may require the adoption of methodological approaches outside the traditional remit of place branding such as action-case research including observing stakeholder interactions (Le Feuvre et al., 2016), participatory methods and community engagement tools (Cilliers and Timmermans, 2014; Dionisio et al., 2016). Here, researchers can draw on the tools and methods of urban governance and place making (Pierce et al., 2011) to examine relational networks and complex social interactions.

Further work is needed to understand the attitudes and actions of different participants (Le Feuvre et al., 2016) in place branding, including those in power, towards collaboration. This should help elucidate discourses of engagement in urban branding campaigns. This knowledge is vital to revealing the alignment of stakeholder groups towards the goals and methods of place branding, as well as the perceptions of stakeholders towards each other, so as to identify additional barriers prohibiting genuine and effective participation and engagement. Beyond the dominant stakeholder approach, understanding inclusion in terms of rights, access and ability to participate is needed. As the review of previous participatory research shows, this requires (at least) a two-dimensional view of participation and engagement that supports a wide range of participants and enables their deep engagement in specific aspects of the ongoing urban branding process.

Extant research shows that residents, among other stakeholders, are integral to urban branding and it is through their behaviour as active citizens engaged in dialogue and actions that shape, influence and reinforce the urban identity that contributes to the brand's co-creation. Existing participatory approaches acknowledge that diverse stakeholder groups are co-producers, consumers and co-owners of the place brand (Hereźniak, 2017), but do not conceive how they can be fully incorporated into the ongoing urban brand governance. Further research is needed to explore alternative approaches and models that give the different constituent groups a recognised role – both a place at the table and a voice that is respected and taken on board. Thus, those with a responsibility for designing participatory structures must ensure that methods and mechanisms for genuine participation and deep engagement are inclusive, durable and enduring 'so that an authentic dialogue can ensue' (Friedmann, 2010: 162).

Note

1.   For example, urban sub-brands can exist simultaneously as in the case of the neighbourhood brands that make up the Manhattan, NYC brand, including SoHo, Greenwich Village, West Village and the Meat Packing District, Upper East Side.

References

Andersson, M. and P. Ekman (2009), 'Ambassador networks and place branding', *Journal of Place Management and Development*, **2** (1), 41–51.

Anon (2009), 'Participation is different from engagement', *Social Media Today*, 21 May, accessed 13 July 2020 at: www.socialmediatoday.com/content/participation -different-engagement.

Boisen, M., Terlouw, K. and B. van Gorp (2011), 'The selective nature of place branding and the layering of spatial identities', *Journal of Place Management and Development*, 5 (2), 135–47.

Braun, E., Eshuis, J., Klijn, E. H. and S. Zenker (2018), 'Improving place reputation: Do an open place brand process and an identity-image match pay off?', *Cities*, **80**, 22–8.

Bregoli, I. (2013), 'Effects of DMO coordination on destination brand identity: A mixed-method study on the city of Edinburgh', *Journal of Travel Research*, **52** (2), 212–24.

Carter, E. W. (2020), *Becoming Communities of Belonging: The Church and People with Disabilities*, Vanderbilt University, accessed 13 July 2020 at: www.wheaton.edu/ media/education/pdf/SPED-03-14-18-Handouts.pdf.

Casais, B. and P. Monteiro (2019), 'Residents' involvement in city brand co-creation and their perceptions of city brand identity: A case study in Porto', *Place Branding and Public Diplomacy*, **15** (4), 229–37.

Casidy, R., Helmi, J. and K. Bridson (2019), 'Drivers and inhibitors of national stakeholder engagement with place brand identity', *European Journal of Marketing*, **53** (7), 1445–65.

Cilliers, E. J. and W. Timmermans (2014), 'The importance of creative participatory planning in the public place-making process', *Environment and Planning B: Planning and Design*, **41** (3), 413–29.

Colomb, C. and A. Kalandides (2010), 'The "Be Berlin" campaign: Old wine in new bottles or innovative form of participatory place branding', in G. Ashworth and M. Kavaratzis (eds), *Towards Effective Place Brand Management: Branding European Cities and Regions*, Cheltenham, UK and Northampton, MA, USA: Edward Elgar Publishing, pp. 173–90.

Dinnie, K. (2018), 'Contingent self-definition and amorphous regions: A dynamic approach to place brand architecture', *Marketing Theory*, **18** (1), 31–53.

Dionisio, M. R., Kingham, S., Banwell, K. and J. Neville (2016), 'Geospatial tools for community engagement in the Christchurch rebuild, New Zealand', *Sustainable Cities and Society*, **27**, 233–43.

Duffy, K. (1995), *Social Exclusion and Human Dignity in Europe: Background Report for the Proposed Inititative by the Council of Europe*, Strasbourg: Council of Europe.

Eshuis, J. and A. Edwards (2013), 'Branding the city: The democratic legitimacy of a new mode of governance', *Urban Studies*, **50** (5), 1066–82.

Eugenio-Vela, J. d. S., Ginesta, X. and M. Kavaratzis (2019), 'The critical role of stakeholder engagement in a place branding strategy: A case study of the Empordà brand', *European Planning Studies*, **28** (7), 1393–412.

Florek, M. (2011), 'Online city branding', in K. Dinnie (ed.), *City Branding: Theory and Cases*, London: Palgrave Macmillan, pp. 82–90.

Florek, M. and A. Insch (2020), 'Learning to co-create the city brand experience', *Journal of International Studies*, **13** (2), 163–77.

Florek, M., Insch, A. and J. Gnoth (2006), 'City council websites as a means of place brand identity communication', *Place Branding*, **2** (4), 276–96.

Friedmann, J. (2010), 'Place and place-making in cities: A global perspective', *Planning Theory and Practice*, **11** (2), 149–65.

Gendel, J. (2019), 'Making our kehillot a place to belong', *USCJ Blog*, 15 April, accessed 13 July 2020 at: https://uscj.org/blog/making-our-kehillot-a-place-to-belong.

Helmi, J., Bridson, K. and R. Casidy (2019), 'A typology of organisational stakeholder engagement with place brand identity', *Journal of Strategic Marketing*, **53** (7), 1445–65.

Hereźniak, M. (2017), 'Place branding and citizen involvement: Participatory approach to building and managing city brands', *International Studies: Interdisciplinary Political and Cultural Journal*, **19** (1), 129–41.

Hereźniak, M. and M. Florek (2018), 'Citizen involvement, place branding and mega events: Insights from Expo host cities', *Place Branding and Public Diplomacy*, **14** (2), 89–100.

Hoenigman Meyer, E. (2019), 'What is diversity, inclusion and belonging?', *Nasdaq*, 21 October, accessed 13 July 2020 at: www.nasdaq.com/articles/what-is-diversity -inclusion-and-belonging-2019-10-21.

Houghton, J. P. and A. Stevens (2011), 'City branding and stakeholder engagement', in K. Dinnie (ed.), *City Branding: Theory and Cases*, Basingstoke: Palgrave Macmillan, pp. 45–53.

Hudak, K. C. (2019), 'Resident stories and digital storytelling for participatory place branding', *Place Branding and Public Diplomacy*, **15** (2), 97–108.

Insch, A. and M. Stuart (2015), 'Understanding resident city brand disengagement', *Journal of Place Management and Development*, **8** (3), 172–86.

Insch, A. and T. Walters (2018), 'Challenging assumptions about residents' engagement with place branding', *Place Branding and Public Diplomacy*, **14** (3), 152–62.

Janiszewska, K. and A. Insch (2012), 'The strategic importance of brand positioning in the place brand concept: Elements, structure and application capabilities', *Journal of International Studies*, **5** (1), 9–19.

Jokela, S. (2020), 'Transformative city branding and the evolution of the entrepreneurial city: The case of "Brand New Helsinki"', *Urban Studies*, **57** (10), 2031–46.

Joo, Y.-M. and B. Seo (2018), 'Transformative city branding for policy change: The case of Seoul's participatory branding', *Environment and Planning C: Politics and Space*, **36** (2), 239–57.

Kalandides, A. (2011), 'City marketing for Bogotá: A case study in integrated place branding', *Journal of Place Management and Development*, **4** (3), 282–91.

Kane, L. (2019), 'The attention economy', *Nielsen Norman Group*, 30 June, accessed 13 July 2020 at: www.nngroup.com/articles/attention-economy/.

Kavaratzis, M. (2008), *From City Marketing to City Branding: An Interdisciplinary Analysis with Reference to Amsterdam, Budapest and Athens*, PhD, Groningen: Rijksuniversiteit Groningen.

Kavaratzis, M. and M. J. Hatch (2013), 'The dynamics of place brands: An identity-based approach to place branding theory', *Marketing Theory*, **13** (1), 69–86.

Kavaratzis, M. and A. Kalandides (2015), 'Rethinking the place brand: The interactive formation of place brands and the role of participatory place branding', *Environment and Planning A*, **47** (6), 1368–82.

Kemp, E., Childers, C. Y. and K. H. Williams (2012a), 'A tale of a musical city: Fostering self-brand connection among residents of Austin, Texas', *Place Branding and Public Diplomacy*, **8** (2), 147–57.

Kemp, E., Childers, C. Y. and K. H. Williams (2012b), 'Place branding: Creating self-brand connections and brand advocacy', *Journal of Product and Brand Management*, **21** (7), 508–15.

Le Feuvre, M., Medway, D., Warnaby, G., Ward, K. and A. Goatman (2016), 'Understanding stakeholder interactions in urban partnerships', *Cities*, **52**, 55–65.

Lichrou, M., Kavaratzis, M. and M. Giovanardi (2017), 'Introduction', in M. Kavaratzis, M. Giovanardi and M. Lichrou (eds), *Inclusive Place Branding: Critical Perspectives on Theory and Practice*, London: Routledge, pp. 12–22.

Maiello, A. and C. Pasquinelli (2015), 'Destruction or construction? A (counter) branding analysis of sport mega-events in Rio de Janeiro', *Cities*, **48**, 116–24.

Mayes, R. (2008), 'A place in the sun: The politics of place, identity and branding', *Place Branding and Public Diplomacy*, **4** (2), 124–35.

Monteiro, P. D. S. (2016), *Stakeholders' Involvement in City Branding: The Participation and Identification of Porto Residents on the Image of the City*, Master's thesis, Porto: Economics and Management School.

North, S. (2014), 'Why do most city branding campaigns fail?', *New Statesman*, 21 August, accesssed 13 July 2020 at: www.citymetric.com/business/why-do-most-city-branding-campaigns-fail.

Pierce, J., Martin, D. G. and J. T. Murphy (2011), 'Relational place-making: The networked politics of place', *Transactions of the Institute of British Geographers*, **36** (1), 54–70.

Rebelo, C., Mehmood, A. and T. Marsden (2020), 'Co-created visual narratives and inclusive place branding: A socially responsible approach to residents' participation and engagement', *Sustainability Science*, **15** (2), 423–35.

Reynolds, L. (2018), *A Critical Approach to Place Branding Governance: From 'Holding Stakes' to 'Holding Flags'*, PhD, Cardiff: Cardiff University.

Ripoll Gonzalez, L. and L. Lester (2018), '"All for one, one for all": Communicative processes of cocreation of place brands through inclusive and horizontal stakeholder collaborative networks', *Communication and Society*, **31** (4), 59–78.

Sadler, D. (1993), 'Place marketing, competitive places and the construction of hegemony in Britain in the 1980s', in G. Kearns and C. Philo (eds), *Selling Places: The City as Cultural Capital Past and Present*, Oxford: Pergamon Press, pp. 175–92.

Sarabia-Sanchez, F. J. and M. J. Cerda-Bertomeu (2017), 'Place brand developers' perceptions of brand identity, brand architecture and neutrality in place brand development', *Place Branding and Public Diplomacy*, **13** (1), 51–64.

Sevin, E. (2011), 'Thinking about place branding: Ethics of concept', *Place Branding and Public Diplomacy*, **7** (3), 155–64.

Sherman, A. (2010), '5 ways cities are using social media to reverse economic downturn', *MashableUK*, 16 December, accessed 13 July 2020 at: https://mashable.com/2020/12/16/cities-social-media-recession/.

Squires, B. (2015), 'Participation vs. engagement: What truly drives success in your corporate wellness program?', *Totalwellness*, 29 January, accessed 13 July 2020 at: https://info.totalwellnesshealth.com/blog/participation-vs.-engagement.-what-truly-drives-success-in-your-corporate-wellness-program.

Strekalova, A. (2018), 'Place branding in Web 2.0: The conceptual contours of new generation of media policy', *Proceedings of the International Scientific Conference 'Competitive, Sustainable and Secure Development of the Regional Economy: Response to Global Challenges'*, *Volgograd State University*, Russia: Atlantis Press, pp. 57–60.

Vallaster, C., Von Wallpach, S. and S. Zenker (2018), 'The interplay between urban policies and grassroots city brand co-creation and co-destruction during the refugee crisis: Insights from the city brand Munich (Germany)', *Cities*, **80** (October), 53–60.

Van Assche, K. and M. C. Lo (2011), 'Planning, preservation and place branding: A tale of sharing assets and narratives', *Place Branding and Public Diplomacy*, **7** (2), 116–26.

Walters, T. and A. Insch (2018), 'How community event narratives contribute to place branding', *Journal of Place Management and Development*, **11** (1), 130–44.

Zenker, S. and C. Erfgen (2014), 'Let them do the work: A participatory place branding approach', *Journal of Place Management and Development*, **7** (3), 225–34.

Zenker, S. and A. Seigis (2012), 'Respect and the city: Resident participation in place marketing', *Journal of Place Management and Development*, **5** (1), 20–34.

Zhang, L. and S. X. Zhao (2009), 'City branding and the Olympic effect: A case study of Beijing', *Cities*, **26** (5), 245–54.

5

The spatial planning–place branding nexus: A research agenda for spatial development

Eduardo Oliveira, Kristof Van Assche and Raoul Beunen

Introduction

Cities and urban regions, broadly defined in this chapter as places, are some of the most dynamic territories worldwide and play a key role in promoting the development of local and regional economies (Zimmermann et al., 2020). Worldwide, local governments and private-sector actors are also calling for greater attention to be paid to their role in addressing some of today's most pressing global challenges, such as climate change and ensuring a sustainable future (Acuto et al., 2018; Rosenzweig et al., 2010). In this quest, the application of the principles and methods of branding to the promotion of the environmental and non-environmental qualities of places quickly turned out to be the 'most wanted' methodology of municipal and regional governments to reinforce the chief objective of positioning themselves on the inter-regional competitive stage (Van Assche et al., 2020; Li and Cai, 2019; Molainen, 2015). Place branding is also employed in support of landscape preservation and development (Porter, 2020), playing a role in regional development processes (Lucarelli and Heldt Cassel, 2020) or as a strategic spatial planning instrument (Oliveira, 2016a). It is reasonable, therefore, to expect that spatial planning and place branding have overlapping and related interests concerning the use, organization and meaning of space and place (Vanolo, 2017; Hae, 2017). In spite of these attempts to disentangle the potential theoretical and empirical linkage between planning and branding, 'much terrain is yet to be uncovered by scientists in the investigation of the existing and potential linkages between spatial planning and place branding' (Van Assche and Lo, 2011: 124). These and other studies evidence that branding countries, cities and regions is more than just catchy slogans, colourful logos, star architecture, bidding for the 'City of Talent' or 'Region of Innovation' status, that are applied as solutions regardless of place-specific amenities and governance settings (cf. Van Assche et al., 2020). We assume, however, that many other possible relations here are imaginable and practicable. In this chapter, we explore the relations and synergies between spatial planning and place branding in the context of widely varying spatial governance systems and their evolution over time (cf. Van Assche et al., 2014). It seems rather obvious that the two fields can enrich each other, and deserve to be considered together as approaches to spatial governance and spatial development in a broad sense. In line with the European Spatial Development Perspective (CEC, 1999) and Goal 11 on *Sustainable Cities and Communities* of the United Nations' Sustainable Development Goals we understand spatial development to be a balanced and sustainable development of cities and urban regions encompassing (1) economic and social cohesion, (2) conservation and management of natural resources, (3) valorization of the cultural heritage and (4) balancing competitive interests in favour of the common good (UN General Assembly, 2015).

The chapter unveils a typology relating spatial planning and place branding through the lenses of spatial governance (e.g. Rivolin, 2017); this is presented as a research agenda to further develop the understanding of planning and branding and their interconnections, as well as their roles in supporting cities and urban regions in reaching social, economic and ecological goals of sustainability. We conclude that if those institutions and actors involved in the development of place branding strategies are unaware of the functioning of spatial governance, i.e. how the relevant local governments, place-based institutions and private actors decide to design, plan, finance and manage a specific spatial planning strategy, place branding cannot reach its full potential and it cannot find a legitimate democratic footing. In the worst scenario, place branding can undermine the democratic legitimacy of itself, of spatial planning and of place-based governance systems as such, hindering, thus, sustainable spatial development.

Planning–Branding nexus: Three possible justifications

It is only recently that research on place branding has significantly broadened its scope to include a wide range of other socio-spatial and spatial-economic issues, and is drawing closer to studies of multiplace actors' governance and participatory planning (Asprogerakas and Mountanea, 2020; Van Assche et al., 2020). The place branding option has been presented as a response to the competitive authentic dialectic of places and, specifically, to areas in need of physical revitalization or urban regeneration and which face post-industrial or other forms of structural, socio-economic change (Evans, 2015). The potentialities and limits for spatial planning and place branding strategies relate to the presence or absence of what can be described as assets, spatial qualities, features, products or flows which can have a value for spatial development. Exploring the relationships between planning and branding is useful for various reasons.

Insights from place branding can enrich the search for new planning approaches. Spatial planning brings together social, economic and ecological aspects at different spatial scales and across multiple sectors of society (Bacău et al., 2020). However, in many cities and urban regions spatial planning, especially strategic spatial planning for the long term, is something that is difficult to grasp and to implement in practice (Hersperger et al., 2018). In many places, spatial planning never has been an influential field, while in some European countries, such as England, the Netherlands or Poland, the former centralized planning systems have lost much of their power due to legal and political reforms (Niedziałkowski and Beunen, 2019; Gunn and Hillier, 2014; Allmendinger and Haughton, 2013). In those situations, where existing forms of planning are not effective or lack institutional support, the insights from place branding can enrich the search for new planning approaches. Thus, place branding would become a valuable addition to the toolbox of planners (Oliveira, 2015a), urban policy makers (Lucarelli, 2018; Kavaratzis, 2018) and place managers (Ashworth and Kavaratzis, 2018; Ntounis and Kavaratzis, 2017; Cleave et al., 2017). For example, defining a place branding strategy involves strategic analysis of urban features (non-environmental qualities) and landscape amenities (environmental qualities), among other methods. Determining a strategic position for a place is the task of spatial planners in support of policy and decision makers (Albrechts, 1999). Therefore, strategic spatial planners, for instance, could play an important role in setting up a place branding strategy, which would facilitate the development of perceptions in the mind of potential investors, visitors as well as new and current residents (Medway et al., 2011).

A spatial-dimension of branding disrupts the corporate/marketing spheres of place branding that still dominates the contemporary branding discourse (cf. Anholt, 2019; Bonakdar and Audirac, 2020). Many critics of place branding have argued that it is essentially a neo-liberal activity that reduces everything, everyone or every place to economic value (Van Assche et al., 2016). Much of the literature on place branding either under or overestimates what branding can actually do to support local business, improve infrastructures and the physical condition of a place, and to contribute to job creation as well as job maintenance and talent retention (Kavaratzis et al., 2015). This is partly because of underlying ideological assumptions (Gotham, 2007) and partly because of a lack of insight in the functioning of governance. This is for example reflected in simplistic recipes and approaches in which place branding is reduced to a marketing strategy through a one-size-fits-all approach (Oliveira, 2016a). It is also reflected in some of the critiques of place branding that focus on the negative consequences of commodification of place – i.e. the process of considering places as a commodity subject to payments or trade (Gerber and Gerber, 2017). Insights from planning literature can enrich understandings of the way narratives, assets and space can be governed, with an eye on democratic decision making on long-term perspectives (Healey, 2006). For example, one of the vectors of Oliveira's (2016b) place branding framework for cities and urban regions proposes that place branding aligned with strategic spatial planning would contribute to envisioning alternative futures through the participation of key actors, organizations and citizens and thus align planning and branding based on narratives. Grenni, Horlings and Soini (2020), through a case study in Finland, contend that place branding is not just what a place is about in the present, but also about joint efforts to make places better and adapted to evolving challenges. They conclude that in a scenario of spatial development, place branding is the co-creation of cultural narratives which support sustainable perspectives for the future. In a study aiming at connecting spatial strategies and place branding through the case study of the region of Ruhr (Germany), Asprogerakas and Mountanea (2020) concluded that branding activities in Ruhr were integrated into a spatial strategy in order to construct new identities based on existing ones.

The planning–branding nexus paves a way for further multidisciplinary collaborations. Theories of spatial governance (e.g. Allmendinger, 2016), of spatial planning (e.g. Fainstein and DeFilippis, 2016) and place branding (Kavaratzis and Ashworth, 2005), can be furthered if they integrate insights from neighbouring disciplines such as critical urban theory (e.g. Vanolo, 2017), landscape research (e.g. de San Eugenio Vela et al., 2017) and sustainability science (e.g. Konecnik Ruzzier et al., 2015), but also on spatial design (e.g. Van Assche et al., 2012). Planning could use insights from place-based value creation stemming from place branding, and place branding can offer more realistic strategies if it includes insights into how places might actually be changed or preserved through coordinated intervention (Lucarelli and Brorström, 2013) and multidisciplinary collaborations (Lucarelli and Heldt Cassel, 2020).

In the next sections, we will first reflect on the endeavour of finding synergies. Second, we will conceptualize assets in place branding and spatial planning are explored. These sections lay the basis for a further exploration of the linkages between spatial planning and place branding in the context of spatial governance. This exploration will focus on the role of planning–branding synergies, specifically on assets and narratives.

Place assets in planning and branding

With a few exceptions, spatial planning has generally neglected place assets (Sandercock, 2003; Throgmorton, 1996). The arrival of participatory approaches to planning brought more stories, more narratives of place and more attention to assets as place qualities (Hersperger et al., 2018; Hospers, 2017). This diversification also brought attention to conflicting place narratives, competing ideas on the nature and ranking of assets and different perspectives on the value of the existing landscape for its desired future form (Harries et al., 2018). In some planning cultures, the conclusion was that planning ought to be about constructing place narratives, later influencing the organization of space (Eshuis et al., 2014), while in other places the immediate focus remained on the organization of space, with long-term projects on narrative identity and spatial development perceived as detracting and distracting, and unfeasible for the existing bureaucracies (Van Assche et al., 2016).

Planning leans on, and transforms landscapes, while place branding relies on and produces synthetic images of place which go beyond objects, details or events (Donner et al., 2017). The landscape itself can often function as a place asset that can frame and enhance other assets (Porter, 2020; Kavaratzis, 2018). Aligned spatial planning and place branding strategies could provide a more realistic view over spatial realities, where identities, assets and the availability and quality of urban amenities such as the quality of transport infrastructures or green infrastructures are paramount for spatial development (Oliveira, 2016a). A lack of planning and branding, obsession with single resources and short-term perspectives, a lack of strategy and of diversity in perspectives, often leads to a degradation of the landscape. Governance systems work then as platforms to maintain long-term and diverse perspectives on spatial development, reminding communities that changes are possible, that some things can be interpreted as future assets and that the landscape itself is worth valuing as a spatial structure, which could accommodate diverse activities fitting alternative futures (Hersperger et al., 2020; Van Assche and Hornidge, 2015).

Place narratives in planning and branding

A focus on narrative dynamics has contributed to increasing the understanding of value dynamics, as narrative underpins any value creation (Kavaratzis, 2012), with local values inspiring local products and narratives of the local selling products and possibly inventing new ones (Feagan, 2007). Place branding is seen as an advanced form of commodification, making everything circulate as 'material' things with a value attached, in a globalized economy (Vanolo, 2017). We, however, would say that indeed the economy is globalized and people are willing to pay for a variety of goods and services, including experiences and places, but that does not imply that everything is reduced to a market price or monetary transaction. Value creation takes place, whether one is aware of that or not, and both planning and branding have partial sets of tools to manage the relation between value creation and places such as cities and regions (Kavaratzis et al., 2015). Putting a price on things is not a panacea, but under certain circumstances it can help to create (dis)incentives to act, to buy, to travel, and (dis)incentives to maintain certain narratives of value (Cleave et al., 2017). Being blind to processes of value creation in place, and refraining from even attempting to manage it, does not stop it, and does not prevent the uglier consequences of capitalism (Van Assche et al., 2016). Place-based assets are those assets that are context-specific and tied to a place (de San Eugenio Vela et al., 2017; Rantisi and Leslie, 2006). They might have pre-existed as narratives, as physical objects or features, then discovered and framed by narrative, or they can be the product of narrative in a literal sense, becoming embodied as a new product after activities inspired by alternative narratives (Harries et al., 2018; Insch and Walters, 2018). Existing products, then, might become assets of a place when connected to a place through narratives; they can add something to the place brand, and the brand can add value to them (Kavaratzis, 2018). For example, when investigating three regions – Tuscany, Italy; Missouri and northern Minnesota in the United States – Van Assche and Lo (2011) noted that a strong place brand allows for strong planning interventions (as in the case of Tuscany). The case of northern Minnesota offers, however, an alternative perspective. The cultural landscape of northern Minnesota was successfully rebranded as a natural landscape. The dialectical relationship between northern Minnesota's image and spatial planning were crucial for the success of this rebranding – translating into protection measures and a more appropriate combination of land use. In addition, the spatial planning strategies implemented by Minnesotan authorities 'improved the quality of the actual product that was branded, so it could obtain more followers' (Van Assche and Lo, 2011: 123).

Both planning and branding strategies are likely to be more effective when they are based on an awareness of locally existing narratives and asset definitions (Van Assche et al., 2016; Jensen, 2007; Healey, 2006; Sandercock, 2003). Existing local narratives can be reinforced through being embedded in larger place brand narratives, through a place branding strategy or through spatial change triggered by planning, for instance by protecting, connecting or creating assets (Van Assche and Lo, 2011). Thus, both narrative and physical space, and the physical conditions of a place, are to an extent amenable to coordinated intervention, to intentional change and to redesign (Oliveira, 2016a), with change in one possibly affecting change in the other. In addition, by establishing a clear and competitive position, highlighting place assets and narratives and bringing together divergent voices into the same place branding storyline, governments and private interest groups are then able to develop shared visions for future spatial development.

Planning–branding nexus: Future research domains

To ensure a future in which humanity thrives together with nature, people around the world will need to coordinate actions and closely cooperate like never before. Cooperation between local and national governments, industry, science and research and non-governmental organizations is indispensable. We argue in this chapter that planning and branding play a role in spatial development but this requires their embeddedness in spatial governance systems (or settings). This also implies that if spatial plans or place brands are becoming disconnected from dominant place assets and place narratives at the community level, they are not likely to have a socio-economic and ecologically sustainable effect. Thus, in the context of spatial governance, different possible relations between planning and branding can be envisioned and assessed. Figure 5.1 shows a six-dimension framework for future research in the spatial planning–place branding nexus. The next subsections explain each of these six dimensions.

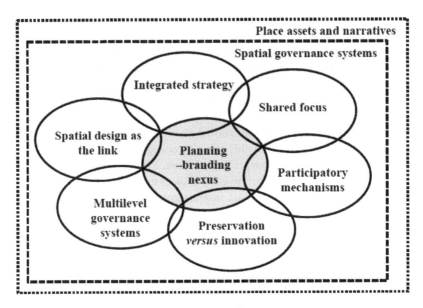

Figure 5.1   A six-dimension framework for future research in place branding

Integrated Strategy

This integrated strategy, in contrast to Oliveira (2015a) who primarily argues in favour of place branding as a strategic planning instrument, is a two-way strategy as argued in Lucarelli and Heldt Cassel (2020). This strategy might work well when the above-mentioned virtuous circle of planning–branding–governance seems within reach. Such joint strategy, which could emphasize either planning or branding depending on the case, does not necessarily require a pre-existing tradition of branding places. It would, however, benefit greatly from a pre-existing planning tradition, which enables spatial transformation (Hersperger et al., 2019; Albrechts, 2015). When assets are already recognized, and already seen in the light of a unifying narrative of place, a combination of planning and place branding in an integrated strategy is easier to envision and accept (e.g. Porter, 2020). Furthermore, strong articulation between place actors, civic participation at the local level and the coordination of spatial policies are also key to effective joint planning and branding strategies. For example, Oliveira (2015b) in the context of inter-regional spatial governance argues for the effectiveness of an integrated place branding strategy for the cross-border region of Galicia (Spain) and northern Portugal. Oliveira (2015b) specifically focused on the cultural assets and linguistic background of northern Portugal that could play a key role in the success of a potential integrated branding strategy because there are similarities, cognitive and spatial proximity, as well as an institutional willingness to position the cross-border region as a whole. Oliveira's proposal of an integrated branding strategy resonates with recent efforts to mitigate the negative effects of the Covid-19 pandemic on the economy of this cross-border region (Eixo Atlántico, 2020).

Shared Focus

One can also relate planning and branding strategies by means of a shared focus. This can be a type of asset that is especially important locally, either to preserve or to create one policy domain especially relevant for the community such as environmental protection, landscape conservation, agriculture and food production, water quality and economic restructuring (Porter, 2020; Van Assche and Hornidge, 2015). It is still possible then to institutionalize one (planning or branding) differently from the other, more lightly than the other, so it supports the activities in the other strategy. This then is an example of policy coordination as a light form of policy integration. Branding could be a flanking measure of planning, and light institutionalization can also be positive for more autonomous decision making (and budgeting) and for flexible adaptation (e.g. by means of project organizations with a limited lifespan). One can also argue that as citizens take part in the branding process and are involved in planning decision making, they contribute to envisioning shared futures for their own place. This is in line with the theoretical considerations presented in Ashworth, Kavaratzis and Warnaby (2015), which argued that place brands provide strategic guidance for spatial development. Thus, place brands could support the envisioning of an aspirational imagined future, which plays well with the focus on what 'ought to be' debated in strategic spatial planning literature (Hersperger et al., 2020; Granqvist et al., 2020; Abis and Garau, 2016).

Participatory Mechanisms

Place branding often works to conceal power struggles and to impose elite-led interests and directions, while suppressing opposing voices or neglecting citizens' needs and hopes (Van Assche et al., 2020). Therefore, a different relation can emerge or be established when spatial planning or place branding is more participatory than the other. One can think of a scenario of transition or reinvention, where a community wants to rethink itself, its future, its assets, and thus a more radically participatory exercise in governance might be in place. This could be a transformation of, or an offshoot of, the planning arena, yet, it could also be a new arena for community reinvention, which can take the character of place branding, in its recent emanations – i.e. involving community change, beyond representation and marketing (Grenni et al., 2020; Kavaratzis, 2018). If one is much more participatory than the other, this can provide a combination of rigidity and flexibility in spatial governance settings, a structure allowing for creativity and institutional experiment, while keeping an eye on the necessary rigidities, i.e. the stabilization of expectations (de San Eugenio Vela et al., 2020; Van Assche et al., 2012). If planning represents the more rigid aspect of governance, part of the checks and balances, it can at the same time help in implementing (and inspiring) some of the visions coming out of the branding-as-reinvention arena. This relation is thus one of keeping in check, and of enabling (Deffner et al., 2020; Stubbs and Warnaby, 2015). Proactive civic participation in a collective strategy and vision for a place may generate trust and legitimize spatial interventions, as participants in the process are likely to find that some visions present a future that certain individuals would like to inhabit; to work, study and play in; visit and develop leisure activities in; while other possible futures are considered highly undesirable.

Preservation versus Innovation

Different relations between planning and branding can occur when they are both linked to the dichotomy of preservation versus innovation. While planning could represent the more conservative side, focusing on preservation of assets or cultural and natural landscape amenities (agricultural land, forest land, wildlife habitats, recreational open areas and culturally significant amenities such as old trees), place branding could do more in terms of changing place narratives. Yet, it could also be the other way around, with branding more focused on the reservation of assets seen as valuable, and planning more oriented on development. Branding then would shift the focus of planning towards context-sensitive spatial development and ongoing redevelopment, fitting new into old (Tobias and Wahl, 2013). The discussion between planning and branding, often embraced separately, can be an internalized and institutionalized site of reflection in governance on this eternal dilemma. It can help to develop innovate concepts and approaches for identifying, preserving and strengthening assets and place narratives. Both innovation and preservation have seemingly objective arguments. Therefore, by structuring an internal and transparent discussion between these viewpoints in governance, the quality of decision making and adaptation is likely to be enhanced. The combination of planning and branding could itself also be seen as an innovation in spatial governance. It allows for a framing of the past, e.g. valuable heritage, in the perspective of the present and the future, whereby buildings and places can acquire a new function, a new economic perspective, while preserving and even strengthening those elements and characteristics for which the place is valued. The policies and practices of Dutch heritage management were, for example, innovated through such discourse about preservation through development (Bloemers et al., 2010).

Multilevel Governance Systems

Planning and branding can be located at different scales or levels of governance (cf. the 'Russian Doll' model of nested scale hierarchies of place branding in Oliveira and Ashworth, 2017). The relation between planning and branding at one level is likely to be influenced by the relation between the two at another level. This influence can be positive or negative. What happens regularly is that some form of place branding strategy exists at the regional level, with minimal planning presence there, while locally, spatial planning affects decision making more intensively than branding. Such differential emphasis is not necessarily bad and is to some extent part of each context. It does however pose specific requirements for coordination. At each scale, planning and branding can still complement each other, if mechanisms exist for collaboration or at least mutual awareness (cf. Yea and Björner, 2018). Coordination between levels might be necessary to maintain the unity of a narrative, to perform the balancing act recounted above.

Spatial Design as the Link

Design can be the linking element between planning and branding (Radosavljević et al., 2020; Van Assche et al., 2012; Dawson and Higgins, 2009). Specifically, place branding remains blissfully ignorant of some of the more legal-bureaucratic aspects of planning, but pays attention when design comes into play, since this can affect the image more directly. Branding can also inspire and argue for more design-oriented approaches in planning, with design not restricted to one scale or to new developments, but also including issues of the preservation of landscape and other elements in new structures, or the protection and construction of new landscape structures. Spatial design can then take the shape of a separate actor, a brokering organization, or it can be a selection of the projects and policies coming through planning. Pareja-Eastway, Chapain and Mugnano (2013) evaluate the branding process across 13 European cities. The case of Barcelona, which started in 1988 with a strategic plan, involved a process of spatial transformation and reorganization. Spatial planning and spatial design were combined, and with the consensus of a variety of actors, long-term strategic planning highly influenced the final outcome of the whole branding exercise. Barcelona City Council was able, both before the Olympic Games in 1992 and after, to implement assertive strategy making in the urban realm, which reinforced the image of the city as a place for business, tourism, cultural and sporting activities (cf. Oliveira, 2016b).

The way forward

The conscious relating of spatial planning and place branding can in many places offer a useful tool to coordinate the use, conservation and development of natural and cultural landscapes. In this chapter, we emphasize the value in both spatial planning and place branding and demonstrate the potential synergies. Finding those synergies is a matter of discovering a locally and regionally appropriate form of exploring the planning–branding nexus. The benefits can be a stabilization of places and the identification of new economic opportunities through a perspective on place-based value creation. The possible problems are in the realm of the increasing complexity of governance, costly overlaps and, most importantly, a possible democratic deficit, often commented upon by critics of place branding and critics of expert-driven planning (cf. Van Assche et al., 2020; Vanolo, 2017).

Despite our warnings against simply subsuming branding under planning or the other way around, against making one simply part of the other, in some circumstances this might be the way forward. For example, Oliveira (2015a) explores the roles of place branding as an instrument for the attainment of strategic spatial planning goals. Other studies, however, acknowledge that place branding can play a 'dominant' role over spatial planning strategies (Deffner et al., 2020; Pasquinelli and Vuignier, 2020). Our argument is that this cannot be a general recipe, without studying the governance path and configurations of each place (cf. Van Assche et al., 2020). When there is a strong planning tradition, with planning aiming at broader spatial development, when this tradition is proven to be flexible and open to new perspectives and when it is in touch with local perceptions of assets and narratives of place, planning could provide the frame for branding activities. Place branding can make planning more sensitive to value creation then help it to envision a social, economic and ecologically sustainable future. When planning is weak, yet there is a strong sense of place, with a civic tradition of cooperation towards common goals, a new branding framework might be more achievable. Within this frame, elements of spatial planning can come into being. We have debated here that the study of the planning–branding nexus requires attention to the many ways in which spatial planning and place branding can cross-fertilize each other and to the embedding of both in evolving spatial governance systems.

References

Abis, E. and C. Garau (2016), 'An assessment of the effectiveness of strategic spatial planning: A study of Sardinian municipalities', *European Planning Studies*, **24** (1), 139–62.

Acuto, M., Parnell, S. and K. C. Seto (2018), 'Building a global urban science', *Nature Sustainability*, **1** (1), 2–4.

Albrechts, L. (1999), 'Planners as catalysts and initiators of change: The new structure plan for Flanders', *European Planning Studies*, **7** (5), 587–603.

Albrechts, L. (2015), 'Ingredients for a more radical strategic spatial planning', *Environment and Planning B: Planning and Design*, **42** (3), 510–25.

Allmendinger, P. (2016), *Neoliberal Spatial Governance*, London: Routledge.

Allmendinger, P. and G. Haughton (2013), 'The evolution and trajectories of English spatial governance: "Neoliberal" episodes in planning', *Planning Practice and Research*, **28** (1), 6–26.

Anholt, S. (2019), 'Place "branding" revisited', LinkedIn blog post, accessed 24 April 2020 at: www.linkedin.com/pulse/place-branding-revisited-simon-anholt/?trackingId=6e9HuGtwTsK8ZB2leLyBgw%3D%3D.

Ashworth, G. and M. Kavaratzis (2018), 'The roles of branding in public administration and place management: Possibilities and pitfalls', in E. Ongaro and S. Van Thiel (eds), *The Palgrave Handbook of Public Administration and Management in Europe*, London: Palgrave Macmillan, pp. 425–39.

Ashworth, G. J., Kavaratzis, M. and G. Warnaby (2015), 'The need to rethink place branding', in M. Kavaratzis, G. Warnaby and G. J. Ashworth (eds), *Rethinking Place Branding: Comprehensive Brand Development for Cities and Regions*, Cham: Springer International Publishing, pp. 1–12.

Asprogerakas, E. and K. Mountanea (2020), 'Spatial strategies as a place branding tool in the region of Ruhr', *Place Branding and Public Diplomacy*, https://doi.org/10.1057/s41254-020-00168-1.

Bacău, S., Grădinaru, S. R. and A. M. Hersperger (2020), 'Spatial plans as relational data: Using social network analysis to assess consistency among Bucharest's planning instruments', *Land Use Policy*, **92**, https://doi.org/10.1016/j.landusepol.2020.104484.

Bloemers, J.H.F., Kars, H., van der Valk, A. and M. Wijnen (eds) (2010), *The Cultural Landscape Heritage Paradox: Protection and Development of the Dutch Archaeological-Historical Landscape and Its European Dimension*, Amsterdam: Amsterdam University Press.

Bonakdar, A. and I. Audirac (2020), 'City branding and the link to urban planning: Theories, practices, and challenges', *Journal of Planning Literature*, **35** (2), 147–60.

CEC (Commission of the European Communities) (1999), *European Spatial Development Perspective: Towards Balanced and Sustainable Development of the Territory of the EU*, Luxembourg: Office for Official Publications of the European Communities.

Cleave, E., Arku, G., Sadler, R. and J. Gilliland (2017), 'Is it sound policy or fast policy? Practitioners' perspectives on the role of place branding in local economic development', *Urban Geography*, **38** (8), 1133–57.

Dawson, E. and M. Higgins (2009), 'How planning authorities can improve quality through the design review process: Lessons from Edinburgh', *Journal of Urban Design*, **14** (1), 101–14.

de San Eugenio Vela, J., Nogué, J. and R. Govers (2017), 'Visual landscape as a key element of place branding', *Journal of Place Management and Development*, **10** (1), 23–44.

Deffner, A., Karachalis, E., Psatha, E., Metaxas, T. and K. Sirakoulis (2020), 'City marketing and planning in two Greek cities: Plurality or constraints?', *European Planning Studies*, **28** (7), 1333–54.

Donner, M., Horlings, L., Fort, F. and S. Vellema (2017), 'Place branding, embeddedness and endogenous rural development: Four European cases', *Place Branding and Public Diplomacy*, **13** (4), 273–92.

Eixo Atlántico (2020), 'Eixo Atlántico contributes to the European Commission proposals for the recovery of the tourism sector', accessed 13 May 2020 at: www .eixoatlantico.com/es/noticias/eixoatlantico/4791-el-eixo-atlantico-aporta-a-la -comision-europea-propuestas-para-la-recuperacion-del-sector-del-turismo.

Eshuis, J., Klijn, E. and E. Braun (2014), 'Place marketing and citizen participation: Branding as strategy to address the emotional dimension of policy making?', *International Review of Administrative Sciences*, **80** (1), 151–71.

Evans, G. (2015), 'Rethinking place branding and place making through creative and cultural quarters', in M. Kavaratzis, G. Warnaby and G. J. Ashworth (eds), *Rethinking Place Branding Comprehensive Brand Development for Cities and Regions*, Cham: Springer International Publishing, pp. 135–58.

Fainstein, S. S. and J. DeFilippis (2016), *Readings in Planning Theory*, Oxford: Wiley.

Feagan, R. (2007), 'The place of food: Mapping out the "local" in local food systems', *Progress in Human Geography*, **31** (1), 23–42.

Gerber J.-D. and J.-F. Gerber (2017), 'Decommodification as a foundation for ecological economics', *Ecological Economics*, **131**, 551–6.

Gotham, K. (2007), '(Re)branding the big easy: Tourism rebuilding in post-Katrina New Orleans', *Urban Affairs Review*, **42** (6), 823–50.

Granqvist, K., Humer, A. and R. Mäntysalo (2020), 'Tensions in city-regional spatial planning: The challenge of interpreting layered institutional rules', *Regional Studies*, https://doi.org/10.1080/00343404.2019.1707791.

Grenni, S., Horlings, L. G. and K. Soini (2020), 'Linking spatial planning and place branding strategies through cultural narratives in places', *European Planning Studies*, **28** (7), 1355–74.

Gunn, S. and J. Hillier (2014), 'When uncertainty is interpreted as risk: An analysis of tensions relating to spatial planning reform in England', *Planning Practice and Research*, **29** (1), 56–74.

Hae, L. (2017), 'Traveling policy: Place marketing and the neoliberal turn of urban studies in South Korea', *Critical Sociology*, **44** (3), 533–46.

Harries, B., Byrne, B., Rhodes, J. and S. Wallace (2018), 'Diversity in place: Narrations of diversity in an ethnically mixed, urban area', *Journal of Ethnic and Migration Studies*, **45** (17), 3225–42.

Healey, P. (2006), 'Transforming governance: Challenges of institutional adaptation and a new politics of space', *European Planning Studies*, **14** (3), 299–320.

Hersperger, A. M., Oliveira, E., Pagliarin, S., Palka, G., Verburg, P., Bolliger, J. and S. Grădinaru (2018), 'Urban land-use change: The role of strategic spatial planning', *Global Environmental Change*, **51**, 32–42.

Hersperger, A. M., Grădinaru, S., Oliveira, E., Pagliarin, S. and G. Palka (2019), 'Understanding strategic spatial planning to effectively guide development of urban regions', *Cities*, **94**, 96–105.

Hersperger, A. M., Bürgi, M., Wende, W., Bacău, S. and S. R. Grădinaru (2020), 'Does landscape play a role in strategic spatial planning of European urban regions?', *Landscape and Urban Planning*, **194**, https://doi.org/10.1016/j.landurbplan.2019.103702.

Hospers, G.-J. (2017), 'People, place and partnership: Exploring strategies to revitalise town centres', *European Spatial Research and Policy*, **24** (1), 65–79.

Insch, A. and T. Walters (2018), 'Challenging assumptions about residents' engagement with place branding', *Place Brand and Public Diplomacy*, **14** (3), 152–62.

Jensen, O. (2007), 'Culture stories: Understanding cultural urban branding', *Planning Theory*, **6** (3), 211–36.

Kavaratzis, M. (2012), 'From "necessary evil" to necessity: Stakeholders' involvement in place branding', *Journal of Place Management and Development*, **5** (1), 7–19.

Kavaratzis, M. (2018), 'Place branding: Are we any wiser?', *Cities*, **80**, 61–3.

Kavaratzis, M. and G. J. Ashworth (2005), 'City branding: An effective assertion of identity or a transitory marketing trick?', *Tijdschrift voor Economische en Sociale Geografie*, **96** (5), 506–14.

Kavaratzis, M., Warnaby, G. and G. J. Ashworth (2015), *Rethinking Place Branding: Comprehensive Brand Development for Cities and Regions*, Cham: Springer International Publishing.

Konecnik Ruzzier, M., Petek, N. and M. Ruzzier (2015), 'Incorporating sustainability in branding: I feel Slovenia', *IUP Journal of Brand Management*, **12** (1), 1–15.

Li, Q. and X. Cai (2019), 'Regional brand development from the perspective of brand relations spectrum: Taking Changle as an example', *Proceedings of the 2019 International Conference on Management, Education Technology and Economics*, Paris: Atlantis Multitude.

Lucarelli, A. (2018), 'Place branding as urban policy: The (im)political place branding', *Cities*, **80**, 12–21.

Lucarelli, A. and S. Brorström (2013), 'Problematising place branding research: A meta-theoretical analysis of the literature', *The Marketing Review*, **13** (1), 65–81.

Lucarelli, A. and S. Heldt Cassel (2020), 'The dialogical relationship between spatial planning and place branding: Conceptualizing regionalization discourses in Sweden', *European Planning Studies*, **28** (7), 1375–92.

Medway, D., Warnaby, G. and S. Dharni (2011), 'Demarketing places: Rationales and strategies', *Journal of Marketing Management*, **27** (1/2), 124–42.

Molainen, T. (2015), 'Challenges of city branding: A comparative study of 10 European cities', *Place Branding and Public Diplomacy*, **11** (3), 216–25.

Niedziałkowski, K. and R. Beunen (2019), 'The risky business of planning reform: The evolution of local spatial planning in Poland', *Land Use Policy*, **85**, 11–20.

Ntounis, N. and M. Kavaratzis (2017), 'Re-branding the High Street: The place branding process and reflections from three UK towns', *Journal of Place Management and Development*, **10** (4), 392–403.

Oliveira, E. (2015a), 'Place branding as a strategic spatial planning instrument', *Place Branding and Public Diplomacy*, **11** (1), 18–33.

Oliveira, E. (2015b), 'Constructing regional advantage in branding the cross-border Euroregion Galicia – northern Portugal', *Regional Studies, Regional Science*, **2** (1), 341–9.

Oliveira, E. (2016a), 'Place branding as a strategic spatial planning instrument: A theoretical framework to branding regions with references to northern Portugal', *Journal of Place Management and Development*, **9** (1), 47–72.

Oliveira, E. (2016b), 'Place branding in strategic spatial planning: A content analysis of development plans, strategic initiatives and policy documents for Portugal 2014–2020', *Journal of Place Management and Development*, **8** (1), 23–50.

Oliveira, E. and G. J. Ashworth (2017), 'A strategic spatial planning approach to place branding: Challenges and opportunities', in A. Campelo (ed.), *Handbook on Place Branding and Marketing*, Cheltenham, UK and Northampton, MA, USA: Edward Elgar Publishing, pp. 22–40.

Pareja-Eastway, M., Chapain, C. and S. Mugnano (2013), 'Success and failures in city branding policies', in S. Musterd and Z. Kovács (eds), *Place-Making and Policies for Competitive Cities*, Chichester: Wiley-Blackwell, pp. 149–71.

Pasquinelli, C. and R. Vuignier (2020), 'Place marketing, policy integration and governance complexity: An analytical framework for FDI promotion', *European Planning Studies*, **28** (7), 1413–30.

Porter, N. (2020), 'Strategic planning and place branding in a World Heritage cultural landscape: A case study of the English Lake District, UK', *European Planning Studies*, **28** (7), 1291–314.

Radosavljević, U., Đorđević, A., Lalović, K., Živković, J. and Z. Đukanović (2020), 'Educational projects for linking place branding and urban planning in Serbia', *European Planning Studies*, **28** (7), 1431–451.

Rantisi, N. and D. Leslie (2006), 'Branding the design metropole: The case of Montreal, Canada', *Area*, **38** (4), 364–76.

Rivolin, A. J. (2017), 'Global crisis and the systems of spatial governance and planning: A European comparison', *European Planning Studies*, **25** (6), 994–1012.

Rosenzweig, C., Solecki, W., Hammer, S. A. and S. Mehrotra (2010), 'Cities lead the way in climate-change action', *Nature*, **467** (7318), 909–11.

Sandercock, L. (2003), 'Out of the closet: The importance of stories and storytelling in planning practice', *Planning Theory and Practice*, **4** (1), 11–28.

Stubbs, J. and G. Warnaby (2015), 'Rethinking place branding from a practice perspective: Working with stakeholders', in M. Kavaratzis, G. Warnaby and G. J. Ashworth (eds), *Rethinking Place Branding: Comprehensive Brand Development for Cities and Regions*, Cham: Springer International Publishing, pp. 101–18.

Throgmorton, J. (1996), *Planning as Persuasive Storytelling: The Rhetorical Construction of Chicago's Electric Future*, Chicago, IL: University of Chicago Press.

Tobias, S. and P. M. Wahl (2013), 'Can place branding support landscape conservation in city-regions? A case study from Switzerland', *Land Use Policy*, **30** (1), 266–75.

UN General Assembly (2015), *Transforming Our World: The 2030 Agenda for Sustainable Development*, New York: United Nations.

Van Assche, K. and M. Chien Lo (2011), 'Planning, preservation and place branding: A tale of sharing assets and narratives', *Place Branding and Public Diplomacy*, **7** (2), 116–26.

Van Assche, K. and A. Hornidge (2015), *Rural Development: Knowledge and Expertise in Governance*, Wageningen: Wageningen Academic.

Van Assche, K., Beunen, R. and M. Duineveld (eds) (2014), *Evolutionary Governance Theory: An Introduction*, Cham: Springer International Publishing.

Van Assche, K., Beunen, R. and M. Lo (2016), 'Place as layered and segmentary commodity: Place branding, smart growth and the creation of product and value', *International Planning Studies*, **21** (2), 164–75.

Van Assche, K., Beunen, R. and E. Oliveira (2020), 'Spatial planning and place branding: Rethinking relations and synergies', *European Planning Studies*, **28** (7), 1274–90.

Van Assche, K., Beunen, R., Duineveld, M. and H. De Jong (2012), 'Co-evolutions of planning and design: Risks and benefits of design perspectives in planning systems', *Planning Theory*, **12** (2), 177–98.

Vanolo, A. (2017), *City Branding: The Ghostly Politics of Representation in Globalising Cities*, New York: Routledge.

Yea, L. and E. Björner (2018), 'Linking city branding to multi-level urban governance in Chinese megacities: A case study of Guangzhou', *Cities*, **80**, 29–37.

Zimmermann, K., Galland, D. and J. Harrison (eds) (2020), *Metropolitan Regions, Planning and Governance*, Cham: Springer Nature Switzerland AG.

PART II

Contexts

6 Place branding and locational decisions: Taking a behavioural economics perspective?

Aleks Vladimirov and Gary Warnaby

Introduction

Urban places are regarded as existing within the context of increasingly intense spatial competition for inward investment, residents, tourists, etc., which is manifest in a variety of ways (see, for example, Kotler et al., 1999). This has arisen, particularly, from the complex and dynamic relationships between the local and the global, interacting at different geographic locations and scales, as locational choices available to hypermobile capital and people have greatly increased (Castells and Hall, 1994; Rogerson, 1999).

The consequent attempts by towns and cities to capitalise on this through enhancing their competitiveness (see Begg, 1999) – and the associated implications for governance – have been conceptualised in notions of urban entrepreneurialism (see Harvey, 1989; Jessop, 1998), which has led to the adoption of a logic which incorporates place marketing and branding activities (see Warnaby, 2009). Arguably, however, this focus is the consequence of perspectives often transferred from the domains of marketing and economics without modification to the specific place context (e.g. Kotler and Gertner, 2002). Indeed, applying the principles of market competition to such a complex phenomenon as place, as if it were reduced to a mere problem of efficient allocation of homogenous commodified resources, has already been discussed as inappropriate in the emergent field of place branding, and in the geography discipline more generally (see, for example, Harvey, 2012; Kavaratzis, Warnaby and Ashworth, 2015).

In this chapter, we address these issues by considering these characteristics of place, and analysing how this might affect the decisions of those individuals and organisations faced with locational choices in terms of choosing where to live, work and invest. We begin by discussing the nature of 'place' more generally, and the consequent implications for locational decisions, before moving to consider – through the lens of behavioural economics – the process(es) by which these decisions may be made. We conclude by mapping out an agenda for further research in this somewhat neglected aspect of place marketing/branding research.

Shaping place?

A useful starting point for our discussion is Agnew's (1987) tripartite definition of place as *location, locale* and a *sense of place*. *Location* is defined in terms of the point on the Earth's surface where the place is to be found, and indeed, locational advantage is a common trope in place marketing messages (see Ward, 1998). *Locale* relates to the settings in which both informal and institutional social relations are constituted – described by Cresswell in terms of 'the material setting for social relations – the actual shape of place within which people conduct their lives' (2004: 7). Agnew's third dimension refers to the emotional attachment that people have to place, and the resulting *sense of place* 'reinforces the social-spatial definition of place from the *inside*' (Agnew, 1987: 27 – original emphasis), potentially creating an identification between individual and place.

Indeed, everyone comes from somewhere, and arguably the place where we are from is forever a part of our perceived identity, and may engender a strong sense of attachment. Hidalgo and Hernandez's (2001: 274) definition of place attachment as 'a positive affective bond between an individual and a specific place, the main characteristic of which is the tendency of the individual to maintain closeness to such a place', points to a deeper question about the nature of place and our relationship(s) to it. However, from a specific place marketing/branding perspective, this sense of attachment may be hard to transmit to those who do not share the same direct experience of a place. Furthermore, it could be argued that our place identities are becoming more complex as people migrate and cultures intersect in the context of a globalised world.

Agnew's definition highlights the complex and dynamic mix of a specific 'location', and what goes on within that location to create a dynamic and evolving 'locale', which in turn may be experienced as – and through – a more phenomenologically oriented and subjective 'sense of place' (see Cresswell, 2004). Such complexity is an interesting area for further research given the tendency for place marketing/branding messages, created in order to attract people and capital, to be somewhat reductionist and homogenised (see, for example, Clegg and Kornberger, 2010). Often, such activities are more concerned with prioritising capital attraction over improvement of the quality of life of those within a place (Rogerson, 1999), and worse, sometimes result in the marginalisation of certain groups over others in the hunt for global capital investment (Harvey, 2012).

Mayer (1989, cited in Harvey, 2012) highlights the fact that, in the contemporary city, whilst there may be a veneer of economic consolidation, it is not a 'pluralism' of lifestyles and consumption patterns that prevails; rather that an understanding of the ideals and definitions of 'the good life' among certain target segments are the most important determinants of place marketing messages. This raises questions about how specific locales are represented, often creating place images through assemblages of stereotypical attributes and facilities (frequently conceptualised in terms of 'hard' and 'soft' conditions – see Musterd and Murie, 2010) that contribute to a place 'product' (see Warnaby and Medway, 2015), and/or creating associations with the place in question to develop place brands (Zenker and Braun, 2017).

Improvements in those place attributes that are deemed attractive to selected target segments, and rising up 'league tables' relating to various aspects of place (i.e. the numerous quality of life, and foreign direct investment confidence indexes that are promulgated by various media organisations, etc.) have been an important means of promoting and communicating place attractiveness (Rogerson, 1999). Developments such as Richard Florida's work on the 'creative class' (2004, 2008; Florida and Adler, 2018) provides a set list of attractive amenities that constitute what has been termed 'quality of place', defined in terms of:

> the bundle of goods and services that come under the broad rubric of amenities…
> these amenities are not mere fleeting phenomena but can be more appropriately
> thought of as the inherited, acquired, and built up characteristics of places – for
> example, as embodied in its parks, neighbourhoods, cultural and educational insti-
> tutions, and broad social milieu. In plainer language, it is what makes Paris – Paris,
> London – London, and New York – New York. (Arora et al., 2000: 2)

However, important questions arise about the match between personal aspirations for quality of life and what a place has to offer, and – specific to the focus of this chapter – how individuals might make decisions about where they choose to live and work. One possible lens through which to examine this issue is that of behavioural economics.

Choosing place?

Much of Florida's (2004) work on 'creative cities' arguaby relies on assumptions of the axiomatic economic rationality (Gigerenzer, 2019) inherent in neoclassical economics. However, such assumptions are increasingly challenged by the growing field of behavioural economics. Pendleton et al. (2019, citing Thaler, 2016) summarise the three core tenets of neoclassical economic theory; namely, that individuals (1) have well-defined, stable preferences along with unbiased beliefs; (2) make optimal choices based on these beliefs and preferences; and (3) are primarily motivated by self interest.

In challenging these assumptions, the interdisciplinary field of behavioural economics has been steadily gaining prominence. Behavioural economists have investigated how the actual behaviour of the human actor in most economic theory may not always match the expectations of more traditional economists. These axiomatic expectations of rationality – embodied in the notion of 'homo economicus' (Thaler and Sunstein, 2009) – have been steadily replaced by a more overt, non-rational perspective on the nature of human judgement, which we discuss below.

Heuristics and Biases

Some behavioural economists follow in the footsteps of what is now called the heuristics-and-biases research programme, pioneered by Tversky and Kahneman (1974). These researchers have focused mainly on investigating deviations from the expected, more overtly rational behaviour of homo economicus, which are manifested in the notion of bias, and Ghisellini and Chang (2018) suggest that there are now over 200 different biases that have been identified. Biases are deviations from rationality, resulting from the reliance on 'heuristics', which are considered to be second-best, sub-optimal coping strategies that replace the logical decision making of homo economicus. Kahneman (2003) views heuristics as types of 'cognitive shortcuts' or 'rules of thumb' that simplify decisions and represent a process of often substituting a difficult question with an easier one that can be answered by the individual. An example related to place that can illustrate this view of human judgement could be that answering a complex question, such as in which location a person feels that her quality of life would be maximised, gets substituted with an easier question asking where previous memories of good quality of life can be retrieved.

Kahneman (2011) further developed a framework describing how such cognitive shortcuts are best described as the result of the workings of two systems of thinking which often work congruently, but sometimes are at odds – a fast, intuitive one (System 1), and another which is more deliberate and slower (System 2). System 1 decision making is seen as second best, and replaces the often necessary use of a more rational System 2 approach. This results in bias. Kahneman's (2011) explanations about why people enact this substitution is grounded in the interpretation of a philosophical view of human nature as 'boundedly rational', as proposed by Simon (1987). Looking at the bounded nature of people's cognitive, emotional and social abilities, Kahneman (2011) finds a reason that explains why people would not 'think slow' all the time due to their limitations. This interpretation of bounded rationality highlights the constraints of rationality without removing our ability to reason in a broader, more intuitive sense. However, by only focusing on the individual as a unit of analysis, the heuristics-and-biases programme arguably does not provide enough scope to understand how these intuitive judgements serve the individual in their broader social and natural environment, and to address this issue we now move to consider the 'fast-and-frugal' research programme.

Fast-and-Frugal Heuristics

The fast-and-frugal behavioural economics research programme championed by Gerd Gigerenzer regards the application of heuristics as an 'ecologically rational' strategy that exploits the structure of the environment to achieve outcomes (see Gigerenzer and Goldstein, 1996; Gigerenzer, Todd and ABC Research Group, 1999; Gigerenzer, 2008; Gigerenzer and Brighton, 2009). This perspective differs from the heuristics-and-biases programme, described above, insofar as when considering the performance of a heuristic in helping to solve a problem, it highlights the plurality of paths that can be taken to achieve the same goal.

In mapping heuristics in depth, Gigerenzer and Brighton (2009) have shown that heuristics may be implicit to the individual until clearly teased out. However, once identified, they can also be formalised into tools that can improve the performance of others in relation to the same task. A demonstration of this effect, often mentioned by Gigerenzer, shows how a baseball catcher does not follow the rationally expected mechanism of calculating the trajectory of a ball in the air that has to be caught. Moreover, when experts are asked how they do it, the catchers do not explicitly calculate the ball's trajectory, but what they do is lock their gaze onto the ball and modify the speed of running to allow them to be in the right position. This heuristic that shows deviation from rationality is then taught to non-experts and improves performance.

This extension of the goals of rationality to actual performance is the key departure between the Kahneman and Tversky heuristics-and-biases school and Gigerenzer's fast-and-frugal-heuristics tradition (Gigerenzer, 2019). This stems from the fast-and-frugal school's following in the tradition of evolutionary psychology, where the individual is not regarded as a stand-alone unit, but rather as an actor making decisions related to their environment. This is based on an interpretation of Simon's (1987) notion of 'bounded rationality' as entailing a mind–environment relationship that should always be studied together as an inseparable 'scissor', where the one blade of the scissor is the mind and the other is the environment. Following this interpretation, Gigerenzer and Selten (2002: 545–6) define a heuristic in terms of: 'a strategy that ignores part of the information, with the goal of making decisions more quickly, frugally, and/or accurately than more complex methods'. This view has implications for how heuristics should be studied by examining how they relate to our broader context, the more imminent domain of decision making and the goals we are pursuing.

Gigerenzer (2019: 7) highlights the original Greek meaning of heuristic as 'serving to find out or discover' and shows how, historically, it was a word that referred to a useful tool for solving problems that cannot easily be handled by logic or probabilistic inference. Given this variance of heuristics away from the trammelled tracks of axiomatic logic, Gigerenzer and Selten (2002: 545) have suggested three overarching processual stages that heuristics share: (1) *search rules*, which specify in what direction the search extends in the search space; (2) *stopping rules*, which specify when the search is stopped; and (3) *decision rules*, which specify how the final decision is reached.

Such an in-depth view of heuristics as multi-stage strategies with a focus on the evolutionary fit between mind and environment is not as prominent in the theorising of Kahneman (2003) and the heuristics-and-biases programme. Nonetheless, there is a general consensus between these two major schools of behavioural economics which assumes that people may not necessarily use logically coherent rationality to make decisions about where to locate. The multiple ways in which people's judgements are non-rational that have been studied in other domains may well extend to their relationships to place, and to decisions about which particular location would best improve their quality of life.

Locational decisions and behavioural economics: Towards a research agenda?

Influencing locational decisions by organisations and individuals that are external to the place to the benefit of particular destinations has been a factor underpinning the recent development of place marketing/branding. Ward (1994: 53) argues that early place marketing activities were motivated by 'two distinct though closely related impulses' – a 'boosterist' desire for growth through the accumulation of urban economic functions, and a more defensive 'regenerative' desire to avoid decline by diversifying the economic base of the locale. Boosterism characterised early place marketing activity in North America (see for example Short et al., 1993 on the development of place marketing in Syracuse), where for many areas of peripheral industrialisation and urbanisation, economic success was dependent on the pursuit of external investment and entrepreneurship (Ward, 1998). By contrast, regeneration has characterised place marketing within traditional industrial areas of the United Kingdom and Europe in order to counteract the decline of traditional industrial activity.

Bailey (1989, cited in Kotler, Haider and Rein, 1993: 77) identifies three genera-tions of 'economic development marketing' from the 1930s onwards as *smoke-stack chasing, target marketing* and *product development*. The emphasis of the first-generation 'smokestack chasing' was on the creation of manufacturing jobs in a locale by luring facilities from other locations by means of promoting better business climates through low operating costs and government subsi-dies. Kotler et al. (1993) argue that the objectives, rationale and methods of place marketing remained little changed over the next four decades, and it was not until the 1970s and 1980s that place marketers began to target their activ-ities more effectively. This second generation of 'target marketing' focused on the creation of employment within those manufacturing and service industries currently enjoying profitable growth. The underlying rationale for these activ-ities was on competitive operating costs, the suitability of the community for the target industries (in terms of their skills and capabilities, etc.) and the pro-motion of good quality of life (particularly regarding recreation and climate).

The third generation of 'product development', from the early 1990s onwards, arguably takes a more strategic perspective. The emphasis is on employment creation, not only in those industries that are currently successful, but also in industries that it is anticipated will provide high-quality jobs in the future. The underlying rationale is to prepare the locality for effective competition and growth in the contemporary global economy by offering competitive operating costs, human and intellectual resources adaptable to future change and a good quality of life (with the emphasis on cultural and intellectual development).

While Bailey's model is based on evidence from the United States, Short and Kim (1999: 98) argue that 'it is suitable for wider generalization', and according to Kotler et al. (1993: 78), it reflects 'the growth, development, and sophistication of place competition in a changing world economy'. Subsequent work by Kavaratzis and Ashworth (2008) has provided a more detailed and theoretically oriented exposition of the place marketing developmental timeline, but their processual stages are broadly analogous with those proposed by Bailey. Moreover, Kavaratzis and Ashworth extend the developmental timeline into the new millennium, with an acknowledgement of the role of place *branding*, which – to reprise the work of Agnew (1987) and Cresswell (2004) mentioned earlier – has a more overt focus on those phenomenological aspects relating to the creation of a 'sense of place' through attempts to create and manage emotional and psychological associations with the locale in question.

Much of the existing research into place marketing and branding has focused on *how* places themselves have responded to the challenges of an increasingly competitive spatial environment and the specific activities those responsible for their marketing have undertaken in order to satisfy the imperatives arising from boosterist and regenerative motivations to improve the economic situation of their locale. Numerous texts exist which seek to provide an understanding and, to a greater or lesser degree, a prescriptive planning process outlining activities to be undertaken to improve a place's competitive position at a variety of spatial scales (see for example Kotler et al., 1993, 1999; Dinnie, 2008; Moilanen and Rainisto, 2009). Whilst such texts acknowledge the need to understand how target markets/place buyers 'make their choices' (Kotler et al., 1993, 1999), we would argue that there are numerous avenues down which future research could develop in terms of developing a more detailed understanding of two key questions: (1) how locational decisions are made; and (2) how might place branders possibly influence these decisions.

Fundamental to answering the first of these questions is some investigation of the actual utility of taking a behavioural economics perspective on the study of locational decisions: in other words, how are locational decisions made by individuals, either acting for their own ends or on behalf of the organisations they are a part of. These issues have been initially discussed above in relation to heuristics and biases, and the extent to which they deviate from the standard rationality of traditional economic thought. In addition, other, more specific, themes which can serve to identify further questions for future investigation can be articulated. These could include:

- The extent, and precise nature of, the systematic errors (biases) – and whether there are common structures to the heuristics – that influence locational decision making, of both supply-side and demand-side actors.
- Determining any distinctions between locational choice System 1 and System 2 decisions that can provide a link to understanding the relationship between heuristic and bias.
- Whether bounded rationality provides a better lens through which to study the process of place branding.
- How does the mind–environment interaction relate to locational choice?

Regarding the second point relating to how place branders might possibly influence these locational decisions, issues relating to the factors at their disposal in order to do this potentially become important. One factor here is the nature of the place itself and the extent to which particular elements of it can be commodified to attract specific audiences.

Existing research has investigated the notion of places as 'products', which Ashworth and Voogd (1990) suggest could be thought of as referring to the place as a whole (i.e. the 'nuclear product') and to the specific services, facilities and attributes that occur at/within the place (i.e. 'contributory elements'). Similarly, Van den Berg and Braun (1999) identify three levels of (urban) place marketing, comprising Level 1, the individual urban goods and services that can be marketed as discrete attractions/facilities; but which can also be combined to create Level 2, namely clusters of related services, which can be marketed to attract particular segments of place users; but which can also in turn coalesce to create an overall perception of Level 3, the urban agglomeration as a whole. Whilst such notions of the 'assemblage' of the place product seemingly focus on its materiality, perceptions of city competitiveness, which can be influential in choices relating to inward investment, might also incorporate 'soft' factors relating to such issues as workforce skills and productivity, quality of life, etc. Thus, important questions for future research relate to:

- Perceptions of the relative importance of the individual elements comprising the place product 'assemblage'.
- How – and why – such perceptions are held by both organisations and individuals faced with relocation.
- Whether these place perceptions can be influenced according to the context of the locational decision; for example, whether individuals make the decision from choice (for example, organisations seeking to expand into new geographic areas), or whether the decision is 'forced' (for example, if the

existing workforce of these organisations have to make a choice between their current domicile – to which they might feel a strong sense of attachment for a range of personal and family reasons – or a new location where they would have to, among other things, potentially recreate the social networks that have supported them to date).

- Mirroring broader discussions in the marketing literature relating to the stereotypical differences between organisational buyer behaviour (as more rational?) and consumer buyer behaviour (as more overtly 'emotional'?), are such stereotypes an accurate reflection of locational decisions, which has implications for the means by which – and the extent to which – they can be influenced.

Concluding comments

In conclusion, perhaps the process-oriented nature of behavioural economics research can provide a new perspective that can help tease out some detail and nuance regarding the similarities and differences between traditional buyer behaviour and choosing a location. Both the heuristics-and-biases and fast-and-frugal-heuristics schools of thought in behavioural economics can serve to provide a broader framework for understanding human reasoning that is more varied than the traditional, neoclassical economic assumptions of rational choice.

After all, the rational pursuit of the maximisation of wealth should take us wherever we can maximise our financial opportunity. But a behavioural economics perspective can help us understand how place attachment could be seen as ecologically rational if we choose to investigate how the advantages inherent in the familiarity of our surroundings, social relationships and sense of belonging to a place can contribute to the betterment of our quality of life. When the BBC attempted to move staff from London to Greater Manchester there was an evident split between those who were willing to relocate and those who stayed put despite facing redundancy if they did not move (see Holmwood, 2009). Such a case of people deciding to forego relocating despite a clear economic disadvantage is just one example that goes against the 'boosterist' place marketing tradition that is often built on attracting those who seek a better economic opportunity. Such behaviour may be seen as biased when studied from the outside, but as this chapter has argued, a bias can often be just the tip of an iceberg that showcases part of a deeper, ecologically rational heuristic that helps an individual or organisation to choose a location.

References

Agnew, J. A. (1987), *Place and Politics: The Geographical Mediation of State and Society*, Boston, MA: Allen and Unwin.

Arora, A., Florida, R., Gates, G. J. and M. Kamlet (2000), *Human Capital, Quality of Place, and Location*, Pittsburgh, PA: Carnegie Mellon University.

Ashworth, G. and H. Voogd (1990), *Selling the City: Marketing Approaches in Public Sector Urban Planning*, London: Belhaven Press.

Bailey, J. T. (1989), *Marketing Cities in the 1980s and Beyond: New Patterns New Pressures, New Promises*, Chicago, IL: American Economic Development Council.

Begg, I. (1999), 'Cities and competitiveness', *Urban Studies*, **36** (5–6), 795–809.

Castells, M. and P. Hall (1994), *Technopoles of the World*, London: Routledge.

Clegg, S. R. and M. Kornberger (2010), 'An organizational perspective on space and place branding', in F. M. Go and R. Govers (eds), *International Place Branding Yearbook 2010: Place Branding in the New Age of Innovation*, Basingstoke: Palgrave Macmillan, pp. 3–11.

Cresswell, T. (2004), *Place: An Introduction*, Oxford: Blackwell Publishing.

Dinnie, K. (2008), *Nation Branding: Concepts, Issues, Practice*, Oxford: Butterworth-Heinemann.

Florida, R. (2004), *The Rise of the Creative Class: And How It's Transforming Work, Leisure, Community and Everyday Life*, New York: Basic Books.

Florida, R. (2008), *Who's Your City? How the Creative Economy Is Making Where You Live the Most Important Decision of Your Life*, New York: Basic Books.

Florida, R. and P. Adler (2018), 'The patchwork metropolis: The morphology of the divided postindustrial city', *Journal of Urban Affairs*, **40** (5), 609–24.

Ghisellini, F. and B. Y. Chang (2018), *Behavioral Economics: Moving Forward*, New York: Springer.

Gigerenzer, G. (2008), 'Moral intuition = fast and frugal heuristics?', in W. Sinnott-Armstrong (ed.), *Moral Psychology, Vol 2. The Cognitive Science of Morality: Intuition and Diversity*, Cambridge, MA: MIT Press, pp. 1–26.

Gigerenzer, G. (2019), 'Axiomatic rationality and ecological rationality', *Synthese*, 1–18, https://doi.org/10.1007/s11229-019-02296-5.

Gigerenzer, G. and H. Brighton (2009), 'Homo heuristicus: Why biased minds make better inferences', *Topics in Cognitive Science*, **1** (1), 107–43.

Gigerenzer, G. and D. G. Goldstein (1996), 'Reasoning the fast and frugal way: Models of bounded rationality', *Psychological Review*, **103** (4), 650–69.

Gigerenzer, G. and R. Selten (eds) (2002), *Bounded Rationality: The Adaptive Toolbox*, Cambridge, MA: MIT Press.

Gigerenzer, G., Todd, P. M. and ABC Research Group (1999), *Simple Heuristics That Make Us Smart*, Oxford: Oxford University Press.

Harvey, D. (1989), 'From managerialism to entrepreneurialism: The transformation in urban governance in late capitalism', *Geografiska Annaler*, **71B**, 3–17.

Harvey, D. (2012), *Rebel Cities: From the Right to the City to the Urban Revolution*, London: Verso Books.

Hidalgo, M. C. and B. Hernandez (2001), 'Place attachment: Conceptual and empirical questions', *Journal of Environmental Psychology*, **21**, 273–81.

Holmwood, L. (2009), 'Nearly 60% of BBC managers snub move to Salford Quays', *The Guardian*, 7 July, accessed 27 January 2020 at: www.theguardian.com/media/2009/jul/03/bbc-staff-salford-move.

Jessop, B. (1998), 'The narrative of enterprise and the enterprise of narrative: Place marketing and the entrepreneurial city', in T. Hall and P. Hubbard (eds), *The Entrepreneurial City: Geographies of Politics, Regimes and Representations*, Chichester: John Wiley & Sons, pp. 77–99.

Kahneman, D. (2003), 'Maps of bounded rationality: Psychology for behavioral economics', *American Economic Review*, **93**, 1449–75.

Kahneman, D. (2011), *Thinking, Fast and Slow*, New York: Macmillan.

Kavaratzis, M. and G. Ashworth (2008), 'Place marketing: How did we get here and where are we going?', *Journal of Place Management and Development*, **1** (2), 150–65.

Kavaratzis, M., Warnaby, G. and G. J. Ashworth (eds) (2015), *Rethinking Place Branding: Comprehensive Brand Development for Cities and Regions*, Heidelberg: Springer.

Kotler, P. and D. Gertner (2002), 'Country as brand, product, and beyond: A place marketing and brand management perspective', *Journal of Brand Management*, **9** (4), 249–61.

Kotler, P., Haider, D. H. and I. Rein (1993), *Marketing Places: Attracting Investment, Industry, and Tourism to Cities, States and Nations*, New York: Free Press.

Kotler, P., Asplund, C., Rein, I. and D. Haider (1999), *Marketing Places Europe: Attracting Investments, Industries, and Visitors to European Cities, Communities, Regions and Nations*, Harlow: Financial Times Prentice Hall.

Moilanen, T. and S. Rainisto (2009), *How to Brand Nations, Cities and Destinations: A Planning Book for Place Branding*, Basingstoke: Palgrave Macmillan.

Musterd, S. and A. Murie (2010), 'The idea of the creative or knowledge-based city', in S. Musterd and A. Murie (eds), *Making Competitive Cities*, Chichester: Wiley-Blackwell, pp. 17–32.

Pendleton, A., Lupton, B., Rowe, A. and R. Whittle (2019), 'Back to the shop floor: Behavioural insights from workplace sociology', *Work, Employment and Society*, **33** (6), 1039–57.

Rogerson, R. J. (1999), 'Quality of life and city competitiveness', *Urban Studies*, **36** (5–6), 969–85.

Short, J. R. and Y.-H. Kim (1999), *Globalisation and the City*, Harlow: Longman.

Short, J. R., Benton, L. M., Luce, W. B. and J. Walton (1993), 'Reconstructing the image of an industrial city', *Annals of the Association of American Geographers*, **83** (2), 207–24.

Simon, H. (1987), 'Models of bounded rationality: Empirically grounded economic reason', *Journal of Macroeconomics*, **20** (2), 425.

Thaler, R. H. and C. R. Sunstein (2009), *Nudge: Improving Decisions about Health, Wealth, and Happiness*, London: Penguin.

Tversky, A. and D. Kahneman (1974), 'Judgment under uncertainty: Heuristics and biases', *Science*, **185** (4157), 1124–31.

Van den Berg, L. and E. Braun (1999), 'Urban competitiveness, marketing and the need for organising capacity', *Urban Studies*, **36** (5–6), 987–99.

Ward, S. V. (1994), 'Time and place: Key themes in place promotion in the USA, Canada and Britain since 1870', in J. R. Gold and S. V. Ward (eds), *Place Promotion: The Use of Publicity and Marketing to Sell Towns and Regions*, Chichester: John Wiley & Sons, pp. 53–74.

Ward, S. V. (1998), *Selling Places: The Marketing and Promotion of Towns and Cities 1850–2000*, London: E. & F. N. Spon.

Warnaby, G. (2009), 'Towards a service-dominant place marketing logic', *Marketing Theory*, **9** (4), 403–23.

Warnaby, G. and D. Medway (2015), 'Rethinking the place product from the perspective of the service-dominant logic of marketing', in M. Kavaratzis, G. Warnaby and G. Ashworth (eds), *Rethinking Place Branding: Comprehensive Brand Development for Cities and Regions*, Heidelberg: Springer, pp. 33–50.

Zenker, S. and E. Braun (2017), 'Questioning a "one size fits all" city brand: Developing a branded house strategy for place brand management', *Journal of Place Management and Development*, **10** (3), 270–87.

7 Global city branding

Adriana Campelo

In recent years, the world has rediscovered Salvador.
It was enchanted by its people that embrace, celebrate, vibrate, and like to be together.
But it also protects. Ours. Yours. The world.
The city which has always had its doors open, needs to retreat.
We want you to come, but not now! Soon, in a while. We are taking care of what matters the most. For you to discover an even stronger Salvador. And with all the warmth that only we have.
Save this dream. Visit later. (YouTube, 2020)

With this narrative, the city of Salvador has launched the #VisitLater campaign (www.salvadordabahia.com) asking tourists to not come now, but to postpone holiday trips for the future. The campaign was prompted by the lockdown caused by Covid-19. Despite the lack of action of the Brazilian central government regarding preventing the spread of the pandemic (it is internationally known that the Brazilian central government did not follow the World Health Organization advice and did not provide the 27 states including the Federal District and the 5,570 Brazilian cities and towns with enough guidance to face the Covid-19 crisis) (IBGE, 2016), Salvador and many other cities and states in Brazil are taking leadership to avoid the spread of the pandemic and to minimise the effects of the outbreak of the disease. Political decision making at the city level regarding the global pandemic might affect the city's image as much as a long-term place branding campaign. It is peculiar, to say the least, and certainly unexpected to witness a city whose economy is based on the tourism industry advertising a visit later campaign. The year of 2020 will be remembered as the year that many tourist cities did not welcome their visitors.

There are a number of cities around the world facing problems and global affairs which are, in fact, the legacy of planetary urbanisation; for instance, rising sea levels and extreme events (heat waves, droughts, tornadoes and hurricanes), to name a couple of examples. According to the United Nations, the ratio of the world's urban population is expected to increase from 55 per cent in 2018 (some 4.2 billion people) to 68 per cent by 2050 (Ritchie and

Roser, 2018). Climate change, urban resilience, civil rights, migration, disease outbreaks and global pandemics are megatrends that demand action alongside local economic development and more mundane 'housekeeping-type' responsibilities. This chapter aims to discuss the role of cities taking leadership on such global agendas and how this impacts city branding, particularly in terms of urban resilience and climate change. It starts with a discussion of the Resilient Cities programme which is concerned with urban resilience and place making. Then, implementation of resilience strategies is presented in the context of discussion regarding Theory of Change (ToC). Following this, concepts relating to social-ecological systems theory are discussed, and cities' initiatives in terms of climate change are examined. Finally, political decision making on global issues and contemporary challenges is considered.

Urban resilience and place making

According to the Rockefeller Foundation (2019), resilience is 'the capacity of individuals, communities, institutions, businesses, and systems within a city to survive, adapt, and grow no matter what kinds of chronic stresses and acute shocks they experience'. This definition is based on an interdisciplinary study aiming to move forward resilience thinking and its potential to improve cities and community well-being (Polèse, 2010; Martin-Breen and Anderies, 2011; Kupers, 2014; Fiksel, Goodman and Hecht, 2014). The Rockefeller Foundation has pioneered a bold effort to help cities 'around the world become more resilient to the physical, social, and economic challenges that are a growing part of the 21st century' (Rockefeller Foundation, 2019). Other international bodies and organisations are also promoting and furthering resilient thinking and advancing action in many fields; some examples of leadership in this domain include the ICLEI Local Governments for Sustainability Network, the European Union's Urban Agenda, the Sendai Framework for Disaster Risk Reduction and the Habitat III New Urban Agenda (Wardekker et al., 2020). In my role as Chief Resilience Officer for Salvador, Brazil as part of the Rockefeller initiative, I have always challenged the definition of urban resilience to include the capacity of cities, communities and systems to *develop* capacity and to develop the local economy instead of growing gross domestic product, no matter what kind of acute shocks and chronic stresses cities are exposed to.

The concept of urban resilience has expanded its spectrum throughout a variety of urban systems, which makes it malleable and contextual as each city has different challenges and problems. Béné et al. (2018) pointed out three epistemological lineages influencing urban resilience accounts and practices: disaster and civil defence, ecological resilience and social resilience (Polèse, 2010; Fiksel et al., 2014). In fact, the three lineages mentioned by the authors are intertwined as human, ecosystems, climate and planetary boundaries are all part of the same equation. Cities which took part in the 100 Resilient Cities network programme have witnessed and experienced the flexibility of this concept during the process of developing a Resilience Strategy. The programme, recently rebranded as Resilient Cities Network, supported city members by providing: 1) grant funding to hire a chief resilience officer, an innovative new position within municipal government to work directly with city leaders in developing a city resilience strategy; 2) support from an international consultancy firm to design a strategy to make the city more resilient and to help cities plan for more integrated solutions to the challenges posed from globalisation, urbanisation and climate change – including important social and economic impacts; 3) direct pro bono support from a 100 Resilient Cities platform of partners, which provides critical tools, services and technical assistance from organisations like Swiss Re, Microsoft, the World Bank and many other non-governmental organisations, companies and institutions; and 4) partnerships between cities connected through a peer-to-peer network, leading to groundbreaking cross-city partnerships and solutions.

Cities from Addis Ababa to Porto Alegre, from Chennai to Paris have different challenges and reasons to implement resilience strategies. A central point for each strategy may be aging infrastructure, flooding, rising sea levels, climate hazards or economic and social inequality. The practicalities of designing a resilience strategy and the use of the City Resilience Framework (CRF) developed by Arup Consultancy have enlarged the concept of resilience itself while making it more contextual. The CRF is a tool to create a city profile revealing acute shocks and chronic stresses alongside the strengths and weaknesses of the city across four dimensions, 12 goals and 52 indicators. It recognises the uniqueness of every city and also how resilience is manifested in every place. The CRF aims to provide a lens through which the complexity of cities and the numerous factors that contribute to a city's resilience can be understood. The 12 key indicators mentioned above have the purpose of grasping and describing the fundamental attributes of a resilient city. According to Rockefeller Foundation and Arup (2015), the CRF is organised by qualities, indicators and categories (see Figure 7.1). Explaining the CRF from the outside cycle to inner cycles, one can start with the cycle of categories. There are four categories: the health and well-being of individuals (people); infrastructure and environment (place); economy and society (organisation); and, finally, leadership and strategy (knowledge). Each category helps to envisage a best case which represents a resilient city, and a worst case which equates to breakdown or collapse. The categories lead to the 12 indicators organised into the next cycle. These provide a holistic articulation of resilience which equates to the elements of a city's immune system. This can help demonstrate a weakness in one area that may compromise the city's resilience. The indicators are performance focused in that they are used to describe the outcome of actions to build resilience, not the actions themselves. These actions can be taken by, and be under the responsibility of, multiple stakeholders. The inner cycle is named qualities with a function to distinguish a resilient city from one that is simply liveable, sustainable or prosperous. The CRF's three cycles – categories, indicators and qualities – each contribute to a richer articulation of resilience. This tool is very helpful to create common knowledge amongst a city's stakeholders and within cities to understand commonalities and areas of exchange learning and support. It is very helpful to identify where there are critical gaps, where action and investment to build resilience will be most effective or where deeper analysis or understanding is required (Rockefeller Foundation and Arup, 2015). Due to its participatory nature, collected data are both quantitative and qualitative and, as a result, several aspects of urban resilience are unveiled, which express the ethos of each city and the plasticity of the concept (Wardekker et al., 2020; Croese, Green and Morgan, 2020).

From 2013 to 2015, the 100 Resilient Cities network programme launched three global calls to invite cities to take part in the movement and to become a sponsored member. Cities willing to join the network had to submit an application followed by a series of interviews with city leaders, including the mayor. Selection was based on the quality of the application and evidence of strong city leadership and commitment to build resilience. Being a member of a global and international network provided cities, especially smaller ones, with opportunities to partner with big metropolises. The Argentinian city of Santa Fe with around 390,000 inhabitants, for example, has collaborated with Paris; and Paynesville, Liberia is partnered with Cape Town and Montevideo. The membership of the network provides cities with para-diplomatic credentials within the global urban scene. The resilient cities are scattered in all corners of the planet, in Asia, Central America and the Caribbean, Europe, the Middle East and North Africa, North America, Oceania, South America and Sub-Saharan Africa (see Table 7.1). Hence, this membership and support for partnering on a global scale arguably grants participants the status of a global city.

In 2019 the Rockefeller Foundation ended the 100 Resilient Cities programme and from this emerged the Resilient Cities Network also pioneered by the Foundation. The new entity is based on four principles: 1) city-led – mayors, city leaders and chief resilience officers will participate in the governance of the network; 2) impact-focused – the work will prioritise resilient projects that aim to improve the lives of the poor and vulnerable; 3) regionally driven – activities will be designed with more flexibility to cater to member cities' needs; and 4) partnership-based network – to attain self-sustainability in the near future (Rockefeller Foundation 2020).

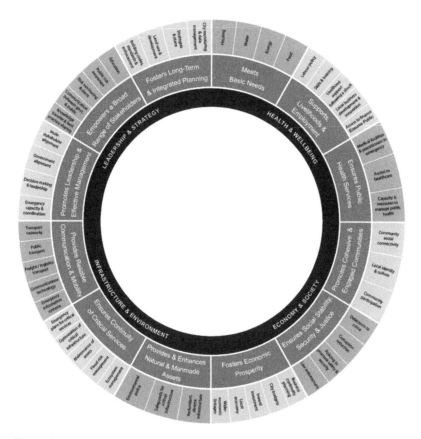

Figure 7.1   City Resilience Framework (CRF)

Aspirational cities

Becoming a resilient city is not a title to be conquered. Instead, it is an aspiration for urban planning and city making which requires long-term vision and political will.

Table 7.1   Global Resilient Cities: members

Accra, Ghana	Guadalajara (Metro),	Pittsburgh, United States
Addis Ababa, Ethiopia	Mexico	Porto Alegre, Brazil
Amman, Jordan	Haiyan, China	Pune, India
Athens, Greece	Honolulu, United States	Quito, Ecuador
Atlanta, United States	Houston, United States	Ramallah, Palestine
Bangkok, Thailand	Huangshi, China	Rio de Janeiro, Brazil
Barcelona, Spain	Jaipur, India	Rome, Italy
Belfast, United Kingdom	Jakarta, Indonesia	Rotterdam, The
Belgrade, Serbia	Juarez, Mexico	Netherlands
Berkeley, United States	Kigali, Rwanda	Salvador, Brazil
Boston, United States	Kyoto, Japan	San Francisco, United
Boulder, United States	Lagos, Nigeria	States
Bristol, United Kingdom	Lisbon, Portugal	San Juan, Puerto Rico
Buenos Aires, Argentina	London, United Kingdom	Santa Fe, Argentina
Byblos, Lebanon	Los Angeles, United States	Santiago de los
Calgary, Canada	Louisville, United States	Caballeros, Dominican
Cali, Colombia	Luxor, Egypt	Republic
Can Tho, Vietnam	Mandalay, Myanmar	Santiago (Metro), Chile
Cape Town, South Africa	Medellin, Colombia	Seattle, United States
Chennai, India	Melaka, Malaysia	Semarang, Indonesia
Chicago, United States	Melbourne, Australia	Seoul, South Korea
Christchurch, New	Mexico City, Mexico	Singapore, Singapore
Zealand	Milan, Italy	St Louis, United States
Colima, Mexico	Minneapolis, United	Surat, India
Da Nang, Vietnam	States	Sydney, Australia
Dakar, Senegal	Montevideo, Uruguay	Tbilisi, Georgia
Dallas, United States	Montreal, Canada	Tel Aviv, Israel
Deyang, China	Nairobi, Kenya	The Hague, The
Durban, South Africa	Nashville, United States	Netherlands
El Paso, United States	New Orleans, United	Thessaloniki, Greece
Glasgow, United Kingdom	States	Toronto, Canada
Greater Manchester,	New York, United States	Toyama, Japan
United Kingdom	Norfolk, United States	Tulsa, United States
Greater Miami and the	Oakland, United States	Vancouver, Canada
Beaches, United States	Panama City, Panama	Vejle, Denmark
	Paris, France	Washington, DC, United
	Paynesville, Liberia	States
		Wellington, New Zealand
		Yiwu, China

Resilient thinking is extremely transformative for cities because of its potential to integrate urban systems, to incorporate cities' own strengths, goals and local capacity to overcome disturbance and to develop and to improve systems (Malalgoda, Amaratunga and Haigh, 2013; Meerow, Newell and Stults, 2016). As a public policy it represents an innovation because it takes an integrative approach in opposition to the traditional departmentalised and fragmented manner of planning and implementing policies. A resilient policy breaks silos, fosters connectivity between areas and aims to advance in collaboration and enable all collaborators to benefit from the dividends of resilience. By doing so, it creates an environment for innovation and for co-benefits among many areas such as infrastructure, mobility, health and the economy. The resilience dividend accounts for this innovation in public policy – it is the proactivity of designing and implementing integrative solutions to face contemporary challenges presented in urban life (Rodin, 2014).

During the last ten years resilience frameworks have emerged and evolved over time to integrate disciplines such as climate change and disaster response with socioeconomic inequality and development planning (Hallegatte et al., 2012; Béné et al., 2018). This resilient thinking aims to integrate disciplines to deliver a holistic approach for public policies. The approach has placed resilience as one aspect of urban planning, alongside mobility, health, sanitation and so forth. However, the challenge to implement these frameworks is not a small one. Cities are complex entities and policies require governance and leadership to be executed. Apart from support for designing and building a tailor-made strategy, cities have benefited from being part of a city network and joining a global movement.

Programmes to promote resilient initiatives are often developed based on Theory of Change (ToC). This is partially because resilient strategies and recovery programmes are frequently funded by philanthropic organisations and/or multilateral agencies which require a methodology to be navigated in contexts of uncertainty. Although authors agree that there is little consensus on defining ToC (Stein and Valters, 2012; Ringhofer and Kohlweg, 2019), it is largely understood as a methodology for strategic planning, and for implementing and monitoring programmes. Often, it is applied in the fields of social and economic development and international relations. Vogel (2012) considers ToC an approach based on outcomes in which achievement is the result of initiatives and programmes intended to support designed and desired changes in specific contexts.

The use of ToC to support development and community building programmes is connected to work developed by the Aspen Institute (www.aspeninstitute .org) in the late 1990s and to the Center for Theory of Change (www .theoryofchange.org). Reading both websites and other publications, one can easily recognise concepts that define the very nature of ToC; these concepts are also easily identified in the literature. They include outcome-based interventions, reflective practice, social change, complex contexts, multifaceted interventions and empowerment (Vogel, 2012; van Es, Guijt and Vogel, 2015; Mayne, 2015).

ToC is connected with place branding theory if the latter is considered to be a programmatic intervention in a highly unpredictable context that is culturally embedded and politically bounded. Adopting a bottom-up branding development approach (Aitken and Campelo, 2011; Lucarelli and Brorström, 2013), one finds resonance with what Hivos (van Es et al., 2015) describes about ToC as a thinking and action approach to navigate the complexity of social change. My perspective to work with place branding has two purposes: the first is a way to reinforce places and community identities by acknowledging and promulgating habits, traditions and practices; the second is a strategy to promote social and economic development. In that sense, community engagement is part of intervention processes. ToC, as is explicit in its very name, is a strategy to promote an intervention aiming to achieve positive results. Similarly, a place branding strategy is a way of action with a specific purpose. Both have to deal with social uncertainties and cultural aspects to be implemented.

Stein and Valters (2012) present a comprehensive review of ToC in the field of international development. This offers a variety of visions that consider ToC as a way of action, a roadmap or a blueprint. Fashioned by demands for change at its heart, ToC action brings together how and why a particular action would result in desirable change. A programmatic ToC strategy as a rule has clear connections between activities and outcomes, and reasons to achieve foreseen and desirable change. ToC has increasingly become mainstream, informing and supporting implementation of community development projects (Vogel, 2012; Ringhofer and Kohlweg, 2019).

The concern to implement result-based initiatives with evidence of learning processes and planned outcomes is a major reason for ToC to be adopted by institutions dedicated to social development, multilateral agencies and international foundations. The field of economic development is naturally entangled with social, cultural and political complexities which need to be taken into consideration to enable and to make viable programme implementation. International cooperation helps to accelerate innovation and to share and galvanise knowledge efficiently on the ground. By sharing global principles and knowledge, it is crucial to translate it to the local and contextualised reality and practice.

Public planning for smart and intelligent cities, resilience strategy and climate action plans have huge transformational potential by generating knowledge, by opening avenues of possibilities and by laying new grounds for innovation. If the potential for change is enormous, implementing challenges is equally vast. An interesting analysis of ToC in a city context is provided by Ibrahim, El-Zaart and Adams (2017), who discuss the Smart Sustainable City.

The authors highlight the significant volume of changes required, including political will, urban planning, financial feasibility and necessary infrastructure. Decisions and changes to be taken can have long-term impacts, such as investments in artificial intelligence, optical fibre and technology as cities are interweaved with social exchanges and evolve from the very basis of those exchanges. It is important to use a theory able to include local features and to evaluate and monitor long-range planning. Innovative and groundbreaking initiatives need to adopt a holistic approach to deliver desired outcomes and to leverage capacity promoting positive impacts in the city. The rationale for choosing ToC is reasonable due to the complexity of dimensions existing in cities.

Be resilient, be green

There is a close link between urban resilience and climate change. It may be determined by the origins of the concept, by the primary fields of research or by the agenda adopted by cities using both themes in an interconnected way (Meerow and Neuner, 2020). From a theoretical perspective resilient thinking is largely entrenched in systems theory and in social-ecological systems. Although the idea and understanding of resilience has its roots in many disciplines such as psychology, engineering, physics and environmental studies (Martin-Breen and Anderies, 2011; Rodin, 2014), the resilient approach to urban planning has embraced social and ecological dimensions to include nature and humanity as part of connected systems (Adger, 2000; Du Plessis, 2008; Andersson et al., 2014). The Stockholm Resilience Centre (2015) defines a social-ecological system as 'a coupled system of humans and nature that constitutes a complex adaptive system with ecological and social components that interact dynamically through various feedbacks'. Ruiz-Mallén (2020) discusses the metaphor of cities of resilience, highlighting the need to connect socioeconomic and ecological systems to create urban resilience.

Cities are very complex systems where institutional, economic and social systems are evolving and adapting continuously (Grove, 2009). The pressure on planetary boundaries and global warming have brought back to city management an imperative to rethink the space of nature and climate issues within cities, and hence to move beyond disaster response. The use of resilient thinking to develop public policies fosters a more holistic type of urban planning that is not only adaptive to shocks and stresses, but is also innovative in order to build solutions.

Analysing the list of resilient cities and cities committed to reducing green-houses gas emissions, one quickly realises that there is a group of at least 40 cities that feature in both groups. Indeed, cities adopting resilience strategies are also taking responsibility for the climate agenda. The Paris Agreement is a commitment made by countries with the United Nations Framework Convention on Climate Change to keep the increase in global average temperature to well below 2 °C above pre-industrial levels; and to pursue efforts to limit the increase to 1.5 °C. Cities are taking leadership by developing climate action plans and trying to reduce greenhouse gas emissions (Hakelberg, 2014; Gordon and Johnson, 2017). Being prepared to reconcile with climate change consequences means being climate resilient and there is no choice for cities other than to adapt to climate change.

These efforts are largely supported by international networks, international non-governmental organisations and multilateral agencies. International networks which support urban resilience and climate action share a collaborative ethos and follow the same trend by helping cities to create local capacity, influence public policy and by trying to stimulate the private sector towards zero carbon and sustainable solutions. The C40 Cities Climate Leadership Group has a very specific mission to help cities reduce their carbon footprint and to deliver the Paris Agreement (Lee, 2013; Fuhr, Hickmann and Kern, 2018; Croese et al., 2020). Although it began with only 40 cities around the world, C40 currently has 96 affiliated cities across all continents, representing 25 per cent of global domestic product (C40 Cities, 2020). Membership is based on two criteria: one based on city population (megacities) and the second based on how innovative the city is, for example Copenhagen and Curitiba, Brazil are considered innovative cities and they do not have large populations. Cities making up the membership of C40 are displayed in Tables 7.2 and 7.3.

In order to accomplish their goal, C40 offers funding and knowledge exchange (Lee and Van de Meene, 2012) for cities to develop climate action plans and to strengthen their actions around sustainable architecture, renewable energy, green economy and low-carbon districts. All these themes are cutting-edge points in the global agenda. In October 2019, during the C40 World Mayors Summit in Copenhagen, C40 cities announced the Global Green New Deal, through which:

> Cities have reaffirmed their commitment to protecting our environment, strengthening our economy, and building a more equitable future by cutting emissions from the sectors most responsible for the climate crisis – transportation, buildings, industry, and waste – to keep global heating below the 1.5 °C goal of the Paris Agreement. (C40 Cities, 2019)

Table 7.2   C40 Cities Network: megacities

Abidjan, Côte d'Ivoire	Lima, Peru
Accra, Ghana	Lisbon, Portugal
Addis Ababa, Ethiopia	London, United Kingdom
Amman, Jordan	Los Angeles, United States
Athens, Greece	Madrid, Spain
Bangkok, Thailand	Medellín, Colombia
Barcelona, Spain	Melbourne, Australia
Bengaluru, India	Mexico City, Mexico
Berlin, Germany	Miami, United States
Bogotá, Colombia	Milan, Italy
Boston, United States	Montréal, Canada
Buenos Aires, Argentina	Moscow, Russia
Cape Town, South Africa	Nairobi, Kenya
Chengdu, China	Nanjing, China
Chennai, India	New York, United States
Chicago, United States	Paris, France
Curitiba, Brazil	Philadelphia, United States
Dakar, Senegal	Phoenix, United States
Dar es Salaam, Tanzania	Qingdao, China
Delhi NCT, India	Quezon City, Philippines
Dhaka, Bangladesh	Rio de Janeiro, Brazil
Dubai, United Arab Emirates	Rome, Italy
Durban (eThekwini), South Africa	Salvador, Brazil
Fuzhou, China	San Francisco, United States
Guadalajara, Mexico	Santiago, Chile
Guangzhou, China	Sao Paulo, Brazil
Hangzhou, China	Seattle, United States
Hanoi, Vietnam	Seoul, Republic of Korea
Hong Kong, China	Shenzhen, China
Houston, United States	Sydney, Australia
Istanbul, Turkey	Tel Aviv-Yafo, Israel
Jakarta, Indonesia	Tokyo, Japan
Johannesburg, South Africa	Toronto, Canada
Karachi, Pakistan	Warsaw, Poland
Kolkata, India	Washington, DC, United States
Kuala Lumpur, Malaysia	Wuhan, China
Lagos, Nigeria	Yokohama, Japan

Table 7.3   C40 Cities Network: innovator cities

Amsterdam, The Netherlands	Portland, OR, United States
Auckland, New Zealand	Quito, Peru
Austin, United States	Rotterdam, The Netherlands
Copenhagen, Denmark	Stockholm, Sweden
Freetown, Sierra Leone	Tshwane, South Africa
Heidelberg, Germany	Vancouver, Canada
New Orleans, United States	Venice, Italy
Oslo, Norway	Zhenjiang, China

This collective action adopted by mayors to join forces around decisions that will impact the entire world is very political. The collective decision to putting inclusive climate action at the centre of all urban decision making aims to secure the transition to a carbon-free economy and society. These networks are bringing cities together in the international arena; they are also providing mayors with political ground to articulate their political position and programmes. Indeed, adopting positions on global warming, levels of carbon emissions and the sustainable economy affects how cities are perceived by tourists, visitors, skilled immigrants and, ultimately, by their citizens.

Resilient, carbon-free and post-pandemic cities

City branding is a vast and debatable field for research and for practice. As an instrument of urban planning it can embrace tourism strategies, economic development, citizen ownership and regional integration (Kavaratzis and Ashworth, 2006; Gnoth, 2007; Medway and Warnaby, 2008; Dinnie, 2011; Braun, 2012). Developed organically or as a result of an orchestrated management strategy, city branding depends on political will and, sometimes, might be included in political agendas (Lucarelli, 2018). In fact, the very decision to portray a city's people and culture reveals the politics of local identity – it is not only what is portrayed but also *how* content is portrayed and presented that matters (Campelo, Aitken and Gnoth, 2011).

Cities are taking global responsibility and building global reputations by joining international networks. The effort to do so requires political leadership and patronage as cities start operating at both local and global levels on administrative issues. Undertaking activities with other cities within global networks not only helps advance knowledge but also accelerates innovation. There is a specific kind of collaborative attitude that is extremely important to highlight. Collaboration is the core value to fight climate change, to build a resilient planet and to face contemporary uncertainties.

Looking back at the place branding and place marketing literature during the first decade of the millennium (Kotler and Gertner, 2002; Anholt, 2007), places and cities were positioning themselves to compete against each other to attract foreign direct investment (FDI), tourists, the Olympic Games and other big events (Papadopoulos, 2004; Dinnie, 2004). The climate emergency and the speed of innovation have changed this logic. The motto of 'leave no one behind' is vital for climate change and very vividly repeated by climate advocates. The same motto fits well for the Covid-19 pandemic. We should be committed to 'leave no one behind' – we countries, cities and citizens. Both the climate emergency and Covid-19 are impacting humanity profoundly and pointing us as a society in a direction that is unknown and uncertain. City image and reputation seem to be stretched and strengthened when they opt to deal with planetary and humanitarian issues. The way cities include (or not) climate planning and action within their priorities, and the measures taken during the pandemic, affect the image and reputation of those cities. Investors, students and tourists might take into account these two issues in any decisions they make towards investing in, moving to, or visiting cities in the future.

Many cities are now inviting people to come later. Many cities are taking the responsibility of dealing with Covid-19 at a municipal level because of the lack of national leadership. Cities, via international networks, are also coming together to support each other in their decisions on social distancing policy and lockdown. Good examples of cities and states helping each other in this way, while their central governments do very little, can be found in the United States and Brazil. Here, cities are collaborating with one another to design a post-pandemic economic recovery plan (Global Resilient Cities Network, 2020).

A new avenue of future research should be taken into consideration for place branding theory. Sustainability, resilience, carbon neutrality and dealing with the pandemic are aspects currently well linked to a place's image. How cities and countries are acting now will impact their reputations for a long time into the future. All these themes are not temporary issues that we have to deal with. They are matters that will continue to affect our economies, how we produce and how we consume. They are subjects that will influence how we will define ourselves as a society. City branding is about how cities portray themselves to be consumed by citizens and tourists, and to be the place where communities celebrate their history, heritage, culture and identity. In my perception, city branding is also a field of research to discuss how cities are dealing with the paramount challenges of our times. How can city branding include resilience in the research agenda? How can city branding theory evolve to embrace climate emergency action as an avenue of research? What are the city assets to develop a noteworthy brand? Is collaboration the main new asset in city branding? These all represent critical enquiries for any future research agenda in place branding.

References

Adger, W. N. (2000), 'Social and ecological resilience: Are they related?', *Progress in Human Geography*, **24** (3), 347–64.

Aitken, R. and A. Campelo (2011), 'The four Rs of place branding', *Journal of Marketing Management*, **27** (9–10), 913–33.

Andersson, E., Barthel, S., Borgström, S., Colding, J., Elmqvist, T., Folke, C. and Å. Gren (2014), 'Reconnecting cities to the biosphere: Stewardship of green infrastructure and urban ecosystem services', *Ambio*, **43** (4), 445–53.

Anholt, S. (2007), *Competitive Identity: The New Brand Management for Nations, Cities and Regions*, London: Palgrave Macmillan.

Béné, C., Mehta, L., McGranahan, G., Cannon, T., Gupte, J. and T. Tanner (2018), 'Resilience as a policy narrative: Potentials and limits in the context of urban planning', *Climate and Development*, **10** (2), 116–33.

Braun, E. (2012), 'Putting city branding into practice', *Journal of Brand Management*, **19** (4), 257–67.

C40 Cities (2019), 'Mayors announce support for Global Green New Deal; recognize global climate emergency', accessed 16 July 2020 at: www.c40.org/press_releases/global-gnd.

C40 Cities (2020), 'The power of C40 Cities', accessed 18 July 2020 at: www.c40.org/cities.

Campelo, A., Aitken, R. and J. Gnoth (2011), 'Visual rhetoric and ethics in marketing of destinations', *Journal of Travel Research*, **50** (1), 3–14.

Croese, S., Green, C. and G. Morgan (2020), 'Localizing the Sustainable Development Goals through the lens of urban resilience: Lessons and learnings from 100 Resilient Cities and Cape Town', *Sustainability*, **12** (2), 550, https://doi.org/10.3390/su12020550.

Dinnie, K. (2004), 'Place branding: Overview of an emerging literature', *Place Branding and Public Diplomacy*, **1** (1), 106–10.

Dinnie, K. (2011), *City Branding: Theory and Cases*, Basingstoke: Palgrave Macmillan.

Du Plessis, C. (2008), 'Understanding cities as social-ecological systems', *World Sustainable Building Conference*, Melbourne, 21–25 September, accessed 16 July 2020 at: https://researchspace.csir.co.za/dspace/handle/10204/3306.

Fiksel, J., Goodman, I. and A. Hecht (2014), 'Resilience: Navigating toward a sustainable future', *Solutions*, **5** (5), 38–47.

Fuhr, H., Hickmann, T. and K. Kern (2018), 'The role of cities in multi-level climate governance: Local climate policies and the 1.5 C target', *Current Opinion in Environmental Sustainability*, **30** (February), 1–6.

Global Resilient Cities Network (2020), 'Cities for a resilient recovery', accessed 18 July 2020 at: www.resilientcitiesnetwork.org/recovery.

Gnoth, J. (2007), 'The structure of destination brands: Leveraging values', *Tourism Analysis*, **12** (5–6), 345–58.

Gordon, D. J. and C. A. Johnson (2017), 'The orchestration of global urban climate governance: Conducting power in the post-Paris climate regime', *Environmental Politics*, **26** (4), 694–714.

Grove, J. M. (2009), 'Cities: Managing densely settled social-ecological systems', in F. S. Chapin, III, G. P. Kofinas and C. Folke (eds), *Principles of Ecosystem Stewardship: Resilience-Based Natural Resource Management in a Changing World*, New York: Springer, pp. 281–94.

Hakelberg, L. (2014), 'Governance by diffusion: Transnational municipal networks and the spread of local climate strategies in Europe', *Global Environmental Politics*, **14** (1), 107–29.

Hallegatte, S., Shah, A., Brown, C., Lempert, R. and S. Gill (2012), 'Investment decision making under deep uncertainty: Application to climate change', World Bank Policy Research Working Paper 6193.

IBGE (2016), *Cidades e Estados*, accessed 18 July 2020 at: www.ibge.gov.br/cidades-e -estados.html?view=municipio.

Ibrahim, M., El-Zaart, A. and C. Adams (2017), 'Theory of change for the transformation towards smart sustainable cities', in *2017 Sensors Networks Smart and Emerging Technologies*, IEEE, doi:10.1109/SENSET.2017.8125067.

Kavaratzis, M. and G. J. Ashworth (2006), 'City branding: An effective assertion of identity or a transitory marketing trick?', *Place Branding and Public Diplomacy*, **2** (3), 183–94.

Kotler, P. and D. Gertner (2002), 'Country as brand, product, and beyond: A place marketing and brand management perspective', *Journal of Brand Management*, **9** (4), 249–61.

Kupers, R. (ed.) (2014), *Turbulence: A Corporate Perspective on Collaborating for Resilience*, Amsterdam: Amsterdam University Press.

Lee, T. (2013), 'Global cities and transnational climate change networks', *Global Environmental Politics*, **13** (1), 108–27.

Lee, T. and S. Van de Meene (2012), 'Who teaches and who learns? Policy learning through the C40 cities climate network', *Policy Sciences*, **45** (3), 199–220.

Lucarelli, A. (2018), 'Place branding as urban policy: The (im)political place branding', *Cities*, **80**, 12–21.

Lucarelli, A. and S. Brorström (2013), 'Problematising place branding research: A meta-theoretical analysis of the literature', *The Marketing Review*, **13** (1), 65–81.

Malalgoda, C., Amaratunga, D. and R. Haigh (2013), 'Creating a disaster resilient built environment in urban cities', *International Journal of Disaster Resilience in the Built Environment*, **4** (1), 72–94.

Martin-Breen, P. and J. M. Anderies (2011), 'Resilience: A literature review', Institute of Development Studies, accessed 16 July 2020 at: https://opendocs.ids.ac.uk/opendocs/ handle/20.500.12413/3692.

Mayne, J. (2015), 'Useful theory of change models', *Canadian Journal of Program Evaluation*, **30** (2), 119–42.

Medway, D. and G. Warnaby (2008), 'Alternative perspectives on marketing and the place brand', *European Journal of Marketing*, **42** (5/6), 641–53.

Meerow, S. and F. G. Neuner (2020), 'Positively resilient? How framing local action affects public opinion', *Urban Affairs Review*, https://doi.org/10.1177/1078087420905655.

Meerow, S., Newell, J. P. and M. Stults (2016), 'Defining urban resilience: A review', *Landscape and Urban Planning*, **147**, 38–49.

Papadopoulos, N. (2004), 'Place branding: Evolution, meaning and implications', *Place Branding and Public Diplomacy*, **1** (1), 36–49.

Polèse, M. (2010), 'The resilient city: On the determinants of successful urban economies', *Working Paper, no. 2010-03, Centre – Urbanisation, Culture, Société*, Institut National de la Recherche Scientifique, University of Québec, Montreal.

Ringhofer, L. and K. Kohlweg (2019), 'Has the theory of change established itself as the better alternative to the logical framework approach in development cooperation programmes?', *Progress in Development Studies*, **19** (2), 112–22.

Ritchie, H. and M. Roser (2018), 'Urbanization', *Our World in Data*, accessed 16 July 2020 at: https://ourworldindata.org/urbanization.

Rockefeller Foundation (2019), *100 Resilient Cities*, accessed 20 March 2020 at: www.r ockefellerfoundation.org/100-resilient-cities.

Rockefeller Foundation (2020), *Global Resilient Cities Network*, accessed 15 May 2020 at: www.rockpa.org/project/global-resilient-cities-network.

Rockefeller Foundation and Arup (2015), *City Resilience Framework*, accessed 16 July 2020 at: www.slideshare.net/RockefellerFound/city-resilience-framework -45626832/acessed.

Rodin, J. (2014). *The Resilience Dividend: Being Strong in a World Where Things Go Wrong*, New York: Public Affairs.

Ruiz-Mallén, I. (2020), 'Co-production and resilient cities to climate change', in J. Nared and D. Bole (eds), *Participatory Research and Planning in Practice*, Cham: Springer, pp. 1–11.

Stein, D. and C. Valters (2012), 'Understanding theory of change in international development', *Justice and Security Research Programme, Paper 1*, accessed 16 July 2020 at: www.alnap.org/system/files/content/resource/files/main/stein.pdf.

Stockholm Resilience Centre (2015), 'Applying resilience thinking: Seven principles for building resilience in social-ecological systems', *Stockholm Resilience Centre*, Stockholm University, accessed 16 July 2020 at: www.stockholmresilience.org/ research/research-news/2015-02-19-applying-resilience-thinking.html.

van Es, M., Guijt, I. and I. Vogel (2015), 'Hivos ToC guidelines: Theory of change thinking in practice', accessed 16 July 2020 at: www.openupcontracting.org/assets/2017/ 09/Hivos-ToC-guidelines-2015.pdf.

Vogel, I. (2012), 'Review of the use of "theory of change" in international development', *Review Report for the UK Department of International Development*, accessed 16 July 2020 at: www.theoryofchange.org/pdf/DFID_ToC_Review_VogelV7.pdf.

Wardekker, A., Wilk, B., Brown, V., Uittenbroek, C., Mees, H., Driessen, P., Wassen, M., Molenaar, A., Walda, J. and H. Runhaar (2020), 'A diagnostic tool for supporting policymaking on urban resilience', *Cities*, **101**, https://doi.org/10.1016/j.cities.2020 .102691.

YouTube (2020), 'Salvador: Visite depois', accessed 20 July 2020 at: www.youtube.com/ watch?v=KpXpqsbx9ik.

8

The Nordic wave in place branding: Global implications and relevance

Cecilia Cassinger, Andrea Lucarelli and Szilvia Gyimóthy

Introduction

In a relatively short time, Nordic place branding has emerged as a field of academic research and practice. The evolution, expansion, and geographical spread of place branding in the Nordic region are studied in several ways and echoed in recent journal articles and special issues (e.g. Pamment, 2016). The Nordic region is not only represented in terms of chronicling Swedish, Norwegian, Icelandic, Finnish, and Danish cases or brand strategies, but also by authors predominantly based in Nordic countries and institutions (e.g. Lucarelli and Berg, 2011; Lucarelli and Brorström, 2013; Cassinger and Eksell, 2017). Furthermore, there is a strong focus on the Nordic as an ideological and socio-cultural construct in research publications, which either explore the essential character of geospecific brands or phenomena (see the interest in Nordic food and Nordic screen productions) or position the Nordic in trans-local and international contexts.

Despite the large number of studies addressing Nordic place brands and branding, little attention is given to the practices of place branding within the Nordic welfare states. The unusual open access to the field of practice granted to researchers (at least compared to Anglo-Saxon and European standards), and the particular political, institutional, and cultural environment of the Nordic has not been fully unpacked. The limited scope of previous studies on place branding paired with a widespread international interest in the Nordic as a brand, geographical place, moral orientation, and (normative) discourse calls for more research into the global relevance of Nordic place branding (see Durand, 2018).

This chapter is concerned with the Nordic region as a context fostering a distinct place branding scholarship and practice. The aim of the contribution is to examine the global relevance and implication of the growing body of research dealing with Nordic place branding. To this end, the Nordic is approached not only as a geographical context of place branding, but also as an approach – an ideological mindset – that shapes place branding concepts, strategies, and tactics. More specifically, we attempt to position – what we refer to as – the *Nordic wave* as a hybrid scholarly approach, which bridges across managerial and critical schools as well as sensitively engaging with place branding practitioners. These distinct features allow the Nordic wave in place branding to travel in different geopolitical and scholarly directions, and by manner of cross-pollination, expand place branding research and practices on an international scale.

In the following discussion, the contours of the Nordic wave are first outlined as a means of considering previous and contemporary research. From this, three paths of conceptual investigation pertaining to place branding are identified: *poetics*, *practices*, and *politics*. Thereafter, in a more systematic fashion, the scholarly relevance of Nordic place branding research is presented. By means of conclusions, three specific areas of contribution are identified along with future directions for research.

The Nordic wave in place branding

The Nordic region is made up of five nation-states, Denmark, Finland, Iceland, Norway, and Sweden, and the semi-autonomous regions and provinces of the Aaland Islands, Faroe Islands, Greenland including the Inuit land areas, and the cultural region of Sapmi. Sapmi, which belongs to the indigenous Sami population in the Nordic region, cuts across Finland, Sweden, Norway, and parts of Murmansk in Russia. In total, the Nordic region is populated by around 27 million people (Nordic Council of Ministers, 2019) who share similarities in terms of language, history, culture, values, and ideals. Such claimed values include cooperation, consensus, solidarity, democracy, freedom, social cohesion, and gender equality, and are mobilised in the international branding strategy of the region by the Nordic Council. Thus, in a Nordic context it notes the importance of:

> *Openness* and a belief in everyone's right to express their opinions. *Trust* in each other and also, because of proximity to power, trust in leaders in society. New ways of thinking, focusing, creativity, and *innovations*. *Sustainable* management of the

environment and development of natural resources. *Compassion*, tolerance, and conviction about equal value of all people. (Nordic Council of Ministers, 2019: 14)

Yet, the values of the Nordic countries and regions differ and have developed unique characters in relation to one another over time (Hannerz, 1990). In order to avoid stereotyping the Nordic brand on the basis of essential myth-ical place qualities, it is here thought of as an ocean wave to emphasise that place brands are not stable, but multiple and enacted in diverse and multiple settings (Ren, Gad, and Bjørst, 2019). Waves appear as unique disturbances in the ocean that are reiterated during certain periods of time. Unlike schools and paradigms, waves have no boundaries, they move in different directions. Waves are counter-expressions of essentialism, since they evolve, disappear, and are replaced by new waves. Due to their liquid properties, waves spread into different areas of the ocean and may thus encounter or merge with other waves that are directed towards different shores (i.e. continental or European approaches).

The Nordic wave exemplifies traditions and qualities of scholarship on the relation between the Nordic concept and place branding. The Nordic is here understood in broad terms as an idea (Czarniawska-Joerges and Sevón, 2005), an ideological orientation, and myth, as well as a regional space in relation to which theories, concepts, and practices of place branding emerge and develop specifically linked to a locale, but with global reflection. It is by using the allegory of a wave among other waves (i.e. other research approaches and schools of thought, see below), that this chapter can be considered to be both an attempt to synthesise the evolution, expansion, and geographical spread of a Nordic approach to place branding, as well as an attempt to consider some more nebulous related terms and concepts (e.g. Nordic cuisine, feminist foreign policy, etc.) as they are glocally deterritorialised in diversified branding practices, policies, and concepts around the world.

Next, the Nordic wave is further explicated by presenting streams of research that build on the existing body of scholarly studies on Nordic place brand-ing (e.g. Lucarelli and Hallin, 2015; Gyimóthy, 2017; Cassinger, Lucarelli, and Gyimóthy, 2019). These research streams not only summarise previous research studies, but also pave the way for how future research may modify or even challenge taken-for-granted concepts, practices, and methodologies in international place branding to reveal new ways of thinking and doing place brand research and practice.

Poetics

The first stream of research deals with the poetics of the Nordic and Nordicity, in other words the way what is considered, or imagined, as Nordic emerges or appears, and is translated into different locations in different historical periods, as well as being evident in different practices and theories. It follows that studies within such streams of research include those dealing with ways of constructing and representing core issues such as Nordicity or consensus culture in place branding practices (e.g. Byrkjeflot, Pedersen, and Svejenova, 2013; Ooi and Pedersen, 2017; Andersen et al., 2019). Studies of poetics reflect on successful or less successful stories of place brands in the Nordic region (Hall, 2008; Brorström and Parment, 2016). Further studies within this field deal with the way branding practices are framed – for example where Nordic place branding practices are considered to be specific, peculiar, and foundational (Jansson, 2012; Danbolt, 2016). Despite the difference in focus, empirical material, and scope, it follows that studies belonging to this research stream have an analytical approach primarily focusing on critically assessing key narratives, rhetorical strategies, genealogical-historical and emerging storytelling templates in various empirical contexts, and on multiple geographic scales. Research based on the 'poetics' is attentive to examining not only the 'how' but also the 'why, where, when, and who' for place branding practices, policies, and concepts. Focus is on how such place branding approaches have been 'declined' or translated, and how they represent a specific idea, myth, and socio-cultural context which is considered to be Nordic.

Further studies for advancing this research agenda could look at the translation and narratives of other subordinate or superordinate mythical objects, for example, Nordic bathing (e.g. the Finnish sauna) and hiking rituals (e.g. the Norwegian practice *gå på tur*). Moreover, they may want to unpack the impact of Nordic cultural characteristics of being moderate (*lagom*) and having grit (*sisu*) in the emergence of specific place branding practices, either at the national level or inter-regionally in border areas like Lapland; or they can analyse specific localised *branded* practices having inter-regional but also international impact, such as touring (*tura*) the (in)famous market of infra-Scandinavian cruises. Finally, researchers could study the adaptation of Nordic *branded* welfare policies in the international context, such as the adoption of Nordic ideals into China's elderly market (Shi, 2006), or the adoption of Nordic/Norse alphabets when labelling specific enterprises in foreign markets, for example, coffee shop names in Central and Eastern European countries (Gurinović et al., 2018).

Practices

The second research stream is preoccupied with Nordic placemaking practices, that is, distinct strategic, tactical, and aesthetic approaches that place brands on high latitudes deploy to position themselves in global markets. It acknowledges the different branding challenges facing streamlined Nordic highlights and the insignificant majority of small places. Contrasted with the cool and cosmopolitan vibrancy of Nordic urban centres, most regional brands in the Nordic rural periphery are marginalised by being unknown, secluded, depopulated, or just remarkably insignificant (cf. Rodríguez-Pose, 2018). This is partially attributable to their vague contours, due to vast administrative territories, unclear or illegible brand narratives, and scarcity of profiled landmarks and industries. From a touristic and investment point of view, these could be quickly written off as 'places that don't matter', and which are highly challenged to turn their apparent liabilities into assets (Avraham, 2014). However, empirical studies exploring contemporary Nordic placemaking practices in different contexts (e.g. indigenous heritage sites, coastal and island destinations) indicate the emergence of unconventional and innovative approaches that challenge and transgress the conventional (or conformist) frames of place branding (e.g. Cassel, 2019). This approach may be termed 'tactical ruralism' (Gyimóthy, 2019), and entails creative translations and eclectic cross-appropriations between contemporary consumer cultures and local manifestations of them. Tactical ruralism arises in local contexts with limited and modest branding capacities, which are overcome by deploying unconventional or translocal placemaking resources.

Subaltern Nordic 'underdogs' explicitly adopt contemporary market ideologies (responsible consumption, sustainability, diversity) and product branding tactics (designing recognisable labels and distinct appellations) to turn the odds in their own favour with legitimate or legible narrative constructions. This echoes the notion of a reversely engineered terroir (Paxson, 2010), in which exclusive place narratives are underpinned by moral, ethical, and health rationales, rather than measurable quality claims based on traditions and history. Short of regular, documented tourist attractions, exogenous (market) agendas and manipulative rhetoric approaches are adopted (Suchman, 1995; Elbe and Emmoth, 2014). This strand of research should be further consolidated by studies that not only explore but compare and conceptualise place branding practices breaking with dominant narratives and institutional logics. There is a need to capture the processual nature of strategies that use the Nordic soil or terroir to develop geospecific products (Gyimóthy, 2017), as well as to chart sensuous and affective design strategies capitalising on extreme climatic and ambient givens (e.g. Nordic food products). In addition, future research studies could look into translocal entrepreneurial constellations through which peripheral places and actors are brought to the fore of global market attention.

Politics

The third research stream deals with the political aspects of Nordic place branding. Previous research predominantly understands the politics of place branding as a neoliberal form of governance (e.g. Eshuis and Klijn, 2012). However, attempts are made to capture additional configurations of politics in the Nordic region given its historical emphasis on welfare policies and social democracy (see Lucarelli, 2019). For example, the idea of a 'Nordic exception' was important to the construction and branding of a common Nordic identity during the Cold War (Browning, 2007). The Nordic exception mainly referred to the mode by which the Nordic countries differentiated themselves as rational and peaceful in contrast to the rest of the war-like Europe. Today, the Nordic exception is predominately used to describe Nordic economic and political models that may be transferred to other countries. Foremost, it is the economic and political organisation of the Nordic countries that is presented as an exception. A recent example of Nordic exceptionalism is the feminist foreign policy introduced by the Swedish government in 2015. The feminist foreign policy may be understood as embedded in a global discourse of gender equality to ensure sustainable development, peace, and international security, as well as in a domestic political discourse to signal a move towards a progressive and less consensus-driven foreign policy (Aggestam, Bergman-Rosamond, and Kronsell, 2019). In addressing gender inequality as a global social injustice, and using the United Nations as a vehicle for distributing the policy, Sweden's feminist foreign policy may be viewed as a way of rebranding the Nordic model by making it relevant again in an international context (Browning, 2018). Feminist foreign policy contributes to shaping the image of Sweden as a good state; thus strengthening the Swedish nation brand (Jezierska and Towns, 2018; Cassinger, 2019). The Nordic model reminds us that brands mediate places both as moral orientations and as markets to invest in (Aronczyk, 2009). At the same time, striving to serve as a humanitarian example for others to follow, promoting equality and welfare models, is not without problems. Such claims may also come with an implicit self-esteem of moral superiority associated with exclusion, struggle, and intolerance. This is underscored in the promotion of the Nordic regional brand by the Nordic Council. The brand platform for the Nordics states:

> When the Nordics collaborate on a unified branding of the Nordic countries, it is not about achieving world domination. It's not about asserting our superior culture,

THE NORDIC WAVE IN PLACE BRANDING 123

wonderful nature and creativity. It's not even about conquering investments, growing tourism and creating jobs. It is about inviting. Inspiring. About conversation and cooperation, exchange of thoughts and ideas. It's about making the Nordic perspective applicable as a human competitive parameter. We are not going to show the Nordics to the world, we will show the Nordics in the world. (The Nordics, 2020)

In view of the transformations within Europe since the Cold War, it has been increasingly difficult to maintain Nordic exceptionalism as a utopian idea to promote the region (Browning, 2007). It is also apparent that the Nordic region has its own problems to deal with, even though it might wish to serve as a moral example for other jurisdictions. For example, the rise of new nationalism and right-wing populism has polarised the Nordic political landscape and turned provincialism against cosmopolitanism. Moreover, there are several ongoing disputes concerning geographical borders in the Nordic region (Ren et al., 2019; Adler-Nissen and Gad, 2014; Bergmann, 2017) and a lack of cultural diversity. Further studies on the political aspects of place branding in the Nordic region may want to unmask the underlying morality of Nordic place brands by considering these and other struggles in further depth.

Global relevance of the Nordic wave

This section turns its attention to the global relevance of Nordic place branding. It assembles the key insights from previous research into a comprehensible Nordic approach towards place branding that can be distinguished from other approaches in the field. Table 8.1 shows the position of the Nordic wave in-between the management and critical approaches in international place branding research. The Nordic approach outlined in the table represents a distinct ideological mindset of place branding, positioned not only in relation to academics and practitioners, but also among other stakeholders (e.g. visitors, politicians, media, citizens, as well as Nordic and non-Nordic audiences) that are involved in place branding processes in the Nordic region and beyond. Overall, the Nordic type of scholarship, research design, stakeholder interaction, and collaboration collectively lend themselves to a distillation of those unique features which characterise the Nordic place branding approach. In what follows, three peculiarities are presented in greater depth: 1) global reflexivity and responsibility, 2) legitimisation of place branding practices, and 3) shifting geopolitical boundaries.

The first feature of the Nordic wave approach is its impact on different stakeholders working and dealing with place branding practices and theories. At the same time, it highlights a sense of global reflexivity and translocal responsibility in two instances.

Table 8.1   The Nordic wave in place branding research

	Management approach	Critical approach	Nordic wave
Conceptualisation	Multi-disciplinary Instrumentalist Essentialist ontology Concept-driven	Interdisciplinary Deconstructionist Determinist ontology Issue-driven	Transdisciplinary Constructionist Relational ontology Problem-driven
Methodological approach	Critical realist Post-positivist	Critical postmodernist	Interventionist (engaged scholarship, participatory)
Scale and scope of research	Mono-dimensional Compartmentalised Colonialist	Two-dimensional Relativist Post-colonialist	Multi-dimensional Process-based De-colonialist
Knowledge objective	Technical Functionalist	Emancipatory Agnostic	Therapeutic Diagnostic
Ideological orientation	Market-driven capitalism Growth	Anti-capitalist Inclusive	Sustainability Social welfare
Place branding metaphor	Heterotopia	Dystopia	Utopia

Source: Cassinger et al. (2019: 238).

First, the Nordic approach impacts the way place branding relates to globalisation and glocalisation. The Nordic approach is in line with Roudometof's (2016) third way of globalisation, according to which glocalisation is not subsumed under globalisation or vice versa. Understood as glocalisation, Nordic branding may be considered as an autonomous concept and theoretical lens. Nordic branding practices, policies, and concepts thus are emerging as deterritorialised in the sense that they are related to cultures or imaginaries, which are not necessarily detached from, nor fully attached to, specific physical locations. Instead, global flows of ideas and practices set conditions for the construction and diffusion of imagining communalities, such as the Nordic lifestyle or Nordic sustainability, which lie beyond nationality, language, ethnicity, and country (Hannerz, 1990).

Second, it follows that a Nordic global responsibility refers not only to how different concepts and theories are treated within Nordic scholarship (i.e. research that attempts to appropriate and transform foreign concepts, theories, and models), but also how the scientific process of creating and transforming place branding concepts and creating best practices impact positively, as well as negatively, on place branding per se. In other words, the Nordic research approach has a globalised outlook while, at the same time, being cautious of narratives which present the Nordic as a dominant role model to be imitated in other parts of the world. The metaphor of the wave is chosen specifically because it suggests the ability of the Nordic approach to originate powerful waves (i.e. ideas, concepts, theory, practices) related to the locale, while consistently and persistently spreading across the world stage, like, for instance, the branded concept of *hygge* (loosely translated as togetherness and comfort; see Andersen et al., 2019). It is possible that such institutionalised place branding concepts and practices make the Nordic regional brand more resilient during times of change and serve as a form of protection from negative rumours. Finally, we suggest a capacity of local Nordic practices to modify or change the course of international waves that pass through via the construction of hybridity, visible, for example, in the increased emphasis on social responsibility and humanitarian issues (e.g. gender equality) in destination branding campaigns (Handayani, 2018).

Further to the above, we suggest an emphasis on translocal responsibility in terms of how researchers, embedded in Nordic political and societal contexts, attempt to engage with the so-called third mission of academics. This implies a dialogic and translocal engagement (i.e. consulting, advising, debating, partaking) with practitioners in different spatial settings, encouraging their various and sometimes alternative practices to be brought together and shared. This will open up an emerging triple helix of place branding networks rooted in new collaborations between researchers, practitioners, and public authorities; these collaborations can consolidate in the form of complex and productive knowledge transfer constellations, as demonstrated in the next section.

Legitimisation of Place Branding Practices and Research Funding

A second feature that sets the Nordic wave beyond previous approaches is the embeddedness of place branding scholarship in the Nordic socio-cultural and political context. The Nordic approach is characterised by enduring practitioner–academic collaborations and development activities informed by research, which positions academics to take complex roles in political and policy decision making, urban and regional planning processes, or more mundane and creative placemaking activities. This scholarly responsibility is indeed fundamental; it contributes to legitimising place branding practices to a broad set of audiences, especially if those are financed by means of tax-funded public (or semi-public) resources. Reaching consensus around the values of the place brand across political parties, in councils, parliaments, and communities at large is a peculiar feature of Nordic place branding, and justification processes regarding the long-term vision and objective of the place brand is of perennial importance. Nordic ideas of fairness and justice also have implications for Nordic research funding policies. Driven by the principle of reducing inequities and providing equal chances to marginalised communities, regional development and research funding positively discriminate subaltern perspectives. At first sight, the channelling of disproportionally large amounts to engage with peripheral regions and indigenous communities may seem a noble, if somewhat ineffective approach to direct research focus to 'places that don't matter' (Rodríguez-Pose, 2018). However, by giving academic consideration to subaltern voices, regions, and issues, and participating in branding solutions, researchers are intersecting path-dependent negative trajectories and contribute to building alternative futures – very much in line with the performative, action research-based imperative envisaged by Gibson-Graham (2008).

Shifting Geopolitical Boundaries

The third feature of the Nordic approach refers to its ability to travel across geopolitical boundaries. Despite the centrality of branding in competitive relationships between nation-states and regions in the contemporary world order, international place branding research has had relatively little to say about geopolitics (Browning and Oliveira, 2017b). The symbolic and cultural significance of place branding converges with a general interest within geopolitical studies on 'the renewed relevance of reputation and prestige politics in the context of emergent powers' (Browning and Oliveira, 2017: 483). In the landscape of post-Cold War globalisation, geopolitics merges with geo-economics, which turns place branding into an exertion of soft power (Volcic and Andrejevic, 2011).

Nordic place branding is not an innocent managerial practice, but is involved in continuous boundary-making practices and struggles over Nordicity (Browning, 2007). Borders confine our movement and imagination of where we can and cannot go and what it is possible to think. However, we also learn that borders are not fixed, but can be diminished, expanded, and abolished, though it is always possible to break free from disadvantageous frames. This is especially relevant to the Nordic approach, since the space of what we may call the geobrand is performed through narratives of the region. Following the figure of the wave and the utopian orientation of the Nordic approach, the borders of the Nordic geobrand may be thought of as fluid and flexible, moving back and forth depending on the winds (or external agendas). This is how indigenous territorial borders traditionally have been upheld under the occupation of nation-states. These borders are preserved in memory and called into presence by being the performed spaces in songs and stories about the land (cf. Verran, 1998; Cassel, 2019). Viewing the Nordic approach as a performance of space means that the borders of the geobrand are not fixed once and for all, but may be reconstructed through narration and negotiation.

Discussion and conclusions

The present chapter attempted to unpack the Nordic approach in place branding research by outlining the fluid contours of – what is referred to as – the Nordic wave. It exemplified particular practices and significant place brand phenomena in the region, but more importantly the aim was to compile and structure the growing body of research dealing with Nordic place branding and assess its global relevance and academic implications. The Nordic was approached, not only as a geographical context of place branding, but also as an approach – an ideological mindset – that shapes place branding concepts, strategies, and tactics.

There is a risk of stereotyping the Nordic region in terms of its symbolic features and mythical qualities, characterised by welfare, social equality, and peace. These qualities are also used in the international branding strategy of the Nordic region and can be found in the promotion of individual countries within the region. This contribution seeks to dismantle these mythologies and show that the Nordic countries deal with their own problems related to colonial history, involvement in international armed conflicts, as well as social, ethnic, and territorial marginalisation. Future place branding scholarship, in the Nordic context and elsewhere, will have to address and engage with emerging territorial conflicts between places that 'do not matter' versus those 'shining places' that do, whilst simultaneously navigating backdrops of social polarisation, rising populism, and other associated reactionary and progressive movements in the political landscape. The hybridity of the Nordic scholarly approach, as it has been presented in this chapter, reveals the potential of expanding place branding research and practice to deal with such issues globally.

References

Adler-Nissen, R. and U. P. Gad (2014), 'Introduction: Postimperial sovereignty games in the Nordic region', *Cooperation and Conflict*, **49** (1), 3–32.

Aggestam, K., Bergman-Rosamond, A., and A. Kronsell (2019), 'Theorising feminist foreign policy', *International Relations*, **33** (1), 23–39.

Andersen, L. P., Kjeldgaard, D., Lindberg, F., and J. Östberg (2019), 'Nordic branding: An odyssey into the Nordic myth market', in S. Askegaard and J. Östberg (eds), *Nordic Consumer Culture*, Cham: Palgrave Macmillan, pp. 213–38.

Aronczyk, M. (2009), 'How to do things with brands: Uses of national identity', *Canadian Journal of Communication*, **34** (2), 291–6.

Avraham, E. (2014), 'Spinning liabilities into assets in place marketing: Towards a new typology', *Place Branding and Public Diplomacy*, **10** (3), 174–85.

Bergmann, E. (2017), *Nordic Nationalism and Right-Wing Populist Politics: Imperial Relationships and National Sentiments*, London: Palgrave Macmillan.

Brorström, S. and A. Parment (2016), 'Various-sized municipalities dealing with growth issues: Different issues but the same solutions?', *Scandinavian Journal of Public Administration*, **20** (4), 73–89.

Browning, C. S. (2007), 'Branding Nordicity: Models, identity and the decline of exceptionalism', *Cooperation and Conflict*, **42** (1), 27–51.

Browning, C. S. (2018), 'Nation branding and policy transfer: Insights from Norden', *EL-CISD Working Paper*, 2018 (22), Brussels: Institute for European Studies.

Browning, C. S. and A. Oliveira (2017), 'Introduction: Nation branding and competitive identity in world politics', *Geopolitics*, **22** (3), 481–501.

Byrkjeflot, H., Pedersen, J. S., and S. Svejenova (2013), 'From label to practice: The process of creating new Nordic cuisine', *Journal of Culinary Science and Technology*, **11** (1), 36–55.

Cassel, S. H. (2019), 'Branding Sámi tourism: Practices of indigenous participation and place-making', in C. Cassinger, A. Lucarelli and S. Gyimóthy (eds), *The Nordic Wave in Place Branding: Poetics, Practices, Politics*, Cheltenham, UK and Northampton, MA, USA: Edward Elgar Publishing, pp. 139–52.

Cassinger, C. (2019), 'Market-mediated feminism and the Nordic: A commentary on the political dimension of place branding', in C. Cassinger, A. Lucarelli and S. Gyimóthy (eds), *The Nordic Wave in Place Branding: Poetics, Practices, Politics*, Cheltenham, UK and Northampton, MA, USA: Edward Elgar Publishing, pp. 227–34.

Cassinger, C. and J. Eksell (2017), 'The magic of place branding: Regional brand identity in transition', *Journal of Place Management and Development*, **10** (3), 202–12.

Cassinger, C., Lucarelli, A., and S. Gyimóthy (eds) (2019), *The Nordic Wave in Place Branding: Poetics, Practices, Politics*, Cheltenham, UK and Northampton, MA, USA: Edward Elgar Publishing.

Czarniawska-Joerges, B. and G. Sevón (eds) (2005), *Global Ideas: How Ideas, Objects and Practices Travel in a Global Economy*, Frederiksberg: Liber and Copenhagen Business School Press.

Danbolt, M. (2016), 'New Nordic exceptionalism: Jeuno JE Kim and Ewa Einhorn's The United Nations of Norden and other realist utopias', *Journal of Aesthetics and Culture*, **8** (1), 30902.

Durand, A. (2018), *Marketing and Globalization*, London: Routledge.

Elbe, J. and A. Emmoth (2014), 'The use of rhetoric in legitimation strategies when mobilizing destination stakeholders', *Journal of Destination Marketing and Management*, **3** (4), 210–17.

Eshuis, J. and E.-H. Klijn (2012), *Branding in Governance and Public Management*, New York: Routledge.

Gibson-Graham, J. K. (2008), 'Diverse economies: Performative practices for "other worlds"', *Progress in Human Geography*, **32** (5), 613–32.

Gurinović, M., Milešević, J., Kadvan, A., Nikolić, M., Zeković, M., Djekić-Ivanković, M., Dupouy, E., Finglas, P., and Glibetić, M. (2018), 'Development, features and application of DIET ASSESS & PLAN (DAP) software in supporting public health nutrition research in Central Eastern European Countries (CEEC)', *Food Chemistry*, **238** (January), 186–94.

Gyimóthy, S. (2017), 'The reinvention of terroir in Danish food place promotion', *European Planning Studies*, **25** (7), 1200–16.

Gyimóthy, S. (2019), 'Tactical ruralism: A commentary on Nordic placemaking practices', in C. Cassinger, A. Lucarelli, and S. Gyimóthy (eds), *The Nordic Wave in Place Branding: Poetics, Practices, Politics*, Cheltenham, UK and Northampton, MA, USA: Edward Elgar Publishing, pp. 153–8. doi:10.4337/9781788974325.00022.

Hall, C. M. (2008), 'Santa Claus, place branding and competition', *Fennia-International Journal of Geography*, **186** (1), 59–67.

Handayani, B. (2018), 'The paradox of authenticity and its implications for contemporary and "bizarre" tourism campaigns', in *Digital Marketing and Consumer Engagement: Concepts, Methodologies, Tools and Applications*, Hershey, PA: IGI Global, Business Science Reference, pp. 1353–70.

Hannerz, U. (1990), 'Cosmopolitans and locals in world culture', *Theory, Culture and Society*, **7** (2–3), 237–51.

Jansson, D. (2012), 'Branding Åland, branding Ålanders: Reflections on place identity and globalization in a Nordic archipelago', *Place Branding and Public Diplomacy*, **8** (2), 119–32.

Jezierska, K. and A. Towns (2018), 'Taming feminism? The place of gender equality in the "Progressive Sweden" brand', *Place Branding and Public Diplomacy*, **14** (1), 55–63.

Lucarelli, A. (2019), 'Nordic, Scandinavia or Schondia? A commentary on Nordic brand constructions', in C. Cassinger, A. Lucarelli and S. Gyimóthy (eds), *The Nordic Wave in Place Branding: Poetics, Practices, Politics*, Cheltenham, UK and Northampton, MA, USA: Edward Elgar Publishing, pp. 68–74.

Lucarelli, A. and P. O. Berg (2011), 'City branding: A state-of-the-art review of the research domain', *Journal of Place Management and Development*, **4** (1), 9–27.

Lucarelli, A. and S. Brorström (2013), 'Problematising place branding research: A meta-theoretical analysis of the literature', *The Marketing Review*, **13** (1), 65–81.

Lucarelli, A. and A. Hallin (2015), 'Brand transformation: A performative approach to brand regeneration', *Journal of Marketing Management*, **31** (1–2), 84–106.

Nordic Council of Ministers (2019), 'Strategy for international branding of the Nordic region 2019–2021', *PolitikNord* 2019: 709, Copenhagen: Nordisk Ministerråd, accessed 20 July 2020 at: http://dx.doi.org/10.6027/PN2019-709.

Ooi, C. S. and J. S. Pedersen (2017), 'In search of Nordicity: How new Nordic cuisine shaped destination branding in Copenhagen', *Journal of Gastronomy and Tourism*, **2** (4), 217–31.

Pamment, J. (2016), 'Introduction: Why the Nordic region?', *Journal of Place Branding and Public Diplomacy*, **12** (2–3), 91–8.

Paxson, H. (2010), 'Locating value in Artisan cheese: Reverse engineering terroir for new-world landscapes', *American Anthropologist*, **112** (3), 444–57. doi:10.1111/j .1548-1433.2010.01251.x.

Ren, C., Gad, U. P. and L. R. Bjørst (2019), 'Branding on the Nordic margins: Greenland brand configurations', in C. Cassinger, A. Lucarelli and S. Gyimóthy (eds), *The Nordic Wave in Place Branding: Poetics, Practices, Politics*, Cheltenham, UK and Northampton, MA, USA: Edward Elgar Publishing, pp. 160–74.

Rodríguez-Pose, A. (2018), 'The revenge of the places that don't matter (and what to do about it)', *Cambridge Journal of Regions, Economy and Society*, **11** (1), 189–209.

Roudometof, V. (2016), 'Theorizing glocalization: Three interpretations', *European Journal of Social Theory*, **19** (3), 391–408.

Shi, S. J. (2006), 'Left to market and family – again? Ideas and the development of the rural pension policy in China', *Social Policy and Administration*, **40** (7), 791–806.

Suchman, M. C. (1995), 'Managing legitimacy: Strategic and institutional approaches', *Academy of Management Review*, **20** (3), 571–610.

The Nordics (2020), 'About the Nordics', accessed 20 July 2020 at: www.thenordics .com/about.

Verran, H. (1998), 'Re-imagining land ownership in Australia', *Postcolonial Studies: Culture, Politics, Economy*, **1** (2), 237–54.

Volcic, Z. and M. Andrejevic (2011), 'Nation branding in the era of commercial nationalism', *International Journal of Communication*, **5**, 598–618.

9 The tale of three cities: Place branding, scalar complexity and football

Steve Millington, Chloe Steadman, Gareth Roberts and Dominic Medway

Introduction

This chapter explores the intertwining of place, branding, and football through telling *The Tale of Three Cities* – Manchester City Football Club (MCFC), the city of Manchester, and City Football Group (CFG). More specifically, through exploring the branding strategies of MCFC over time, this chapter unravels the porous, dynamic, and sometimes reverse trajectories between the global and local, and glocal and grobal, which are central to place and football branding. Building on earlier work (Edensor and Millington, 2008), we demonstrate how close associations to place thwart efforts of brands to go fully 'grobal'.

Initial academic interrogation of the complex relations between global–local spatial scales uncritically produced binary and static oppositions between the global and local (Cox, 1993), with the local 'fetishised' as something to be rescued from the homogenising clutches of globalisation (Andrews and Ritzer, 2007). However, more recent literature provides multilayered, dynamic, and porous accounts of geographical scales (Andrews and Ritzer, 2007; Brenner, 1998). For instance, 'glocal' is now regularly deployed to capture the leaky boundaries between the global and local (Robertson, 1995); whilst, to deepen this analysis, 'grobal' – an amalgamation of 'growth' and 'global' – has been added to the growing lexicon of concepts examining the complex spatialities of globalisation (Andrews and Ritzer, 2007). The term 'grobal' thus explains how global processes can sometimes overwhelm the local, rather than the global and local always slotting seamlessly together as implied by the bridging concept 'glocal' (Andrews and Ritzer, 2007; Medway et al., 2019; Ritzer, 2007),

due to a focus on continuous growth across global borders without consideration of preserving local values, identities, or cultures.

However, discussions of scalar entanglements are limited in place branding
literature. This is surprising given well-rehearsed anxieties about globalisation
producing a dystopic end-state of 'nothingness' (Ritzer, 2007), with localities
becoming standardised, 'placeless' (Relph, 1976) and 'non-places' (Augé,
1992). A further concern is how the appropriation of place branding by
policy-makers might also contribute to the homogenisation of places, through
place marketing and placemaking designed to appeal to international target
markets (Rantisi and Leslie, 2006). To counter anxiety about the flattening
of place, emergent research focuses on attempts to reconnect consumers
with local cultures. This encompasses craft produce (Sjölander-Lindqvist,
Skoglund, and Laven, 2020), how local distinction and perceived 'authenticity'
could regenerate high streets (Hubbard, 2019), and concerns about overtourism in relation to destination branding (Séraphin et al., 2019). Such work
amplifies the importance of addressing the relative neglect of spatial scales and
tensions within place branding, for which this chapter addresses and contributes an emergent research agenda.

The complexity of spatial scales

Since the mid-1970s, globalisation has become a popular term (Kelly, 1999)
used to reflect the time–space compression, intensified social and cultural
connectivity, and sense of the 'world as a single place' associated with contemporary developed societies (Kelly, 1999; Giulianotti and Robertson, 2004).
Traditionally, geographical scales (e.g. local, regional, national, global, etc.)
were presented as relatively bounded, static, and hierarchical; for example,
the perceived binaried distinctions between the global and local (Andrews
and Ritzer, 2007; Brenner, 1998; Cox, 1993). It led to what Kelly (1999: 382)
refers to as a 'caricature' of the world, with culture no longer seen as mean-
ingfully connected to place. This reflects the 'narrative of loss' (Arefi, 1999:
179) found in much place-based literature, which argues globalisation has
led to places becoming homogenised, inauthentic, and disembedded from
the local. However, for Brenner (1998: 464; original emphasis), geographical
scales are: 'complex, socially contested territorial scaffolding upon which
multiple overlapping *forms of territorial organization* converge, coalesce, and
interpenetrate'.

Therefore, whilst the 'serious leakage' (Cox, 1993: 436) between spatial scales was initially overlooked, since the 1990s an emergent stream of critical literature has considered geographical scales as dynamic, porous, unbounded, relational, and dialectical (Andrews and Ritzer, 2007; Brenner, 1998; Cox, 1993; Kelly, 1999; Medway et al., 2019). Thus, 'glocal' and 'glocalisation' have been coined to capture the fluid, dialectical, and interpenetrative relationship between the global and local (Robertson, 1995), including the adaptation of global products to suit local audiences. Andrews and Ritzer (2007), however, argue discussions of glocalisation often neglect a critical appreciation of how the 'grobal' – the continuous expansionist aims of nations and organisations – can overwhelm the 'glocal', as explained in the introduction. Rather than the global and local neatly slotting together, they suggest researchers should examine the underexplored interplays between the 'glocal' and 'grobal' (cf. Hoogenboom, Bannick, and Trommel, 2010). Reflecting the challenges places might face in terms of appealing to both the local catchment and visitors, user perceptions of (in)authenticity, and overtourism, the above reveals the importance of considering the complexity of spatial scales within place branding, in order for places to retain character, vitality, and viability in today's competitive globalised environment.

Scalar tensions in place branding

Place branding literature has bourgeoned over the last three decades, with an exponential year-on-year increase in the number of articles from 1988 to 2009 (Lucarelli and Berg, 2011). This proliferation can be understood through the lens of an increasingly neoliberal environment (Rantisi and Leslie, 2006), and resultant competition between places. As Boisen (2007) suggests, if policy-makers perceive their places as being in competition, they are likely to embark on policies designed to improve the competitive position of their places. It follows that branding can be seen as a hegemonic, widely adopted strategy employed by different places to ensure they can compete in this environment (Kornberger and Carter, 2010).

Yet, whilst Dinnie (2008: 15) defines place branding as 'the unique, multi-dimensional blend of elements that provide (places) with culturally grounded differentiation and relevance for all of its target audiences', concerns continue to surround homogenous 'top-down' branding strategies (Ntounis and Kavaratzis, 2017). In this regard, Omholt (2013) indicates place branding needs to develop a collective capacity for genuine stakeholder engagement. Thus, as research and practice has evolved, top-down place branding has been eschewed in favour of participatory, 'bottom-up' branding that is embedded in interactive processes with local stakeholders (Eshuis and Edwards, 2013; Omholt, 2013; Kavaratzis and Kalandides, 2015). As Zenker (2011) suggests, the greater the depth of participation, the higher the level of satisfaction, commitment and trust people have with the place brand created.

Despite the shift towards participatory branding – which arguably favours the local – constituting a key aspect of progression in the field, there has been little conceptual development in respect of associated scalar tensions. Boisen, Terlouw, and van Gorp (2011: 138) contend places are not distinct entities but part of a scalar hierarchy through which identities at different scales are selectively layered. Warnaby and Medway (2013: 348) suggest this manifests both in terms of administrative jurisdictions, as well as in the physical spaces they occupy, as 'such spatial identities as perceived by audiences may overlap, contradict or complement places defined in territorial-administrative terms'. Likewise, Giovanardi (2015: 611) argues place branding 'can no longer be viewed as nested in a static hierarchy, but instead must co-exist and interpenetrate in a tangled and sometimes surprising manner'. As such, the typical scales of place branding activity – city/region/nation (Herstein, 2012) – can no longer be considered binaried or static. Cities for example, are an aggregate of other places and spaces within their boundaries, with this scalar disaggregation applying within and across each of these 'traditional' spatial scales (Boisen, 2007). The 'porous' accounts of geographical scales described above, therefore, have implications for 'interscalar' (Giovanardi, 2015) place brand formation and consumption, and should be taken into account to avoid what Lucarelli (2018: 261) has termed the 'territorial trap'.

Place branding and football are closely interwoven, thus making it a fruitful context for unravelling the complexities of spatial scales, and to avoid such territorial trappings. Football clubs, for example, can promote the place in which they are embedded (Bale, 2000); as van den Berg, Braun, and Otgaar (2016) observe, sports events are important to city marketing campaigns, since they enhance city competitiveness and attractiveness to local communities and tourists. The Visit Manchester (2020) website, for instance, promotes stadium tours and matches at Manchester United's Old Trafford ground and Manchester City's Etihad Stadium to attract visitors, proclaiming: 'Manchester is synonymous with football; it's written in our DNA'. Indeed, 10.8 per cent of visits to the north west of England include seeing a live football match (Visit Britain, 2015), with Old Trafford attracting 109,000 overseas visitors and the Etihad Stadium 33,000 in 2014 (Brooks-Sykes, 2016). Football tourists are also likely to spend more on average per stay in the United Kingdom compared to the typical visitor, thus boosting local economies (Brooks-Sykes, 2016). The next section, therefore, explores how such associations between place, football, and branding involve intricate scalar interrelations and considerations.

Football branding and place

The globalisation of football is now well documented (Giulianotti, 2002). Once reliant on match-day attendance, the highest-performing clubs have diversified their commercial activity to include branded merchandise, hospitality packages, and sponsorship deals (Abosag, Roper, and Hind, 2012). English Premier League clubs, for example, currently share over £5 billion from broadcasting rights (Buraimo, 2019), with match-day revenue contributing a small percentage of total income. Indeed, these elite clubs aim to extend their brand through global media channels, augmented by lucrative tours of growing football markets, or 'friendly globalisation' (Menary, 2018). Consequently, football markets are fragmenting beyond the confines of longstanding local fans to geographically dispersed 'consumers', who perhaps do not share such a passionate relationship with the clubs themselves (Giulianotti, 2002; Tapp and Clowes, 2002).

However, geographical association or origin (Pike, 2011) remains an immutable core attribute of the world's leading global football brands, thus challenging processes of 'grobalisation'. Unlike the franchise model in the United States, where sports club mobility is more commonplace, it is unthinkable, for example, that Barcelona FC would relocate to Madrid, no matter what the commercial benefits. There has been one attempt in English football, where Wimbledon FC relocated to Milton Keynes to form MK Dons; but this provoked such a backlash from Wimbledon supporters that they refused to follow the new club, and actually formed their own, Wimbledon AFC, to maintain the connection to their original locale (Cook and Anagnostopoulos, 2017). As this case exemplifies, within football fan cultural identity, the connection between club and place remains a prominent marker in claims of what it means to be a 'true' supporter (Davis, 2015). Hence, it is not surprising that the 'grobal' ambitions of football clubs can be resisted by local supporters who refuse to view their team as a dislocated brand (Abosag et al., 2012), and hold a generally negative view of supposedly detached touristic spectators during matches (Steadman et al., 2020).

Subsequently, whilst football is often considered the 'global game' (Richelieu and Desbordes, 2009; Rowe, 2003), football clubs remain intimately rooted in place; despite the geographical mobility of fans, players, and managers, they retain symbolic ties to 'home' (Giulianotti and Robertson, 2004). Most English football clubs, for example, are named after a town or city (Bale, 2000; Medway et al., 2019), with club headquarters, home stadia, strip colours, and core supporters typically embedded in the place from which that club originated (Giulianotti and Robertson, 2004). Whilst football brands are communicated through tangible elements such as merchandise and billboards, local support- ers form a crucial aspect of the unpredictable and intangible 'core' product pro- moted, i.e. the match and its attendant atmospheres (Guschwan, 2015), with fans as 'pro-sumers' of match experiences (Couvelaere and Richelieu, 2005). Home stadia are important architectural repositories of supporter affects, emotions, and memories, with stadium relocations potentially rupturing these topophilic connections fans form with their club (Bale, 2000; Giulianotti, 2002), and any associated match-day routines (Edensor and Millington, 2010; Steadman et al., 2020), geographical memories, and identities (Edensor and Millington, 2008; Guschwan, 2015; Hague and Mercer, 1998).

Whereas studies of football branding overwhelmingly focus on the grobal (Hinson et al., 2020), we draw on the notion of brands as 'half-finished frames' (Goffman, 1974) which cannot generate meanings to which people automat- ically subscribe, but must connect to spatially embedded identities, memo- ries, and emotions (Edensor and Millington, 2008). Indeed, brands are not passively received; they are social texts co-produced between marketers and consumers (Hatch and Rubin, 2006; Holt, 2002). Fans interpret football brands from a 'horizon of expectations' (Hatch and Rubin, 2006) informed by their geographically embedded experiences with the club. Thus, whilst brands might be conceptualised as complex and fluid (Lury, 2004), historical associations to place hinder the capacity of even the most powerful football brands to ever go fully 'grobal' – an argument we will now unravel further.

The Tale of Three Cities: Manchester City Football Club branding story

Giulianotti and Robertson (2004: 555) assert that football provides a revealing context to analyse the 'complex interplay of universalizing and localizing forces'. To move beyond static and binaried accounts of the global–local nexus, and account for fluid, shifting, and complex flows intertwining the glocal and grobal, Hoogenboom et al. (2010) adopt a longitudinal approach. They thereby illustrate how, over time, brands might follow non-linear and multidirectional trajectories spanning multiple spatial scales. We take inspiration from their framework to analyse how football brands negotiate tensions between their indispensable geographical associations with place, and expansionist global ambitions (Edensor and Millington, 2008). We will now explore four of what we call 'transects'[1] of MCFC branding strategies over time, alongside considerations of the entangled global–local and glocal–grobal scalar interplays.

Transect 1: From the Grobal to the Local – *This Is Our City*

The first branding transect emphasises MCFC's locally embedded connections to the city of Manchester in the United Kingdom. Following decades of on-field and off-field calamities, whilst local rivals Manchester United enjoyed unprecedented success, MCFC started the 2003 season in the new City of Manchester Stadium (now the Etihad Stadium), having spent 80 years at their previous home ground, Maine Road (Edensor and Millington, 2010; Steadman et al., 2020). The move was supposed to mark MCFC's rebirth; however, reflecting a long absence from the top flight, the club initially suffered from poor results, with fan expectations quickly dropping. This raised the question of: how do you brand a mediocre team? Local fans also experienced a lingering sense of dislocation following the disruptive stadium move (Edensor and Millington, 2010; Steadman et al., 2020). In response, the club hired an advertising agency in 2005 to develop a new branding campaign – *This Is Our City* – which knowingly constructed MCFC as Manchester's embedded 'local team', in opposition to its disembedded 'global other', Manchester United (Edensor and Millington, 2008). Despite simultaneously trying to grobalise the brand during this time, through an international network of supporter clubs and online media, and growing the club's presence in China through the calculated signing of international player Sun Jihai – the club's first Asian player – this campaign aimed to cultivate the loyalty and passion of *existing* local supporters. As Matt Lowery (Assistant Club Secretary) explained: 'We simply can't afford to be complacent. We enjoy a tremendous loyalty from our core fans… if this really is Manchester's club we should be spreading that message around the city' (*The Guardian*, 2005).

The campaign therefore drew on slogans, imagery, and narratives associated with club and fan histories within the city of Manchester. Online advertising for a new kit, for example, made geographical and temporal associations with the working-class terraced housing and alleyways of Moss Side, the neighbourhood in which the former Maine Road ground was embedded. This landscape deliberately resonated with sentiments expressed by fans comparing their experiences between the old and new stadia (Edensor and Millington, 2010). Another online advert featured a photograph by Shirley Baker, famous for recording working-class life in 1960s Manchester. Overlaying the image, depicting young boys playing football against a backdrop of terraced streets, was the slogan 'Always was… Always will be'. The deployment of these nostalgic sites and spaces of Maine Road tapped into myths around MCFC fans as working class and locally rooted Mancunians, in contrast with the new embourgeoised, and increasingly geographically dispersed, football 'consumer' (Giulianotti, 2002).

As well as drawing on historical imagery of places such as Maine Road, the campaign sprawled into the city of Manchester itself, reaffirming the club's local-rootedness. For example, 48 billboards in MCFC colours were strategically placed around central Manchester, proclaiming *This Is Our City* and using slogans such as *Pure* or *Réal* Manchester. As Edensor and Millington (2008) suggest, the play on Real/*Réal* not only undergirds notions of authenticity, but also makes playful reference to a time when MCFC regularly played in European club competition in their 1970s 'glory days', prior to more recent successes. This word play also conceivably signals the club's wider global ambitions, thus revealing the complex scalar paradoxes involved in the campaign. Graffiti-style adverts for MCFC matches also began to appear in Manchester's trendy Northern Quarter cultural district. Such interventions were designed not only to appeal to MCFC fans' Mancunian embeddedness and sense of rooted cosmopolitanism, but to also brazenly antagonise fans of rivals Manchester United.

Given consumers sometimes resist branding efforts (Holt, 2002), fans acknowledged *This Is Our City* as a deliberative campaign instigated by the club's management. However, by tapping into 'pre-existing structures of feeling, belief, and identity' (Edensor and Millington, 2008: 174), through which individuals both 'locate themselves and define their locality' (Hague and Mercer, 1998: 113), supporters were largely acquiescent (Edensor and Millington, 2008). The campaign remained locally embedded and sensitive to the club and fans' geographical context, positioning the MCFC brand as 'locally authentic', distinguished from the 'inauthentic global'. The MCFC brand at this time was thus less promiscuously available to global audiences. *This Is Our City*, therefore, illustrates how sports branding can provide a sense of locality and differentiation in a globalising world (Guschwan, 2015). Yet, whilst cultivating the loyalty of local fans may make commercial sense for a struggling team, things rapidly changed for MCFC in 2008, with a takeover by the wealthy Sheikh Mansour family of Abu Dhabi, which held ambitions to grow MCFC into a global football brand. This development is now explored further.

Transect 2: From the Local to the Grobal – Branding the City of Manchester through Football

The second branding transect examines the repositioning of a 'local' brand within a global network, reflective of how branding can involve 'jumping' between multiple scales (Ntounis and Kanellopoulou, 2017). Scott (2000) describes the interweaving of significant cultural and social institutions and spaces into broader place branding narratives. We might also consider football clubs as cultural assets within a milieu of local features projecting images that function as branding devices for a place's capabilities, ambitions, and aspirations (Giulianotti, 1999; van den Berg et al., 2016). Since the 1970s, sports-led development has become a key feature of cities' regeneration strategies, such as Birmingham, Glasgow, and Sheffield (Gratton, Shibli, and Coleman, 2005). Building on Peck and Ward (2002), we focus on the transformation of poverty-stricken east Manchester into an international sporting destination following MCFC's 2008 takeover and changing fortunes.

More specifically, the 2008 investment from Abu Dhabi accelerated the development of the area around MCFC's home stadium to accommodate new training facilities; a second football stadium for the youth and women's teams; a complex of community football pitches; sports science research facilities; and a school and college, together with MCFC's administrative base. The new owners expanded the main stadium and sold naming rights to Etihad Airways. This deal extended to the entire site, subsequently renamed the Etihad Campus, to replace its previous incarnations of SportsCity and Eastlands – an advanced example of toponymic commodification (Medway et al., 2019). Consequently, the Etihad brand has become embedded and synonymous with Manchester, reflecting the city's neoliberal 'entrepreneurial script' (Peck and Ward, 2002). Sir Richard Leese, leader of Manchester City Council, has celebrated such developments:

> The relationship between Etihad Airways and MCFC further supports Manchester's international profile and global connectivity and the city's ability to attract leading brands to invest and create job opportunities. It is great news for Manchester, reinforcing our sporting, transport and economic growth priorities and is particularly welcome news for east Manchester. (*Manchester Evening News*, 2011)

We suggest, therefore, that the repositioning of MCFC as a global club aligns with the strategic desires of the city's political elite, seeking to portray Manchester as a future global city, and is a key driver of a grobal strategy for both club and local authority. The above reaffirms the interweaving of place, place branding, and football (van den Berg et al., 2016).

The connection between the city of Manchester and Abu Dhabi, however, is not necessarily a one-way process. Middle Eastern brands, such as Etihad and Emirates, are notable for exploiting the global exposure of football teams (Al Masari and O'Connor, 2013), committing $1.4 billion between 2006 and 2021 in sponsorship deals with MCFC and several others, including Arsenal, Paris Saint-Germain, and Real Madrid (Thani and Heenan, 2017). However, as Thani and Heenan suggest, both airlines act as proxies for national state authority, with these deals being more about repositioning the United Arab Emirates, rather than promoting those places where the clubs receiving this sponsorship are embedded. Etihad, for instance, established direct plane routes between Manchester and Abu Dhabi, and MCFC fans can take advantage of discounted holidays promoted to them through in-stadium adverts by the Abu Dhabi Department of Culture and Tourism. The creation of the Etihad Campus, therefore, demonstrates the interwoven nature of football, place, and place branding; and, as we reveal in the next section, such interrelationships are further complicated by the multiple glocalities and cities, which might be a target of the grobal ambitions of Abu Dhabi.

Transect 3: Entangling the Grobal with Multiple Glocals – *The City Way*

The third transect traces how football branding can play out in multiple glocalities, to occupy both the grobal and the glocal (Hinson et al., 2020). It maps the construction of *City* as a global umbrella brand encompassing multiple international football brands and cities, including – but extending far beyond – MCFC and the city of Manchester. The relative simplicity of football matches renders the game particularly open to consumption by global audiences (Giulianotti and Robertson, 2004); and thus the global flow of media and money that are hallmarks of the twenty-first century (Guschwan, 2015: 374). However, as Evans and Norcliffe (2016) explain, cultivating football supporters at club level remains dependent on how branding appeals to specific national and local cultural contexts. Indeed, as Andrews and Ritzer (2007) note, grobal brands can appeal to multiple glocals, whereby the product is customised for different national markets. We also see this in sport: mega-events such as the Olympic Games provide an example of multiplicity in sports branding as they involve numerous glocalities (Andrews and Ritzer, 2007). This multiplicity is also evidenced by football brands.

In 2013, MCFC's owners established a holding company, CFG, jointly owned by the Abu Dhabi United Group, together with Chinese media and American financial interests. Central to this grobal strategy is multiple club ownership, whereby CFG now owns majority shares in MCFC, New York City, and

Melbourne City; has acquired six further clubs (Montevideo City Torque, Girona FC, Lommel SK, Mumbai City, Sichuan Jiuniu FC, and Yokohama F. Marinos); and established player development agreements with two further clubs (NAC Breda and Atlético Venezuela CF). In total, CFG now incorporates 25 men's, women's, and youth teams, as well as establishing a further 25 subsidiary companies, with operations in 12 countries. They have also invested in:

- Sapphire Sports – a United States-based sport venture capital fund.
- Global Soccer Centres – a network of recreational football centres across North America.
- Professional ESports teams in Manchester, New York, Melbourne, and China.

CFG's overarching mission is 'creating globally connected football communities', and it has established the brand – *City* – to achieve this. Here, *City* is constructed as a global umbrella brand that connects multiple clubs and cities around the world. Although the *City* in question might be the one playing in Manchester, New York, or Melbourne, nevertheless they are all *City*. In a competitive global market, brand distinction rests on *The City Way*, summarised by Omar Berrada in 2015 (Commercial Director, City Football Marketing):

> One of our key objectives is to win – and to win not just at Manchester City, but at all of our clubs. The other aspect is how you win. We want to play a very specific type of football – a classy, beautiful style of football that we believe resonates with football fans around the world. It allows brands to have the best of both worlds: a consistent global marketing platform… as well as the ability to deliver messages that are very specific to the local markets of our clubs around the world. (*Marketing Week*, 2015)

Clubs in New York, Montevideo, Melbourne, and Girona have been subject to name changes, new colours, and badges to align with the *City* brand. Whilst retaining some local distinctions, therefore, each club is recognisably linked to *City*. Although the Manchester version of *City* remains prominent, the deployment of *City* to signify a winning attitude and particular style is a more fluid and globally available brand concept. The multiple club ownership model, therefore, enables CFG to establish multiple brands in the world's core and expanding football markets.

Regardless of accusations of financial irregularity levelled at the club by European governing body UEFA (*The Guardian*, 2020), which once threatened to dent their ambitions, under Sheikh Mansour's ownership, MCFC has become one of the world's most valuable clubs and brands (Deloitte, 2020), and remains core to CFG's grobal ambitions as a parent brand to be consumed both at home and across the world. However, as the position of MCFC within the glocal–grobal nexus becomes increasingly complex, not all of MCFC's core supporters appear to be buying into the club's new elevated position.

Transect 4: From Multiple Glocals back to the Local – Reclaiming the Local

The final transect reveals how fan disenchantment with commercialisation is driving MCFC's (re)emphasis on the local. Andrews and Ritzer (2007: 142) draw attention to the potential loss of control of the parent brand as 'the fundamental grobal–glocal problematic', a particularly heightened concern in the context of sports branding, which can 'frequently be subject to forms of defensive resistance by glocal constituencies' (2007: 147). Indeed, football 'consumers' can be reflexive (Edensor, 2015) and reticent to see their club as a 'brand' (Abosag et al., 2012). As Edensor and Millington (2008) demonstrate, football branding can generate fan anxieties that clubs will become detached from local roots to lure global audiences, resonating with Arefi's (1999: 179) 'narrative of loss'. Despite increasing global reach and an unprecedented period of success, local MCFC supporters appear to be experiencing a growing sense of disconnection to the club. As Steadman et al. (2020) find, local core supporters are beginning to feel *overwhelmed* by the grobal, and increasingly detached from the club which they believe is becoming a disconnected 'brand'. Due to MCFC's grobal strategy, supporters are also becoming sensitised to the presence of new spectators during matches, rehearsing a common trope within fan culture which positions 'real fans' against glory hunters, tourists, or 'plastic fans' (Edensor, 2015). To exemplify, as one fan in Steadman et al.'s (2020: 12) study of football match atmospheres remarked: 'People who don't really have the passion for the club, who just come here for a day out. That's the "un-real" fans… Selfie sticks and spend two hundred pounds in the shop and… then fly off wherever… The club is pandering for those types of fans' (John, Group discussion 1).

MCFC is facing related challenges around core local fans lacking feelings of topophilic connectedness at the club's new Etihad Stadium (Edensor and Millington, 2010; Steadman et al., 2020), reflecting Relph's (1976) notion of placelessness, and wider concerns around the 'disenchanted homeliness' (Ritzer and Stillman, 2001: 101) of contemporary sports stadia. Whereas Maine Road, and its wider neighbourhood, comprised variegated, loose, complex spaces, the Etihad Campus confronts fans with a smoother and more regulated environment in danger of becoming a 'non-place' (Augé, 1992). As one fan opines:

> Park up near a pub, then have a couple of pints. Go to the ground [Maine Road] and buy some Bovril and maybe a Wagon Wheel. At half time grab a pie and a cup of tea. After the match go to the pub again – usually a different one – or a local curry house and talk about the match... Where do you go for a decent pint near Eastlands [The Etihad]? (*Manchester Confidential*, quoted in Edensor and Millington, 2010: 152)

The above has together contributed to issues around atmosphere at the Etihad Stadium – a crucial intangible element of football brands (Guschwan, 2015), which fans 'pro-sume' (Couvelaere and Richelieu, 2005). Indeed, Steadman et al. (2020) draw attention to the term *The Emptihad* – a jibe regularly deployed by rival fans and critics concerning the swathes of empty seats at MCFC home matches. During match days there is concern shared by both supporters and management that the atmosphere is poor, and that fans are quiet and do not come to games ready to spur the team on, often arriving late and leaving early: 'It was not full. I don't know why. [Wednesday] gives a chance to go back to Wembley. Hopefully they will support us more' (Pep Guardiola, *BBC Sport*, 2020). With the broader objective to win competitions and leagues, whilst promoting MCFC to a global multimedia audience, empty seats and dispassionate crowds challenge the parent brand attributes of *The City Way*, as well as the brand image of MCFC. Atmosphere in this case is an emotional and performative extension of the *City* brand, with certain expectations about how fans should display their loyalty.

Despite atmosphere being unpredictable, unlike other brand attributes (Guschwan, 2015), the club is currently enacting material and sensory place-making strategies in the sites and spaces surrounding the Etihad. It is hoped this will (re)foster a sense of local fan belonging and enhance atmosphere (Edensor, 2015), in turn improving brand image. The main intervention is focused on the introduction of *City Square*, a permanent fan zone incorporating bars, eateries, and a main stage at the centre for live music and onstage interviews. Place activation has also been stimulated through buskers and a plethora of activities for younger people, in addition to enhancing the walking routes from the city centre, with strategic positioning of activities and parades en route. Further illustrating a reorientation back to the local, the stadium exterior has been adorned with huge photographs depicting the history of the club from its humble nineteenth-century origins to the present-day successes, alongside narratives expressing local fans' match-day memories. Moreover, in a development which echoes the previous *This Is Our City* campaign, the club's new home shirt, launched in July 2020, incorporates a design which acknowledges creative mosaics found in Manchester's Northern Quarter cultural district in an attempt to reinscribe MCFC's embeddedness in place, whilst appealing to the local capital of MCFC supporters.

Although such interventions might be viewed cynically as an attempt to encourage fans to spend more time and money at the stadium, MCFC thus appears to have embarked on an innovative placemaking programme to enhance brand image. Nevertheless, there is always the underlying challenge that atmosphere cannot be easily and corporately manufactured in football, but must be carefully co-produced (Edensor, 2015; Steadman et al., 2020). Thus, drawing on marketing messages which explicitly call on fan loyalty, attempts by MCFC to improve atmosphere chimes with well-established notions within fan culture – notably, celebrating passion and the trope of 'real' fans getting behind their team. This final transect, therefore, reveals a broader challenge to football branding, as it seems stretching too far from their geographical associations continues to restrain the grobal ambitions of clubs.

Conclusions

This chapter explored the branding strategies deployed by MCFC, the city of Manchester, and CFG to reveal the interweaving, shifting, and multidirectional flows between geographical scales (Hoogenboom et al., 2010). First, we explored MCFC's *This Is Our City* campaign, branding which played upon the club's and supporters' locally embedded connections to Manchester (Edensor and Millington, 2008), which demonstrates how sports branding can provide a sense of locality and differentiation in a globalising world (Guschwan, 2015). Second, we mapped MCFC's rising 'grobal' ambitions following the 2008 takeover by the Abu Dhabi United Group, and subsequent sponsorship deals with Etihad Airways and development of the Etihad Campus. This illustrates complex interplays between Manchester's global branding aspirations, and attempts by the United Arab Emirates to reposition itself as a global destination. Third, we focused on the creation of *City* as a global umbrella brand for multiple football clubs and cities, including MCFC and Manchester. It unravels how a once locally embedded brand can be positioned within multiple glocalities through the adoption of a more fluid and globally available product concept. Finally, we explored concerns expressed by core supporters in Manchester about feeling overwhelmed by the grobal, which has provoked attempts to reconnect fans and 'reclaim' the local.

Subsequently, this chapter makes two key contributions to place branding. First, building on Rowe (2003) and Edensor and Millington (2008), we demonstrate how place embeddedness restrains football brands from ever going fully 'grobal'. We further suggest there are limits to how much a *place* brand can stretch away from its locally embedded roots before disenfranchisement results. Much research has been conducted into the requirement for 'authenticity' in place branding (Anholt, 2004; Murray, 2001); yet, little attention has been paid to the *implications* of extending a place brand too far, however authentic it is deemed to be. We suggest, therefore, there is fruitful ground to explore, beyond football, the complexity of the grobal–glocal nexus. For example, 'locals' in a given place may experience similar levels of resultant disconnection, and erosion of embedded place attachments, as place branding might strip away depth to render the qualities of place more amenable to non-localised place consumers.

Second, whilst existing literature discusses how sports teams help to promote the place from which they originate (e.g. Bale, 2000; van den Berg et al., 2016), we found in the case of MCFC that not only is the city of Manchester thereby promoted, but also the United Arab Emirates and other cities under the *City* umbrella brand. Such findings demonstrate how places cannot be considered bounded objects to be neatly packaged for consumers; nor should the 'local' be fetishised, as arguably occurs in participatory place branding (Kavaratzis and Kalandides, 2015). Rather, extending geographical insights into the realm of place branding, spatial scales must be considered as interpenetrative, overlapping, and ever shifting, with the attendant porosity and multiplicity of places considered during the branding process.

To conclude, future work could challenge literature which demonises the 'global' for its associations with placelessness, as well as that which enthusiastically celebrates the 'local'. Specifically, we call for additional work regarding scalar tensions within place branding. Researchers in this field are, therefore, encouraged to explore further the leaky boundaries between spatial scales in place branding contexts, rather than accepting the traditional view of places as neat and boundaried objects for promotion.

Note

1. Transect is a geographical term denoting a line of enquiry. However, unlike trajectory which suggests unstoppable linearity, transect conveys that one can

cut across, or move around in multiple directions, such lines of enquiry to detect changes over time and space.

References

Abosag, I., Roper, S., and D. Hind (2012), 'Examining the relationship between brand emotion and brand extension among supporters of professional football clubs', *European Journal of Marketing*, **46** (9), 1233–51.

Al Masari, H. J. and S. O'Connor (2013), 'Sport marketing in the modern age: A case study of Etihad Airways' sponsorship of Manchester City Football Club', in M. Sulayem, S. O'Connor, and D. Hassa (eds), *Sport Management in the Middle East: A Case Study Analysis*, London: Routledge, pp. 65–86.

Andrews, D. and G. Ritzer (2007), 'The grobal in the sporting local', *Global Networks*, **7** (2), 135–53.

Anholt, S. (2004), *Brand New Justice: How Branding Places and Products Can Help the Developing World*, Oxford: Elsevier Butterworth-Heinemann.

Arefi, M. (1999), 'Non-place and placelessness as narratives of loss: Rethinking the notion of place', *Journal of Urban Design*, **4** (2), 179–93.

Augé, M. (1992), *Non-Places: Introduction to an Anthropology of Supermodernity*, New York: Verso.

Bale, J. (2000), 'The changing face of football: Stadiums and communities', *Soccer and Society*, **1** (1), 91–101.

BBC Sport (2020), 'Manchester City: Pep Guardiola did not intend to offend fans over FA Cup attendance', *BBC Sport*, 28 January, accessed 5 March 2020 at: www.bbc.co.uk/sport/football/51285173.

Boisen, M. (2007), 'City marketing in contemporary urban governance', Paper presented at the *51st World Conference of the International Federation of Housing and Planning*.

Boisen, M., Terlouw, K., and B. van Gorp (2011), 'The selective nature of place branding and the layering of spatial identities', *Journal of Place Management and Development*, **4** (2), 135–47.

Brenner, N. (1998), 'Between fixity and motion: Accumulation, territorial organization and the historical geography of spatial scales', *Environment and Planning D: Society and Space*, **16** (4), 459–81.

Brooks-Sykes, N. (2016), 'How football tourism boosts the Manchester economy', *The Marketing Manchester blog*, accessed 1 March 2020 at: https://marketingmanchesterblog.wordpress.com/2016/08/11/football-tourism-boosts-manchester-economy/.

Buraimo, B. (2019), 'Exposure and television audience demand: The case of English Premier League football', in P. Downward, B. Frick, B. R. Humphreys, T. Pawlowski, J. E. Ruseski, and B. P. Soebbing (eds), *The SAGE Handbook of Sports Economics*, London: Sage, pp. 171–80.

Cook, D. and C. Anagnostopoulos (2017), 'MK Dons and AFC Wimbledon: Moving the goalpost and rising from the ashes', in S. Chadwick, D. Arthur, and J. Beech (eds), *International Cases in the Business of Sport*, Abingdon: Routledge, pp. 138–45.

Couvelaere, V. and A. Richelieu (2005), 'Brand strategy in professional sports: The case of French soccer teams', *European Sports Management Quarterly*, **5** (1), 23–46.

Cox, K. (1993), 'The local and the global in the new urban politics: A critical view', *Environment and Planning D: Society and Space*, **11** (4), 433–48.

Davis, L. (2015), 'Football fandom and authenticity: A critical discussion of historical and contemporary perspectives', *Soccer and Society*, **16** (2–3), 422–36.

Deloitte (2020), 'Deloitte football money league 2020: Eye on the prize', *Deloitte*, accessed 5 March 2020 at: www2.deloitte.com/uk/en/pages/sports-business-group/articles/deloitte-football-money-league.html.

Dinnie, K. (2008), *Nation Branding: Concepts, Issues, Practice*, Oxford: Butterworth-Heinemann.

Edensor, T. (2015), 'Producing atmospheres at the match: Fan cultures, commercialisation and mood management in English football', *Emotion, Space and Society*, **15**, 82–9.

Edensor, T. and S. Millington (2008), '"This is Our City": Branding football and local embeddedness', *Global Networks*, **8** (2), 172–93.

Edensor, T. and S. Millington (2010), 'Going to the match: The transformation of the match-day routine at Manchester City FC', in S. Frank and S. Steets (eds), *Stadium Worlds: Football, Space, and the Built Environment*, London: Routledge, pp. 146–62.

Eshuis, J. and A. Edwards (2013), 'Branding the city: The democratic legitimacy of a new mode of governance', *Urban Studies*, **50** (5), 1066–82.

Evans, D. and G. Norcliffe (2016), 'Local identities in a global game: The social production of football space in Liverpool', *Journal of Sport and Tourism*, **20** (3–4), 217–32.

Giovanardi, M. (2015), 'A multi-scalar approach to place branding: The 150th anniversary of Italian unification in Turin', *European Planning Studies*, **23** (3), 597–615.

Giulianotti, R. (1999), *Football: A Sociology of the Global Game*, Cambridge: Polity Press.

Giulianotti, R. (2002), 'Supporters, followers, fans, and flaneurs: A taxonomy of spectator identities in football', *Journal of Sport and Social Issues*, **26** (1), 25–46.

Giulianotti, R. and R. Robertson (2004), 'The globalization of football: A study in the glocalization of the "serious life"', *British Journal of Sociology*, **55** (4), 545–68.

Goffman, E. (1974), *Frame Analysis: An Essay on the Organization of Experience*, Cambridge, MA: Harvard University Press.

Gratton, C., Shibli, S., and R. Coleman (2005), 'Sport and economic regeneration in cities', *Urban Studies*, **42** (5–6), 985–99.

Guschwan, M. (2015), 'The football brand dilemma', *Soccer and Society*, **17** (3), 372–87.

Hague, E. and J. Mercer (1998), 'Geographical memory and urban identity in Scotland: Raith Rovers FC and Kirkcaldy', *Geography*, **83** (2), 105–16.

Hatch, M. and J. Rubin (2006), 'The hermeneutics of branding', *Brand Management*, **14** (1–2), 40–59.

Herstein, R. (2012), 'Thin line between country, city, and region branding', *Journal of Vacation Marketing*, **18** (2), 147–55.

Hinson, R., Osabutey, E., Kosiba, J., and F. Asiedu (2020), 'Internationalisation and branding strategy: A case of the English Premier League's success in an emerging market', *Qualitative Market Research: An International Journal*, https://doi.org/10.1108/QMR-12-2017-0188.

Holt, D. (2002), 'Why do brands cause trouble? A dialectical theory of consumer culture and branding', *Journal of Consumer Research*, **29** (1), 70–90.

Hoogenboom, M., Bannick, D., and W. Trommel (2010), 'From local to grobal, and back', *Business History*, **52** (6), 932–54.

Hubbard, P. (2019), 'Enthusiasm, craft, and authenticity on the High Street: Micropubs as "community fixers"', *Social and Cultural Geography*, **20** (6), 763–84.

Kavaratzis, M. and A. Kalandides (2015), 'Rethinking the place brand: The interactive formation of place brands and the role of participatory place branding', *Environment and Planning A*, **47** (6), 1368–82.

Kelly, P. (1999), 'The geographies and politics of globalization', *Progress in Human Geography*, **23** (3), 379–400.

Kornberger, M. and C. Carter (2010), 'Manufacturing competition: How accounting practices shape strategy making in cities', *Accounting, Auditing and Accountability Journal*, **23** (3), 325–49.

Lucarelli, A. (2018), 'Co-branding public place brands: Towards an alternative approach to place branding', *Place Branding and Public Diplomacy*, **14**, 260–71.

Lucarelli, A. and P. Berg (2011), 'City branding: A state-of-the-art review of the research domain', *Journal of Place Management and Development*, **4** (1), 9–27.

Lury, C. (2004), *Brands: The Logos of the Global Economy*, London: Routledge.

Manchester Evening News (2011), 'Manchester City announce deal to rename Eastlands as the Etihad Stadium', *Manchester Evening News*, 8 July, accessed 13 March 2020 at: www.manchestereveningnews.co.uk/news/greater-manchester-news/manchester -city-announce-deal-to-rename-1221094.

Marketing Week (2015), 'City Football Group's commercial director on growing the Man City brand globally', *Marketing Week*, accessed 13 March 2020 at: www .marketingweek.com/city-football-groups-commercial-director-on-growing-the -man-city-brand-globally.

Medway, D., Warnaby, G., Gillooly, L., and S. Millington (2019), 'Scalar tensions in urban toponymic inscription: The corporate (re)naming of football stadia', *Urban Geography*, **40** (6), 784–804.

Menary, S. (2018), 'Game on: The commercialisation and corruption of the pre-season friendly', *Soccer and Society*, **19** (2), 301–17.

Murray, C. (2001), *Making Sense of Place: New Approaches to Place Marketing*, Leicester: Comedia.

Ntounis, N. and E. Kanellopoulou (2017), 'Normalising jurisdictional heterotopias through place branding: The cases of Christiania and Metelkova', *Environment and Planning A*, **49** (10), 2223–40.

Ntounis, N. and M. Kavaratzis (2017), 'Re-branding the high street: The place branding process and reflections from three UK towns', *Journal of Place Management and Development*, **10** (4), 392–403.

Omholt, T. (2013), 'Developing a collective capacity for place management', *Journal of Place Management and Development*, **6** (1), 29–42.

Peck, J. and K. Ward (2002), *City of Revolution: Restructuring Manchester*, Manchester: Manchester University Press.

Pike, A. (2011), 'Placing brands and branding: A socio-spatial biography of Newcastle Brown Ale', *Transactions of the Institute of British Geographers*, **36** (2) 206–22.

Rantisi, N. and D. Leslie (2006), 'Branding the design metropole: The case of Montréal, Canada', *Area*, **38** (4), 364–76.

Relph, E. (1976), *Place and Placelessness*, London: Pion.

Richelieu, A. and M. Desbordes (2009), 'Football teams going international: The strategic leverage of branding', *Journal of Sponsorship*, **3** (1), 10–22.

Ritzer, G. (2007), *The Globalization of Nothing 2*, London: Sage.

Ritzer, G. and T. Stillman (2001), 'The postmodern ballpark as a leisure setting: Enchantment and simulated de-McDonaldization', *Leisure Studies*, **23** (2), 99–113.

Robertson, R. (1995), 'Glocalization: Time-space homogeneity-heterogeneity', in M. Featherstone, S. Lash and R. Robertson (eds), *Global Modernities*, London: Sage, pp. 25–44.

Rowe, D. (2003), 'Sport and the repudiation of the global', *International Review for the Sociology of Sport*, **38** (3), 281–94.

Scott, A. (2000), *The Cultural Economy of Cities*, London: Sage.

Séraphin, H., Zaman, M., Olver, S., Bourliataux-Lajoinie, S., and F. Dosquet (2019), 'Destination branding and overtourism', *Journal of Hospitality and Tourism Management*, **38** (4), 1–4.

Sjölander-Lindqvist, A., Skoglund, W., and D. Laven (2020), 'Craft beer: Building social terroir through connecting people, place, and business', *Journal of Place Management and Development*, **13** (2), 149–62.

Steadman, C., Roberts, G., Medway, D., Millington, S., and L. Platt (2020), '(Re)thinking place atmospheres in marketing theory', *Marketing Theory*, https://doi.org/10.1177/1470593120920344.

Tapp, A. and J. Clowes (2002), 'From "carefree casuals" to "professional wanderers": Segmentation possibilities for football supporters', *European Journal of Marketing*, **36** (11/12), 1248–69.

Thani, S. and T. Heenan (2017), 'The ball may be round but football is becoming increasingly Arabic: Oil money and the rise of the new football order', *Soccer and Society*, **18** (7), 1012–26.

The Guardian (2005), 'Football calls for help in selling the brand', *The Guardian*, 6 October, accessed 1 March 2020 at: www.theguardian.com/football/2005/oct/06/newsstory.sport11.

The Guardian (2020), 'Manchester City could face Premier League sanctions over FFP breaches', 15 February, accessed 14 April 2020 at: www.theguardian.com/football/2020/feb/15/manchester-city-premier-league-sanctions-ffp-breaches.

van den Berg, L., Braun, E., and A. Otgaar (2016), *Sports and City Marketing in European Cities*, London: Routledge.

Visit Britain (2015), 'Inbound football tourism research', *Visit Britain*, accessed 1 March 2020 at: www.visitbritain.org/inbound-football-tourism-research.

Visit Manchester (2020), 'Things to see and do', *Visit Manchester*, accessed 1 March 2020 at: www.visitmanchester.com/things-to-see-and-do.

Warnaby, G. and D. Medway (2013), 'What about the "place" in place marketing?', *Marketing Theory*, **13** (3), 345–63.

Zenker, S. (2011), 'How to catch a city? The concept and measurement of place brands', *Journal of Place Management and Development*, **4** (1), 40–52.

10 Sustainable Development Goals in place branding: Developing a research agenda

Anette Therkelsen, Laura James and Henrik Halkier

Introduction

Since the adoption of the 2030 Agenda for Sustainable Development by the United Nations (UN) member states in September 2015, the 17 Sustainable Development Goals (SDGs) have received significant attention from politicians, public institutions as well as private businesses. More specifically, national policies and local development plans have been formulated with reference to the SDGs, public institutions brand themselves as dedicated to the SDGs, and private companies are working to integrate the SDGs into their business development strategies. As a result, various aspects of sustainability are becoming associated with places, and place-ranking lists, such as the *Sustainable Development Report* (Sachs et al., 2019) and the *Global Destination Sustainability Index* (GDSI, 2020; Targeted News Service, 2017; McCartney and Leong, 2018), testify that meeting SDGs can provide a competitive edge for a place. Limited research attention has, however, been dedicated to the implications for place branding of these SDG-oriented practices. Given that such practices are anticipated to assume even greater importance as 2030 draws closer, scholarly investigation of the implications is required.

Research into place branding has undergone significant developments within the past three decades, which in many ways is a reflection of how place branding practices themselves have changed. First, problems inherent in the interplay between symbolic representation and physical/sociocultural placemaking have received increased research attention, and the significance of placemaking efforts has been highlighted (Jensen, 2007; Eckstein and

Throgmorton, 2003; Therkelsen and Halkier, 2010). As the SDGs are concerned with major challenges facing societies, change in a variety of social and economic practices will be needed. It is therefore important to study whether this is reflected in public authorities' approach to place branding, or whether efforts center on symbolic representation with little influence on wider policy and practice. This is underscored by a 2019 analysis (Sachs et al., 2019), which concludes that there is more rhetoric than action in UN nations' approach to the SDGs. A second development in place branding research concerns the difficulties in developing a place brand that appeals to multiple external and internal markets; i.e. competing for new market shares and at the same time maintaining place engagement and attachment among residents. In particular, local residents' involvement in place branding efforts has caught researchers' attention (Colomb and Kalandides, 2010; Jernsand and Kraff, 2015; Kavaratzis, 2012; Ren and Gyimóthy, 2013), which seems to fit well with an SDG-based approach, as sociocultural sustainability is one of its founding principles. This may, however, be in possible conflict with the needs and wishes of external target groups, and places need to find ways of combining competitive with more altruistic approaches to place branding. Third, and in many respects as a consequence of the other two research trajectories, place branding has developed from mainly a marketing discipline to span several research fields, including policy studies, human geography, planning and consumer studies (Hankinson, 2010; Kavaratzis, 2005; Therkelsen and Halkier, 2010).

Taking policy studies, human geography and consumer studies as its disciplinary starting points, this chapter argues that these three developments are critical to future research into SDG-related place branding. It will bring together the perspectives of public authority strategizing and consumer place consumption and, on the basis of this interdisciplinary perspective, identify SDG-related research agendas to be pursued in the future. We begin by expanding on reasons why place branding scholars need to pay attention to the UN SDGs by combining a historical perspective with present-day examples of SDG-related practices. The representation–placemaking conundrum and the multiple-market dilemma structure the following discussion, and the chapter concludes by summarizing the directions for future studies.

The United Nations Sustainable Development Goals: Origin and emerging practices

Since the 1972 Earth Summit, the UN has had global environmental and developmental needs among its main concerns (UNDP, 2020). Perhaps apart from the years following the publication of the Brundtland Report (Brundtland et al., 1987), it was not, however, until the adoption of the 17 SDGs in 2015 that sustainability issues were the subject of wider public attention and engagement. A central reason for this may be found in a shift towards a more global approach to sustainability, in that ambitions in relation to less economically developed countries, epitomized by the Millennium Development Goals, were supplemented by concerns pertaining to the whole world, in particular that of climate change. Indeed, it is arguably the integration of the climate issue into the SDGs that has struck a chord with the general public. This coincided with the escalating climate debate of the late 2010s – a debate fueled not least by visible climate changes and the Fridays For Future demonstrations that have spread across the globe (FridaysForFuture, 2020).

The influence of the 2030 Agenda for Sustainable Development on the practices of various actors and sectors is becoming increasingly visible. Consultants offer both companies and places advice on how to move towards the SDGs, with the explicit purpose of turning the goals into a competitive advantage for private firms (e.g. McKinsey and Company, 2019), or with more altruistic purposes of making cities and countries better places to live. An example of the latter is the *Sustainable Development Solutions Network* that, in cooperation with the German government, guides cities on how to turn SDG 11, *Sustainable cities and communities*, into practice (SDSN, 2020). Zooming further in on actors and sectors relevant in a place branding context, a UN World Tourism Organization report (2017) offers recommendations to tourism policy-makers and private tourism businesses based on SDG implementations in 64 countries. Of the points the report makes, it is worth highlighting two here: first, not all SDGs are equally important to all types of place actors – for the tourism sector *Decent work and economic growth* (SDG 8), *Responsible consumption and production* (SDG 12) and *Partnerships for the goals* (SDG 17) are identified as being most relevant. This may make partnerships for the goals across sectors difficult, and may obstruct place-wide processes for SDG implementation. Disintegrated national, regional or local policy-making may be the outcome of this, and the opportunities, including competitive ones, that umbrella place branding efforts may result in may be missed (Therkelsen and Halkier, 2008). Second, the report points out that for private tourism businesses competitiveness is the main driver of sustainability, however, there is a widespread lack of knowledge on how investment in sustainable business operations can increase competitiveness, and ultimately profitability.

The issue of competitiveness is likewise highly relevant for governments and other public bodies. Among nation states, for instance, a competitive agenda is present in the shape of ranking lists like the yearly *Sustainable Development*

Report (Sachs et al., 2019), which presents an SDG index and dashboard for all UN member states. The report concludes that politicians are not meeting the promises made in 2015, in that countries have mainly endorsed the SDGs in official statements but not in budget documents. In other words, there is a gap between rhetoric and action. The climate (SDG 13) and biodiversity (SDG 14 and 15) are singled out as the areas that require most attention.

All in all, a schism between competitive and altruistic purposes seems to exist when place actors engage with the SDGs: while private actors by definition must be concerned with the former, corporate social responsibility points towards the latter – and, paradoxically, the pursuance of multifaceted SDGs may generate a competitive race among public actors keen to boost their position in the 'altruistic places' league. If measures to address, for instance, urgent environmental problems are not somehow translated into profitability, this may have dire consequences for both private and public actors. The gap between rhetoric and action may also partly be a consequence of a lack of knowledge of how to use SDGs as a template for place development as well as business actions, and thereby turn SDGs into an advantage for the individual place and private firm. The discussion below will delve further into these two issues.

Sustainable Development Goals-based place branding: Between rhetoric and action

Relatively little research has examined the connections between place branding and sustainability (Maheshwari, Vandewalle and Bamber, 2011; Acharya and Rahman 2016), and those studies that do exist identify environmental sustainability as the main focus. In their recent review of the literature on sustainability and place branding, Taecharungroj, Muthuta and Boonchaiyapruek (2019), for example, found very few place branding initiatives based on a holistic understanding of sustainability, but report on several examples of places that have focused on the 'green' or 'environmental' dimension as the basis for their brand (e.g. Kalandides, 2011; Pant, 2005). The work of Joss (2015) and De Martin et al. (2015) on eco-cities and low carbon cities show that even when a relatively narrow environmental definition of sustainability is applied, a very large range of policies can form the basis of 'green' place brands. Given the fuzzy and contested nature of sustainability as a concept, it is likely that this will also be the case in relation to branding based on the SDGs. At the same time, the all-embracing and potentially conflicting nature of the goals implies that SDG-based place brands will inevitably have to be based on the selective prioritizing of some goals at the expense of others. With its focus on the tourism sector, the UN World Tourism Organization report (2017) underscores this observation, but also points to disintegrated place branding approaches that may be the outcome of having SDGs as a template for place branding efforts. Researching which SDGs will be integrated in place brands, for which reasons and with what outcomes are, in other words, important future research tasks.

The SDGs are concerned with global challenges that all societies face, and building a place brand around these comprehensive goals therefore implies changes in a wide range of place-related practices (Valencia et al., 2019). An important question for future research will therefore be how the introduction of SDG concerns will affect the relationship between symbolic representation and physical/cultural placemaking activities. The research literature has generally moved away from focusing on communication-centered place promotion towards more holistic approaches (Eckstein and Throgmorton, 2003; Jensen, 2007; Kavaratzis, 2004; Ma et al., 2019; Richards, 2017; Therkelsen, Halkier and Jensen, 2010), in which placemaking, e.g. around physical structures or cultural events, attempts to ensure a reasonable degree of concurrence between how a place is being presented communicatively and how it is being experienced by residents and external interests. Though such place branding efforts require significantly higher levels of long-term resource commitment, they also seem to be more successful (Maheshwari et al., 2011; Richards, 2017; Ma et al., 2019). Examples of such long-term commitment are, for instance, Vancouver's urban sustainability strategy 'Greenest City' (Affolderbach and Schulz, 2017; McCann, 2013; Scerri and Holden, 2014), Växjö's 'green' place brand based on energy, transport and housing policies (Andersson and James, 2018) and the sustainability branding of the Øresund region (Anderberg and Clark, 2013). These examples may be characterized by what McCann (2013) terms 'policy boosterism', which is 'the active promotion of locally developed and/or locally successful policies, programs, or practices across wider geographical fields as well as to broader communities of interested peers' (2013: 5). It has, however, been argued that there is a risk of 'cherry picking' policies that target easy-to-solve problems in order to generate 'quick wins' rather than long-term solutions (Andersson, 2016; Andersson and James, 2018; Valencia et al., 2019). That this may be the case in relation to SDG-related practices is underscored by the conclusions of the aforementioned *Sustainable Development Report* (Sachs et al., 2019). The relationship between communication and placemaking is hence a central issue with regard to SDG selectivity in the branding process, and this will require place branding researchers to draw on a wide range of disciplines in order to assess government claims of progress with regard to, for example, clean-tech systems, social inclusion and decent working conditions.

The multiple-market dilemma: Balancing competitive and altruistic appeals

As the preceding discussion has indicated, competing for new market shares through the creation of an attractive place brand, and at the same time maintaining place engagement and attachment among residents, is a particular challenge of SDG-based place branding. Broad stakeholder involvement is needed if the environmental and sociocultural sustainability issues facing societies are to be addressed, but at the same time, private firms and public authorities are concerned with profit and growth to ensure continued development and prosperity. Hence altruistic and competitive approaches and goals may compete and thereby complicate SDG-based place branding.

Research has demonstrated that commitment among residents to place branding efforts is both a prerequisite for maintaining local place attachment and for developing a successful brand towards external target groups (Hankinson, 2007; Kavaratzis and Ashworth, 2005). For this reason, place development and branding efforts that take their starting point in the resources of the place – its natural and cultural resources and not least the practices, demands and perceptual universe of its residents – stand a better chance of becoming effective and viable (Colomb and Kalandides, 2010; Jernsand and Kraff, 2015; Kavaratzis, 2012). Engagement in climate issues, not least among younger generations, points towards populations that are keen on becoming involved. Experiments with citizen involvement in, for instance, neighborhood development initiatives in socially disadvantaged urban areas (Frantzeskaki, Steenbergen and Stedman, 2018; Magnussen, Dalby and Stensgaard, 2019) demonstrate that high levels of motivation and a renewed sense of place can be achieved among citizens when a participatory approach to place development is chosen. Such experiments, characterized by mixed agency between place branding organizations and residents, may be useful when trying to engage individual residents and whole communities in SDG-based place branding efforts. However, this simultaneously opens up numerous complications; for instance, regarding who is to represent the local perspective, how local participation may be orchestrated and how, simultaneously, to ensure brand appeal to external target groups. This calls for further scrutiny.

What makes place branding efforts meaningful to residents may also be a reflection of the type of location they inhabit. Urban and rural places, as well as countries situated in different parts of the world, face different sustainability challenges and have different resources available to address them. This is likely to influence residents' engagement. Moreover, events disrupting the everyday lives of people in given places at given points in time and which, rightly or wrongly, are ascribed to climate change, may influence citizens' engagement in sustainability initiatives. The massive forest and bush fires in Australia in 2019–20 and the repeated flooding of residential areas in Central and Northern Europe in recent years are just two examples of such disruptive events that have escalated the climate change debate and popular call for action. Comparative studies across locations and events could significantly increase our insight into these matters.

Citizen engagement in sustainability issues is predominantly based on altruistic arguments, such as wanting to save the flora and fauna of the earth, creating a better place to live free of pollution and ensuring the future of our children. These may, however, clash with private efforts and public policies concerned with 'quick wins' rather than long-term solutions (Andersson, 2016; Andersson and James, 2018; Valencia et al., 2019) in that competitive advantages towards attractive markets may overrule 'doing good'. Inter-place competition built around pre-SDG sustainability has been around for several years (Affolderbach and Schulz, 2017; Andersson and James, 2018) and has been supported by a number of instruments to measure such competition. For instance, the *Anholt Ipsos Nation Brands Index* includes '(p)ublic opinion about national government competency and fairness, as well as its perceived commitment to global issues such as peace and security, justice, poverty and the environment' (Ipsos Public Affairs, 2019: 1), reflecting the current salience of sustainability as a dimension of place brands. An example of more specialized indices is the *Global Destination Sustainability Index* (Targeted News Service, 2017; McCartney and Leong, 2018), which has instituted a ranking system that functions as a voluntary third-party certification (Cidell, 2015) for tourist destinations, and thereby creating new 'ritualistic features' (Cassinger and Eksell, 2017) of place branding through standardized reporting of sustainability indicators and publicity rituals associated with the announcement of annual rankings. Along these lines, the UN has implemented an SDG index and dashboard which on a yearly basis measures the progress of all UN nations on the 17 SDG goals and 232 indicators (Sachs et al., 2019). This could be seen as a very extensive checklist through which individual places can compare themselves to their peers in terms of progress with regard to sustainable development. The rise of sustainability indexing has not only potential implications for place branding practices in localities across the globe, but also affects the associated research agenda. Understanding how the indices are designed in terms of goals included or excluded and indicators chosen will obviously be important, but so will the ways in which these rankings become part of the local branding process through stakeholder interaction. This will potentially influence the balance between communicative and placemaking activities.

Conclusion

This chapter has identified several future research avenues within the area of SDG-based place branding. So far, the UN SDGs seem mainly to have left a mark on the rhetorical strategies of cities and countries, and it remains to be seen how the SDGs will influence place development practices across the world in future. Quick wins versus long-term solutions will be one of the issues that researchers need to examine further, and to that end a cross-disciplinary approach is needed in order to assess whether viable solutions to pressing environmental and sociocultural issues are being implemented. In relation to this, the attention of place branding researchers should be directed at the relationship between symbolic representation and physical/cultural placemaking, and whether and how such activities mutually support each other. This should help determine the significance and strength of a given place branding campaign both in relation to internal and external markets.

Future research also needs to pay attention to SDGs and place branding in relation to different sectors, locations, suppliers and target groups. The all-embracing nature of the goals may be able to accommodate the multitude of interests of various stakeholders related to a given place and form the basis for a collective long-term effort towards a common goal. Analyses, however, indicate that selective prioritizing of some goals at the expense of others by public authorities leads to piecemeal place branding approaches where some stakeholders and sectors are left without influence. Thus, what appears to be a framework that could accommodate all interests may not be able to solve stakeholder battles over influence. These are intriguing questions to examine further.

The chapter has also highlighted how the multiple-market dilemma of place branding may play out in the context of an SDG-based effort. Though a participatory approach in terms of resident involvement goes hand in hand with sociocultural sustainability and recognizes that residents occupy a double role as both stakeholders constituting/contributing to the place and as target groups for branding efforts, external markets cannot be neglected. The ability to balance sometimes conflicting market interests is a pressing issue in all place branding efforts, however, it may be accentuated in SDG-based place branding as it seems to be the fundamental preconditions for people's lives that are at stake here, i.e. biodiversity and stable natural conditions, a healthy living environment and the future of our children. Such altruistic engagements and arguments demand long-term solutions, but this may clash with more competitive mindsets of private and public stakeholders, who may favor short-term solutions to ensure a position in the inter-place competitive game. Future case studies will determine the validity of such hypotheses, just as they need to consider the demands of external markets, a proportion of which in time become internal markets (i.e. residents) with long-term interests.

All in all, plenty of opportunities and dilemmas present themselves in the context of SDG-based place branding. These are in need of further analysis on the basis of case material, just as cooperation with practitioners may facilitate the development of practical solutions to some of the potential difficulties in SDG-based place branding efforts.

References

Acharya, A. and Z. Rahman (2016), 'Place branding research: A thematic review and future research agenda', *International Review on Public and Nonprofit Marketing*, **13** (3), 289–317.

Affolderbach, J. and C. Schulz (2017), 'Positioning Vancouver through urban sustainability strategies? The Greenest City 2020 Action Plan', *Journal of Cleaner Production*, **164**, 676–85.

Anderberg, S. and E. Clark (2013), 'Green sustainable Øresund region: Or eco-branding Copenhagen and Malmö?', in I. Vojnovic (ed.), *Urban Sustainability: A Global Perspective*, East Lansing, MI: Michigan State University Press, pp. 591–610.

Andersson, I. (2016), '"Green cities" going greener? Local environmental policy-making and place branding in the "Greenest City in Europe"', *European Planning Studies*, **24** (6), 1197–215.

Andersson, I. and L. James (2018), 'Altruism or entrepreneurialism? The co-evolution of green place branding and policy tourism in Växjö, Sweden', *Urban Studies*, **55** (15), 3437–53.

Brundtland, G. H., Khalid, M., Agnelli, S., Al-Athel, S. and B. Chidzero (1987), *Our Common Future*, New York: United Nations.

Cassinger, C. and J. Eksell (2017), 'The magic of place branding: Regional brand identity in transition', *Journal of Place Management and Development*, **10** (3), 202–12.

Cidell, J. (2015), 'Performing leadership: Municipal green building policies and the city as role model', *Environment and Planning C: Government and Policy*, **33**, 1–14.

Colomb, C. and A. Kalandides (2010), 'The "be Berlin" campaign: Old wine in new bottles or innovative form of participatory place branding?', in G. J. Ashworth and M. Kavaratzis (eds), *Towards Effective Place Brand Management: Branding European*

Cities and Regions, Cheltenham, UK and Northampton, MA, USA: Edward Elgar Publishing, pp. 173–90.

De Martin, J., Joss, S., Schraven, D., Zhan, C. and W. Margot (2015), 'Sustainable-smart -resilient-low-carbon-eco-knowledge cities; making sense of a multitude of concepts promoting sustainable urbanization', *Journal of Cleaner Production*, **109**, 25–38.

Eckstein, B. and J. A. Throgmorton (eds) (2003), *Story and Sustainability: Planning, Practice and Possibility for American Cities*, Cambridge, MA: MIT Press.

Frantzeskaki, N., Steenbergen, F. and R. C. Stedman (2018), 'Sense of place and exper-imentation in urban sustainability transitions: The Resilience Lab in Carnisse, Rotterdam, The Netherlands', *Sustainability Science*, **13**, 1045–59.

FridaysForFuture (2020), www.fridaysforfuture.org, accessed 20 February 2020.

GDSI (2020), Global Destination Sustainability Index, www.gds-index.com/destinations/explore/index/2019.

Hankinson, G. (2007), 'The management of destination brands: Five guiding principles based on recent developments in corporate branding theory', *Brand Management*, **14** (3), 240–54.

Ipsos Public Affairs (2019), *Anholt Ipsos Nation Brands Index NBI*, Paris: Ipsos Public Affairs, pp. 1–4.

Hankinson, G. (2010), 'Place branding research: A cross-disciplinary agenda and the views of practitioners', *Place Branding and Public Diplomacy*, **6** (4), 300–15.

Jensen, O. B. (2007), 'Culture stories: Understanding cultural urban branding', *Planning Theory*, **6** (3), 211–36.

Jernsand, E. M. and H. Kraff (2015), 'Participatory place branding through design: The case of Dunga beach in Kinsumu, Kenya', *Place Branding and Public Diplomacy*, **11** (3), 226–42.

Joss, S. (2015), 'Eco-cities and sustainable urbanism', in W. D. James (ed.), *International Encyclopedia of the Social and Behavioral Sciences*, 2nd edition, London: Elsevier, pp. 829–37.

Kalandides, A. (2011), 'City marketing for Bogotá: A case study in integrated place branding', *Journal of Place Management and Development*, **4** (3), 282–91.

Kavaratzis, M. (2004), 'From city marketing to city branding: Towards a theoretical framework for developing city brands', *Place Branding*, **1** (1), 58–73.

Kavaratzis, M. (2005), 'Place branding: A review of trends and conceptual models', *The Marketing Review*, **5** (4), 329–42.

Kavaratzis, M. (2012), 'From "necessary evil" to necessity: Stakeholders involvement in place branding', *Journal of Place Management and Development*, **5** (1), 7–19.

Kavaratzis, M. and G. J. Ashworth (2005), 'City branding: An effective assertion of identity or a transitory marketing trick?', *Tijdschrift Voor Economische En Sociale Geografie*, **96** (5), 506–14.

Ma, W., Schraven, D., de Bruijne, M., de Jong, M. and H. Lu (2019), 'Tracing the origins of place branding research: A bibliometric study of concepts in use (1980–2018)', *Sustainability*, **11** (11), 1–20.

Magnussen, R., Dalby, H. V. and G. A. Stensgaard (2019), 'Education for co-production of community-driven knowledge', *Electronic Journal of e-Learning*, **17** (3), 222–33.

Maheshwari, V., Vandewalle, I. and D. Bamber (2011), 'Place branding's role in sustain-able development', *Journal of Place Management and Development*, **4** (2), 198–213.

McCann, E. (2013), 'Policy boosterism, policy mobilities, and the extrospective city', *Urban Geography*, **34** (1), 5–29.

McCartney, G. and V. M. W. Leong (2018), 'An examination of the impact of green impressions by delegates toward a trade show', *Journal of Convention and Event Tourism*, **19** (1), 25–43.

McKinsey and Company (2019), *SDG Guide for Business Leaders: A Practical Guide for Business Leaders to Working with the SDGs as a Competitive Factor*, https://vl.dk/wp-content/uploads/2019/06/20190612-SDG-Guide-full-version.pdf.

Pant, D. R. (2005), 'A place brand strategy for the Republic of Armenia: "Quality of context" and "sustainability" as competitive advantage', *Place Branding and Public Diplomacy*, **1** (3), 273–82.

Ren, C. and S. Gyimóthy (2013), 'Transforming and contesting nation branding strategies: Denmark at the Expo 2010', *Place Branding and Public Diplomacy*, **9** (1), 17–29.

Richards, G. (2017), 'From place branding to placemaking: The role of events', *International Journal of Event and Festival Management*, **8** (1), 8–23.

Sachs, J., Schmidt-Traub, G., Kroll, C., Lafortune, G. and G. Fuller (2019), *Sustainable Development Report 2019*, New York: Bertelsmann Stiftung and Sustainable Development Solutions Network, https://sdgindex.org.

Scerri, A. and M. Holden (2014), 'Ecological modernization or sustainable development? Vancouver's Greenest City Action Plan: The city as "manager" of ecological restructuring', *Journal of Environmental Policy and Planning*, **16** (2), 261–79.

Sustainable Development Solutions Network (SDSN) (2020), *Getting Started with the SDGS in Cities: A Guide to Local Stakeholders*, https://sdgcities.guide.

Taecharungroj, V., Muthuta, M. and P. Boonchaiyapruek (2019), 'Sustainability as a place brand position: A resident-centric analysis of the ten towns in the vicinity of Bangkok', *Place Branding and Public Diplomacy*, **15** (4), 210–28.

Targeted News Service (2017), 'Global Destination Sustainability Index releases first ever city ranking', *The Association Magazine*, accessed 6 July 2020 at: www.meetingmediagroup.com/article/global-destination-sustainability-index-releases-first-ever-city-ranking.

Therkelsen, A. and H. Halkier (2008), 'Contemplating place branding umbrellas: The case of coordinated national tourism and business promotion in Denmark', *Scandinavian Journal of Hospitality and Tourism*, **8** (2), 159–75.

Therkelsen, A. and H. Halkier (2010), 'Branding provincial cities: The politics of inclusion, strategy and commitment', in A. Pike (ed.), *Brands and Branding Geographies*, Cheltenham, UK and Northampton, MA, USA: Edward Elgar Publishing, pp. 200–12.

Therkelsen, A., Halkier, H. and O. B. Jensen (2010), 'Branding Aalborg: Building community or selling place?', in G. Ashworth and M. Kavaratzis (eds), *Towards Effective Place Brand Management: Branding European Cities and Regions*, Cheltenham, UK and Northampton, MA, USA: Edward Elgar Publishing, pp. 136–55.

United Nations Development Programme (UNDP) (2020), *Sustainable Development Goals: Background on the Goals*, accessed 6 July 2020 at: www.undp.org/content/undp/en/home/sustainable-development-goals/background.html.

United Nations World Tourism Organization (2017), *Tourism and the Sustainable Development Goals: Journey to 2030 – Highlights*, file://id.aau.dk/Users/at/Documents/SDG%20&%20tourism/UNWTO%20report%20on%20SDG.pdf.

Valencia, S. C., Simon, D., Croese, S., Nordqvist, J., Oloko, M., Sharma, T., Buck, N. T. and I. Versace (2019), 'Adapting the Sustainable Development Goals and the New Urban Agenda to the city level: Initial reflections from a comparative research project', *International Journal of Urban Sustainable Development*, **11** (1), 4–23.

11 Keeping pace with the digital transformation of place

Brendan James Keegan

Introduction

Digital platforms are increasingly important in modern life, offering unprecedented access to information and services at a rapid pace. Such interactions produce significant amounts of data which are utilized for purposes of interest, by both the owners and users of such platforms. These data establish fertile ground for understanding human behaviour through empirical study. Accordingly, scholars have shown interest in the digitalization of place branding practices (Sevin, 2014; Hanna and Rowley, 2015; Kim et al., 2017; Uşaklı, Koç and Sönmez, 2017; Breek et al., 2018), and there have been notable attempts to offer critical commentaries on the complexities arising from the practice of digital adoption (e.g. Oliveira and Panyik, 2015). Whilst such studies present a viable picture of digital transformation through numerous case studies *in situ* and impressionistic reflections, there is a distinct requirement to establish a holistic view of the phenomenon.

Systematic literature reviews are useful tools for keeping pace with popular trends in disparate disciplines (Tranfield, Denyer and Smart, 2003). One of the benefits of systematic reviews is the ability to illustrate trends and patterns in empirical interrogations and conceptualizations of topics, and this approach is popular with place branding scholars (Jones and Kubacki, 2014; Acharya and Rahman, 2016; Cleave and Arku, 2017; Boisen et al., 2018). However, reviews such as these have disadvantages, particularly with their methodological application. Webster and Watson (2002) suggest the use of exclusion protocols to ensure clarity in the focus of reviews. Consequently, systematic reviews of place branding research employ limiting exclusion policies which only permit publications from marketing journals (e.g. Vuignier, 2016; Cleave and Arku, 2017). For example, Jones and Kubacki's (2014) review narrowed their selection of relevant articles to the fields of business, branding and tourism to examine the impact of social issues on place branding. With exclusion policies being commonplace in application, they equate to a knowledge conundrum in place branding whereby sources in disciplines such as geography and architecture can be overlooked. Additionally, systematic reviews can sometimes draw their conclusions from a quite small number of papers, which is understandable for niche topics, but runs the risk of narrative bias. Cleave and Arku (2017), for example, used 39 sources for their review of the influence of place branding from a geographic perspective.

Hence, this chapter seeks to offer a broader view of the relationship between digital transformation of place branding by clustering together a flotilla of work from a range of disciplines using the lens of place management. In doing so, a trifecta of place management frames the systematic literature review, namely, place marketing, placemaking and place maintenance. As a result, a better understanding of the impact of digital transformation of place branding is produced which may be of value to researchers and practitioners alike. After reflecting on the range of studies thematically, notable gaps are identified which the chapter encapsulates in a further research agenda. Three new potential avenues for future research are suggested; specifically, the use of artificial intelligence and machine learning operations in understanding a wider array of user interactions with places, digital automation processes supporting users' experiences of places and the use of sentiment analysis to compliment place management strategies.

The chapter continues with an overview of definitions and concepts used, followed by an overview of the methodology used in the systematic collection and review of studies that consider digital transformation in place branding. Then, a commentary on notable trends and knowledge gaps in this body of research is made through the place management lens. Following this, a future research agenda is provided, building upon prior gaps identified. The chapter concludes by arguing that future place branding scholars may consider the place management trifecta as a guide to their investigative endeavours.

Definitions and concepts

To perform any commentary on place branding, it is worth addressing definitional perplexity. Skinner (2008) points out the issues surrounding the use of place branding as an umbrella term and its relation with the marketing of places. She provides a useful argument by positing the subtle nuances of place branding and the relationship between place promotion activities and the management of places. Hence, it is not a new (let alone unworthy) endeavour to try to provide an alternative viewpoint of place branding as this chapter hopes to do. By unpicking the component parts of concepts, it may be possible to learn more about its capabilities and future potential.

To navigate the murky waters of the place branding identity debate (Warnaby and Medway, 2013), the chapter gladly adopts Parker's (2008: 5) mantra that place management strives to 'make places better'. Hence, instead of seeking to add fuel to the definitional place branding merry-go-round, this chapter adopts three facets of place management (marketing, making and maintenance) which are relevant to digital transformation to frame the systematic literature review. In so doing, the resultant trifecta establishes a viable lens to make sense of the body of work in this field as well as guide a further research agenda. Let me next clarify each facet of the trifecta.

By place marketing, I refer to the activities involved in the promotion of places, which of course involves branding as well as other marketing functions. For brevity's sake, Skinner (2008) attests to the concept of place marketing as a place management function, enacted through an outside-in approach by multiple stakeholders, whereas place branding privileges the marketing communications domain through an inside-out approach. As both the marketing and branding of places are of importance, the rest of the discussion will adopt place branding as a composite of both sides of the debate, as digital transformation has influenced both the management and promotional functions of place management.

Making places or placemaking indicates activities taken by users in the enhancement of places, transforming them into more liveable spatial entities. Paulsen (2010) suggests that the goal of placemaking is to create a space that is useful and meaningful. Typically, this type of strategy would involve the input of planners, residents, etc. to influence the dimensions of places. In turning our attention to the digital sphere, online communities are rapidly becoming important platforms for debate relating to places (Breek et al., 2018); hence, there is potential to consider the influence of digital technologies and channels in modern-day placemaking (Fredericks et al., 2015).

The final element of the trifecta is place maintenance, which represents ongoing curation activities by stakeholders who already interact with that place. Benson and Jackson (2013) distinguish place maintenance from placemaking, claiming the former is a process of ensuring longevity of places through ongoing action. There are obvious links here to Graham and Thrift's

(2007) notion of maintenance and repair work to maintain distinct assemblages and spatialities. Arguably, the mundane and quotidian nature of much maintenance work lacks the allure of innovative placemaking initiatives, yet it is equally as important to place management (e.g. Denis and Pontille, 2014). For example, Memmott (1980) considered the role of place maintenance and its contribution to placefulness through an ethnographic study of aboriginal cultural practices which offers us a user grounding for understanding this concept: 'In classical Aboriginal cultures examples [of place maintenance] included burning areas of country, cleaning plant growth from sacred sites, seasonal rebuilding of villages and camps, sweeping domiciliary spaces and replenishing rock art ochres. The various forces listed above, imbue stability to place character' (Memmott, 1980: 498). It is certainly the case that digital platforms can play a role in supporting the organization and implementation of place maintenance, as this systematic review will show.

To summarize, the trifecta of place management presents three facets which are important in their own right, yet also have interlinked associations. Place marketing has strong connections with placemaking, and vice versa. Place maintenance activities can also underpin the other two facets. For this chapter, therefore, these three facets will be treated as individual, yet interdependent, guiding categories for the purposes of the systematic review.

Lastly, in this chapter I refer to digital transformation as the use of 'platforms' in conjunction with the place management trifecta. An often used piece of jargon in IT and digital communications fields, 'platforms' refers to media communication destinations such as websites, email, mobile, search engines, etc.; essentially, any digital destination that can be used to communicate with stakeholders and customers. Digital platforms are commonly used by place branding organizations for the purposes of the trifecta. Indicative platforms are listed in Table 11.1 with notable examples.

Table 11.1   Digital transformation platforms in place management

Facet	Digital platforms	Example
Place marketing and branding	Websites, Search engines, Social media, Video, Mobile applications, Email, VR	Destination websites
Place making	Social media, Blogs, Mobile applications	Localised Facebook groups
Place maintenance	Digital-physical automated devices	Shotstopper

The next section of the chapter will provide an overview of the systematic collection and analysis of studies that incorporate digital transformation in place branding through the place management trifecta, culminating in a broad view of the discipline. As a result, the alignment of these studies allows for thematic clustering and identification of patterns and notable gaps.

Systematically reviewing digital transformation in place branding literature

A systematic literature review was performed to identify previous studies which have reported findings or theorized upon the utilization of digital platforms and their role within a place marketing/branding context. This operation involved the identification of search strings such as in the following example:

"Digital" AND "Place*" Branding OR Marketing...

Subsequently, these strings were applied using a combination of databases through Harzing's *Publish or Perish* which indexes *Google Scholar*, *Crossref* and *Web of Science*.

For the first round of searches, 2,242 results were returned with many erroneous responses, and these were exported to a .csv Excel file format and were prepared for sorting, using pivot table operations. Initial screening removed a large volume of results that were not relevant to the search strings. In all, 771 sources showed the terms digital with some affiliation to place within the title, abstract, keywords and main body of the sources provided. The next stage performed the first cleaning of the dataset to remove erroneous or non-relevant results, such as branding articles not within a place context. Exclusion factors were then applied to omit duplicate sources, incorrect citations and non-cognate results (for example, the term digital rights management featured in the initial results due to the search string, yet had no connection to place branding). Next, the results were obtained through direct download into the Mendeley reference manager. At this juncture, 331 results were deemed to be appropriate based on title and abstract screening and were prepared for further analysis.

In terms of disciplines, it was not surprising that marketing, geography, economics, management and tourism featured. However, unexpected domains also emerged. In particular, the video gaming industry provided commentary on digital space and place, and its component constructs (Boellstorff, 2019), which is useful for our understanding of digital placemaking. Other serendipitous results emerged from architectural studies featured in the results by way of insights relating to digital installations and their role in the transformation of spaces and places (Chousein, 2016; Hespanhol et al., 2017). An overview of results can be found in Table 11.2.[1]

Table 11.2   Digital research in place marketing, making and maintenance

	No. of results	Most common publication sources
Place marketing	252	*Place Branding and Public Diplomacy* (26), *Journal of Place Management and Development* (14), *Rethinking Place Branding* (6)
Placemaking	54	*Journal of Place Management and Development* (5), *Place Branding and Public Diplomacy* (5)
Place maintenance	12	*Urban Forestry and Urban Greening* (1), *Cities and Health, Urban Affairs Review* (1), *Sustainability* (1)

Digital transformation of place marketing

The dataset indicates that digital transformation of place branding has had the most impact upon marketing. Understandably so, as the primary focus is to convey an image of a place to an audience, digital communication methods can play a role. A number of themes within this sub-set of the dataset were identified; in particular, the reliance on social media as the most commonly used platform for investigations. The dataset indicates a prevalence of place branding studies focusing on social media, through the use of Facebook and Twitter (Ntalianis et al., 2015; Kim et al., 2017; Barcelos, Dantas and Sénécal, 2019; Ebrahimi, Hajmohammadi and Khajeheian, 2019). Furthermore, a common trend identified from empirical studies in this facet is the analysis of openly available social media data to understanding the outcomes of place marketing (e.g. Petrikova, Jaššo and Hajduk, 2020).

One such example is del Mar Gálvez-Rodríguez et al. (2020), who examined varying dimensions of Facebook posts used by destination marketing organizations and analysed social media destination pages over a six-year data collection period. Their findings offer valuable insights into the types of social media posts that outperform others. Furthermore, sentiment analysis of social media data is used to evaluate attitudinal interpretations through vast swathes of content (Micu et al., 2017), which will feature later in this chapter's future research agenda. Previously, scholars did not offer such depth in their interpretive analysis of digital transformation in place marketing, favouring retrospective examination of the performance of social media in place marketing scenarios (Lazaridou, Vrana and Paschaloudis, 2017; Uşaklı et al., 2017; Taneja and Bala, 2019). For instance, Molinillo et al. (2019) claim to investigate the engagement of citizens, but refer to the notion of social media engagement (propensity to like, comment and share); offering little in terms of users' impressions of smart city communication. This highlights an important knowledge gap, whereby only limited studies examine the wider impact of the digital transformation of place marketing amongst a wider range of stakeholders than social media users (Hanna and Rowley, 2015; Cleave et al., 2017; Breek et al., 2018).

It is also noteworthy that very few studies in this section of the dataset consider the impact of destination websites and search engine ranking performance for place marketing (Míguez González, 2011; Fernandez-Cavia et al., 2013). Arguably, these two fundamental digital platforms (websites and search engines) are central to most digital marketing campaigns, yet place branding scholars seem to have overlooked them. Perhaps this is due to the easier access to openly available social media data such as Facebook comments versus performing an in-depth assessment of search engine ranking performance, or website traffic.

Notably, a cursory glance over the dataset suggests an overtly positive tone to research that considers the digital transformation of place marketing, which begs the question why are the disadvantages, issues and challenges involved in digital transformation not covered to any great extent? Critical reflections are presented, whereby a place marketing initiative has not been successful (Pareja-Eastaway, Chapain and Mugano, 2013; Oliveira and Panyik, 2015; Lupo, 2018; Kompaniets and Rauhut, 2019). However, recent debates around user privacy would suggest that a blithe view of the benefits of digital transformation is ill advised. Further work in this area would be welcomed, not least for its potential to enhance place marketing practice.

Digital placemaking

The next facet represents an emergent area in practice, yet research is slow to keep pace with developments. Indeed, the term 'digital placemaking' frequently appears in the results (Govers, Kaefer and Ferrer-Roca, 2017; Breek et al., 2018; Vallicelli, 2018; Nisi, Prandi and Nunes, 2020), yet, oddly, remains undefined within academic works. Numerous interpretations of digital placemaking are available, predominantly within the commercial sectors of architecture (e.g. Digital Placemaking Institute, 2020), planning (e.g. Bristol and Bath Creative Research and Design, 2020) and digital design (e.g. Chousein, 2016). Calvium has published numerous articles on the topic of digital placemaking and considers it to be 'the augmentation of physical places with location-specific digital services, products or experiences to create more attractive destinations for all' (Calvium, 2018).

From this perspective, an overtly positive viewpoint of the potential of digital technology in the enhancement of spaces and places is provided. Encouragingly, this indicates a niche and emerging area where a range of interested parties are thinking about the digital transformation of placemaking. However, I would offer the suggestion that digital placemaking offers the opportunity to equally detract from spaces and places, and that future studies would remain objective as to the shiny allure of digital transformation and remain grounded in their approaches to investigating this topic.

Usage of digital technology in support of efficient interaction by way of smart city applications dominates the digital placemaking facet (e.g. Koeck and Warnaby, 2014; de Noronha, Coca-Stefaniak and Morrison, 2017; Nisi et al., 2020). However, the predominant focus is on the outcomes and results of a smart city implementation, whereas very few works explore digital placemaking strategies in detail (e.g. Aurigi, Willis and Melgaco, 2016; Wang, 2019). In other words, the 'traditional' smart city perspective of digital placemaking is the 'use of digital technology within a dedicated public urban space to specifically communicate with the public' (Anon, 2016: p. 1); whereas an emerging stream of studies in this facet identifies examples of strategic digital placemaking initiatives (e.g. Fredericks et al., 2018), which extends far beyond a unidirectional information dissemination to more inclusive placemaking. Furthermore, one wonders whether the focus on the notion of 'smart' is appropriate in such cases. What does smart mean in these instances? It would certainly be considered smart by large corporations to obtain vast amounts of user data for marketing research purposes, under the guise of a smart city application. Yet recent high-profile cases of data privacy issues and nefarious activities in election campaigns have tarnished the public perception of open exchanges of user data to third parties (Bright, Wilcox and Rodriguez, 2019). Therefore, this chapter proposes a shift away from the traditional smart city notion, towards more inclusive placemaking which is supported by digital platforms.

Digital place maintenance

The third and final area identified in the systematic literature review was the identification of studies that examined the notion of place maintenance. As mentioned previously, there are elements of place maintenance which have strong associations with the other two facets of the place management trifecta. However, the systematic review has also identified a small body of studies in this area that hone in on efforts by community stakeholders to engage in ongoing efforts to improve spaces and places (Benson and Jackson, 2013). As such, this final facet represents an important distinction between placemaking and marketing, which can be viewed as activities that are enacted in the pursuit of drawing attention to places.

Notably, there was some difficulty in obtaining results, due to the nature of the keywords used, which tended to conflict with the phrase 'in-place' and 'maintenance'. Hence, alternative keywords were adopted which yielded better results, e.g. 'place' AND 'management'. As a result of this revised search protocol, four key areas were identified in the literature obtained whereby digital transformation featured, namely *crime*, *pollution*, *mobility* and *general upkeep*.

Crime featured as a significant focus for place maintenance. Works by Eck and Madensen identify that such facets of place management can feature reducing crimes such as drug dealing and violence in bars (Madensen and Eck, 2003). Whilst their early works seem to assert the role of place maintenance, only recently has digital transformation featured in this endeavour, presenting an interesting future area for investigation (Eck and Madensen-Herold, 2018). For example, our ShotSpotter exemplar used in Table 11.1 is particularly relevant here, in which a digital gunfire detection system uses acoustic sensors to isolate the sound of gunfire and alert the police. The sensors are placed at a 30 foot elevation under a mile apart. When shots are fired anywhere in the coverage area, ShotSpotter triangulates their location to within 10 feet and reports the activity to police. In effect we see digital management and transformation of place through a place maintenance function.

Another area of place maintenance identified was the application of digital technology to tackle the issue of noise pollution (Carson et al., 2020). Equally, Dempsey and Burton's (2012) work looked at management practices of urban spaces through the use of digital platforms, culminating in the idea of 'place-keeping', i.e. long-term management activities after placemaking activities have occurred. More recently, Faraji and Nozar (2019) promoted a smart parking programme using magnetic sensors pointing to a central digital display platform with the aim of addressing air pollution. And, sentiment analysis of social media data proposed by Sdoukopoulos et al. (2018) identifies indicators for sustainable urban mobility (e.g. cleanliness, air quality, congestion, public transport affordability). By examining residents' opinions and sentiments expressed on social media platforms, planning decisions in mobility would be supported through such place maintenance indicators (e.g. perception of emissions and air quality for cyclists).

Lastly, the benefits and challenges of urban area upkeep were identified by Nam and Dempsey (2019), who assert the value of nature-based interventions in enhancing users' health and wellbeing. They argue that user needs are addressed through place maintenance processes and one particularly important notion is the idea of 'Friends of' groups on Facebook. Whilst these types of groups are commonplace in placemaking terms, there is a subtle differentiation here whereby the ongoing maintenance of places, such as continued upkeep of parks by collection of litter, imbues a sense of place and belonging by the members (Parker, Roper and Medway, 2015). Usage of social media in this manner is only notionally discussed by the authors, yet offers a lucrative avenue for further research. Yet, it is clear that digital transformation has played a role in the efforts of communities to engage in place maintenance activities and hence a contribution to this theme is evident, despite the lower numbers of studies involved.

Future research agenda

The chapter has adopted a place management lens to reflect upon digital transformation in place branding research. Each of the three facets involved represents a valuable contribution to our understanding of place management. However, the review also highlights unanswered questions that remain in each facet, before proposing three key areas which have been overlooked.

Harnessing the Trifecta

Not surprisingly, place marketing studies were the most common within the dataset. However, very few holistic studies consider the viewpoints of the communities who are influenced by such activities. The majority of studies in this area focus on the individuals responsible for marketing or branding activities, whilst overlooking the community members and vice versa. However, future studies might incorporate both the community view (from the wide-scale collection of social media data) as well as the outcomes of place marketing activities (digital ticket sales, destination website traffic, search engine keyword popularity, footfall traffic, etc.).

The chapter also supports the notion that digital placemaking research is an emergent area of interest and practice, and more studies are welcome here. Given the extremely difficult conditions imposed on daily life by the Covid-19 virus, more research into placemaking initiatives which use digital platforms to recreate the lived experience would be useful for the future. Place maintenance had the fewest results from the systematic review and therefore much more could be done to understand how digital transformation might play a role in assisting this facet, by considering how community projects are using digital platforms to raise awareness of and facilitate their activities.

It is also worth considering the inter-relationships between the trifecta. Notably, some studies identified by this review aimed to perform a case study of place branding, however, they also enhance our knowledge of placemaking and maintenance at the same time (e.g. Cleave et al., 2017; Breek et al., 2018; Källström and Hultman, 2019). Likewise, the processes involved with placemaking can certainly draw attention to and produce new visitors, effectively performing a marketing function. Similarly, by investigating place maintenance projects in communities, we learn more about placemaking. Perhaps future studies will speak to all three aspects of the trifecta too. The systematic review did not reveal many contributions to all three and perhaps this suggests a potential area for further investigation. Next, I suggest three key areas as a future research agenda for the digital transformation of place branding.

Artificial Intelligence and Machine Learning

The timescale to which the systematic review was performed was not restricted and incorporated studies from 2019 and 2020. What has emerged as a key omission was any discussion of artificial intelligence (AI) in the studies identified in recent publications. I believe this to be an important omission to highlight, as AI is currently being hailed in hyperbolic terms as a significant tool for innovation in marketing. As a result, a wide spectrum of business processes are being altered by innovative technological solutions such as rapid identification of customers who would be more receptive to incentives and concomitant avoidance of those unlikely to purchase (Davenport et al., 2020). Advances in programmatic advertising models also allow for a highly efficient segmentation of customer groups based on a plethora of behaviours which would have been difficult for humans to perform at pace. As McGuigan (2019) rightly points out, this approach is a replication of television advertising techniques from the 1950s, albeit in larger volumes. Regardless, it is wise to acknowledge the potential of artificial intelligence and machine learning processes and their contribution to the goals of the place management trifecta.

Considering the traditional tenets of human geography, artificial intelligence and machine learning processes may also be useful in assessing people's interactions with spaces and places. Through a widespread collection and analysis of a broad range of data, the decision-making processes can be assisted by digital technology. Arguably, by removing the human element in the analysis of data produced by large volumes of user interactions with places, an unvarnished representation of reality emerges, which may help change management perspectives and approaches in relation to the place management trifecta. Furthermore, the potential for even larger-scale research projects is now evident, with opportunities emerging to conduct machine learning experiments on large datasets from sources such as footfall and weather data to develop predictive models regarding place (e.g. Mumford et al., 2020).

Automation of Processes

Similar to AI and machine learning processes, automation of digital processes is becoming commonplace. However, automation processes are relatively simple to instigate and would demand a lower budget for place managers and planners. This could be useful for place maintenance in a similar manner to the ShotSpotter application. Furthermore, brands are increasingly using automation for marketing purposes whereby customers are faced with an automated system that will provide key information to expedite the customer journey. There could be a case of use of automation processes that will pinpoint areas of places based on user signifiers such as food preferences and previous trips, etc. Automation could also extend to regular users of places, by suggesting alternative routes through cities with lower pollution in support of health and wellbeing. In effect, use of AI and automation represents the shift from the smart city ideology to a customer-centric mindset, which I argue moves places towards more inclusive placemaking that can only be afforded by digital technology. A cautionary note, however, is that over-automation is already being reported as a significant detractor of customer experiences (Willis and Aurigi, 2020), so a careful balance between automation and human intervention is required.

(Improved) Social Media Sentiment Analysis

Advances in the sentiment analysis of social media data have been made through recent improvements in analytics (Micu et al., 2017). More rigorous approaches to deciphering sentiment on topics relating to places could be an advantageous activity. For example, using sentiment analysis to identify patterns and trends within users' interactions with places might facilitate a more bottom-up approach to the marketing, making and maintenance of places. Trend mapping of user sentiment on social media using NVIVO could also provide clearer insights into user connections with places pre- and post-experience or visit. Lastly, sentiment analysis techniques can unearth negative opinions of places such as cleanliness, air quality, etc. Further scrutiny of negative sentiment would be a welcome solution to the dearth of critical works which examine the detrimental effects of digital transformation.

Conclusion

This chapter has provided a framework of place branding research by considering the influence of digital transformation. In doing so, an alternative view of the relationship between digital transformation of place branding is provided by focusing on three facets of place management, namely place marketing, making and maintenance. Hence, in order to understand the potential of place branding, we need to look at its digital transformation through the place management trifecta, considering that place branding arguably has a legitimate stake in each of the three facets. By aligning the collective knowledge in these three areas, notable trends and patterns have been identified and discussed, as well as notable gaps in the current knowledge base. A future research agenda for researchers considering the impact, detriment and outcomes observed with digital transformation in places is also provided. Three primary areas for further research areas are identified, namely artificial intelligence, automation processes and social media sentiment analysis.

Note

1.   The dataset is openly available at http://bit.ly/DigitalPlaceSLR.

References

Acharya, A. and Z. Rahman (2016), 'Place branding research: A thematic review and future research agenda', *International Review on Public and Nonprofit Marketing*, **13** (3), 289–317.

Anon (2016), '"Digital placemaking" at the heart of designing smart cities', *Premium Official News*, 1–2.

Aurigi, A., Willis, K. and L. Melgaco (2016), 'From "digital" to "smart" upgrading the city', MAB: Proceedings of the 3rd Conference on Media Architecture Biennale, June, 10, 1–4.

Barcelos, R. H., Dantas, D. C. and S. Sénécal (2019), 'The tone of voice of tourism brands on social media: Does it matter?', *Tourism Management*, **74** (March), 173–89.

Benson, M. and E. Jackson (2013), 'Place-making and place maintenance: Performativity, place and belonging among the middle classes', *Sociology*, **47** (4), 793–809.

Boellstorff, T. (2019), 'The ability of place: Digital topographies of the virtual human on ethnographia island', *Current Anthropology*, **61** (February), S109–S122.

Boisen, M., Terlouw, K., Groote, P. and O. Couwenberg (2018), 'Reframing place promotion, place marketing, and place branding: Moving beyond conceptual confusion', *Cities*, **80**, 4–11.

Breek, P., Hermes, J., Eshuis, J. and H. Mommaas (2018), 'The role of social media in collective processes of place making: A study of two neighborhood blogs in Amsterdam', *City and Community*, **17** (3), 906–24.

Bright, L. F., Wilcox, G. B. and H. Rodriguez (2019), '#DeleteFacebook and the consumer backlash of 2018: How social media fatigue, consumer (mis)trust and privacy concerns shape the new social media reality for consumers', *Journal of Digital and Social Media Marketing*, **7** (2), 177–88.

Bristol & Bath Creative R&D (2020), *Bristol & Bath Creative Research & Design*, accessed 14 July 2020 at: https://bristolbathcreative.org.

Calvium (2018), *Digital Placemaking Guide*, accessed 5 December 2019 at: https://calvium.com/resources/digital-placemaking/.

Carson, B., Cooper, C., Larson, R. and L. Rivers (2020), 'How can citizen science advance environmental justice? Exploring the noise paradox through sense of place', *Cities and Health*, https://doi.org/10.1080/23748834.2020.1721222.

Chousein, B. C. (2016), 'Martin Tomitsch discusses "digital placemaking" for the Media Architecture Biennale 2016', *World Architecture*, accessed 5 August 2019 at: https://worldarchitecture.org/architecture-news/cevge/martin_tomitsch_discusses_digital_placemaking_for_the_media_architecture_biennale_2016.html.

Cleave, E. and G. Arku (2017), 'Putting a number on place: A systematic review of place branding influence', *Journal of Place Management and Development*, **10** (5), 425–46.

Cleave, E., Arku, G., Sadler, R. and E. Kyeremeh (2017), 'Place marketing, place branding, and social media: Perspectives of municipal practitioners', *Growth and Change*, **48** (4), 1012–33.

Davenport, T., Guha, A., Grewal, D. and T. Bressgott (2020), 'How artificial intelligence will change the future of marketing', *Journal of the Academy of Marketing Science*, **48** (1), 24–42.

de Noronha, I., Coca-Stefaniak, J. A. and A. M. Morrison (2017), 'Confused branding? An exploratory study of place branding practices among place management professionals', *Cities*, **66**, 91–8.

del Mar Gálvez-Rodríguez, M., Alonso-Cañadas, J., Haro-de-Rosario, A. and C. Caba-Pérez (2020), 'Exploring best practices for online engagement via Facebook with local destination management organisations (DMOs) in Europe: A longitudinal analysis', *Tourism Management Perspectives*, **34**, 100636.

Dempsey, N. and M. Burton (2012), 'Defining place-keeping: The long-term management of public spaces', *Urban Forestry and Urban Greening*, **11** (1), 11–20.

Denis, J. and D. Pontille (2014), 'Maintenance work and the performativity of urban inscriptions: The case of Paris subway signs', *Environment and Planning D: Society and Space*, **32** (3), 404–16.

Digital Placemaking Institute (2020), 'What is digital placemaking?', *Digital Placemaking Institute*, accessed 10 July 2020 at: http://digital-placemaking.org/.

Ebrahimi, P., Hajmohammadi, A. and D. Khajeheian (2019), 'Place branding and moderating role of social media', *Current Issues in Tourism*, **23** (14), 1723–31.

Eck, J. E. and T. D. Madensen-Herold (2018), 'Place management, guardianship, and the establishment of order', in D. S. Nagin, F. T. Cullen and C. L. Jonson (eds), *Deterrence, Choice, and Crime: Contemporary Perspectives*, New York: Routledge, pp. 269–307.

Faraji, S. J. and M. J. Nozar (2019), 'Smart parking: An efficient approach to city's smart management and air pollution reduction', *Journal of Air Pollution and Health*, **4** (1), 53–72.

Fernandez-Cavia, J., Díaz-Luque, P., Huertas, A., Rovira, C., Pedraza-Jimenez, R., Sicilia, M., Gómez, L. and M. I. Míguez (2013), 'Destination brands and website evaluation: A research methodology', *Revista Latina de Communicación Social*, 10.4185/RLCS-2013-993en.

Fredericks, J., Tomitsch, M., Hespanhol, L. and I. McArthur (2015), 'Digital pop-up: Investigating bespoke community engagement in public spaces', in *Proceedings of the Annual Meeting of the Australian Special Interest Group for Computer Human Interaction*, pp. 634–42.

Fredericks, J., Hespanhol, L., Parker, C., Zhou, D. and M. Tomitsch (2018), 'Blending pop-up urbanism and participatory technologies: Challenges and opportunities for inclusive city making', *City, Culture and Society*, **12**, 44–53. doi: 10.1016/j.ccs.2017.06.005.

Govers, R., Kaefer, F. and N. Ferrer-Roca (2017), 'The state of academic place branding research according to practitioners', *Place Branding and Public Diplomacy*, **13** (1), 1–3.

Graham, S. and N. Thrift (2007), 'Out of order: Understanding repair and maintenance', *Theory, Culture and Society*, **24** (3), 1–25.

Hanna, S. A. and J. Rowley (2015), 'Towards a model of the Place Brand Web', *Tourism Management*, **48**, 100–12.

Hespanhol, L., Häusler, M. H., Tomitsch, M. and G. Tscherteu (2017), *Media Architecture Compendium: Digital Placemaking*, Stuttgart: Avedition.

Jones, S. and K. Kubacki (2014), 'Branding places with social problems: A systematic review (2000–2013)', *Place Branding and Public Diplomacy*, **10** (3), 218–29.

Källström, L. and J. Hultman (2019), 'Place satisfaction revisited: Residents' perceptions of "a good place to live"', *Journal of Place Management and Development*, **12** (3), 274–90.

Kim, S. E., Lee, K. Y., Shin, S. I. and S. B. Yang (2017), 'Effects of tourism information quality in social media on destination image formation: The case of Sina Weibo', *Information and Management*, **54** (6), 687–702.

Koeck, R. and G. Warnaby (2014), 'Outdoor advertising in urban context: Spatiality, temporality and individuality', *Journal of Marketing Management*, **30** (13–14), 1402–22.

Kompaniets, O. R. and D. Rauhut (2019), 'Literary tourism in Sweden: Examples of failure and success', in *6th Corfu Symposium on Managing and Marketing Places*, Corfu, 6–9 May, pp. 161–4.

Lazaridou, K., Vrana, V. and D. Paschaloudis (2017), 'Museums+ Instagram', in V. Katsoni, A. Upadhya and A. Stratigea (eds), *Tourism, Culture and Heritage in a Smart Economy: Third International Conference IACuDiT, Athens 2016*, Cham: Springer, pp. 73–84.

Lupo, C. V. (2018), *Social Media Marketing Strategies in Landscape Industry Small Businesses*, PhD thesis, Walden University.

Madensen, T. D. and J. E. Eck (2003), 'Violence in bars: Exploring the impact of place manager decision-making', *Crime Prevention and Community Safety*, **10** (2), 111–25.

McGuigan, L. (2019), 'Automating the audience commodity: The unacknowledged ancestry of programmatic advertising', *New Media and Society*, **21** (11–12), 2366–85.

Memmott, P. (1980), *Lardil Properties of Place: An Ethnological Study in Man–Environment Relations*, University of Queensland, St. Lucia.

Micu, A., Micu, A. E., Geru, M. and R. C. Lixandroiu (2017), 'Analyzing user sentiment in social media: Implications for online marketing strategy', *Psychology and Marketing*, **34** (12), 1094–100.

Míguez González, M. I. (2011), 'Websites and place branding for seven Galician cities: An exploratory study', *Catalan Journal of Communication and Cultural Studies*, **3** (2), 297–304.

Molinillo, S., Anaya-Sánchez, R., Morrison, A. M. and J. A. Coca-Stefaniak (2019), 'Smart city communication via social media: Analysing residents' and visitors' engagement', *Cities*, **94** (June), 247–55.

Mumford, C., Parker, C., Ntounis, N. and E. Dargan (2020), 'Footfall signatures and volumes: Towards a classification of UK centres', *Environment and Planning B: Urban Analytics and City Science*, doi: 10.1177/2399808320911412.

Nam, J. and N. Dempsey (2019), 'Place-keeping for health? Charting the challenges for urban park management in practice', *Sustainability (Switzerland)*, **11** (16), 4383.

Nisi, V., Prandi, C. and N. J. Nunes (2020), 'Towards eco-centric interaction: Urban playful interventions in the Anthropocene', in A. Nijholt (ed.), *Making Smart Cities More Playable: Exploring Playable Cities*, Singapore: Springer Nature Singapore, pp. 235–61.

Ntalianis, K., Kavoura, A., Tomaras, P. and A. Drigas (2015), 'Non-gatekeeping on social media: A reputation monitoring approach and its application in tourism services', *Journal of Tourism and Services*, **6** (10), 19–44.

Oliveira, E. and E. Panyik (2015), 'Content, context and co-creation: Digital challenges in destination branding with references to Portugal as a tourist destination', *Journal of Vacation Marketing*, **21** (1), 53–74.

Pareja-Eastaway, M., Chapain, C. and S. Mugano (2013), 'Successes and failures in city branding policies', in S. Musterd and Z. Kovács (eds), *Place-Making and Policies for Competitive Cities*, Chichester: John Wiley & Sons, pp. 149–71.

Parker, C. (2008), 'Extended editorial: Place – the trinal frontier', *Journal of Place Management and Development*, **1** (1), 5–14.

Parker, C., Roper, S. and D. Medway (2015), 'Back to basics in the marketing of place: The impact of litter upon place attitudes', *Journal of Marketing Management*, **31** (9), 1090–112.

Paulsen, K. (2010), 'Placemaking', in R. Hutchinson (ed.), *Encyclopedia of Urban Studies*, Thousand Oaks, CA: Sage, pp. 600–4.

Petrikova, D., Jaššo, M. and M. Hajduk (2020), 'Social media as tool of SMART city marketing', in N. V. M. Lopes (ed.), *Smart Governance for Cities: Perspectives and Experiences*, Cham: Springer Nature, pp. 55–72.

Sdoukopoulos, A., Nikolaidou, A., Pitsiava-Latinopoulou, M. and P. Papaioannou (2018), 'Use of social media for assessing sustainable urban mobility indicators', *International Journal of Sustainable Development and Planning*, **13** (2), 338–48.

Sevin, H. E. (2014), 'Understanding cities through city brands: City branding as a social and semantic network', *Cities*, **38**, 47–56.

Skinner, H. (2008), 'The emergence and development of place marketing's confused identity', *Journal of Marketing Management*, **24** (9–10), 915–28.

Taneja, G. and A. Bala (2019), 'Current scenario of social media marketing', in *Proceedings of 10th International Conference on Digital Strategies for Organizational Success*.

Tranfield, D., Denyer, D. and P. Smart (2003), 'Towards a methodology for developing evidence-informed management knowledge by means of systematic review', *British Journal of Management*, **14** (3), 207–22.

Uşaklı, A., Koç, B. and S. Sönmez (2017), 'How "social" are destinations? Examining European DMO social media usage', *Journal of Destination Marketing and Management*, **6** (2), 136–49.

Vallicelli, M. (2018), 'Smart cities and digital workplace culture in the global European context: Amsterdam, London and Paris', *City, Culture and Society*, **12** (March), 25–34.

Vuignier, R. (2016), 'Place marketing and place branding: A systematic (and tentatively exhaustive) literature review', hal-01340352, accessed 24 July 2020 at: https://hal .archives-ouvertes.fr/hal-01340352/document.

Wang, W. (2019), 'A study of digitally enhanced people–space interaction: A place-centric perspective', *Space and Culture*. doi: 10.1177/1206331219881352.

Warnaby, G. and D. Medway (2013), 'What about the "place" in place marketing?', *Marketing Theory*, **13** (3), 345–63.

Webster, J. and R. T. Watson (2002), 'Analyzing the past to prepare for the future: Writing a review', *MIS Quarterly*, **26** (2), 8–23.

Willis, K. S. and A. Aurigi (2020), *The Routledge Companion to Smart Cities*, London: Routledge.

PART III

Experience

12 Posthuman phenomenology: What are places like for nonhumans?

Jack Coffin

Introduction

Thomas Nagel (1974) once asked: *what is it like to be a bat?* More recently, Ian Bogost (2012) has sought to answer a broader puzzle: *what it's like to be a thing?* Both point to what might be described as a *posthuman phenomenology*. The term phenomenology derives from philosophy, describing philosophical reflections on the nature of experience (Grayling, 2019). In principle, phenomenology can encompass the study of human experience but also the experience of animals, smart objects, and everything else. However, in social theory the term phenomenology is almost exclusively associated with *human* experience, such as the 'sense of place' that emerges when humans engage with spatial environments (Agnew, 1987; Cresswell, 2004). Scholars who seek to challenge an experiential emphasis in the literature tend to turn to other perspectives, such as assemblage theory (see Roffe, 2016), rather than rework these underlying anthropocentric assumptions. Thus, although posthuman phenomenology may be tautological in the technical sense, given that phenomenology can already encompass all manner of experiences, in practice it may be useful to develop and deploy this phrase as a discrete discursive resource, especially within traditionally humanistic disciplines such as place branding.[1]

Esoteric speculations about the nature of nonhuman experience may not appear particularly relevant to place branding, which 'is very much a practitioner-led field' (Therkelsen, Halkier, and Jensen, 2010: 138). Yet, it could be countered that considering the phenomenon of nonhuman experience is crucial in an era of accelerating technological change and deepening environmental concern. Posthuman philosophers aver anthropocentric assumptions, especially the often taken-for-granted hierarchy between humans – as agentic, self-aware, and significant subjects – and nonhumans – as inert, unconscious, and largely insignificant objects (Barad, 2003; Braidotti, 2006, 2016; Bettany, 2016). In contrast, posthumanists present reality as reiterative rhizomes of relational activity (Deleuze and Guattari, 1987), with characteristics like agency, consciousness, and importance being emergent *effects* of non/human net working (Latour, 2005), rather than pre-existing *essences* of individual entities. Those that embrace this rhizomatic worldview are encouraged to reconsider the human–nonhuman relationship with regard to theory, but also in practical and political terms (Law, 2009). For example, Haraway (2003) once argued that humans and animals are not autonomous entities with clear-cut boundaries, but rather 'companion species' with co-constitutive relationships (see also Haraway, 2008). Drawing inspiration from this theoretical argument, Bettany and Daly (2007) demonstrated empirically how humans and dogs co-consume products and services, rejecting the taken-for-granted hierarchy between 'owners' and 'pets'. This, in turn, suggests new opportunities for brand managers, service providers, and even policy-makers to engage more sensitively and successfully with these symbiotic entanglements. In a similar vein, this chapter proposes a posthuman research agenda for place branding, focusing on the topic of posthuman phenomenology to illustrate the benefits of more-than-human theorisations.

Place branding is a discipline that remains anthropocentric in its focus on the experiences of human placemakers. Nonhumans have often been implicitly acknowledged under the category of 'materiality', with place brands conceptualised as mixtures of meanings and materials that must be managed (Cresswell and Hoskins, 2008; Therkelsen et al., 2010). However, this tacit theorisation elides the role of nonhumans as entities that can experience places and contribute to placemaking processes. In recent years marketing theorists have begun to foreground the materiality of place and its nonrepresentational effects (Hill, Canniford, and Mol, 2014; Cheetham, McEachern, and Warnaby, 2018), resonating with calls for multisensory place branding (Medway and Warnaby, 2017) and branding practices that consider forces that operate beneath, between, and beyond moments of conscious reflection (Coffin, 2019). However, these theoretical innovations do not necessarily result in a fully fledged appreciation of nonhumans and their emplaced experiences. This chapter draws on Bogost's (2012) notion of 'alien phenomenology' to consider how these experiences, however strange and unfamiliar from an anthropocentric point of view, are worth considering given their theoretical, practical, and ethical implications. In doing so, the chapter follows a well-established critical streak within place branding scholarship, expanding the extant concern with excluded human stakeholders (Warnaby and Medway, 2013; Giovanardi,

Kavaratzis, and Lichrou, 2019) to consider nonhumans as well. This chapter first unpacks the core concept of posthuman phenomenology before applying it to two key examples – animal experiences and artificial experiences – and considering how such experiences may operate at speeds and scales beyond everyday human experience. The chapter concludes by emphasising the practical and political consequences of posthuman phenomenology. As discussed throughout the remaining sections, this ethics of inclusion may pose many difficult questions, but is a worthwhile endeavour to help make place branding more equitable, ecological, and enriching for all.

Posthuman phenomenology

Phenomenology is the philosophy of experience (Grayling, 2019), so research can be described as phenomenological if (a) it represents an attempt to theorise experience *per se*, or (b) if it emphasises the role of experience in relation to a given topic. Place branding can be considered phenomenological in both senses. Heavily influenced by the work of various phenomenological geographers, the discipline's eponymous concept is understood as inherently experiential (Warnaby and Medway, 2013). Cresswell (2004) defines place as space made meaningful, giving the example of a university student who transforms a rented room into their home-away-from-home with material objects and via significant events. This example foregrounds a process ontology in which places do not simply exist, but are instead continually (re)created by the subjective experience of 'dwelling' in a space (Seamon, 1993). From a phenomenological perspective, the term space suggests a more abstract point of view, in contrast to the more embodied experience associated with the word place (Agnew, 1987; Cresswell, 2013). In the terminology of marketing and consumer research, 'the notion of space traditionally refers to something anonymous, whereas place distinctively accounts for the meaningful experience of a given site; that is, it is "consumed space"' (Visconti et al., 2010: 512). Accordingly, place describes a 'kaleidoscope' of experience that emerges from the unorganised interactions of heterogeneous spatial stakeholders at multiple scales simultaneously, with place branding denoting an attempt to manage and mobilise the more positive and profitable experiences whilst mitigating more shadowy and subversive spatial effects (Warnaby and Medway, 2013). Experience has an almost axiomatic status in the discipline of place branding, such that major contributions to the field are often achieved by augmenting or altering this core concept in some way. For instance, Medway and Warnaby's (2017) manifesto for multisensory place branding represents a call to appreciate the multisensuousness of human experience, challenging the ocularcentric focus of conventional theory and practice.

Much like the multisensory manifesto, posthuman phenomenology should not be thought of as a break from tradition. Rather, it is an opportunity to expand the epistemological imagination of place branding, opening up new lines of research inquiry and new possibilities for practical intervention. Although phenomenological researchers have a history of adopting anthropocentric assumptions about the concept of experience, there is no reason to assume that posthumanism and phenomenology are mutually exclusive. There are certainly a number of 'more-than-human' geographers who have considered the emplaced experiences of animals and other nonhumans (Cresswell, 2013). For years animal geographers have studied how possums live alongside humans in Australia (Power, 2009), how anglers attempt to 'think like a fish' in the rivers of Yorkshire (Bear and Eden, 2011), or how cougars contribute to the ongoing negotiation of human gender identity in North America (Collard, 2012). Such empirical studies point toward a more inclusive conceptualisation of experience, one which does not assume that a 'sense of place' (Agnew, 1987) is an exclusively human phenomenon. Indeed, these studies suggest that the folk theories of fishermen and other spatial stakeholders actually acknowledge nonhuman experience more readily than many academic theorisations, such as those that presently prevail within the place branding literature. However, appreciating that nonhumans *can* experience place is only the first step in developing a posthuman phenomenology of place brands. One must also question *how* nonhumans experience place.

Ian Bogost (2012) has proposed the term 'alien phenomenology' to describe attempts to philosophise the broad topic of nonhuman experience. The term is apt because nonhuman experiences are likely to be unfamiliar, as Nagel's (1974) example of chiropteran echolocation attests, and can only be indirectly understood via metaphor and other figurative techniques (see also Harman, 2018; Hoffman and Novak, 2018). Despite these difficulties, Bogost (2012) argues that attempts to understand such alien experiences are important, perhaps even existentially so, in an era of runaway climate change and increasingly sophisticated forms of artificial intelligence (see also Haraway, 2008; Morton, 2013). At the same time, the term *alien* has extra-terrestrial associations that may prove problematic, somewhat exoticising nonhuman experience as something otherworldly, unknowable, and even dangerous. At the very least it suggests a division between human phenomenology and nonhuman phenomenology. In contrast, posthuman perspectives seek to blur such boundaries and appreciate the non/human hybrids that emerge from everyday practices (Barad, 2003; Haraway, 2003, 2008; Braidotti, 2006, 2016), as in the case of companion consumers (Bettany and Daly, 2007) or humans who treat smart assistants as part of the family (Hoffman and Novak, 2018). The term posthuman phenomenology may therefore be preferable, especially for scholars that seek to engage with nonacademic audiences and must therefore consider the wider cultural connotations of any conceptual terminology. It also helps to form a distinction between Bogost's (2012) recent work and the posthuman philosophical tradition more generally. The 'panpsychic' proposition that everything may be able to experience the world reoccurs throughout the history of philosophy, most notably in the work of Deleuze, Nietzsche, and Spinoza (Grayling, 2019), and sets a long-established posthuman precedent against which alien phenomenology is merely the most recent articulation. Thus, while alien phenomenology suggests a more specific interest in asking *how* nonhumans experience the world, posthuman phenomenology may be used more broadly to also encapsulate conceptual and empirical studies of *when*, *where*, and *why* such experiences might be relevant.

Animal phenomenology

The experiences of animals are likely to be the most accessible example of posthuman phenomenology and its relevance. It is relatively uncontroversial to argue that animals experience the world around them, with the mental faculties of some animals facilitating levels of conscious awareness that may be similar to humans in terms of sophistication but markedly different in qualitative terms (Nagel, 1974). The vast and rapidly growing market for pet food, toys, and other products suggests a widespread acknowledgement of animal experience (Bettany and Daly, 2007). Relatedly, pet hotels and other specialist spaces are becoming increasingly popular (Tickle, 2017), pointing to an implicit appreciation of fauna phenomenology. However, it may be more difficult to convince people that nomadic, domesticated, and territorial species may all experience spaces in ways that go beyond basic forms of environmental awareness and recognition. Although animals and humans may not share a similar sense of place, this does not preclude the possibility that animals may experience place differently, and that these differing experiences may have practical, political, and personal implications for place branding scholars and practitioners. At a basic level, an animal's engagement with an environment is shaped, at least in part, by their experience of it (Gibson, 1979), and these engagements shape human experience in turn (Philo, 1995; Power, 2009). Everyday examples abound: what would London's Trafalgar Square be without its pigeons (Escobar, 2014),[2] and how might a public park feel without any dogs (Fletcher and Platt, 2018)? Although animals are unlikely to perceive a place as a brand, this co-sensuality of place means that place branding must be considered as an anthropocentric practice that *affects* animals but is also *affected by* them.

If animals experience places differently to humans, then decisions that make a place brand more attractive for humans may come at the detriment of animals' experiences. Escobar (2014) describes how pigeons and other animals were 'displaced' by attempts to refashion Trafalgar Square for a human public. Here displacement can denote physical movements but also experiential divestments, whereby a once beloved place loses its status as a special space following a redevelopment or other dramatic change (Maclaran and Brown, 2005). Critical scholars have highlighted how place branding practices can ignore and diminish certain actors' attachments to a place (Warnaby and Medway, 2013), sometimes encouraging or even compelling them to relocate (Giovanardi et al., 2019). Animals may also be subject to such displacements, ranging from the macro-scale of urban development to the micro-scale of the suburban garden (Ginn, 2014). This suggests an ethical stance where animals are considered in the place branding process, 'building *with* wildlife' (Sage et al., 2014) rather than against or merely alongside it. Of course, one cannot consult animals directly, so ecologists and other experts may be beneficial as proxy representatives, giving voice to these under-represented stakeholders. Such suggestions augment existing calls for a more inclusive, or 'bottom-up', approach to place branding (Warnaby and Medway, 2013; Cheetham et al., 2018), and a posthuman research agenda could contribute to such progressive place branding practices by providing new insights into animal phenomenology. In lieu of animal interviews and other forms of first-hand discourse, researchers will be reliant on the observational data. White (2020: 13) conducted '18 months of ethnographic fieldwork' to explicate the politically charged 'domestications' of Mongolian animals wrought by China's Belt and Road Initiative. Such long-term immersion may be somewhat idealistic within the 'publish or perish' culture of contemporary academia, but the ethnographic ideal of observing actors *in situ* is certainly worth pursuing in some form. As noted by Oliveira and Ashworth (2017: 24), place branding 'requires more than advertising, promotional or communication strategies' but also 'spatial planning and spatial development to influence the physical appearance of the place, contributing, thereby, to improvement of its image'. As melds of meaning *and* materiality (Cresswell and Hoskins, 2008; Therkelsen et al., 2010), place branding campaigns are likely to put in motion changes that may be detrimental to an animal's sense of place. By attempting to understand animal phenomenology, posthuman scholarship can help practitioners to mitigate any negative effects and maximise human–animal synergies.

While an interest in animal phenomenology may be driven by the ethical and political sensibilities of critical scholarship, even mainstream practitioner-oriented research may seek to accommodate animal experiences because of their practical, human-centric consequences. As noted earlier, animal geographers have demonstrated that human placemakers can imagine how animals experience place and act accordingly (Bear and Eden, 2011), and may feel considerable guilt when human and animal experiences come into conflict (Ginn, 2014). Thus, if the experientially informed actions of animals can affect how humans experience a place, then place branding campaigns may benefit from considering how to work animals into their strategies. Place branding practices can contribute to the stigmatisation and marginalisation of certain animals in order to naturalise anthropocentric reterritorialisations, as in the case of reframing pigeons as pests in order to legitimise their displacement from public squares (Jerolmack, 2008; Escobar, 2014). Conversely, animals may be centralised as part of the place product, as illustrated by safari parks (Flack, 2016). Both extremes demonstrate how animals may be objectified as 'pests' or 'assets' to be managed by place branding practices, but a posthuman research agenda might seek to conceptualise animals as co-consumers and co-producers of the place experience. For instance, Fletcher and Platt (2018: 211) describe how 'walking is more than *just* walking' for dog walkers, instead constituting 'a highly sensual and complex activity'. Drawing on Bettany and Daly's (2007) notion of Companion Species Consumption, it might be argued that walking becomes a con-sensual experience. A dog may become distracted by a scent imperceptible to their human companion, dragging the duo off course, while a human may avoid shadowy areas that a dog may not regard as unsafe, bringing both back to the beaten path. If posthuman scholarship can draw insights from such symbioses, then practitioners may be able to develop coeval experiences into their place brand. Sticking to the example of dog walking, cities might create and promote more canine-companion spaces to attract new residents, but a more exotic example might be the cadre of conservation projects that provide eco-tourists opportunities to experience life amongst turtles and other endangered animals. Yet, while the practical insights of posthuman phenomenology may prompt tourist boards and local governments to promote experiences *with* animals as part of their place brand-ing activities, critical scholars should not lose sight of the political implications of such experiences *for* animals. The ethics of elephant riding, as a popular but cruel practice, is a contemporary case in point (Marshall, 2017; Wilson, 2018; Frazier, 2019).

Artificial phenomenology

Posthuman phenomenology need not restrict its enquiries to animals, however, and may also be applied to the experience of artificial intelligence. In their study of smart assistants in the home, Hoffman and Novak (2018) explicated a theory of artificial consciousness, which might be extended to suggest that spatially sensitive objects can become sophisticated enough to develop a sense of place. Many places are already populated by increasingly intelligent objects that incorporate sensors and geolocation technologies, and given the ubiquity of smartphones and satellites almost any space can be considered 'sensible' from an artificial perspective. Although designed by humans, an artificial sense of place is likely to be quite dissimilar to the anthropic perception of emplacement, especially as the Internet of Things becomes more established and the combination of interconnected sensors with machine learning creates a kind of hive consciousness. Such pronouncements may sound like science fiction, but the possibility is not so outlandish given the current rate of technological development, and thanks to the work of Yuval Noah Harari (2015, 2018) such ideas are increasingly legitimate within the public discourse. Yet although films and other forms of popular culture tend to promote anthropocentric representations of artificial intelligence, digital phenomenology is likely to be far more 'alien' in its composition (Bogost, 2012). It benefits business to make smart assistants and robots that are anthropomorphic, but in the future artificial objects may design themselves to unfamiliar ends.

More than theoretical musings, considering the rapidly developing sense of place amongst artificially intelligent objects and infrastructures may have many practical implications for place branding. For one, the manifesto for multisensory place branding (Medway and Warnaby, 2017) may need updating, given that machines can be built to sense magnetic fields, pollution levels, or nonvisible bands in the electromagnetic spectrum, such as infrared and ultraviolet. Recent research has emphasised the importance of smell in shaping the human experience of place (Canniford, Riach, and Hill, 2018), and how a 'city of smells' might be marketed (Henshaw et al., 2015), but how might an artificial intelligence experience the city as polluted and respond accordingly? In addition to experiencing places differently, artificially intelligent objects may also experience places where humans do not, and perhaps cannot, tread. *Exempli gratia*, posthumanist scholars have studied places like landfills and nuclear sites (Bennett, 2009; Hird, 2012), places designed to be kept apart from most humans for decades, centuries, or even millennia. While these places may be undesirable and even dangerous for organic bodies, machinic forms may be resistant to toxins and radiation, thus enabling artificial experiences of these misanthropic places. Depending on its code, a mobile artificial intelligence may even desire to visit such environments, which may provide opportunities for place branding researchers (e.g. data gathering by artificial assistants) and practitioners (e.g. virtual reality tours of irradiated sites or ocean floors). However, it may be countered that designing artificially intelligent bodies to desire danger is somewhat unethical, effectively objectifying these sentient beings as instruments of human profiteering, and certainly ideological, insofar as it inflects (or infects) these bodies with the profit-maximising ideology of capitalism.

Reflecting on artificial phenomenology will only become more important in the years ahead, given the current popularity of 'smart city' projects and similar attempts to embed sensory systems into everyday life (e.g. the Internet of Things). If successful, smart nonhumans will not only be sensuous subjects but also powerful actors who can reshape urban, suburban, and rural places by informing human decision makers and thus influencing placemaking processes. Although artificial intelligence is usually presented as politically neutral and objective, recent research has shown how facial recognition follows the racist assumptions of its designers and their data set (Breland, 2017; Perkins, 2019), and argues that smart assistants can reproduce gender biases (Bogost, 2018; Rawlinson, 2019). City planners and other spatial stakeholders must be careful to avoid deifying smart systems as the solution to human problems, instead adopting a more critical position where artificial intelligence is an aid but not an arbiter. Then again, as systems become smarter they may be able to rewrite their own code and diverge from human phenomenology. The increasingly alien thinking of artificial intelligence may become problematic if smart cities and other spatial infrastructures are allowed to automate decisions like traffic flows, water systems, or transportation. More efficient cities may result in better place experiences for human residents and visitors, resulting in more favourable associations for place brands, but may also diminish opportunities for surprise and serendipity, not to mention the loss of human interaction as robots replace human employees. As they become increasingly influential, the question of *how* intelligent objects make sense of place should be a significant concern for place branding scholars and practitioners, not to mention activists and citizens. Zuboff (2019) and Harari (2020) have helped to bring the issue of pervasive surveillance into the public discourse, yet the parallel concern of pervasive placemaking by machinic intelligence has yet to be considered. Considering artificial phenomenology may help to make shared spaces 'smarter' whilst steering away from the more dangerous, destructive, and dehumanising scenarios.

Phenomenology beyond the anthroposcale

The topic of automation draws attention to a key difference between human phenomenology and artificial phenomenology – speed. Computational processing operates in a very different way to organic cognition (despite the popularity of the brain-as-computer trope in some circles), so perceptions of time are likely to be quite different for smart objects. This means that their automated activities are likely to be implemented before humans are even aware that a decision has been made. The same is also true of animals. An animal with a shorter lifespan or nomadic tendencies may be more affected by seasonal or even daily changes, which may alter the ways in which place brand managers may incorporate their needs into their bottom-up consultation. Conversely, some artificial systems or animal species may operate at a slower pace, resulting in a longer-term sense of place that goes beyond the short-term key performance indicators imposed on some Destination Management Organisations by the competitive pressures of global tourism. The viral video of an orangutan defending its home from diggers, originally aired on Sir David Attenborough's *Climate Change: The Facts*, is a salient reminder that animals often make lifelong investments in particular territories. These are investments that may be far more intense and existential than human 'place attachments' (c.f. Manzo and Devine-Wright, 2013; Debendedetti, Oppewal, and Arsel, 2014), given that humans often have other places to live and visit (Warnaby and Medway, 2013). It is already widely acknowledged that places change over time (Cresswell, 2004), and that they are products of historical as well as geographical forces (Pred, 1984), thus prompting researchers to analyse the rhythms of human and nonhuman placemakers (McEachern, Warnaby, and Cheetham, 2012; Cheetham et al., 2018). However, the anthropocentric assumptions of traditional phenomenology engender an emphasis on human rhythms and timeframes, with nonhumans considered only if they synchronise with anthropological experience (Morton, 2013). In contrast, posthuman perspectives encourage scholars to speculate about the emplaced phenomenology of actors who operate at other speeds (Coffin, 2019). A sheep, a sheepdog, and a shepherd may all appreciate a field differently thanks to their differing relationships to time, and all would experience it differently from a satellite passing overhead or a smart agricultural sensor in the grass.

In addition to speed, nonhumans also differ in terms of scale. Although artificial assistants may be located in the home, they are connected to a vast invisible infrastructure (Hoffman and Novak, 2018), representing an extreme form of distributed cognition that contrasts sharply with the localised phenomenology of human embodiment. Each smart object connects to an extensive web of subterranean cables, satellites, and servers that collectively generate a huge carbon footprint (Webb, 2020), as well as connecting to data processing centres across the world where anonymous employees listen to domestic soundscapes in order to 'improve service quality' (BBC, 2020). Such scales are difficult to imagine and are often easily forgotten in daily life, yet each represents a complex enmeshment of non/human phenomenologies that may affect place branding practices in a variety of ways. For instance, how might smart cities or artificially assisted tourist destinations be marketed in light of such ecological and ethical considerations? Here Morton's (2013) concept of the hyperobject may be useful, as it describes arrangements that are so large that they operate at scales beyond the perceptual limits of everyday human experience. He gives the topical example of the climate, which is difficult for humans to perceive directly and whose changes can only be indirectly intuited through various technologies. An artificial intelligence may be able to experience the climate more directly if it operates at a similar scale across billions of interconnected sensors, helping humans to design places and place brands that are more ecological in their orientation.

In terms of animal phenomenology, it may seem trivial to point out that rats, humans, and elephants may all experience a place differently due to their relative size, resulting in alternative approaches to place design and branding. For instance, compare the width of roads in places that had to accommodate cavalry or war elephants versus those that only had human and small domestic animals to consider. Yet, scalar differences are not just quantitative or extensive but also result in qualitative differences in the place experience:

> Take the example of a lake with well-defined geographical borders. Now, two differently scaled organisms inhabiting this lake can be presented with an entirely different reality. A small bacterium, whose weight is negligible relative to the viscosity of water, will be presented with a medium that allows it to move around only if it keeps its motor (its flagellum) on all the time; a large fish, on the other hand, can throw its much larger weight around, and can therefore swim using a thrust and glide maneuver. To put this in more subjective terms: one and the same object, the lake, will appear much more viscous to one organism, and much less viscous to another. (DeLanda in DeLanda and Harman, 2017: 23)

In attempting to understand animal phenomenology and the responses that result, scholars should not lose sight of these scalar distinctions. While a bacterium, fish, and human may differ dramatically in terms of their qualitative experience, smaller scalar differences may still produce significant, albeit more subtle, phenomenological distinctions. The suburban garden may be a small private space for a human, but for a slug it represents a large landscape of opportunities and threats; this affords the possibility for slugs and humans to co-exist peacefully, with slugs occupying a territory that they experience as sizeable, but which humans consider small enough to enable more desirable fauna and flora to survive and thrive (Ginn, 2014).

Concluding remarks: The pragmatics and politics of posthuman place branding

Posthuman perspectives can be very productive in challenging conventional theorisations and enabling new ways of thinking to emerge (Hill et al., 2014), especially ones which are more appropriate for the techno-environmental enmeshments of contemporary societies (Haraway, 2008; Bogost, 2012; Morton, 2013; Braidotti, 2016). This chapter has explored the potential of posthumanism phenomenology to challenge the implicit anthropocentrism of mainstream place branding. This, in turn, encourages scholars and practitioners to consider (a) how place branding practices affect nonhumans, (b) how these nonhumans contribute to the place experiences of humans, and (c) the practical, political, and ethical implications of these experiential enmeshments across multiple speeds and scales. Animal phenomenology and artificial phenomenology were developed as illustrative examples, but the broader conceptual category of posthuman phenomenology can also accommodate the experiences of other nonhuman entities. There is certainly evidence that plants have some awareness of their surroundings (Chamovitz, 2012; Wohlleben, 2017; Gagliano, 2018), and arguments have been made that 'plant blindness' is a pervasive and problematic tendency across contemporary human civilisations (Wandersee and Schussler, 1999). The phenomenology of flora may be an avenue for future research, especially insofar as plants impact on the place experiences of humans and may justify the creation of 'dumb cities' as ecological alternatives to the data-driven conurbations of contemporary urban planning (Fleming, 2020).

This chapter developed the concept of posthuman phenomenology because experience is a core concept in place branding that is worth critically reconceptualising. However, posthuman phenomenology should not be considered an end destination but rather a point of departure for a wider posthuman research agenda for place branding. Drawing inspiration from the posthuman philosophy of Deleuze and Guattari (1987), Coffin (2019) argues that mainstream managers often overlook the subconscious spatial forces that surround and suffuse moments of conscious reflection and experience. If place brands are more than just images and narratives (Warnaby and Medway, 2013), then practitioners would certainly benefit from theoretical accounts that incorporate such nonrepresentational phenomena (see also Hill et al., 2014). Studies of nonhuman experience and other posthuman phenomena may necessitate more creative methodological approaches, including ethnographic observation (White, 2020) but also metaphor (Bogost, 2012; Harman, 2018), anthropomorphism (Hoffman and Novak, 2018), and fiction (Sherry, 2020). It may also necessitate a more critical realpolitik. A recurring theme in this chapter has been the observation that posthumanism expands the ethical and political sensitivities of critical *scholarship*, but whether this can translate into praxis is uncertain. As shown by Escobar's (2014) account of pigeons and Ginn's (2014) study of slugs, dealing with conflicts between stakeholders can be difficult and may result in deadly conclusions for some parties. Although animal welfare, environmental degradation, and technological development are prominent concerns in the public discourse, a truly posthuman perspective may necessitate sacrifices that brand managers and other human stakeholders may find difficult to accept. A posthuman research agenda for place branding must create a compelling case for more-than-human sensibilities that reaches beyond the ivory towers of academia. In an era of potentially cataclysmic climate change (Morton, 2013; Campbell and Deane, 2019), a more ecological and equitable approach to place branding may be an existential necessity.

Notes

1. Place branding should not be conflated with place marketing or place management; these are concepts which share some overlap in practice yet remain distinct in theory (Skinner, 2008). In line with the title of this edited volume, the term *place branding* is used throughout this chapter. It is used to describe how nebulous geographical phenomena are transformed into valuable branded assets through the careful curation of cultural connotations.
2. It is actually rather ironic that the Trafalgar Square place brand is so commonly associated with pigeons, given that much of the rebranding activity was focused around *displacing* these feathery dwellers (Escobar, 2014). As noted by Jerolmack (2008), pigeons have suffered from decades of demonisation in the popular press, becoming problematic pests rather than companion consumers.

References

Agnew, J. (1987), *Place and Politics: The Geographical Mediation of State and Society*, Boston, MA: Allen and Unwin.

Barad, K. (2003), 'Posthumanist performativity: Toward an understanding of how matter comes to matter', *Signs: Journal of Women in Culture and Society*, **28** (3), 801–31.

BBC (2020), 'Panorama – Amazon: What they know about us', *British Broadcasting Corporation*, 17 February, accessed 12 May 2020 at: www.bbc.co.uk/iplayer/episode/m000fjdz/panorama-amazon-what-they-know-about-us.

Bear, C. and S. Eden (2011), 'Thinking like a fish? Engaging with nonhuman difference through recreational angling', *Environment and Planning D: Society and Space*, **29** (2), 336–52.

Bennett, J. (2009), *Vibrant Matter: A Political Ecology of Things*, Durham, NC: Duke University Press.

Bettany, S. (2016), 'A commentary: Where (and what) is the critical in consumer-oriented actor-network theory?', in R. Canniford and D. Bajde (eds), *Assembling Consumption: Researching Actors, Networks and Markets*, Abingdon: Routledge, pp. 187–97.

Bettany, S. and R. Daly (2007), 'Figuring companion-species consumption: A multi-site ethnography of the post-canine Afghan hound', *Journal of Business Research*, **61** (5), 408–18.

Bogost, I. (2012), *Alien Phenomenology, or What It's Like to Be a Thing*, Minneapolis, MN: University of Minnesota Press.

Bogost, I. (2018), 'Sorry, Alexa is not a feminist', *The Atlantic*, 24 January, accessed 19 May 2020 at: www.theatlantic.com/technology/archive/2018/01/sorry-alexa-is-not-a-feminist/551291/.

Braidotti, R. (2006), 'Posthuman all too human: Towards a new process ontology', *Theory, Culture and Society*, **23** (7/8), 197–208.

Braidotti, R. (2016), 'Posthuman critical theory', in D. Banerji and M. R. Paranjape (eds), *Critical Posthumanism and Planetary Futures*, New Delhi: Springer, pp. 13–32.

Breland, A. (2017), 'How white engineers built racist code – and why it's dangerous for black people', *The Guardian*, 4 December, accessed 19 May 2020 at: www.theguardian.com/technology/2017/dec/04/racist-facial-recognition-white-coders-black-people-police.

Campbell, N. and C. Deane (2019), 'Bacteria and the market', *Marketing Theory*, **19** (3), 237–57.

Canniford, R., Riach, K., and T. Hill (2018), 'Nosenography: How smell constitutes meaning, identity and temporal experience in spatial assemblages', *Marketing Theory*, **18** (2), 234–48.

Chamovitz, D. (2012), *What a Plant Knows: A Field Guide to the Senses of Your Garden*, Oxford: Oneworld Publications.

Cheetham, F., McEachern, M., and G. Warnaby (2018), 'A kaleidoscopic view of the territorialized consumption of place', *Marketing Theory*, **18** (4), 473–92.

Coffin, J. (2019), 'Deleuzoguattarian place marketing: Becoming, between, beneath and beyond', *Journal of Place Management and Development*, https://doi.org/10.1108/JPMD-01-2019-0003.

Collard, R. (2012), 'Cougar figures, gender, and the performances of predation', *Gender, Place and Culture*, **19** (4), 518–40.

Cresswell, T. (2004), *Place: A Short Introduction*, Oxford: Blackwell Publishing.

Cresswell, T. (2013), *Geographic Thought: A Critical Introduction*, Chichester: Blackwell.

Cresswell, T. and G. Hoskins (2008), 'Place, persistence, and practice: Evaluating historical significance at Angel Island, San Francisco, and Maxwell Street, Chicago', *Annals of the Association of American Geographers*, **98** (2), 392–413.

Debendedetti, A., Oppewal, H., and Z. Arsel (2014), 'Place attachment in commercial settings: A gift economy perspective', *Journal of Consumer Research*, **40** (5), 904–23.

DeLanda, M. and G. Harman (2017), *The Rise of Realism*, Cambridge: Polity Press.

Deleuze, G. and F. Guattari (1987), *A Thousand Plateaus*, translated by B. Massumi, London: Athlone.

Escobar, M. (2014), 'The power of (dis)placement: Pigeons and urban regeneration in Trafalgar Square', *Cultural Geographies*, **21** (3), 363–87.

Flack, A. (2016), 'Lions loose on a gentleman's lawn: Animality, authenticity and automobility in the emergence of the English safari park', *Journal of Historical Geography*, **54** (October), 38–49.

Fleming, A. (2020), 'The case for… Making low-tech "dumb" cities instead of "smart" ones', *The Guardian*, 15 January, accessed 14 May 2020 at: www.theguardian.com/cities/2020/jan/15/the-case-for-making-low-tech-dumb-cities-instead-of-smart-ones?utm_source=dlvr.it&utm_medium=twitter.

Fletcher, T. and L. Platt (2018), '(Just) a walk with the dog? Animal geographies and negotiating walking spaces', *Social and Cultural Geography*, **19** (2), 211–29.

Frazier, D. (2019), 'In Thailand, you can ride an elephant. But should you?', *New York Times*, 19 June, accessed 19 May 2020 at: www.nytimes.com/2019/06/19/travel/thailand-elephant-tourism-humane.html.

Gagliano, M. (2018), *Thus Spoke the Plant: A Remarkable Journey of Groundbreaking Scientific Discoveries and Personal Encounters with Plants*, Berkeley, CA: North Atlantic Books.

Gibson, J. (1979), *The Ecological Approach to Visual Perception*, Boston, MA: Houghton Mifflin.

Ginn, F. (2014), 'Sticky lives: Slugs, detachment and more-than-human ethics in the garden', *Transactions of the Institute of British Geographers*, **39** (4), 532–44.

Giovanardi, M., Kavaratzis, M., and M. Lichrou (2019), 'Critical perspectives on place marketing', in M. Tadajewski, M. Higgins, J. Denegri-Knott, and R. Varman (eds), *The Routledge Companion to Critical Marketing*, London: Routledge, pp. 115–34.

Grayling, A. (2019), *The History of Philosophy*, London: Penguin.

Harari, Y. (2015), *Homo Deus: A Brief History of Tomorrow*, London: Penguin.

Harari, Y. (2018), *21 Lessons for the 21st Century*, London: Penguin.

Harari, Y. (2020), 'Yuval Noah Harari: The world after coronavirus', *Financial Times*, 20 March, accessed 31 March 2020 at: www.ft.com/content/19d90308-6858-11ea-a3c9-1fe6fedcca75.

Haraway, D. (2003), *The Companion Species Manifesto: Dogs, People, and Significant Otherness*, Chicago, IL: Prickly Paradigm.

Haraway, D. (2008), *When Species Meet*, Minneapolis, MN: University of Minnesota Press.

Harman, G. (2018), *Object-Oriented Ontology: A New Theory of Everything*, London: Penguin, Random House.

Henshaw, V., Medway, D., Warnaby, G., and C. Perkins (2015), 'Marketing the "city of smells"', *Marketing Theory*, **16** (2), 153–70.

Hill, T., Canniford, R., and J. Mol (2014), 'Non-representational marketing theory', *Marketing Theory*, **14** (4), 377–94.

Hird, M. (2012), 'Knowing waste: Towards an inhuman epistemology', *Social Epistemology: A Journal of Knowledge, Culture and Policy*, **26** (3–4), 453–69.

Hoffman, D. and T. Novak (2018), 'Consumer and object experience in the Internet of Things: An assemblage theory approach', *Journal of Consumer Research*, **44** (6), 1178–204.

Jerolmack, C. (2008), 'How pigeons became rats: The cultural-spatial logic of problem animals', *Social Problems*, 55 (1), 72–94.

Latour, B. (2005), *Reassembling the Social: An Introduction to Actor-Network-Theory*, Oxford: Oxford University Press.

Law, J. (2009), 'Actor network theory and material semiotics', in B. S. Turner (ed.), *The New Blackwell Companion to Social Theory*, Oxford: Wiley-Blackwell, pp. 141–58.

Maclaran, P. and S. Brown (2005), 'The center cannot hold: Consuming the utopian marketplace', *Journal of Consumer Research*, 32 (2), 311–23.

Manzo, L. and P. Devine-Wright (eds) (2013), *Place Attachment: Advances in Theory, Methods and Applications*, Abingdon: Routledge.

Marshall, C. (2017), 'Elephant tourism is "fuelling cruelty"', *BBC News*, 6 July, accessed 19 May 2020 at: www.bbc.co.uk/news/science-environment-40501667.

McEachern, M., Warnaby, G., and F. Cheetham (2012), 'Producing and consuming public space: A "rhythmanalysis" of the urban park', in Z. Gürhan-Canli, C. Otnes, and R. Zhu (eds), *NA – Advances in Consumer Research*, 40, 873–4.

Medway, D. and G. Warnaby (2017), 'Multisensory place branding: A manifesto for research', in A. Campelo (ed.), *Handbook on Place Branding and Marketing*, Cheltenham, UK and Northampton, MA, USA: Edward Elgar Publishing, pp. 147–59.

Morton, T. (2013), *Hyperobjects: Philosophy and Ecology after the End of the World*, Minneapolis, MN: University of Minnesota Press.

Nagel, T. (1974), 'What is it like to be a bat?', *The Philosophical Review*, 83 (4), 435–50.

Oliveira, E. and G. Ashworth (2017), 'A strategic spatial planning approach to regional branding: Challenges and opportunities', in A. Campelo (ed.), *Handbook on Place Branding and Marketing*, Cheltenham, UK and Northampton, MA, USA: Edward Elgar Publishing, pp. 22–40.

Perkins, T. (2019), '"It's techno-racism": Detroit is quietly using facial recognition to make arrests', *The Guardian*, 17 August, accessed 19 May 2020 at: www.theguardian.com/us-news/2019/aug/16/its-techno-racism-detroit-is-quietly-using-facial-recognition-to-make-arrests.

Philo, C. (1995), 'Animals, geography, and the city: Notes on inclusions and exclusions', *Environment and Planning D: Society and Space*, 13 (6), 655–81.

Power, E. (2009), 'Border-processes and homemaking: Encounters with possums in suburban Australian homes', *Cultural Geographies*, 16 (1), 29–54.

Pred, A. (1984), 'Place as historically contingent process: Structuration and the time-geography of becoming places', *Annals of the Association of American Geographers*, 74 (2), 279–97.

Rawlinson, K. (2019), 'Digital assistants like Siri and Alexa entrench gender biases, says UN', *The Guardian*, 22 May, accessed 19 May 2020 at: www.theguardian.com/technology/2019/may/22/digital-voice-assistants-siri-alexa-gender-biases-unesco-says.

Roffe, J. (2016), 'The concept of the assemblage and the case of markets', in R. Canniford and D. Bajde (eds), *Assembling Consumption*, London: Routledge, pp. 42–56.

Sage, D., Dainty, A., Tyggestad, K., Justesen, L., and J. Mouritsen (2014), 'Building *with* wildlife: Project geographies and cosmopolitics in infrastructure construction', *Construction Management and Economics*, 32 (7–8), 773–86.

Seamon, D. (ed.) (1993), *Dwelling, Seeing and Designing: Toward a Phenomenological Ecology*, Albany, NY: State University of New York Press.

Sherry, Jr., J. F. (2020), 'Grave goods', *Marketing Theory*, https://doi.org/10.1177/1470593119897782.

Skinner, H. (2008), 'The emergence and development of place marketing's confused identity', *Journal of Marketing Management*, **24** (9–10), 915–28.

Therkelsen, A., Halkier, H., and O. B. Jensen (2010), 'Branding Aalborg: Building community or selling place?', in G. Ashworth and M. Kavaratzis (eds), *Towards Effective Place Brand Management: Branding European Cities and Regions*, Cheltenham, UK and Northampton, MA, USA: Edward Elgar Publishing, pp. 136–55.

Tickle, L. (2017), 'Luxury cat hotels and "fur-jazzles": Pet care goes upmarket', *The Guardian*, 15 June, accessed 19 May 2020 at: www.theguardian.com/small-business -network/2017/jun/15/luxury-cat-hotels-and-fur-jazzles-pet-care-goes-upmarket.

Visconti, L., Sherry, J., Borghini, S., and L. Anderson (2010), 'Street art, sweet art? Reclaiming the "public" in public place', *Journal of Consumer Research*, **37** (3), 511–29.

Wandersee, J. and E. Schussler (1999), 'Preventing plant blindness', *The American Biology Teacher*, **61** (2), 82–6.

Warnaby, G. and D. Medway (2013), 'What about the "place" in place marketing?', *Marketing Theory*, **13** (3), 345–63.

Webb, B. (2020), 'Dirty streaming: The internet's big secret', *BBC*, 5 March, accessed 12 May 2020 at: www.bbc.co.uk/iplayer/episode/p083tb16/dirty-streaming-the -internets-big-secret.

White, T. (2020), 'Domesticating the Belt and Road: Rural development, spatial politics, and animal geographies in Inner Mongolia', *Eurasian Geography and Economics*, **61** (1), 13–33.

Wilson, A. (2018), 'How ethical is the elephant "sanctuary" you're visiting?', *The Guardian*, 11 August, accessed 19 May 2020 at: www.theguardian.com/travel/2018/ aug/11/how-ethical-is-the-elephant-sanctuary-youre-visiting.

Wohlleben, P. (2017), *The Hidden Life of Trees: What They Feel, How They Communicate*, London: William Collins.

Zuboff, S. (2019), *The Age of Surveillance Capitalism*, London: Profile Books.

13 Co-creation of place brands?

Jenny Rowley and Sonya Hanna

Introduction

Place and destination brands must be aligned with the evolving identity of a place. For the purpose of this chapter, we regard place identity as the essence of a place, and acknowledge that place identity is probably the most elusive and paradoxical of concepts (Kavaratzis and Kalandides, 2015). The place identity, and its associated experiences, is co-created by a myriad of stakeholders, ranging from destination marketing organisations (DMOs), other private- and public-sector organisations, residents, tourists, other associated places, and, in social media, bloggers. This chapter seeks to distil the diverse literature on co-creation and its relationship to the co-creation of place brands, as a guide to future research and practice. The chapter commences with a review of the key theoretical concepts underpinning the co-creation of place brands, including value creation and brand co-creation. Next, it acknowledges the centrality of place experience co-creation to place branding. Place experience co-creation includes customer-to-customer (C2C) co-creation, the antecedents of co-creation processes in tourism, and resident pro-tourism behaviours. The co-creation of the place brand is then discussed with reference to place brand architectures (place-to-place associations), stakeholders (residents and tourists), and social media. The chapter acknowledges the benefits and challenges of the successful co-creation of place brands, and provides suggestions for practice and for future research.

Theoretical foundations

Prior to exploring the co-creation of place brands, it is important to pay due consideration to the concept of co-creation. We argue there are three key strands of theory and research that inform this concept:

1. Value creation and co-creation, that have their foundations in the literature of service-dominant logic (Grönroos and Voima, 2013; Aitken and Campelo, 2011; Vargo and Lusch, 2004).
2. Multi-stakeholder brand meaning co-creation, in the general branding literature (Pera, Occhiocupo, and Clarke, 2016; Gryd-Jones and Kornum, 2013; Vallaster and Von Wallpach, 2013).
3. Engagement with, and valuing of the contribution of multiple-stakeholder groups, in both place management and development, and place branding (Bounincontri et al., 2017; Aurelli and Forlani, 2016).

Transcending these key strands, there is an increasing recognition of the growing importance of digital and social media spaces as arenas in which brand meaning can be developed, and the contribution of various stakeholder groups to this process (Oliveira and Panyik, 2015; Andehn et al., 2014).

Value Creation and Co-creation

The notions of value creation and co-creation are complex and have been explored from a variety of different perspectives, and contexts. Service-dominant (S-D) logic (Vargo and Lusch, 2004) typically acknowledges two spheres of action, the provider sphere and the customer sphere. The provider sphere focuses on the creation of value-in-exchange (based on the value embedded in a resource), and the customer sphere focuses on the creation of value-in-use (value perceived and determined by the customer) (Grönroos and Voima, 2013). Warnaby (2009) suggests that despite the context specificity and the complexity of cities, an S-D place marketing logic model can be proposed with 'place consumers and customers', 'place product elements', and 'city' (holistic place product) as the three key interacting components.

Zwass (2010: 13) suggests that 'co-creation is the participation of consumers along with producers in the creation of value in the marketplace' and introduces two types of co-creation – sponsored and autonomous. Sponsored co-creation is conducted by consumer communities, or by individuals on behalf of an organisation, whereas, in autonomous co-creation, individuals or consumer communities produce marketable value through voluntary activities, independently of any established organisation. Other researchers have extended the theory to consider types of value, and the contexts in which customers are creating value for other customers. For example, Sheth, Newman, and Gross (1991) proposed a multi-dimensional value model, with the following dimensions: social, emotional, functional, epistemic, and conditional; whilst Pera et al. (2016) present reputation enhancement, experimentation, and relationship building as the *motivators* for participation in value co-creation, and trust, inclusiveness, and openness as fundamental *enablers*.

Whilst research taking an S-D approach may acknowledge the importance of the co-creation activities of customers, and their role in resource integration, consumers view co-creation from the perspective of the value that they create for the organisation. The relatively recent Customer-dominant logic (C-D) relocates value-creating activities into customers' own life contexts, making the activities invisible to organisations, such that organisations cannot use marketing or other communications to intervene in these activities or to support customers in facilitating value outcomes that may lead to positive brand associations (Medberg and Heinonen, 2014). More recently, Rihova et al. (2018) examined C2C co-creation practices in five festivals and identified four value-outcome categories (affective, social, functional, and network value) and outlined the opportunities that arise from facilitating C2C co-creation practices.

In summary, the concept of value creation and co-creation is becoming increasingly important to understanding businesses and communities, and their interactions. S-D logic (Vargo and Lusch, 2004) continues to be extremely important in highlighting the significance of value in the relationship between the provider sphere and the consumer sphere. Arguably, C-D logic offers even greater potential for understanding the dynamics associated with places and their resident and visiting communities, the development of sophisticated value creation practices, and typologies of value-outcome categories.

Brand Meaning Co-creation

Theory relating to co-creation has also been applied to the more specific realm of co-creation of brands. Later, we consider the co-creation of place brands, but this section first explores the nature of brand co-creation in general.

There is acknowledgement that brand identity and meaning are socially constructed as a result of the consequences of complex interactions between multiple stakeholders (Essamri, McKechnie, and Winklhofer, 2019; Gryd-Jones and Kornum, 2013). Consumer co-creation radically refocuses the business around customer value creation, as discussed above. Consumers, often through brand communities, actively create brandscapes (Thompson and Arsel, 2004) and brand cultures (Muniz and O'Guinn, 2001). However, whilst acknowledging the role of consumer participation in co-creation, it is also important to widen the ambit of co-creation to embrace multiple-stakeholder groups. Gryd-Jones and Kornum (2013) refer to this as the stakeholder ecosystem, a concept that embraces both the networked nature of the relationships between stakeholders and the complex set of sub-cultures that contribute to this ecosystem. Importantly, Iglesias, Ind, and Alfaro (2013) specifically acknowledge that many aspects of this co-creation process lie outside of the boundaries of the firm.

Whilst co-creation can have positive outcomes, there are two main challenges associated with it. The first is that as stakeholders become powerful when they combine their resources and skills and create social spaces to interact with each other and the firm, they may communicate an image that is inconsistent with that which the firm seeks to project (Cova, Pace, and Skalen, 2015). Additionally, co-creation is reliant on the firm's awareness and ability to attract stakeholders/consumers 'and offer them resources and a collaborative and creative milieu in which to communicate, debate, critique, innovate and utilise their skills and knowledge for their own interest as well as that of the brand' (Essamri et al., 2019: 368). According to Vallaster and Von Wallpach (2013), virtual spaces, and most notably social media, are a suitable arena for co-creation as they facilitate free expression, reflection on brand experiences, and the sharing of brand associations with other stakeholders. Virtual spaces and social media extend stakeholder participation in brand-related discourse and increase the interrelatedness between stakeholders (Asmussen et al., 2010). However, it has to be recognised that online and social media stakeholder communications, especially in highly visible areas such as tourism, are likely to contribute to the generation of a fluid and evolving brand identity, which in turn may pose its own unique challenges.

Place and destination co-creation

This section commences with a review of the nature of co-creation and some of its benefits and challenges in different contexts. It then considers co-creation as the result of the relationships between the brands associated with a place, focusing on place brand architectures. This acts as a precursor to a more focused analysis on place and destination co-creation through digital and social media channels, an arena that offers some unique opportunities for co-creation.

Co-creation

The literature acknowledges the diversity of stakeholder groups associated with a place and, most importantly, the understanding of co-creation as 'a shared reality, dynamically constructed through social interaction' (Ballantyne and Aitken, 2007: 365). On this basis, it is important not only to consider the number of and types of stakeholders, but also to consider how the interaction of these various perspectives generates new brand meanings and a consensus on the essence of the brand, and the processes whereby the brand meaning emerges and evolves. Brand meanings are created by shared beliefs and realities and the interaction between suppliers, stakeholders, and consumers is at the heart of the paradigm of co-creation (Aitken and Campelo, 2011; Grönroos, 2000). Believing that brand meanings are socially constructed, culturally dependant, and 'community' owned represents a radical shift in the notion of brands, brand ownership, and brand leadership (Ballantyne and Aitken, 2007).

Various perspectives have been adopted in the pursuit of understanding place brand co-creation, including place experience co-creation. Focusing on tourists and residents, research highlights that the context and purpose of co-creation differs between these groups. Residents typically have a relatively long-term view of, multiple associations with, and perspectives emerging from their interaction with the place that forms a key aspect of their life. Their interactions may be associated with their roles as residents, workers, sports fans, volunteers, students, shoppers, and 'tourists'. Tourists, however, have a more limited interaction with a place. For some this may constitute one short visit, whereas others may be regular visitors. Residents may have a wide variety of attitudes regarding tourists. Some may resent their presence, others may acknowledge the economic and wider benefits they bring, and some may participate in pro-tourism behaviours (Ribeiro et al., 2017). There is significant evidence that the attitudes and behaviours of host communities are pivotal in supporting tourism development (e.g. Sinclair-Maragh and Gursoy, 2016), given that the success of a place's tourism industry relies on residents' hospitality and their active support (Alegre and Cladera, 2009). In a study of the Cape Verde Islands, Ribeiro et al. (2017) found that economic factors have a direct influence on resident pro-tourism behaviours. Further, the relationship between non-economic factors (residents' degree of welcoming tourists) was only mediated by positive attitudes, whereas attitudes to both positive and negative impacts have a direct influence on residents' pro-tourism development behaviour. As part of a research programme also based in an island context, Aitken and Campelo (2011) demonstrate the embeddedness of place identities in the minds of the residents of the Chatham Islands in New Zealand,

and demonstrate the importance of a bottom-up approach to co-creation in order to achieve brand ownership, as a basis for brand authenticity, commitment, and brand sustainability.

Research also focuses on tourists' involvement in the co-creation of the place experience as distinct from the co-creation of the place brand. For example, Bounincontri et al. (2017) explored the main antecedents and consequences of experience co-creation in tourism. Buhalis and Sinarta (2019: 564) suggest that 'technology has transformed value creation from a product centred process to a consumer-centric approach'. They also suggest that the integration of real-time consumer intelligence, dynamic big data mining, artificial intelligence, and contextualisation can transform service co-creation, so as to engage consumers in experience co-creation in real time. Rihova et al. (2018) conducted interviews at five United Kingdom festivals. On this basis, they proposed 18 C2C co-creation practices: insulating, territoriality, non-confirming, communicating, sharing, collaborating, acknowledging, advising, conversing, helping, relating, confiding, conforming, trading, initiating, embracing, fun making, and rekindling. Taking a rather different focus for co-creation, Pasquinelli (2014) analyses the process associated with the development of a brand that embraces the relational space of two cities, the NewcastleGateshead brand. The research focuses on the formation and development of an organisational identity within the relational space of the two cities, framed by an institutional collaboration crossing local administrative borders. However, the branding process was challenging because it was implemented in order to bring together two organisational entities, with different histories and processes.

Place Brand Architecture and Co-branding

The concepts of brand architecture and co-branding explore the relationships between brands. When brand owners work together to contribute to the identity of a place, they are engaging in co-creation at an organisational level. Traditional branding theory views relationships between brands from the perspective of owner managers and under the control of brand managers such that together the brands form the organisation's brand portfolio (Sanchez, 2004). Place brand architectures are much 'looser', with each of the constituent brands being to a greater or lesser extent independent of the dominant brand. For example, the brand 'Manchester' could be viewed as one of the umbrella brands for other places, such as Stockport and Didsbury, as well as for organisations in its 'region' such as Manchester United, the Manchester Museum, or the Palace Theatre. In contrast to the NewcastleGateshead example discussed earlier, such places have varying levels of formal association with the Manchester brand and with its DMO, Marketing Manchester. To acknowledge this unique relationship between the brands associated with a place, Hanna and Rowley (2015) introduced the concept of the Place Brand Web. Using the place brand of Liverpool, they differentiate between sub-brands (brands fully managed by the DMO, Marketing Liverpool) and co-brands (brands that have established co-branding relationships with the DMO). They also identify a range of 'types of organisations in the region' that may have either an explicit or implicit association with the brand 'Liverpool', including local and national government, universities and colleges, and sports, regeneration, commercial, tourism, leisure, cultural, and social organisations.

A brand portfolio, or web, may be managed through either a house-of-brands or branded-house strategy, giving different levels of autonomy to the brands in the portfolio and, for the organisations/places involved, flexibility in their use and development of brands (Hsu, Fournier, and Srinivasan, 2016; Aaker and Joachimsthaler, 2000). Datzira-Masip and Poluzzi (2014) suggest that the Balearic Islands use the house-of-brands strategy since the individual islands such as Majorca are more visible than the brand of the archipelago, whereas the Maldives use the branded-house strategy since the names and characteristics of the single islands are unrecognised, but the generic characteristics of the Maldives are well known. More recently, Zenker and Braun (2017) point to the complexity of city branding and offer insights into the use of a branded-house strategy for place brand management to accommodate the diversity of the place offering and the various associations customers might have with the place. They propose a city branded-house strategy that embraces both a shared city umbrella brand and specific sub-brands for individual target groups.

Managing a network of relationships between a 'loose' collection of brands is challenging given the interactive and evolutionary nature of place brand architectures (Kotsi et al., 2018; Van der Zee, Gerrets, and Vanneste, 2017; Freire, 2016). Models based on corporate co-branding such as the 'corporate brand association base' (Uggla, 2006) that link the corporate brand with its surrounding environment through partner associations may be more viable. Using the corporate co-branding approach, for place brands, partner associations may include other places or service brands, persons with strong associations with a place, and institutional cultural associations. In co-branding, relationships are consensual and involve a shared commitment to various aspects of the brand, including its symbolic and narrative representations. Recent studies in the hotel sector (Dioko and So, 2012; Tasci and Guillet, 2011; Tasci and Denizci, 2010) reveal that both synergies and spillover effects can be realised through destination co-branding.

Place brand co-creation through digital and social media channels

Social media offers significant potential for brand co-creation, through contributions from place and destination marketers, bloggers, and 'place users', and can be viewed as a 'new' venue for place-meaning formulation (Andehn et al., 2014). Boyd, Golder, and Lotan (2010) suggest that social media has 'a unique conversational architecture'. This architecture offers firms not only an opportunity for persistent engagement with consumers, but also for customised and triggered engagement (Cabiddu, De Carlo, and Piccoli, 2014). More specifically, online and social media platforms can facilitate and strengthen the dynamic interactions within online communities, making it possible to share brand stories with others and to participate jointly in the co-creation process. Zwass (2010) suggests that the interconnectivities of consumers in online brand communities generates relationship marketing and loyalty, which, in turn, contributes to the co-creation of the value associated with a brand. Some organisations invite consumer groups to co-create a brand's ideology, use, and persona (Cova and Pace, 2006), in order to create a sense of belonging to a brand community alongside a brand self-congruence effect.

A recent contribution develops a taxonomy of value co-creation on the social media platform Weibo (Ge and Gretzel, 2018). Their taxonomy includes actors (organisations, focal firms, local stakeholders, travel trade, media), consumers (influencers, general users), and actions (liking, tagging, reporting, commenting). Each of these action categories have sub-actions, with the list under 'commenting' including enhancement, validation, promotion, entertainment, personalisation, negotiation, and socialisation. Other researchers have adopted different theoretical lenses, such as customer engagement, and associated motivational factors, including personal and community-related benefits (Munar and Steen Jacobsen, 2014). Harrigan et al. (2017) develop scales that can be used to measure, for example, customer engagement with tourism brands.

However, the management of social media interactions and data by DMOs is a challenge and can lead to co-destruction in which social media users harm destination brands through their posts (Lund, Cohen, and Scarles, 2019). Brand community 'members' sometimes appropriate the brand, and together reshape the brand's identity, image, and reputation (Cova and Pace, 2006). This appropriation is particularly prevalent in social media networks, where it is easier to exert control over brand identity and reputation, leading at times to 'damage to the brand' or a divergence of brand meaning, with different stakeholders projecting different meanings (Cova and White, 2010). For example, in the national referendum campaign supporting Scottish independence, Black and Veloutsou (2017) demonstrate how interactions between the brand, individual consumers, and the brand community facilitated the co-creation of these three identities as a basis for developing good-quality relationships and loyalty. This, in turn, supported co-creation processes with the brand. Hence, central to managing a place brand is an understanding of the extent to which user-generated social media content aligns with the DMO's projections of the place and, in turn, the impact of the level of alignment on place brand equity. One way of exploring the alignment between the identities of the brands associated with a place is through conducting a netnographic analysis of social media content and comparing the outcome of this process with the key themes in DMO communications related to the place identity and brand.

Lund, Cohen, and Scarles (2018: 271) suggest that the extent of global engagement with social media poses a significant challenge for DMOs 'which must cope with a new reality where destination brands are increasingly the product of people's shared tourism experiences and storytelling in social networks, rather than marketing strategies'. The authors propose a conceptual framework of the four technologies of power: storytelling, mobilities, performativities, and performances. They suggest that whilst storytelling is central, the other three technologies are instrumental in increasing the attractiveness of users' stories. Using a case study approach based on VisitDenmark, they explore how a DMO can use these technologies to merge the online and offline worlds, and to participate in collaborative storytelling.

Future research agenda

This chapter seeks to draw together the various theoretical and empirical perspectives that act as a foundation for research into the co-creation of place brands. An understanding of co-creation has become particularly important in recent years as stakeholders and other audiences have been empowered by social media and widespread travel opportunities. In order that a place can project a clear, but also multi-faceted identity, it needs to continue to innovate in partnership with its communities. To accomplish this, it needs to be informed by a rich and evolving research base, which encompasses the diversity of place branding, including:

- Different co-creation *stakeholders* e.g. other places, businesses, organisations and places in the place brand web, and people (tourists and residents).

- Different co-creation *objectives and outcomes*. Even for an individual place there can be a mismatch between objectives and outcomes, especially given the dynamic nature of places.
- Different *platforms for communication and co-creation* – digital, including the web and social media, and place infrastructures including cultural assets, transport links, housing, and geography (e.g. hills and rivers).

More specifically, we suggest the following foci for future research:

1. The nature of co-creation in different place branding contexts, including research on the roles and influence of different stakeholder groups.
2. Wider exploration of the nature and contribution of stakeholders in different settings and contexts, including the identification of strategies for engaging place stakeholders, and understanding the impact (positive or negative) of apathy towards a place.
3. Further theoretical development of the distinction between a stakeholder and a customer and the consequences for the co-creation of place brands.
4. DMOs' contributions and approaches to creating and managing a place brand community.
5. Exploration of the relationship between co-creating the place experience and co-creating the place brand, including consideration of the nature of the contributions from different stakeholder groups and from relevant DMOs.
6. Enhanced understanding of the role of social media in co-creation of the brand, and the differences associated with the different social media platforms (e.g. Twitter versus Facebook).
7. Extension of the use of C-D logic approaches to inform the *motivators* and *enablers* associated with participation in generating place brand value.
8. Exploration of what DMOs do and can do to participate in social media conversations, not only by using social media posting to promote a more positive image of a place, but also to facilitate a sense of identification with, or of belonging amongst, tourists, residents, and other stakeholder groups.
9. Place brand evolution over time and its alignment with the place identity.
10. Further exploration of the range of groups that might be involved in co-creation in different settings, and the contributions that they are able and willing to make.
11. Research on the participation and role of residents in brand meaning and value co-creation to counter the emphasis in existing studies on tourists.

References

Aaker, D. A. and E. Joachimsthaler (2000), 'The brand relationship spectrum: The key to the brand architecture challenge', *California Management Review*, **42** (3), 8–22.

Aitken, R. and A. Campelo (2011), 'The four Rs of place branding', *Journal of Marketing Management*, **27** (9/10), 913–33.

Alegre, J. and M. Cladera (2009), 'Analysing the effect of satisfaction and previous visits on tourism intentions to return', *European Journal of Marketing*, **43** (5/6), 670–85.

Andehn, M., Kazeminina, A., Lucarelli, A., and E. Sevin (2014), 'User-generated place brand equity on Twitter: The dynamics of brand associations in social media', *Place Branding and Public Diplomacy*, **10** (2), 132–44.

Asmussen, B., Haridge-March, S., Occhiocupo, N., and J. Farquhar (2010), 'The internet-based democratisation of brand management: The dawn of a new paradigm or dangerous nonsense?', *Proceedings of the 39th EMAC Conference*, Copenhagen.

Aurelli, S. and F. Forlani (2016), 'The importance of brand architecture in business networks: The case of tourist network contracts in Italy', *Qualitative Market Research: An International Journal*, **19** (2), 133–55.

Ballantyne, D. and R. Aitken (2007), 'Branding in B2B markets: Insights from the service-dominant logic of marketing', *Journal of Business and Industrial Marketing*, **22** (6), 363–71.

Black, I. and C. Veloutsou (2017), 'Working consumers: Co-creation of brand identity, consumer identity and brand community identity', *Journal of Business Research*, **70**, 416–29.

Bounincontri, P., Morvillo, A., Okumus, F., and M. Ban Niekerk (2017), 'Managing the experience co-creation process in tourism destinations: Empirical findings from Naples', *Tourism Management*, **62**, 264–77.

Boyd, D., Golder, S., and G. Lotan (2010), 'Tweet, tweet, retweet: Conversational aspects of retweeting on Twitter', in *2010 43rd Hawaii International Conference on System Sciences*, Honolulu, HI: IEEE, pp. 1–10.

Buhalis, D. and Y. Sinarta (2019), 'Real-time co-creation and nowness service: Lessons from tourism and hospitality', *Journal of Travel and Tourism Marketing*, **36** (5), 563–82.

Cabiddu, F., De Carlo, M., and G. Piccoli (2014), 'Social media affordances: Enabling customer engagement', *Annals of Tourism Research*, **48**, 175–92.

Cova, B. and S. Pace (2006), 'Brand community of convenience products: New forms of customer empowerment – the case of "my Nutella the Community"', *European Journal of Marketing*, **40** (9/10), 1087–105.

Cova, B. and T. White (2010), 'Counter-brand and alter-brand communities: The impact of Web 2.0 on tribal marketing approaches', *Journal of Marketing Management*, **26** (3/4), 256–70.

Cova, B., Pace, S., and P. Skalen (2015), 'Marketing with consumers: The case of a carmaker and its brand community', *Organisation*, **22** (5), 682–701.

Datzira-Masip, J. and A. Poluzzi (2014), 'Brand architecture management: The case of four destinations in Catalonia', *Journal of Destination Marketing and Management*, **3** (1), 48–58.

Dioko, L. A. N. and S. I. So (2012), 'Branding destinations versus branding hotels in a gaming destination: Examining the nature and significance of co-branding effects in the case study of Macao', *International Journal of Hospitality Management*, **31** (2), 554–63.

Essamri, A., McKechnie, S., and H. Winklhofer (2019), 'Co-creating corporate brand identity with online brand communities: A managerial perspective', *Journal of Business Research*, **96**, 366–75.

Freire, J. R. (2016), 'Managing destination brand architecture: The case of Cascais Municipality', *Place Branding and Public Diplomacy*, **12** (1), 78–90.

Ge, J. and U. Gretzel (2018), 'A taxonomy of value co-creation on Weibo: A communication perspective', *International Journal of Contemporary Hospitality Management*, **30** (4), 2075–92.

Grönroos, C. (2000), *Service Management and Marketing: A Customer Relationship Management Approach*, Chichester: Wiley.

Grönroos, C. and P. Voima (2013), 'Critical service logic: Making sense of value creation and co-creation', *Journal of the Academy of Marketing Science*, **41** (2), 133–50.

Gryd-Jones, R. I. and N. Kornum (2013), 'Managing the co-created brand: Value and cultural complementarity in online and off-line multi-stakeholder ecosystems', *Journal of Business Research*, **66**, 1484–93.

Hanna, S. and J. Rowley (2015), 'Towards a model of the Place Brand Web', *Tourism Management*, **48**, 100–12.

Harrigan, P., Evers, U., Miles, M., and T. Daly (2017), 'Customer engagement with tourism social media brands', *Tourism Management*, **59**, 597–609.

Hsu, L., Fournier, S., and S. Srinivasan (2016), 'Brand architecture strategy and firm value: How leveraging, separating, and distancing the corporate brand affects risk and returns', *Journal of the Academy of Marketing Science*, **44** (2), 261–80.

Iglesias, O., Ind, N., and M. Alfaro (2013), 'The organic view of the brand: A brand value co-creation model', *Journal of Brand Management*, **20** (8), 670–88.

Kavaratzis, M. and A. Kalandides (2015), 'Rethinking the place brand: The interactive formation of place brands and the role of participatory place branding', *Environment and Planning A*, **47** (6), 1368–82.

Kotsi, F., Balakrishnan, M. S., Michael, I., and T. Z. Ramsoy (2018), 'Place branding: Aligning multiple stakeholder perception of visual and auditory communication elements', *Journal of Destination Marketing and Management*, 7 (3), 112–30.

Lund, N. F., Cohen, S. A., and C. Scarles (2018), 'The power of social media storytelling in destination branding', *Journal of Destination Marketing and Management*, **8**, 271–80.

Lund, N. F., Cohen, S. A., and C. Scarles (2019), 'The brand value continuum: Countering co-destruction of destination branding in social media through storytelling', *Journal of Travel Research*, https://doi.org/10.1177/0047287519887234.

Medberg, G. and K. Heinonen (2014), 'Invisible value formation: A netnography in retail banking', *International Journal of Bank Marketing*, **32** (6), 590–607.

Munar, A. M. and J. Steen Jacobsen (2014), 'Motivations for sharing tourism experiences through social media', *Tourism Management*, **43**, 46–54.

Muniz, A. M. and T. C. O'Guinn (2001), 'Brand community', *Journal of Consumer Research*, **27** (4), 412–32.

Oliveira, E. and E. Panyik (2015), 'Content, context and co-creation: Digital challenges in destination branding with reference to Portugal as a tourist destination', *Journal of Vacation Marketing*, **21** (1), 53–74.

Pasquinelli, C. (2014), 'Branding as urban collective strategy-making: The formation of NewcastleGatesheads' organisational identity', *Urban Studies*, **51** (4), 727–43.

Pera, R., Occhiocupo, N., and J. Clarke (2016), 'Motives and resources for value co-creation in a multi-stakeholder ecosystem: A managerial perspective', *Journal of Business Research*, **69** (10), 4033–41.

Ribeiro, M. A., Pinto, P., Silva, J. A., and K. M. Woosnam (2017), 'Residents' attitudes and the adoption of pro-tourism behaviours: The case of developing island countries', *Tourism Management*, **61**, 523–37.

Rihova, I., Buhalis, D., Gouthro, M. B., and M. Moital (2018), 'Customer-to-customer co-creation practices in tourism: Lessons from customer-dominant logic', *Tourism Management*, **67**, 362–75.

Sanchez, R. (2004), 'Conceptual analysis of brand architecture and relationships with product categories', *Journal of Brand Management*, **11** (3), 233–47.

Sheth, J. N., Newman, B. I., and B. L. Gross (1991), 'Why we buy what we buy: A theory of consumption values', *Journal of Business Research*, **22** (2), 159–70.

Sinclair-Maragh, G. and D. Gursoy (2016), 'A conceptual model of residents' support for tourism development in developing countries', *Tourism Planning and Development*, **13** (1), 1–22.

Tasci, A. D. A. and R. Denizci (2010), 'Fashionable hospitability: A natural symbiosis for Hong Kong's tourism industry?', *International Journal of Hospitability Management*, **29** (3), 488–99.

Tasci, A. D. A. and B. D. Guillet (2011), 'It affects, it affects not: A quasi-experiment on the transfer effect of co-branding on consumer-based brand equity of hospitality products', *International Journal of Hospitality Management*, **30** (4), 774–82.

Thompson, C. J. and Z. T. Arsel (2004), 'The Starbucks brandscape and consumers' (anticorporate) experiences of glocalisation', *Journal of Consumer Research*, **31** (3), 631–42.

Uggla, H. (2006), 'The corporate brand association base: A conceptual model for the creation of inclusive brand architecture', *European Journal of Marketing*, **40** (7/8), 785–802.

Vallaster, C. and S. Von Wallpach (2013), 'An online discursive inquiry into the social dynamic of multi-stakeholder brand meaning co-creation', *Journal of Business Research*, **66** (9), 1505–615.

Van der Zee, E., Gerrets, A. M., and D. Vanneste (2017), 'Complexity in the government of tourism networks: Balancing between external pressure and internal expectations', *Journal of Destination and Marketing Management*, **6** (4), 296–308.

Vargo, S. L. and R. F. Lusch (2004), 'Evolving a new dominant logic for marketing', *Journal of Marketing*, **68** (1), 1–17.

Warnaby, G. (2009), 'Towards a service-dominant place marketing logic', *Marketing Theory*, **9** (4), 403–23.

Zenker, S. and E. Braun (2017), 'Questioning a "one size fits all" city brand: Developing a branded house strategy for place brand management', *Journal of Place Management and Development*, **10** (3), 270–87.

Zwass, V. (2010), 'Co-creation: Toward a taxonomy and an integrated research perspective', *International Journal of Electronic Commerce*, **15** (1), 11–48.

14 Tourism, the burden of authenticity and place branding

Maria Lichrou and Lisa O'Malley

Introduction

Tourism 'involves the symbolic transmutation of many ordinary objects, places and experiences into sacred ones' (Watson and Kopachevsky, 1994: 648). Nevertheless, the realisation of the tourist visit involves a degree of commodification of places (which become 'destinations') as access is managed and an array of services are provided to make the visit possible (Williams and Shaw, 1992). Consequently, the tourism phenomenon is marked by a paradox: tourism is seen as both sacred and frivolous (Crick, 1996). On the one hand, consumption of tourism is marked by a religious aspect, and is likened to ritual performance and pilgrimage (MacCannell, 1999 [1976]; Graburn, 1983; Seaton, 2002). On the other, tourism, as a frivolous activity, is regarded as a corruptor of authenticity (Boorstin, 1962; Crick, 1996). This is captured in notions of places as 'tourist bubbles' or 'enclaves', which are created and curated for tourism consumption by the tourist industry (MacCannell, 1973; Edensor, 2006). Commodification is the process by which things and activities come to be evaluated primarily in terms of their exchange value in a context of trade, thereby becoming goods and services (Cohen, 1988). Marketers of tourism places are often caught in this paradox: the simultaneous perception of tourism as a quest for authenticity and its effects as a commoditising process. This is essentially the burden of authenticity. In unravelling this conundrum, we consider how applications of marketing management thinking to tourism have exacerbated commodification processes, by homogenising places. We then explore how more recent thinking opens up new possibilities for action, facilitating experience co-creation, the realisation of value and the potential for existential authenticity. This resonates with the turn to participatory place branding practices (e.g. Colomb and Kalandides, 2010; Kavaratzis, Giovanardi and Lichrou, 2017), acknowledging how brands become symbolic resources (e.g. Kavaratzis and Hatch, 2013, 2019) employed by different actors to co-create value.

The marketing of tourism destinations is an important and serious business as success in attracting visitors contributes significantly to local, regional and national economies, providing opportunities for enterprise and employment that allow locals to preserve and/or enhance their way(s) of life. Efforts to professionalise place marketing have resulted in the widespread adoption of market-oriented strategies, involving a focus on selecting target markets, identifying and anticipating tourists' needs, benchmarking against competing destinations, developing coherent place products, articulating compelling brands and organising communication strategies around selected functional and representational qualities (e.g. Ashworth and Goodall, 2013 [1990]; Giovanardi, Lucarelli and Pasquinelli, 2013). Consequently, distinct categories of tourism – cultural tourism, adventure tourism, eco-tourism, heritage tourism, city tourism, etc. – have been identified, with markets segmented a priori in order to receive targeted communications. Within this approach, the creation of value is the responsibility of the destination management authority and value is embedded in the place product. This requires a focus on the qualities of the place that might appeal to a target market, rather than a consideration of the place's unique needs and characteristics (Haywood, 1990). However, because places are multifaceted, contested and dynamic, the conception of places as products fails to capture this complexity (Warnaby and Medway, 2013; Lichrou, O'Malley and Patterson, 2008; Campos, 2012). Socially constructed through myth (Rojek, 2000) and intersubjective drama (Voase, 1999), places are not simply physical settings, but particular expressions of the dialectical relationship between material reality and subjective meaning (Meethan, 2001).

Contemporary tourists appear to be more empowered and more demanding than ever before; they have access to unprecedented amounts of information about the places they visit and are more discerning about the quality of their experiences (Poon, 1994; Robinson and Novelli, 2005). They do not represent a target market in the sense of identifiable homogeneous groups. Rather, they are more complex, have more diversified patterns of behaviour and heterogeneous motivations (Torres, 2002). They seek authentic experiences in which they can actively participate and which 'assist them in the creation of their own identities, while experiencing feelings and related emotional states' (Campos, 2012: 35). The de-differentiation of tourism (Urry, 1990) from other domains of everyday life such as art, culture, sport, hobby, school, work, etc. (Binkhorst and Den Dekker, 2009) further exacerbates the challenges of marketing to clearly defined target markets.

Following years of market-oriented approaches to tourism development and marketing, tourism places have become increasingly similar and are implicated in the serial reproduction of staged cultural experiences (Richards and Wilson, 2006), through the application of standardised place branding practices globally, including hosting mega events and investing in flagship buildings and signature districts (Kavaratzis and Ashworth, 2015). This phenomenon is referred to as the 'McGuggenheimisation' of cultural experiences (Richards and Wilson, 2006). Following the effect of Guggenheim Museum Bilbao in the place's transformation into a city of culture, many cities attempted to emulate Bilbao's success by investing in flagship museum projects. However, the particularities that made the project successful in Bilbao meant that its effect is not easily transferred elsewhere (Franklin, 2016). Furthermore, the repackaging of culture by corporations and localities for the attraction of tourists has resulted in homogeneous, 'comfortingly predictable' tourist spaces, which paradoxically further drive the search for denser, more authentic places (Edensor, 2006).

Given these challenges it is increasingly recognised that efforts to manage and brand destinations as products are problematic in that they ultimately commoditise destinations; reductive in that they ignore the multifaceted, contested and dynamic nature of places; and limited in communicating complexity. This has intensified the shift away from attractions and towards participatory, 'engaging' activities that distinguish destinations at the experiential level (e.g. Tung and Ritchie, 2011; Park and Santos, 2017). Such shifts are mirrored in the wider consumptionscape, where the emphasis on experiences is in the ascendancy (Pine and Gilmore, 2011 [1999]; Prahalad and Ramaswamy, 2003, 2004a, 2004b; Vargo and Lusch, 2004). Experience is now regarded as the locus of value creation, implying that marketers, tourists and local communities 'co-create' destinations. This requires a shift of mindset from marketing *to* tourists to marketing *with* tourists and other stakeholders. Recent work articulates the challenges and opportunities associated with understanding and marketing experiences (Tung and Ritchie, 2011; Park and Santos, 2017) and others explore how new marketing logics might inform tourism (Warnaby, 2009; Park and Vargo, 2012; Warnaby and Medway, 2015). Through the engagement of tourists' operant resources – such as energy, imagination, relationships and skills – co-creation has transformational potential for tourists and destinations (Richards and Wilson, 2006). The aim of this chapter is thus to consider value co-creation, not as a panacea to the serial reproduction of tourism attractions, but as an opportunity for less commodified experiences. We begin by revisiting tourism discourse on authenticity, placing particular attention to the notion of existential authenticity (Wang, 1999).

The quest for authenticity

For MacCannell (1999 [1976]) the tourist is a modern pilgrim who is searching for experiences in places other than his or her own, but cannot escape the 'staged authenticity' (MacCannell, 1973) that is performed by the tourism industry and/or the locals at the destination. As such, authenticity has been discussed in relation to some kinds of tourism – ethnic, historical or cultural tourism – which involve representation of the 'other' or the past. Authentic cultures are assumed to be the cultures that are primitive, timeless and unchanged (Silver, 1993; Echtner and Prasad, 2003). Marketing strategies often invoke fusing the modern and the primitive, claims for a more authentic other, invitations for unique experiences (Silver, 1993), 'authentic' accommodation (Paulauskaite et al., 2017) and new forms of tourism, such as volunteer tourism (Mostafanezhad, 2014) and eco-cultural tourism (Tiberghien, 2019). Arguably, then, conceptions of authenticity often reflect an essentialist perspective (Chhabra, 2008), which has been criticised for reifying particular traditions and cultures as authentic, especially those deemed 'untouched' by the market (Shepherd, 2002). In contrast, constructivists view culture as dynamic and flexible, and question the existence of an original moment (Shepherd, 2002). From this perspective culture is always in progress, and authenticity is better understood as a struggle for competing interests. The experience of authenticity is pluralistic, and something initially artificial may become authentic with the passage of time (Cohen, 1988). Besides, to try and keep a culture 'real' in the objective authenticity sense is to keep it frozen, cryogenised and protected to death (Ritzer and Liska, 1997).

For Wang (1999: 353), 'authenticity is not a matter of black or white, but rather involves a much wider spectrum, rich in ambiguous colours'. Drawing on Berger (1973), he delineates the notion of existential authenticity, which is activity related and involves the realisation of the self through tourist experiences (Wang, 1999; Steiner and Reisinger, 2006). According to Berger (1973) existential authenticity denotes a special state of being in which one is true to oneself, and acts as a counter dose to the loss of 'true self' in public roles and public spheres, central in contemporary Western living (Wang, 1999). It involves both *intrapersonal* and *interpersonal* authenticity as tourists seek 'authenticity of, and between *themselves*' (Wang, 1999: 364, original emphasis). Intrapersonal authenticity is essentially concerned with self-renewal and self-making. It involves both the sensual (authenticity manifesting as bodily sensations) and the symbolic, where the body becomes a display of personal identity (communicating ideals of health, naturalness, youth, fitness, movement, beauty, etc.). Interpersonal authenticity relates to the formation of touristic 'communitas' or relationship making (Wang, 1999). Building on Victor Turner's research on pilgrimage and Michel Maffesoli's notion of tribes, Wang (1999: 364) argues that 'the toured objects of tourism can be just a means or medium by which tourists are called together, and then, an authentic inter-personal relationship between themselves is experienced subsequently'. Communitas is characterised by liminality and 'occurs as an unmediated, pure inter-personal relationship among pilgrims who confront one another as social equals based on their common humanity' (Wang, 1999: 364). Liminality refers to 'any condition outside of or on the peripheries of everyday life' (Turner, 1974: 47).

Tourism offers extensive opportunities for existential authenticity (e.g. Kim and Jamal, 2007); including 'flow' (Csikszentmihalyi, 1975; Weber, 2001), 'peak' (Celsi, Rose and Leigh, 1993; Buckley, 2012), 'extraordinary' (Arnould and Price, 1993) and 'recovery' experiences (Valtonen and Veijola, 2011). Such experiences play an important role in tourists' re-enchantment (Rojek, 2000) with the world and can be transformative not only for their members, but for business practices and society in general (Cova, Kozinets and Shankar, 2007). Flow and extraordinary experiences have been explored within tourism and marketing. Both categories of experience involve 'the merging of action and awareness, attention or clear focus, personal integration, personal control, awareness of power, joy and valuing, and a spontaneous (uninhibited) letting-be of process' (Arnould and Price, 1993: 25). However, drawing on Abrahams (1986), Arnould and Price distinguish extraordinary experience from flow, because extraordinary experience 'implies neither superior levels of effort nor an independent relational mode' (1993: 25). Furthermore, extraordinary experience is characterised by spontaneity, ambiguous expectations and emergent rather than predicted satisfaction. As such, it is not possible for marketers to script and package this type of experience. Extraordinary experiences can be transformative (e.g. Bosangit, Hibbert and McCabe, 2015), because they enable individuals to transcend everyday realm and experience an 'authentic' sense of self and connection to others. Art festivals, for example, are social and spatio-temporal contexts that facilitate cathartic communal experiences (Kozinets, 2002) and help participants feel a sense of freedom and escape from the quotidian existence (Szmigin et al., 2017). Building on Turner (1982), Kozinets proclaims that such experiences can be 'enough to liberate considerable creativity, to release repression, to fulfil some sense of people's hidden potential, to evoke self-expression, and to unleash the potential for self-transformation' (2002: 36).

However, tourists do not always seek extraordinary or commercialised experiences (Carù and Cova, 2003). Simple, more ordinary activities like taking a walk (Carù and Cova, 2003) and even sleeping (Valtonen and Veijola, 2011) allow time for contemplation and recovery and thus engender existential well-being. The implication is that value for tourists may involve moments marked by an absence of commercial activity. Such moments can be 'serendipitous' and 'epiphanic' (Cary, 2004), and as such cannot be pre-determined, orchestrated and delivered as products. Serendipitous implies that authentic experiences are as much a question of time as they are of space, because they occur when something unexpected happens (Park and Santos, 2017), 'a chance encounter, a flat tire, a moment alone on a park bench, a view from a particular angle' (Shepherd, 2015: 68). Such moments are not exclusive to tourism but can 'happen to everyone, whether on vacation, a journey of self-discovery, or at home' (Shepherd, 2015: 68). Yet tourism, as a break from everyday life, both in terms of space and time, can provide a plethora of opportunities for such moments to occur. It is these unexpected moments that tourists tend to remember (Park and Santos, 2017), highlighting the extent to which they represent value for them.

Phenomenological conceptions of value and value creation

The attention of marketers has shifted over the last few decades away from physical products towards services, relationships and experiences. Consequently, our understanding, and perhaps more accurately, our articulation of value creation and the *locus* of value for consumers have changed dramatically. Value creation is now understood as inherently relational and experiential. According to Grönroos and Ravald, 'the prevailing view that value for customers is embedded in products that are outputs of a supplier's manufacturing process, value-in-exchange, has been challenged by the value-in-use notion' (2011: 7). Value-in-use is customer defined and phenomenologically determined. It therefore defies objective definition. Nonetheless, it does have a number of criteria (Holbrook, 1999, 2006a, 2006b). First, assessments of value are personal (they differ from one individual to another), situational (they vary from one evaluative context to another) and comparative (the relative merits of one thing over another are considered relevant at that point in time). In these regards, value is 'an interactive relativistic preference experience' (Holbrook, 1999: 5). Holbrook (1999, 2006a) also delimits three key dimensions of consumer value: (1) extrinsic versus intrinsic value; (2) self-oriented versus other-oriented value; and (3) active versus reactive value. These distinctions become important both as descriptors of consumer value and as prescriptors of marketing strategy.

First, products or experiences with extrinsic value are viewed as utilitarian and appreciated as a means to some end. In contrast, intrinsic value emerges from experiences that are autotelic and appreciated for their own sake (Holbrook, 2006a; Komppula and Gartner, 2013). Intrinsic value is an outcome of experiences only, while extrinsic value is accessed through the objects (products/services) that contribute to those experiences. Existential authenticity is thus clearly aligned with intrinsic value, as it emphasises the experience as the source of meaning, self-renewal and growth. Second, products and experiences with self-oriented value are treasured because they are personal and inner-directed. Correspondingly, we acknowledge other-oriented experiences for what they do for others (Holbrook, 2006a). Third, value is active when we act upon or with a product in the pursuit of an experience, and reactive when products act upon or with us as part of some consumption experience (Holbrook, 2006a; Komppula and Gartner, 2013).

Significantly, interactions can result in different value outcomes or even multiple value outcomes at the same time (Holbrook, 2006a). While conceptually these definitions are useful, in practice it is not always feasible to distinguish intrinsic from extrinsic, self- from other-oriented and active from reactive. Multiple motives and outcomes can be present in a given experience. For example, a visit to a museum could be about an appreciation of heritage, experiencing authentic local culture and/or family entertainment or togetherness. Thus, value is complex, dynamic and context dependent and its management presents significant challenges for tourism marketers.

It is important to note here that co-creation 'results from the interaction of an individual at a specific time and place and within the context of a specific act' and, as such, 'a real co-creation experience is neither company nor product centred' (Binkhorst and Den Dekker, 2009: 315). Thus, it is only when the tourist engages with a consumption experience that value can be created (Smith, 1994). Here, value is created *with* rather than *for* tourists. This means that the tourist participates in value creation, rather than being a recipient of predefined value. Also, and most significantly, it is the tourist that decides what constitutes value in any given context (Holbrook, 2006a). In other words, 'value creation is always uniquely and phenomenologically determined by the beneficiary' (Vargo and Lusch, 2008: 8). The interactive, relative and phenomenological nature of value means that firms are no longer 'producers'

of value *per se*. Rather, their role is reimagined as articulating value proposi-
tions and facilitating tourists in their own value creation processes (Park and
Vargo, 2012). Thus, 'value is not produced', rather the 'resources out of which
value can be created are produced' (Grönroos and Ravald, 2011: 7). Here, the
experience offering, associated meaning and other attributes all constitute the
resources by and through which it is accomplished, and 'anyone and anything
involved in the tourism network' (Binkhorst and Den Dekker, 2009: 313) can
be involved in this process. Service providers and tourism marketers continue
to play an important role (Grönroos, 2000), co-creating value through their
knowledge, skills, processes and performances (Lusch and Vargo, 2006).
Tourists also deploy a range of resources, including energy, physical endow-
ment, emotions, relationships and networks, knowledge, skills and imagination (Arnould, Price and Malshe, 2006) in co-creating value.

Facilitating tourism experience co-creation

'Co-creation is the process by which mutual value is expanded together,
where value to participating individuals is a function of their experiences'
(Ramaswamy, 2011: 195). These include both engagement experiences and
meaningful *human* experiences. Indeed, Ramaswamy (2011) argues that value
is a function of human experience, and experience comes from interactions.
Interactions amongst people in their various roles of tourist, employee, service
provider, resident, etc. allow for the realisation of a variety of experiences.
While some of these relate directly to the engagement platform or activity,
others create/allow/facilitate meaningful human experiences such as interpersonal and intrapersonal authenticity (see Wang, 1999).

One way to facilitate co-creation is through creative tourism. Creativity is
attractive as a policy option for stimulating a range of economic, cultural
and social outcomes, including the advantages produced by networking and
knowledge spillover which engenders further creative activities (Richards,
2011). Creative tourism can include engagement with traditional crafts, languages and gastronomy, perfume making, dance and music making (Richards
and Wilson, 2006). Creative skills are deployed in the co-creation of tourism
experiences and are widely used as the basis for small-scale tourism businesses.
For example, in the provision of special interest holidays, such as painting
or photography holidays, gastronomic experiences and spiritual or 'holistic'
holidays (Smith and Puczkó, 2013). Furthermore, creative tourism can lead
to more flexible and innovative forms of tourism experience which are harder
to imitate than mere services (Alvarez, 2010). By placing the responsibility on

the tourists to develop their own context, it reduces the need for a standard-ised frame of reference (Richards and Wilson, 2006). The experience of the co-creation itself is the basis of a unique value for each individual (Binkhorst and Den Dekker, 2009), and therefore creative tourism appeals to the kind(s) of existential authenticity sought by people in their leisure activities.

Engaging with co-creation requires a shift of attention from first-generation experiences towards the multifaceted interactions between tourists, market-ers and other actors that go beyond the staging or orchestration of experi-ences. First-generation experiences date from the late 1990s and are largely staged – entertainment and fun. Second-generation experiences are based on co-creation and take the individual as the starting point. This form of experi-ence is directed towards the personal social and cultural values that the indi-vidual holds (Boswijk, Thijssen and Peelen, 2007). For example, people use the internet and/or specialised organisations to exchange houses during holidays in order to get a more personal, local, authentic accommodation experience. This is an example of technology allowing consumer to consumer co-created experiences. In this light, places can be thought of as 'experience spaces' or 'experiencescapes', in which the individual consumer is central and an event triggers a co-creation experience. The event has 'a context in space and time, and the involvement of the individual influences that experience' (Prahalad and Ramaswamy, 2003: 14). Value to the individual is thus determined by the personal meaning that he or she obtains from the co-created experience.

Third-generation experiences occur between communities of producers and consumers in which the distinction between the roles effectively disappears (Boswijk et al., 2007). This trajectory away from individual producer/con-sumer roles towards communities is an important one. For example, The Gathering Ireland 2013 (Miley, 2013), a successful initiative by Failte Ireland (the Irish Tourism Board), mobilised and engaged at the grassroots level multiple groups and communities of citizens, entrepreneurs and other actors within Ireland and from the Irish diaspora, facilitating the co-creation of mul-tiple experiences (Mottiar, 2016). The Gathering facilitated local ownership, interpretation and manifestation of various, often idiosyncratic events. This unleashing of creativity enhanced the experiences of locals and tourists result-ing in a highly successful and unique initiative. The Gathering initiative was created as a platform to mobilise every citizen to promote tourism, to revive a sense of community spirit and to promote 'pride' in Ireland (elements that appear to have been lost in the Celtic Tiger years). It asked Irish citizens to fuel economic recovery by inviting family, friends and acquaintances from abroad to visit Ireland (the Irish diaspora is estimated at more than 70 million people), by developing, promoting and participating in diverse events throughout 2013.

The essence of The Gathering was to enable connections and reconnections between the Irish in Ireland and abroad, those who feel Irish, are friends of Ireland and those who want to be Irish. More than 5,000 events were hosted during 2013, attracting between 250,000 and 275,000 additional visitors to Ireland (Miley, 2013; Trew and Pierse, 2018). Of these, 30 per cent related to 'family and clan' while another 26 per cent were community based, illustrating the 'power of the personal and local connection' (Miley, 2013: 20) in making The Gathering a powerful engagement platform.

Part of the success of The Gathering is that it aligned with extant articulations of brand Ireland as being all about 'people, place and pace' (O'Leary and Deegan, 2003: 213). Promoted as a rural idyll populated by a friendly and welcoming people (Baum, Hearns and Devine, 2007), tourists are invited to experience culture, creativity and craic. Tourism has always been an 'industry of every parish' (Failte Ireland, 2005), and the call for grassroots ownership of The Gathering engaged and mobilised the Irish people. Indeed, The Gathering had all the elements necessary as a platform that offered tourists and locals the potential to experience existential authenticity. Fundamentally, it invited and encouraged symbolic displays of Irishness (intrapersonal authenticity) by hosts *and* visitors, as well as numerous events and occasions through which relationships could be enhanced and communitas experienced (interpersonal authenticity).

Events also have a long-term impact on place branding processes by developing collaboration, capacity building and knowledge sharing (Richards, 2015, 2017); and Ireland learned a lot from the initiative (Miley, 2013). Most importantly, events like The Gathering are significant in that they create cultural codes and content that are circulated by local actors and, in this way, 'play an important role in the representation of places' (Richards, 2015: 556). The Gathering was a platform to be used by Irish citizens to promote tourism and the resources produced by Failte Ireland to market The Gathering invoked and reinforced key themes around people, craic and the Cead Mile Failte (a hundred thousand welcomes) that have long been associated with brand Ireland (Baum et al., 2007). Moreover, it also reignited a sense of community and belonging (Miley, 2013) that seems to have reinforced notions of Irishness, pride and sense of place. This created a virtuous circle that reinforces the centrality of Irish people to the experience of Ireland. It is also relevant to note that despite the project's success, the organisers explicitly recommended that the event not be repeated (Miley, 2013). Turning an initiative like The Gathering into an annual event would risk commoditising the experience and standardising the relational networks involved, eroding its spontaneity and organic reinforcement of the place brand.

Engagement platforms (such as The Gathering) facilitate co-creation experiences in time and place. This requires a shift in mindset away from traditional value chains that run from producer to consumer towards links between actors, who may be individuals or firms, social networks, both real and virtual, and market-based enterprises, organisations and coordinating institutions (Richards, 2011). It is through collaboration within these networks that value is created, leading to their reimagination as a value constellation (Binkhorst and Den Dekker, 2009). Tourism marketers, including local authorities and tourist bodies, can facilitate co-creation through the development of relational and creative resources that enable actors to create their own meaningful and transformational experiences. Thus, place branding continues to play an important role in mediating and integrating marketing and promotional activities (Warnaby, 2009; Warnaby and Medway, 2015) that enable meaningful collaboration and co-creation. Creativity is important here, because it is embedded within communities, and itself becomes a resource. Thus, emergent thinking moves away from end results (either in the form of product or experience) towards processes that recognise the role of interaction, constellations and fluidity in the marketing of tourism places. We capture these key ideas in Table 14.1.

This chapter began with the notion that authenticity is a burden for tourism and place branding practices, because tourists essentially destroy what they implicitly seek, and because marketing processes are implicated in the commodification of tourism places. Existential authenticity emerges through interaction in experience, justifying the increasing focus on experiences in contemporary life. Refocusing attention on the processes through which experiences are co-created, and particularly the inimitability of third-generation experiences, is insightful for tourism marketing. Most importantly, while acknowledging that value is determined phenomenologically, it is created through interaction by actors in networks. Together these trends allow us to appreciate different phases of how tourism places are constructed. Conceptualisations of places as destinations or place products adopt a more objectivist position, and assume that value is produced and embedded a priori in the offer. In contrast, recognition of the tourist as ultimate arbiter of his/her value creates the tourism place as an experiencescape, existing for the delectation of the tourist. This shifts understanding to a more subjectivist position. More recently, however, a number of trends suggest that tourism places are better understood from a more relational perspective. While value may be determined by users, it is created in context through interaction. The tourist is not the only stakeholder or most important arbiter of value. Appreciation of the importance of the wider network directs attention towards places as creative value constellations.

Table 14.1   Perspectives on authenticity, experience, value and tourism place

	Objective perspective	Subjective perspective	Relational perspective
Authenticity	Historical or cultural authenticity is a source of value for tourists	Experiences are the source of value for tourists	Dialectical relationship between objective/experiential authenticity. The source of value lies
	Objective authenticity	Experiential authenticity	in the interactions between objects and experiences and actors Existential authenticity
Experience	Largely staged experiences	Focus on the individual tourist as the starting point	Experiences co-created between communities of producers
	First generation	Second generation	and consumers, effectively blurring the boundaries between the two Third generation
Value	Value is produced and embedded in products and services Value-in-exchange	Value is phenomenologically determined by the tourist in context Value-in-use	Value is co-created through interaction between multiple actors and networks Value co-creation
Tourism place	Finished offer, both in functional and representational terms; scripted by service providers and marketers; value is prefigured, and experience largely prefabricated 'Destination'	Place perceived and experienced subjectively by tourists 'Experiencescape'	Meanings are not fixed but negotiated by those who market, visit, live and work there 'Constellation'

Tourism places can really benefit from truly embracing the phenomenological and relational nature of value. Conventional approaches to understanding markets, developing offers and evaluating satisfaction are of limited utility here, particularly those which rely on survey responses and standardised satisfaction scores. Rather, research methods that allow for more emic understandings of tourists' experiences, that accommodate articulations of tourists' determination of value-in-use and that afford access, however fleeting, to authentic experiences, feelings and places will have more to offer (see for example, Bosangit et al.'s (2015) analysis of tourist sensemaking through travel blog analysis). Given that value co-creation includes networks of actors, place branding research should explore how different actors participate in value constellations, how interactions between and amongst them are supported and how meaning is negotiated.

Recognising the importance of experience, co-creation, value and existential authenticity to place actors means that marketing strategy can no longer be usefully fully determined or articulated in advance. Rather than focusing on producing value, tourism places need to focus on producing the resources out of which value can be created. Here the place brand is a symbolic resource that serves to mediate and integrate marketing activities (Warnaby, 2009; Warnaby and Medway, 2015), allowing actors in the value constellation to produce, reproduce, create and co-create experiences and value. This extends the number and diversity of experience platforms, contributing to both authenticity of the tourism place and authenticity of the tourism experience. The example of The Gathering, discussed earlier, illustrates the potential of a fluid, largely unscripted branding event that creates space for diverse experiences to occur; it builds on existing and emergent relational resources and organically feeds into and reinforces the place brand. Rather than an end in itself, the place brand becomes a symbolic resource interpreted, negotiated and appropriated by different actors. The place brand is thus complex, open-ended and elusive (Kalandides, 2012; Kavaratzis and Hatch, 2019), which requires that marketers embrace ambiguity. The ability to truly engage in co-creation is only possible when tourism actors appreciate that place is dynamic, culture is living and value is interactive, relative and phenomenologically determined.

References

Abrahams, R. D. (1986), 'Ordinary and extraordinary experience', in V. W. Turner and E. M. Bruner (eds), *The Anthropology of Experience*, Urbana, IL: University of Illinois Press, pp. 45–72.

Alvarez, M. D. (2010), 'Creative cities and cultural spaces: New perspectives for city tourism', *International Journal of Culture, Tourism and Hospitality Research*, **4** (3), 171–5.

Arnould, E. J. and L. L. Price (1993), 'River magic: Extraordinary experience and the extended service encounter', *Journal of Consumer Research*, **20** (1), 24–45.

Arnould, E. J., Price, L. L. and A. Malshe (2006), 'Toward a cultural resource-based theory of the customer', in R. F. Lusch and S. L. Vargo (eds), *The Service-Dominant Logic of Marketing: Dialog, Debate and Directions*, Armonk, NY: M. E. Sharpe, pp. 320–33.

Ashworth, G. J. and B. Goodall (eds) (2013 [1990]), *Marketing Tourism Places*, Volume 2, Abingdon: Routledge.

Baum, T., Hearns, N. and F. Devine (2007), 'Place, people and interpretation: Issues of migrant labour and tourism imagery in Ireland', *Tourism Recreation Research*, **32** (3), 39–48.

Berger, P. L. (1973), 'Sincerity and authenticity in modern society', *The Public Interest*, **31**, 81–90.

Binkhorst, E. and T. Den Dekker (2009), 'Agenda for co-creation tourism experience research', *Journal of Hospitality Marketing and Management*, **18** (2–3), 311–27.

Boorstin, D. J. (1962), *The Image: A Guide to Pseudo-events in America*, New York: Harper and Row.

Bosangit, C., Hibbert, S. and S. McCabe (2015), '"If I was going to die I should at least be having fun": Travel blogs, meaning and tourist experience', *Annals of Tourism Research*, **55**, 1–14.

Boswijk, A., Thijssen, T. and E. Peelen (2007), *The Experience Economy: A New Perspective*, Amsterdam: Pearson Education.

Buckley, R. (2012), 'Rush as a key motivation in skilled adventure tourism: Resolving the risk recreation paradox', *Tourism Management*, **33** (4), 961–70.

Campos, A. C. (2012), 'Marketing the destination experience', *Discussion Papers Nº10: Spatial and Organizational Dynamics: Marketing*, Faro: University of Algarve.

Carù, A. and B. Cova (2003), 'Revisiting consumption experience: A more humble but complete view of the concept', *Marketing Theory*, **3** (2), 267–86.

Cary, S. H. (2004), 'The tourist moment', *Annals of Tourism Research*, **31** (1), 61–77.

Celsi, R. L., Rose, R. L. and T. W. Leigh (1993), 'An exploration of high-risk leisure consumption through skydiving', *Journal of Consumer Research*, **20** (1), 1–23.

Chhabra, D. (2008), 'Positioning museums on an authenticity continuum', *Annals of Tourism Research*, **35** (2), 427–47.

Cohen, E. (1988), 'Authenticity and commoditization in tourism', *Annals of Tourism Research*, **15** (3), 371–86.

Colomb, C. and A. Kalandides (2010), 'The "Be Berlin" campaign: Old wine in new bottles or innovative form of participatory place branding', in G. Ashworth and M. Kavaratzis (eds), *Towards Effective Place Brand Management: Branding European Cities and Regions*, Cheltenham, UK and Northampton, MA, USA: Edward Elgar Publishing, pp. 173–90.

Cova, B., Kozinets, R. and A. Shankar (2007), 'Tribes, Inc.: The new world of tribalism', in B. Cova, B., R. Kozinets and A. Shankar (eds), *Consumer Tribes*, Oxford: Butterworth-Heinemann, pp. 3–26.

Crick, M. (1996), 'Representations of international tourism in the social sciences: Sun, sex, sights, savings, and servility', in G. Apostolopoulos, S. Leivadi and A. Yiannakis (eds), *The Sociology of Tourism: Theoretical and Empirical Investigations*, London: Routledge, pp. 15–50.

Csikszentmihalyi, M. (1975), *Beyond Boredom and Anxiety*, Washington, DC: Jossey-Bass.

Echtner, C. M. and P. Prasad (2003), 'The context of Third World tourism marketing', *Annals of Tourism Research*, **30** (3), 660–82.

Edensor, T. (2006), 'Sensing tourist spaces', in C. Minca and T. Oakes (eds), *Travels in Paradox: Remapping Tourism*, Lanham, MD: Rowman and Littlefield, pp. 23–45.

Failte Ireland (2005), *A Human Resource Development Strategy for Irish Tourism: Competing through People*, Dublin: Failte Ireland.

Franklin, A. (2016), 'Journeys to the Guggenheim Museum Bilbao: Towards a revised Bilbao effect', *Annals of Tourism Research*, **59**, 79–92.

Giovanardi, M., Lucarelli, A. and C. Pasquinelli (2013), 'Towards brand ecology: An analytical semiotic framework for interpreting the emergence of place brands', *Marketing Theory*, **13** (3), 365–83.

Graburn, N. H. (1983), 'The anthropology of tourism', *Annals of Tourism Research*, **10** (1), 9–33.

Grönroos, C. (2000), *Service Management and Marketing: A Customer Relationship Approach*, Chichester: Wiley.

Grönroos, C. and A. Ravald (2011), 'Service as business logic: Implications for value creation and marketing', *Journal of Service Management*, **22** (1), 5–22.

Haywood, K. M. (1990), 'Revising and implementing the marketing concept as it applies to tourism', *Tourism Management*, **11** (3), 195–205.

Holbrook, M. B. (ed.) (1999), *Consumer Value: A Framework for Analysis and Research*, London: Routledge.

Holbrook, M. B. (2006a), 'Consumption experience, customer value, and subjective personal introspection: An illustrative photographic essay', *Journal of Business Research*, **59** (6), 714–25.

Holbrook, M. B. (2006b), 'Rosepekiceciveci versus CCV', in R. F. Lusch and S. L. Vargo (eds), *The Service-Dominant Logic of Marketing: Dialog, Debate, and Directions*, New York: M. E. Sharpe, pp. 208–21.

Kalandides, A. (2012), 'Place branding and place identity: An integrated approach', *Tafter Journal*, **43** (1), 5.

Kavaratzis, M. and G. Ashworth (2015), Hijacking culture: The disconnection between place culture and place brands', *Town Planning Review*, **86** (2), 155–76.

Kavaratzis, M. and M. J. Hatch (2013), The dynamics of place brands: An identity-based approach to place branding theory', *Marketing Theory*, **13** (1), 69–86.

Kavaratzis, M. and M. J. Hatch (2019), The elusive destination brand and the ATLAS wheel of place brand management', *Journal of Travel Research*, https://doi.org/10.1177/0047287519892323.

Kavaratzis, M., Giovanardi, M. and M. Lichrou (eds) (2017), *Inclusive Place Branding: Critical Perspectives on Theory and Practice*, London: Routledge.

Kim, H. and T. Jamal (2007), 'Touristic quest for existential authenticity', *Annals of Tourism Research*, **34** (1), 181–201.

Komppula, R. and W. C. Gartner (2013), 'Hunting as a travel experience: An auto-ethnographic study of hunting tourism in Finland and the USA', *Tourism Management*, **35**, 168–80.

Kozinets, R. (2002), 'Can consumers escape the market? Emancipatory illuminations from burning man', *Journal of Consumer Research*, **29** (1), 20–38.

Lichrou, M., O'Malley, L. and M. Patterson (2008), 'Place product or place narrative(s)? Perspectives in the marketing of tourism destinations', *Journal of Strategic Marketing*, **16** (1), 27–39.

Lusch, R. F. and S. L. Vargo (2006), 'Service-dominant logic: Reactions, reflections and refinements', *Marketing Theory*, **6** (3), 281–8.

MacCannell, D. (1973), 'Staged authenticity: Arrangements of social space in tourist settings', *American Journal of Sociology*, **79** (3), 589–603.

MacCannell, D. (1999 [1976]), *The Tourist: A New Theory of the Leisure Class*, Berkeley, CA: University of California Press.

Meethan, K. (2001), *Tourism in Global Society: Place, Culture, Consumption*, Basingstoke: Palgrave.

Miley, J. (2013), *The Gathering Ireland 2013: Final Report*, Dublin: The Gathering Project.

Mostafanezhad, M. (2014), 'Locating the tourist in volunteer tourism', *Current Issues in Tourism*, **17** (4), 381–4.

Mottiar, Z. (2016), 'Exploring the motivations of tourism social entrepreneurs: The role of a national tourism policy as a motivator for social entrepreneurial activity in Ireland', *International Journal of Contemporary Hospitality Management*, **28** (6), 1137–54.

O'Leary, S. and J. Deegan (2003), 'People, pace, place: Qualitative and quantitative images of Ireland as a tourism destination in France', *Journal of Vacation Marketing*, **9** (3), 213–26.

Park, S. Y. and C. A. Santos (2017), 'Exploring the tourist experience: A sequential approach', *Journal of Travel Research*, **56** (1), 16–27.

Park, S. Y. and S. L. Vargo (2012), 'The service-dominant logic approach to tourism marketing strategy', in R. H. Tsiotsou and R. E. Goldsmith (eds), *Strategic Marketing in Tourism Services*, Bingley: Emerald Group, pp. 231–46.

Paulauskaite, D., Powell, R., Coca-Stefaniak, J. A. and A. M. Morrison (2017), 'Living like a local: Authentic tourism experiences and the sharing economy', *International Journal of Tourism Research*, **19** (6), 619–28.

Pine, B. J. and J. H. Gilmore (2011 [1999]), *The Experience Economy*, Boston, MA: Harvard Business Press.

Poon, A. (1994), 'The "new tourism" revolution', *Tourism Management*, **15** (2), 91–2.

Prahalad, C. K. and V. Ramaswamy (2003), 'The new frontier of experience innovation', *MIT Sloan Management Review*, **44** (4), 12–18.

Prahalad, C. K. and V. Ramaswamy (2004a), 'Co-creation experiences: The next practice in value creation', *Journal of Interactive Marketing*, **18** (3), 5–14.

Prahalad, C. K. and V. Ramaswamy (2004b), 'Co-creating unique value with customers', *Strategy and Leadership*, **32** (3), 4–9.

Ramaswamy, V. (2011), 'It's about human experiences… and beyond, to co-creation', *Industrial Marketing Management*, **40** (2), 195–6.

Richards, G. (2011), 'Creativity and tourism: The state of the art', *Annals of Tourism Research*, **38** (4), 1225–53.

Richards, G. (2015), 'Events in the network society: The role of pulsar and iterative events', *Event Management*, **19** (4), 553–66.

Richards, G. (2017), 'Sharing the new localities of tourism', in D. Dredge and S. Gyimóthy (eds), *Collaborative Economy and Tourism*, Cham: Springer, pp. 169–84.

Richards, G. and J. Wilson (2006), 'Developing creativity in tourist experiences: A solution to the serial reproduction of culture?', *Tourism Management*, **27** (6), 1209–23.

Ritzer, G. and A. Liska (1997), '"McDisneyization" and "post-tourism": Complementary perspectives on contemporary tourism', in C. Rojek and J. Urry (eds), *Touring Cultures: Transformations of Travel and Theory*, London: Routledge, pp. 96–109.

Robinson, M. and M. Novelli (2005), 'Niche tourism: An introduction', in M. Novelli (ed.), *Niche Tourism*, Oxford: Elsevier Butterworth-Heinemann, pp. 1–14.

Rojek, C. (2000), 'Mass tourism and the re-enchantment of the world? Issues and contradictions in the study of travel', in M. Gottdiener (ed.), *New Forms of Consumption: Consumers, Culture, and Commodification*, Oxford: Rowman and Littlefield, pp. 51–70.

Seaton, A. V. (2002), 'Tourism as metempsychosis and metensomatosis', in G. S. Dann (ed.), *The Tourist as a Metaphor of the Social World*, Wallingford: CABI Publishing, pp. 135–68.

Shepherd, R. J. (2002), 'Commodification, culture and tourism', *Tourist Studies*, 2 (2), 183–201.

Shepherd, R. J. (2015), 'Why Heidegger did not travel: Existential angst, authenticity, and tourist experiences', *Annals of Tourism Research*, 52, 60–71.

Silver, I. (1993), 'Marketing authenticity in third world countries', *Annals of Tourism Research*, 20 (2), 302–18.

Smith, M. and L. Puczkó (2013), *Health and Wellness Tourism*, Abingdon: Routledge.

Smith, S. L. (1994), 'The tourism product', *Annals of Tourism Research*, 21 (3), 582–95.

Steiner, C. J. and Y. Reisinger (2006), 'Understanding existential authenticity', *Annals of Tourism Research*, 33 (2), 299–318.

Szmigin, I., Bengry-Howell, A., Morey, Y., Griffin, C. and S. Riley (2017), 'Socio-spatial authenticity at co-created music festivals', *Annals of Tourism Research*, 63, 1–11.

Tiberghien, G. (2019), 'Managing the planning and development of authentic eco-cultural tourism in Kazakhstan', *Tourism Planning and Development*, 16 (5), 494–513.

Torres, R. (2002), 'Cancun's tourism development from a Fordist spectrum of analysis', *Tourist Studies*, 2 (1), 87–116.

Trew, J. D. and M. Pierse (eds) (2018), *Rethinking the Irish Diaspora: After The Gathering*, Cham: Springer.

Tung, V. W. S. and J. B. Ritchie (2011), 'Exploring the essence of memorable tourism experiences', *Annals of Tourism Research*, 38 (4), 1367–86.

Turner, V. W. (1974), *Dramas, Fields, and Metaphors*, Ithaca, NY: Cornell University Press.

Turner, V. W. (1982), *From Ritual to Theatre: The Human Seriousness of Play*, New York: Performing Arts Journal Publications.

Urry, J. (1990), *The Tourist Gaze*, London: Sage.

Valtonen, A. and S. Veijola (2011), 'Sleep in tourism', *Annals of Tourism Research*, 38 (1), 175–92.

Vargo, S. L. and R. F. Lusch (2004), 'Evolving to a new dominant logic for marketing', *Journal of Marketing*, 68 (1), 1–17.

Vargo, S. L. and R. F. Lusch (2008), 'Service-dominant logic: Continuing the evolution', *Journal of the Academy of Marketing Science*, 36 (Spring), 1–10.

Voase, R. (1999), '"Consuming" tourist sites/sights: A note on York', *Leisure Studies*, 18 (4), 289–96.

Wang, N. (1999), 'Rethinking authenticity in tourism experience', *Annals of Tourism Research*, 26 (2), 349–70.

Warnaby, G. (2009), 'Towards a service-dominant place marketing logic', *Marketing Theory*, 9 (4), 403–23.

Warnaby, G. and D. Medway (2013), 'What about the "place" in place marketing?', *Marketing Theory*, 13 (3), 345–63.

Warnaby, G. and D. Medway (2015), 'Rethinking the place product from the perspective of the service-dominant logic of marketing', in M. Kavaratzis, G. Warnaby and G. J. Ashworth (eds), *Rethinking Place Branding: Comprehensive Brand Development for Cities and Regions*, Heidelberg: Springer, pp. 33–50.

Watson, G. L. and J. P. Kopachevsky (1994), 'Interpretations of tourism as commodity', *Annals of Tourism Research*, 21 (3), 643–60.

Weber, K. (2001), 'Outdoor adventure tourism: A review of research approaches', *Annals of Tourism Research*, 28 (2), 360–77.

Williams, A. M. and G. Shaw (1992), 'Tourism research: A perspective', *American Behavioral Scientist*, 36 (2), 133–43.

15 Making 'sense' of place branding: Adopting a sensemaking, sensefiltering and sensegiving lens

Laura Reynolds and Nicole Koenig-Lewis

Introduction

Place branding has gained popularity due to its capacity in shaping people's perceptions and experiences of a place. The involvement of people in place branding is thus pivotal within what is increasingly premised to be a participatory process (Kavaratzis, 2012; Kavaratzis and Kalandides, 2015). Stakeholder engagement has been propelled as an important tool for involving multiple parties within an increasingly complex place branding process (Hanna and Rowley, 2015). More specifically, there has been heightened focus on the meanings that people assign to the places in which they live, work, visit and invest (Green, Grace and Perkins, 2016; Merrilees, Miller and Herington, 2012), especially as not all gain the same impetus when translated into shared meanings (Boisen, Terlouw and van Gorp, 2011). However, there have been few attempts to explore how these meanings are collectively forged, shared and disseminated through stakeholder engagement, especially between often competing groups.

To address this gap in knowledge, we apply the interconnected sensemaking and sensegiving frameworks (Weick, 1995). Of particular interest to place branding is collective sensemaking, whereby people negotiate and interpret mutual meanings through a group dynamic (Maitlis, 2005; Maitlis and Sonenshein, 2010). We premise that these frameworks offer an important, and yet underexplored, explanation for managing complexity, transition and change at the heart of a participatory approach to place branding. Specifically, we seek to shed light on how stakeholders collectively develop, distil and deliver meanings assigned to the place through stakeholder engagement.

The chapter proceeds as follows: first, we introduce the sensemaking and sensegiving frameworks exploring the importance of the interpretive lens for forging brand meanings through stakeholder engagement. Moreover, we propose a further sensefiltering layer, whereby certain meanings are filtered through engagement, resulting in selective retention and conveyance of a particular version of the place to a wider audience. This is followed by an application of the frameworks to place branding. To investigate this three-stage sensemaking, sensefiltering and sensegiving process within a complex place branding setting, we draw on in-depth interviews with 30 actors from Bath, United Kingdom. Since our focus is on the process of collective sensemaking we look particularly at four key groups, namely the business community, local authority, local community and visitor attractions. Bringing together brand meanings and stakeholder engagement, we explore how brand meanings are forged (sensemaking), filtered (sensefiltering) and conveyed (sensegiving) through stakeholder engagement.

Sensemaking and sensegiving in place branding

Origins of Sensemaking and Sensegiving

Originating in the study of organisations, the sensemaking and sensegiving frameworks centre around the way that people create meaning (Weick, 1995; Weick, Sutcliffe and Obstfeld, 2005). These meanings are communicated through narratives, which can be written, spoken or visualised through language and symbols (Weick, 1995). By individually and collectively reflecting and speaking about events and environments people retrospectively process and make sense of their experiences. As such, the sensemaking and sensegiving process is a multiple-stage social process of abduction, plotting and selective retention (Abolafia, 2010), beginning with narratives, developing a sense of events and ultimately conveying these understandings to a wider audience.

The two frameworks are interconnected, yet important differences exist. Sensemaking refers to the *interpretive process* of creating meaning for individuals and groups, based on singular and shared narratives within a given arena, to produce their own intersubjective accounts of a phenomenon (Weick, 1995). The process of sensemaking is predominately retrospective whereby narratives are translated into meanings to validate current and future action (Weick et al., 2005). In contrast, sensegiving refers to the *process of communicating* the outcomes (Gioia and Chittipeddi, 1991; Weick et al., 2005), and as such is also an interpretive process, whereby actors seek to influence one another through language and persuasion (Maitlis and Lawrence, 2007). Together the twofold process (Rouleau, 2005) helps to explain how meanings are derived within the sensemaking domain, and then projected onto others through the sensegiving process.

Applying the Frameworks to Place Branding

One of the main aims of this chapter is to highlight the potential usefulness of the sensemaking and sensegiving frameworks for understanding how people develop and convey meanings assigned to place brands. There is a heightened recognition that places belong to a range of stakeholders who live, work, visit and invest within its boundaries (Merrilees et al., 2012).

Taking this stakeholder-orientated approach, success can be attained through enabling stakeholder participation in decision-making processes (Klijn, Eshuis and Braun, 2012), and encouraging 'dialogue, debate and contestation' (Kavaratzis and Hatch, 2013: 82). This constructs stakeholders as partners and co-producers, rather than passive participants (Aitken and Campelo, 2011). While a central aspect of this shift has been encouraging greater resident inclusion (Aitken and Campelo, 2011; Braun, Kavaratzis and Zenker, 2013), other studies have also investigated visitors, entrepreneurs (García, Gómez and Molina, 2012) and business leaders seeking inward investment (Jacobsen, 2012). However, previous approaches largely analyse stakeholders as distinct and separate brand audiences, as opposed to exploring how competing stake-holders develop and communicate multiple versions of complex and evolving places.

The literature is beginning to recognise the value of sensemaking frameworks for helping to understand how consumers and other stakeholders attach meaning to a brand (e.g. O'Reilly and Kerrigan, 2013; Iannone and Izzo, 2017; Grenni, Horlings and Soini, 2020). However, more research is needed to explore how these meanings are negotiated, altered and transmitted in a place branding context when competing stakeholders are included. One way to do this is through assessing the brand meaning-making processes.

Conceptualising Place Brand Meanings

Brands are formed from 'a cluster of meanings' (Batey, 2015: 6) that bring together stakeholders' perceptions of a multitude of associations, attributes, benefits and values (Wilson, Bengtsson and Curran, 2014). While originating in conventional branding, brand meanings remain an important and under-explored component of place branding (Green et al., 2016; Green, Grace and Perkins, 2018). Places are imbued with a plethora of functional and symbolic assets (Voase, 2012), bringing together various brand meaning claims (Vallaster and von Wallpach, 2013). Gaining a consensus among stakeholder claims is seldom simple for conventional branding, and even less so for place branding. Inevitably, gaps emerge between the official brand meanings communicated and stakeholders' intrinsic claims (Wilson et al., 2014). As such, there is a growing acceptance that brand meanings develop organically and with them come converging and competing stakeholder claims (Green et al., 2016).

Moreover, a distinction is drawn between the involvement of residents in the internal essence of the place brand versus their involvement in the official communication and marketing practices (Aitken and Campelo, 2011). Whilst the importance of residents making sense of the meanings assigned and sharing with others is highlighted, they are not granted the same ability to convert these meanings into messages in the sensegiving process. Developing these findings, it would be helpful to consider how the process differs further when many groups are considered. For example, Merrilees et al. (2012) looked at the clustering of meanings based on whether stakeholders belonged to the local community or business community.

It is becoming accepted that meaning making is a socially constructed and complex process, whereby multiple stakeholders come together to attach and convey meanings to places, passed on through everyday conversations, traditions and even the clothing a person wears (Green et al., 2018). We build on these developments, recognising the multiplicity of stakeholders' narratives and behaviour, evaluating the dialectical processes whereby these are exchanged, meanings are forged and dominant discourses prevail.

Making Sense through Stakeholder Engagement

Stakeholder engagement, defined as 'the processes whereby stakeholders are identified, their interests surfaced and interactions are managed' (Hanna and Rowley, 2011: 465), has gained popularity in place branding, responding to the call for multiple groups to be brought together. Through two-way communication multiple, and often competing, stakeholder associations relating to the place brand can be considered in tandem (Hanna and Rowley, 2015), enabling stakeholders to develop a shared purpose (Govers, 2013). Stakeholders are resultantly provided a platform to voice their understandings, even when presenting conflicting perspectives (Baker, 2007).

Yet, a disjuncture emerges between stakeholders who can foster relationships through engagement and those who remain excluded (Henninger et al., 2016). Moreover, effectively implementing stakeholder engagement is cumbersome, with stakeholder tensions being heightened by place branding's diffused ownership (Hanna and Rowley, 2015) alongside 'lip service' being utilised rather than meaningful participation (Zenker and Erfgen, 2014). Resultantly, despite the academic call for greater inclusion of stakeholders (Hanna and Rowley, 2011), in practice the branding process remains predominately focused around the communication and promotion of slogans or logos (Green et al., 2016). Thus, there remains a need to explore in-depth the barriers impeding stakeholders' equal access to stakeholder engagement as a means of both developing and delivering their associated brand meanings.

The connections between stakeholder engagement and the sensemaking–sensegiving frameworks have been explored outside of place branding (e.g. Maitlis, 2005; Morsing and Schultz, 2006). These studies pinpoint stakeholder engagement as a means to facilitate actors' roles as both sensemakers and sensegivers. Moreover, the active involvement of stakeholders has moved engagement away from information (sensegiving) or response-orientated approaches (sensemaking to sensegiving), instead allowing for an iterative and ongoing (sensemaking and sensegiving simultaneously) progressive process (Morsing and Schultz, 2006). These developments focus on creating two-way communication, whereby dialogue and activities are created and shaped by, and not simply for, multiple stakeholders (Morsing and Schultz, 2006).

A Three-Stage Framework: Sensemaking, Sensefiltering, Sensegiving

As the extant literature shows, branding a place increasingly calls for the greater inclusion of competing stakeholder groups, bringing with them a myriad of brand meanings and contributing in the sharing and dissemination of these meanings to varying extents through stakeholder engagement practices. We suggest that the sensemaking–sensegiving frameworks can help to explain the way that people associate meanings with the cities they live, work and invest in. Moreover, we begin to highlight the tensions between developing collective meanings and being able to disseminate these more widely, suggesting that there is a missing interim between the sensemaking and sensegiving processes, wherein certain meanings gain favour and translate into communication and action across the city. As such, we propose a three-step approach for place branding (Figure 15.1).

The conceptualisation illustrates the process whereby brand meanings are forged, filtered and conveyed through stakeholder engagement. First, the model explores how multifarious stakeholder brand meanings are captured and *derived* within the sensemaking domain. Second, we inductively add an additional layer, examining the ways these understandings are *distilled* in the sensefiltering domain. Here, we analyse the practices and processes that allow the world to be presented within predefined parameters (Maitlis and Lawrence, 2007). Last, we investigate the sensegiving processes that *deliver* and *maintain* dominant meanings and discourses. Figure 15.1 draws these themes together, pinpointing the nuances across the three interconnected processes and looking at the types of questions that can help when investigating a complex phenomenon. In doing so, an evolving place branding process can be traced through a sensemaking, sensefiltering and sensegiving process. This framework has been applied to a real setting, exploring its application within a complex and transitory city.

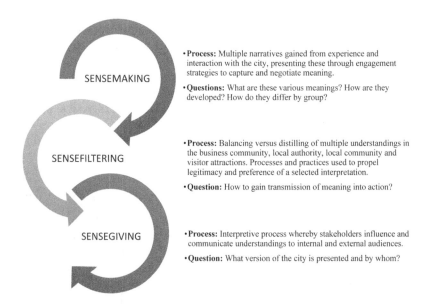

Figure 15.1   Conceptual framework of the place branding sensemaking, sensefiltering and sensegiving process

Application of sensemaking and sensegiving to Bath

Methodology

Bath, with a population of approximately 88,500, receives international recognition as a UNESCO World Heritage Site (WHS), attracting approximately 1 million overnight and 3.8 million day visitors annually, whilst also expanding its key employment areas in finance and insurance (BANES, 2017, 2018). Despite its small size, tensions have emerged surrounding the protection of the WHS status alongside the city's ability to expand its investment and business opportunities. The city is undergoing a transition between the two discourses of continuing to focus its image around the past or to carve out a new innovative future.

To explore the sensemaking, sensefiltering and sensegiving process within Bath we undertook in-depth interviews with 30 key stakeholder informants, each lasting 80 minutes on average. We incorporated four crucial stakeholder groups who played an important role in the presentation and representation of the city; namely the business community, local authority, local community and visitor attractions. To ensure stakeholders held a stake in the engagement processes we selected the sample based on Mitchell, Agle and Wood's (1997) stakeholder salience model, whereby participants demonstrated varying degrees of power, urgency and legitimacy. These stakeholder informants included officials within the local authority, leaders within the destination management organisations, hotel owners, restaurant proprietors, business leaders, city-based entrepreneurs, lobbyists, central organisers and members of resident groups, and key parties responsible for inward investment in the city. To ensure informant anonymity pseudonyms were assigned and descriptive characteristics removed.

The research employed some principles of grounded theory to support the data collection, analysis and abductive development of emergent theory (Gioia, Corley and Hamilton, 2012). Incorporating elements of grounded theory is particularly useful when undertaking a critical qualitative inquiry, encouraging a thorough scrutiny of the data (Charmaz, 2014), whilst allowing the data collection and data analysis to occur in tandem. The three-stage approach to data analysis started with open coding of processes, which helped to guide the proceeding interview structures. This was followed by clustering the processes into collective incidents, and finally these incidents were analysed alongside the existing literature to develop and extend theory (Charmaz, 2014; Gioia et al., 2012). This approach ensured a combination of flexibility, integrity and depth. The simultaneous data collection and analysis ended once theoretical saturation was reached and the data were no longer pointing to new insights and theoretical constructs (Samuel and Peattie, 2016).

Making 'Sense' of Bath

The following sections briefly explore the sensemaking, sensefiltering and sensegiving process in Bath. First, we identify the multiplicity of meanings developed and highlight sources of tension between those pushing for a retention of the past versus those groups wanting change. Second, we analyse the processes and engagement practices that enable the collective meanings to be distilled and select meanings to prevail. Finally, we highlight, briefly, how these meanings can be delivered to other audiences when presenting a given discourse for the city brand. Together, they begin to identify the benefits of applying the frameworks to a study of place branding and offer an explanation as to why a participatory approach to place branding remains cumbersome in practice (Figure 15.2).

SENSEMAKING

- Multiple stakeholders developing personal and collective meanings, guided by their role and involvement
- Not a catchall; use of descriptions, attitudes, values and emotions
- Varied meanings emerge
- Tensions associated with symbolic values and emotions, in particular the push for change alongside preservation of the past

SENSEFILTERING

- Distilling stakeholder perceptions to the exclusion of certain meanings
- Practices and processes used to strengthen and legitimise selected stakeholder meanings into accepted understandings
- Claims of expertise, development of networks of influence, leadership
- Hard to alter power dynamics

SENSEGIVING

- Place brand is officially and unofficially communicated to internal and external stakeholders
- Use of slogans that present city as innovative and beautiful
- Retention of an emphasis on traditional communication tools such as logos and slogans
- Discourse of the past considered outdated, aligned with a new discourse about the future

Figure 15.2 Applying the sensemaking, sensefiltering and sensegiving lens to Bath

Sensemaking in Bath

The interviews confirmed the complexity of brand meanings which are collectively shaped and shared by stakeholders from across Bath. The participants discussed multiple narratives and meanings assigned to the city which were expressed through stories, behaviours, anecdotes and experiences. Moreover, connections were made between the city's past and ambitions for the future, highlighting a temporal and spatial component of sensemaking in a place branding setting.

The narratives ranged from functional descriptions to more symbolic accounts of values assigned to the city. At the functional end of the continuum, stakeholders discussed the city's assets including the historic tangible and intangible infrastructure, e.g. the arts and culture and connection to water. Drawing together Bath's composition of stone, lighting and architectural style, residents refer to these distinctive features as 'Bathness', highlighting the uniqueness of these assets. Based upon the descriptions of the city's assets, participants also discussed values focusing on the beautiful, rejuvenating and recreational nature of the city. While the stakeholders were predominately in agreement over the descriptions of the city, differences and tensions emerged when values assigned to these tangible and intangible features were expressed.

Whilst the dominant discourse rested on the status of the city as a WHS and tourist magnet, increasingly, these are being permeated by new narratives that look to the future and speak of aspirations for change and modernisation. While many of the resident groups discussed the need to remain true to the essence of the city and its heritage, other groups in the business community and local authority were pushing for an alternative vision whereby the past is valued alongside a move toward a more modern and innovative future.

These tensions evidence the power battles inherent within the place branding process (Lucarelli and Giovanardi, 2016), as the combination of the tangible and intangible infrastructure, brand architecture, protocols and myriad of people are inseparable from the brand meanings assigned (Hanna and Rowley, 2011, 2015; Voase, 2012). There is thus an inextricable connection between the place as the product and people's connection to it (Aitken and Campelo, 2011). Of particular importance for Bath is the tension between the need to be transitioning into a twenty-first-century city versus the 'value and trueness' and 'protecting the rich heritage and legacy' of the city:

> What we now need to build up for a 21st century audience. Well you've got your historical bit and your health bit. What we need to build and reimagine for the next generation. It has always been a place that people do business and that's got

> lost a little bit as offices have closed. Now we're building that back up. (Peter, local authority)

Sensefiltering in Bath

During the interviews, we investigated how groups used stakeholder engagement to develop, present and defend their competing narratives surrounding the protection of the past versus the push for change looking to the future. During the filtering process, several mechanisms were used to propel a given vision over another. At the centre of this filtering process were claims of legitimacy, whereby groups used their own resources, influence and leadership capacity to exert claims of authority over the discourse presented.

The absence of strong leadership encouraged greater participation:

> I think again, there's no driver on the bus. I think that's perhaps in the old days, inverted commas, there was a council that did all of that, albeit not very well, but at least everyone knew who that was. Nowadays I'm not sure people know who does what anymore. (Paul, Bath, visitor economy)

This blurring of ownership and leadership is a defining feature of a participatory place branding approach (Hanna and Rowley, 2015), encouraging more parties to get involved to collectively develop a brand. Responding to the lack of a central leadership body, stakeholders instead exerted their own claims to leadership, forging collective alliances. For example, in Bath, a group comprising entrepreneurs and ambassadors from across the city emerged, pushing for a changing logic that moves away from purely heritage and draws upon creativity and innovation. By pooling the resources of its board members, the group was able to yield an influential position:

> So, you can see a whole array of people from different sectors and industries. They're very high powered and creative thinkers. That's the nature of the group. You stuff it full of representatives from different bodies, because they're not meant to represent their organisation, they come as what they have to give and what they want for Bath. (Susan, Bath, business community)

This partnership was central in engagement strategies across the city, using its expertise, connections and strong leadership to encourage its narratives to be retained and helping to replace the discourse of the past with a new future-orientated approach. While previous studies suggested that exerting influence over narratives is easier when running alongside dominant discourses (Humphreys, Ucbasaran and Lockett, 2012), this research indicates that attaining legitimacy through collective resources can help to overcome dominant discourses and recreate new narratives.

Sensegiving in Bath

As the sensefiltering section details, not all meanings manage to percolate through the filtering process. In Bath, the claims presented by the business community and local authority were still dominant, despite the literature suggesting that place branding is becoming more inclusionary and participatory. Furthermore, the use of mechanisms to support the legitimacy of their claims enabled them to overthrow the dominant discourse in Bath by replacing it with an alternative communicated vision.

The messages conveyed included a city-wide branding campaign designed by members of the business community which focused on the beauty and inventiveness of the city. The aligned slogans and identity were taken up by the local authority and later used in their marketing and communication. This highlights the connection between the internal brand meanings and those communicated (Aitken and Campelo, 2011), while confirming that logos and slogans remain common practice despite claims to the contrary.

Conclusion and limitations

This chapter explored the potential capacity of sensemaking and sensegiving frameworks to better understand the ways that stakeholder groups collectively develop brand meanings and project these meanings through stakeholder engagement strategies. Using the extant literatures, we first developed a conceptual sensemaking, sensefiltering and sensegiving process, recognising the tensions of translating greater participation into practice. This enables an exploration of the transition stakeholders make from sensemaking to sensegiving, drawing together two central conceptual components of place branding; namely the development and communication of shared brand meanings through stakeholder engagement. In doing so, the chapter assessed the barriers preventing certain actors from participating in the branding process and explored the consequences of the imbalance for the direction of place branding. These conceptualisations were explored in relation to Bath's complex and evolving branding process, showing how sensemaking, sensefiltering and sensegiving is occurring in practice. Again, the initial findings suggested that a filtering process is a central component of stakeholders' collective approach to making and conveying 'sense' of the places they live, work, visit and invest in.

The chapter conceptually explored the relevance of sensemaking and sensegiving to place branding, applying and extending this lens to Bath. The aim was not to provide an extensive empirical examination, rather to provide a snapshot of the proposed filtering process. It is here where further empirical and theoretical research could explore each stage in more detail, examining the core themes identified in this initial account. Despite the scant research on sensemaking in the place branding field, it has been applied within the sense of place literature (e.g. Jahn, White and Brenkert-Smith, 2020; Hede and Watne, 2013; Nicholds et al., 2017; Reid, Beilin and McLennan, 2020; Tuan, 1991). This literature draws on the uniqueness of places, the symbolic and emotional connection between people and places evoking attachment, identity and a sense of belonging to the place. While there are parallels across the two literatures, this chapter focuses on the transference and filtering of meanings and narratives when seeking to convey a particular image of the city. Future research could expand this scope and evaluate further how stakeholders convey and delineate multidimensional (i.e. feelings, senses, attachment) connections to a place through stakeholder engagement.

References

Abolafia, M. Y. (2010), 'Narrative construction as sensemaking: How a central bank thinks', *Organizational Studies*, **31** (3), 349–67.

Aitken, R. and A. Campelo (2011), 'The four Rs of place branding', *Journal of Marketing Management*, **27** (9–10), 913–33.

Baker, B. (2007), *Destination Branding for Small Cities: The Essentials for Successful Place Branding*, Portland, OR: Creative Leap Books.

BANES (2017), 'Core strategy and placemaking plan', Bath and North East Somerset Council, accessed 29 July 2020 at: https://beta.bathnes.gov.uk/policy-and-documents-library/core-strategy-and-placemaking-plan.

BANES (2018), 'Bath area profile', Bath and North East Somerset Council, accessed 1 September 2018 at: www.bathnes.gov.uk/services/your-council-and-democracy/local-research-and-statistics/wiki/bath-forum-area.

Batey, M. (2015), *Brand Meaning: Meaning, Myth and Mystique in Today's Brands*, New York: Routledge.

Boisen, M., Terlouw, K. and B. van Gorp (2011), 'The selective nature of place branding and the layering of spatial identities', *Journal of Place Management and Development*, **4** (2), 135–47.

Braun, E., Kavaratzis, M. and S. Zenker (2013), 'My city – my brand: The different roles of residents in place branding', *Journal of Place Management and Development*, **6** (1), 18–28.

Charmaz, K. (2014), *Constructing Grounded Theory: A Practical Guide through Qualitative Analysis*, 2nd ed., London: Sage.

García, J. A., Gómez, M. and A. Molina (2012), 'A destination-branding model: An empirical analysis based on stakeholders', *Tourism Management*, **33** (3), 646–61.

Gioia, D. A. and K. Chittipeddi (1991), 'Sensemaking and sensegiving in strategic change initiation', *Strategic Management Journal*, **12** (6), 433–48.

Gioia, D. A., Corley, K. G. and A. L. Hamilton (2012), 'Seeking qualitative rigor in inductive research: Notes on the Gioia methodology', *Organizational Research Methods*, **16** (1), 15–31.

Govers, R. (2013), 'Editorial: Why place branding is not about logos and slogans', *Place Branding and Public Diplomacy*, **9** (2), 71–5.

Green, A., Grace, D. and H. Perkins (2016), 'City branding research and practice: An integrative review', *Journal of Brand Management*, **23** (3), 252–72.

Green, A., Grace, D. and H. Perkins (2018), 'City elements propelling city brand meaning-making processes: Urban reminders, the arts, and residential behaviour', *Marketing Theory*, **18** (3), 349–69.

Grenni, S., Horlings, L. G. and K. Soini (2020), 'Linking spatial planning and place branding strategies through cultural narratives in places', *European Planning Studies*, **28** (7), 1355–74.

Hanna, S. and J. Rowley (2011), 'Towards a strategic place-brand management model', *Journal of Marketing Management*, **27** (5–6), 458–76.

Hanna, S. and J. Rowley (2015), 'Towards a model for the place brand web', *Tourism Management*, **24**, 100–12.

Hede, A. M. and T. Watne (2013), 'Leveraging the human side of the brand using a sense of place: Case studies of craft breweries', *Journal of Marketing Management*, **29** (1–2), 207–24.

Henninger, C. E., Foster, C., Alevizou, P. J. and C. Frohlich (2016), 'Stakeholder engagement in the city branding process', *Place Branding and Public Diplomacy*, **12** (4), 285–98.

Humphreys, M., Ucbasaran, D. and A. Lockett (2012), 'Sensemaking and sensegiving stories of jazz leadership', *Human Relations*, **65** (1), 41–62.

Iannone, F. and F. Izzo (2017), 'Salvatore Ferragamo: An Italian heritage brand and its museum', *Place Branding and Public Diplomacy*, **13** (2), 163–75.

Jacobsen, B. P. (2012), 'Place brand equity: A model for establishing the effectiveness of place brands', *Journal of Place Management and Development*, **5** (3), 253–71.

Jahn, J. L. S., White, M. S. and H. Brenkert-Smith (2020), 'My place or yours? Using spatial frames to understand the role of place in forest management conflicts', *Society and Natural Resources*, **33** (3), 329–46.

Kavaratzis, M. (2012), 'From "necessary evil" to necessary stakeholders: Stakeholders' involvement in place branding', *Journal of Place Management and Development*, **5** (1), 7–19.

Kavaratzis, M. and M. J. Hatch (2013), 'The dynamics of place brands: An identity-based approach to place branding theory', *Marketing Theory*, **13** (1), 69–86.

Kavaratzis, M. and A. Kalandides (2015), 'Rethinking the place brand: The interactive formation of place brands and the role of participatory branding', *Environment and Planning A*, **47** (6), 1368–82.

Klijn, E. H., Eshuis, J. and E. Braun (2012), 'The influence of stakeholder involvement on the effectiveness of place branding', *Public Management Review*, **14** (4), 499–519.

Lucarelli, A. and M. Giovanardi (2016), 'The political nature of brand governance: A discourse analysis approach to a regional brand building process', *Journal of Public Affairs*, **16** (1), 16–27.

Maitlis, S. (2005), 'The social processes of organizational sensemaking', *Academy of Management Journal*, **48** (1), 21–49.

Maitlis, S. and T. B. Lawrence (2007), 'Triggers and enablers of sensegiving in organizations', *Academy of Management Journal*, **50** (1), 57–84.

Maitlis, S. and S. Sonenshein (2010), 'Sensemaking in crisis and change: Inspiration and insights from Weick (1988)', *Journal of Management Studies*, **47** (3), 551–80.

Merrilees, B., Miller, D. and C. Herington (2012), 'Multiple stakeholders and multiple city meanings', *European Journal of Marketing*, **46** (7/8), 1032–47.

Mitchell, R. K., Agle, B. R. and D. J. Wood (1997), 'Toward a theory of stakeholder identification and salience: Defining the principle of who and what really counts', *Academy of Management Review*, **22** (4), 853–86.

Morsing, M. and M. Schultz (2006), 'Corporate social responsibility communication: Stakeholder information, response and involvement strategies', *Business Ethics: A European Review*, **15** (4), 323–38.

Nicholds, A., Gibney, J., Mabey, C. and D. Hart (2017), 'Making sense of variety in place leadership: The case of England's smart cities', *Regional Studies*, **51** (2), 249–59.

O'Reilly, D. and F. Kerrigan (2013), 'A view to a brand: Introducing the film brandscape', *European Journal of Marketing*, **47** (5/6), 769–89.

Reid, K., Beilin, R. and J. McLennan (2020), 'Communities and responsibility: Narratives of place-identity in Australian bushfire landscapes', *Geoforum*, **109**, 35–43.

Rouleau, L. (2005), 'Micro-practices of strategic sensemaking and sensegiving: How middle managers interpret and sell change every day', *Journal of Management Studies*, **42** (7), 1413–41.

Samuel, A. and K. Peattie (2016), 'Grounded theory as a macromarketing methodology: Critical insights from researching the marketing dynamics of Fairtrade Towns', *Journal of Macromarketing*, **36** (1), 11–26.

Tuan, Y.-F. (1991), 'Language and the making of place: A narrative-descriptive approach', *Annals of the Association of American Geographers*, **81** (4), 684–96.

Vallaster, C. and S. von Wallpach (2013), 'An online discursive inquiry into the social dynamics of multi-stakeholder brand meaning co-creation', *Journal of Business Research*, **66** (9), 1505–15.

Voase, R. (2012), 'Recognition, reputation and response: Some critical thoughts on destinations and brands', *Journal of Destination Marketing and Management*, **1** (1–2), 78–83.

Weick, K. E. (1995), *Sensemaking in Organizations*, Thousand Oaks, CA: Sage.

Weick, K. E., Sutcliffe, K. M. and D. Obstfeld (2005), 'Organizing and the process of sensemaking', *Organization Science*, **16** (4), 409–21.

Wilson, J. E., Bengtsson, A. and C. Curran (2014), 'Brand meaning gaps and dynamics: Theory, research, and practice', *Qualitative Market Research: An International Journal*, **17** (2), 128–50.

Zenker, S. and S. Z. C. Erfgen (2014), 'Let them do the work: A participatory place branding approach', *Journal of Place Management and Development*, **7** (3), 225–34.

16 Considering place and the sensorium through the lens of non-representational theory

Simon Cryer

Introduction

The role of the senses in further understanding place is undoubtedly important, and of increasing interest to multidimensional and multidisciplinary perspectives. We experience place wholly through a multisensory medium, and it is perhaps surprising that there have been persistent calls for the exploration of sensory interactions related to place knowledge throughout such a relatively protracted time period of academic attention (see, for example: Schafer, 1977; Porteous, 1990; Rodaway, 1994; Adams and Guy, 2007; Medway, 2015; Campelo, 2017). It is theorised that broader recognition of the interrelationships between place and the lived sensorium will provide deeper insight into how stimulating attributes might be strategically managed, and how sensory engagement might be better employed within place marketing practices (Medway and Warnaby, 2017; Canniford, Riach, and Hill, 2018; Wiedmann et al., 2017; Rodrigues et al., 2019). This chapter aims to elucidate on how we might advantageously engage with the multisensory relationship with place in order to enhance place branding efforts.

Sensory experiences dominate people's engagement with place (Adams et al., 2007; Degen and Rose, 2012). Indeed, Pink (2015: 11) insists that our immediate environment is 'constituted, experienced, understood, evaluated, and maintained through all the senses'. The senses provide us with rich, personal detail when navigating through place, experientially immersing us, often inciting emotional attachment (Pink, 2015). Rouby, Fournel, and Bensafi (2016) concur, suggesting that it is difficult to tune out or switch off our sensorial reception; moreover, several sensory channels will usually process stimulating information simultaneously, bombarding our neural cognitions with emotional cues which instantaneously facilitate our feelings. Put another way, environmental sensory stimuli can produce emotional triggers and ties which are processed almost instantaneously by our senses, often subconsciously, influencing our behaviours and emotional states covertly. Sensory stimulus derived from places, then, directly affects a given place user's experiences, memories, and ultimately their perceptions and images of that place. Bull et al. (2006: 5) neatly summarise why a multisensory approach to appreciating place is imperative: 'The senses mediate the relationship between self and society, mind and body, idea and object. The senses are everywhere. Thus, sensation… is fundamental to our experience of reality, and the sociality of sensation cries out for more concerted attention from cultural studies scholars.'

Porteous (1990) describes the individual sensory aspects of place as 'senses-capes' (for example: landscapes, soundscapes, smellscapes), and by addressing these either directly or as part of the sensorium, place managers can make places more comfortable, attractive, practical, and crucially for place market-ing efforts, *more desirable* for new and established investors (Ward, 1998). Place managers might create something approaching a holistic sensory expe-rience for their target market (Landry, 2007), and encourage a deeper, more embodied impression of place identity for potential and existing consumers (Henshaw and Mould, 2013). In this regard, Daugstad (2008: 413) stresses the importance of the senses in tourism, arguing that tourists have largely moved away from: 'passing through the landscape and only experiencing it through the eyes. The modern tourist wants the personal experience of tasting, feeling, and hearing stories about the landscape, and to experience it first-hand.'

For place branding efforts, a deeper understanding of our sensorial experiences of place could expand the opportunity for a wider appreciation of how place image is established, thus helping to bolster any desired identity messages. Wiedmann et al. (2017) express that the provision of unique and memorable sensory experiences can determine a positive customer–brand relationship, and indeed, this is clearly one of the principal challenges in contemporary brand management practice. Multisensory experiences significantly affect differentiation and positioning of brand image in the mind (Hulten, 2011), and Rodrigues et al. (2019) venture that cities might even be planned as expe-riential conduits, where designed and inherent unique sensory place branding experiences should combine with emotional, behavioural, and intellectual encounters to help to create long and lasting memories for place users. The place experience becomes an integral driving factor in the place user's endur-ing perception, and place image is augmented and sustained. This resonates with Kim's (2018) reinforced findings that the proposition of 'memorable tourism experiences' significantly enhances the future behaviour of place visitors: the hope of unique experiences is particularly attractive to prospective visitors, and the evoked positive memories of those who have already visited may encourage a return.

Challenges

Almost immediately, research efforts dealing with sensescapes and affect are a tricky endeavour. One of the fundamental characteristics of both place and the sensory environment is that neither will keep still long enough for traditional positivist approaches to have any meaningful impact. Places are in constant flux, sensory stimuli are not static and therefore attempting to apply tangible boundaries to research would be futile – smells and sounds, for example, cannot be restrained by research borders, and a good pair of eyes can spot a candle flame up to 30 miles away.

In any case, sensory appreciation itself is perceived individually even if it is simultaneously experienced by many (Porteous, 1990; Lorimer, 2005), and is determined by other fluid influences, such as mood, experience, active and unconscious recollection, and the behaviours of other people (Rodaway, 1994; Degen and Rose, 2012; Rouby et al., 2016). It is clear, therefore, that research into the sensory experience of place should arrive from phenomenological modes of enquiry (Medway and Warnaby, 2017). However, much of the material relating to the sensory experience of place is difficult to uncover. Discussing the sensorium and sensescapes means describing intangible and probably unnoticed phenomena (stimulating sounds, smells, tastes, and tangible touch), and the initiative is particularly slippery in terms of exploration, ratification, representation, and dissemination, yet this information is crucial if place marketers are to become more efficient in achieving their core objective. How, then, can we more effectively investigate the place user's experiential relationship with place?

Non-representational theory offers an approach to exploring the multitudes of sensory experience in a multiplicity of ways, and has the capability to assist with enquiries into the various and conflicting meanings surrounding and permeating our interrelationship with places. Nigel Thrift's reflection of non-representational thinking from the late twentieth century onwards offers a way of considering thought, action, and affect, and presents a set of interconnected tenets which might guide researchers to discover and contemplate 'the embodied movements, precognitive triggers, practical skills, affective intensities, enduring urges, unexceptional interactions, and sensuous dispositions' embedded within the conversation (Lorimer, 2005: 84).

The kaleidoscopic lens of non-representational theory

Non-representational theory, as a collective term used here, relates to the consolidation of Nigel Thrift's writings on space and affect. The core objective of the principle is to augment investigations into everyday life by concentrating on the analysis of practice and mobility, rather than interpretation and representation of static detail. Practices here are considered as a series of intermingling events, flowing from one action to the next, and not framed as clipped individual performances. This allows an insight into performativity of emotions, affect, and embodied actions. It is an attempt to embrace and engage with the complexity of life as it happens. It is less concerned with procedural, technical methods, and more excited about movement, bodily sensation, the unmentionable, and the undiscovered – that which is either problematically difficult or impossible to represent.

Non-representational theory is not a series of regulated mechanical steps to be taken in order to realise some predetermined ending to research. It is rather a means of engaging with life lived with others, 'cognisant of the past, finely attuned to the conditions of the present, and speculatively open to the possibilities of the future' (Ingold, 2015: vii). Lorimer (2005: 83) summarises: 'Non-representational theory is an umbrella term for diverse work that seeks to better cope with our self-evidently more-than-human, more-than-textual, multi-sensual worlds.'

Non-representational theory offers a way of considering that which might be overlooked, attempting to 'make different things significant and worthy of notice' (Thrift, 2008: 224). By exploring phenomena that are 'seldom valued, quickly forgotten or that remain uncaptured altogether' (Hill, Canniford, and Mol, 2014: 384) researchers can gain access into the 'undisclosed and sometimes undisclosable nature of everyday practice' (Cadman, 2009: 456). And it is in this *geography of what happens*' (Thrift, 2008: 2), in the mundane and the missed, the unintentional, the automatic, and the elusive in routines and practices, where new streams of inquiry might be uncovered.

This background detail provides crucial circumstantial support which enables us to enact conceivably more pressing conscious thoughts and actions: an instinctive and ongoing interaction with our environment contextualises our position, consequently informing both reflexive and considered movements and reactions. By way of example, Anderson and Harrison (2010) describe the intricacies of a student arriving late to a class and quickly finding a chair, suggesting that the latecomer would not actively recognise the doorway and door, consider its function as an aperture, contemplate its mechanics, or question its closure behind them – this is before looking for a chair. The background knowledge used here is unspoken, in the moment, and allows the latecomer to perform the conscious activity of swiftly taking their place in the class without governing every action. This example illustrates how people constantly process background interactions without conscious negotiation. The non-representational lens considers that 'the root of action is to be conceived less in terms of willpower or cognitive deliberation and more via embodied and environmental affordances, dispositions, and habits' (Anderson and Harrison, 2010: 7).

When questioned about the influences behind decision making – the minutiae of practice – people can find it difficult to articulate, the nuance of 'ordinary' so inherently profound that the details may never have been considered. Elements of practices can be easily overlooked, regarded as too familiar for notable comment or unmet with ambivalence to the point of innocent ignorance (Hitchings, 2011; Shove, Pantzar, and Watson, 2012), leaving social enquiry short, particularly if the aim of the research concerns behaviours and movements. Finding the small things allows us to augment the possibilities.

Thrift is wholly transparent in explaining that although non-representational theory is presented to be used as a diagnostic tool, it is not permanently fixed, and providing a methodical 'how to' manual was not his objective. It does not offer an epistemological approach to understanding, nor is it a research method. It is not a theory in the traditional sense at all. Rather, it is a way of thinking about thinking. Thrift implies that the guiding theoretical principles are to be leaned on throughout the research process, to be used as a lens through which research can be positioned, performed, and perceived. Thrift describes these guidelines as '*practices* of vocation' (2008: 3) intended to expand the opportunities in exploring and identifying 'what is present in experience' (2008: 2). Vannini (2015: 3) summarises that the principles behind non-representational theory should be held in mind during the entirety of the social science research process as ongoing exercises in creativity, and as vocational routines, intended for the practices of an 'imprecise science concerned more with hope for politico-epistemic renewal than validity'. Rather than a prescriptive method for encounter, non-representational theory offers some tactical suggestions of how we might set about tackling the relationships between place, space, the senses, and life.

All this might sound somewhat uncomfortable in its ambiguity, and one might easily refuse to engage with the principles from sheer objectivist alarm. Non-representational theory appears initially esoteric, and indeed, it is difficult to penetrate. It is assumed that the reader has a solid grounding in a gamut of theoretical inspiration from numerous associated disciplines, listed without conclusion in any number of other writings (see: Jones, 2008; Cadman, 2009; Thorpe and Rinehart, 2010; Cresswell, 2012; Hill et al., 2014; Vannini, 2015). On top of this, Thrift's ideas are notably poetic, open to interpretation, tricky, evocative, and probably abstruse, making non-representational theory a difficult proposition for the burgeoning researcher. Thrift is fully aware of this, and unapologetic, explaining that non-representational theory is intentionally experimental in order to assist 'wild conceptuality' (2008: 19) in the exploration and dissemination of research. The aim is to allow an approach to inquiry without the constraint of rigid boundaries.

Thrift (2008) outlines a set of core tenets for non-representational approaches to thought, insisting that these qualities are cordoned tentatively: any outlines are purposefully blurry to allow for experimentation and unexpected turns in the research process. Each tenet is not ranked in terms of importance, nor are the principles regarded as comparable. There is no order of attack, rather the tenets are to be adopted and applied according to the research situation, leaving room for adaptation and experimentation as appropriate. The tenets are briefly expanded as follows.

On-flow

Non-representational theory attempts to uncover and obtain the 'on-flow' of everyday life, interested in absorbing the movement of (and within) the 'moment', rather than the capture of some frozen descriptive state. The 'moment' is considered to be an in-flux, interrelated exchange between the pre-cognitive management of information (from conversation, body language, or situational ambience) and reactionary cognitive action: the pre-cognitive is deemed to be more than just a supplement to the cognitive.

Donald (2001) describes available consciousness as a slight window of time, probably no longer than 15 seconds, where only a few things can be genuinely attended to. It is susceptible to distraction, and ultimately 'opaque to introspection' (Thrift, 2008: 6). Cognitive action within this conscious window is arrived at by the synthesis of a roiling mass of pre-cognitive thought formation, perception, anticipation, and automatism. Thrift (2008: 7) suggests that 'cognition should be seen as an emergent outcome of strategic joint action for which it acts as a guidance function' for iterative and exploratory pre-cognitive processes. Every action is therefore an interaction (Anderson and Harrison, 2010): we are immersed in an iterative relationality with our environment, constantly running checks on things in our periphery, continually collecting phenomena and updating the moment. 'We live *through* what is happening' (Boyd, 2017: 33), forever adjusting the 'now' and adapting to life's ebb and flow as the world continues to emerge and unfold.

The idea of life being lived in the moment allows us to consider Thrift's 'geography of what happens' as it happens. This continuous performativity allows permanent developing change, the unforeseen, yet it also enables the notion of mundanity as life rolls on (Cadman, 2009). It is in this mundanity where Thrift argues we might find areas of interest through reassessing what we determine to be significant, as 'forces and entities continually come in and out of relation in ways that are contingent, messy, and unpredictable, but, at the same time, full of potential' (Boyd and Edwardes, 2019: 2).

Parts of the sensorium are inevitably on-flow. Some sensory stimuli move and morph, and can appear, strengthen, transform, reduce, and vanish sometimes even before we have registered their existence. Various aspects of sensory stimuli seemingly apparent in place are difficult to notice at all until they are no longer stimulating: we might think about the unexpected physical relief when, for example, a persistent noise halts (a pitched whine from machinery; a distant alarm bell), or when cloud cover provides respite from the baking sun, or when transitioning underfoot from loose sand or shale to solid concrete offers welcome kinaesthetic stability.

On-flow has synergy with the well-trodden interpretation of place as a constantly in motion, figuratively living, breathing entity (for example: Le Corbusier's (2000) approach to urban design in 1929; Amin and Thrift's (2002) notion of the city as collected virtualities and potentialities; Landry's (2007) conception of the city as a 'guzzling beast'). Even Tuan's (1977: 125) allegorical description of place as a pause in space rides with the view that as 'we stand before a prospect, our mind is free to roam'. For Tuan (1977), time flows through place (manifest in architecture, art, the landscape, culture), and history and viable futures are reflected by our mental wandering. The sensorium and our perceptions and reactions do not remain static, nor do the physical arenas which host our experiences; epistemologies and methods which investigate place must also exist and perform in fluid motion to run alongside what is happening in the moment.

Anti-Biographical and Pre-Individual

Thrift (2008) insists that preceding accounts pose a problem when exploring the lived experience: non-representational theory revels in moments and instants of life being lived, and previous individual experiences become an awkward fit. The celebration of individual reports promote 'a spurious sense of oneness' (Thrift, 2008: 8), where a whole story is ringfenced, and no further information or affect can influence. Individuals count for their effect on the performed moment: 'on-flow' remains the focus of inquiry. Biography is deemed to be inextricably linked with the previous; a confirmatory full-stop. Thrift (2008: 8) calls for a 'material schematism', where continuous and involuntary encounter with the world facilitates the interrelation between all kinds of things brought from all manner of spaces. In this completely materialist view, a priori information does not limit the possibilities of what makes up the lived experience: Anderson and Harrison (2010: 14) stipulate 'everything takes-part and in taking part takes place: everything happens, everything acts'. Nothing is excluded, and eschewing the individual and biography removes their latent restrictions. The 'now' of lived life is pertinent, and any individual agency is only consequential in that it might illuminate or contextualise (Thorpe and Rinehart, 2010).

Practices

Thrift (2008: 8) positions 'practices' as non-representational theory's focus: 'if we are looking for something that approximates to a stable feature of a world that is continually in meltdown, that is continually bringing forth new hybrids, then I take practices to be it'. Practices are coordinated, recognisable, routine forms of behaviour, comprising of interdependent elements that require continued performance to substantiate their existence (Reckwitz, 2002; Warde, 2005). As such, practices simultaneously exist as performances. Shove et al. (2012) identify that practices are made up of three elements:

> *Materials.* The actual 'things' we use when we are doing whatever it is that we are doing, that is, objects, technologies, tools, infrastructures, or any other tangible entities.

> *Competences.* The information we know and the experience we call upon, so that we can do whatever it is that we are doing, such as embodied skills, knowledge and know-how, and technique.

> *Meanings.* The significance of the practice in terms of how it relates to society, whether symbolic, ideological, or aspirational. Maller

(2015) adds that meanings are about how and why things are done, guided by cultural expectations and conventions.

Separated, the elements of a practice are abstract, until they are actively combined during the performance of a particular practice; the practice becoming the sum of the interdependent relations between its essential parts. Shove et al. (2012) explain that these three elements are bonded, and the interlinks must be maintained and sustained for the practice to remain recognisable. However, practices are open to change and reconfiguration: if the links are modified or they conclude, the practice will alter or cease to exist.

Practices, then, are inherently stable, but not static. They are not hermetically sealed. The elemental components are in flux, affected by proto-practices yet to exist, by unfaithful and playful repetition, and by the remnants of disintegrated practices gone by. Thrift (2008) relishes the prospects of this metamorphosis and wreckage, noting the possibilities of reusing the detritus in other networks, and recognising the memorial qualities of past events and practices.

By grounding itself in 'the leitmotif of movement in its many forms' (Thrift, 2008: 5), non-representational theory has been practically included as a theory of mobile practices (Cadman, 2009). Theories of practice are a response towards comprehending social action and interaction, interested in how things are done normally, and concerned with the interconnected, reciprocal relationship between human and non-human actors. By emphasising practices as the unit of inquiry, social research might then find the opportunity to uncover and examine overlooked processes within routine, particularly that which is arbitrarily dismissed as unimportant, the unnoticed, the mundane.

Echoes of Bourdieu's (1990) concept of the 'habitus' resonate here: over a period of time, as we mix with familiar people and move through the same places, we become incorporated by particular group identities, and much of our routines and behaviours become naturalised to us, no longer of immediate interest or deliberation. Bourdieu (1990) indicates that once practices are established, quirks and idiosyncrasies meld into the routine, and habitus is sustained. Yet we can turn to the idea of this 'background' as a forum to search for these things that we seldom notice in place. These things may be hard to find – we might not yet realise that they exist, or we might overlook them, or they may be too sensitive or too uncomfortable to raise – however, such phenomena might be crucial in interpreting why particular places and their sensescapes evoke certain emotional responses. In addition, the identification of germane elements of practices materialises their capacity to assist with developing and strengthening the detail of place branding communications.

Things

Non-representational theory 'has always given equal weight to the vast spillage of things' (Thrift, 2008: 9) – 'things' being the materials we use to negotiate and engage with the life lived. In the world we occupy, things become crucial enablers of how the body encounters and experiences life. Crucially, the body and its interaction with things allows us to facilitate otherwise inaccessible sensory experiences through the use of tools, clothing, machinery, and such.

Thrift (2008) is keen to identify that the body is not separated from the world. The body is also a thing, and things are continually brought into relation with us through encounter: we are always in movement, and we do not move as a single entity. Furthermore, the body has the ability to co-exist with and assimilate things, producing a constantly evolving entity with constantly evolving reaches. The body is therefore a 'tool-being' working in tandem with things to create hybrid assemblages. Considerable importance is placed on this interaction, and Thrift (2008: 10) is careful to explain that the body/things interrelation is fluid, that the body external does not present an 'ineffable perceptual membrane'. There is a permanently present sense of touch in attendance throughout the material body, extending through the things we interact with, informing our proprioception, and helping us to assess our next action. Thrift considers the relationship between things, time, space, nature, and the body to be contemporaneously blended, melding to produce what Thorpe and Rinehart (2010: 1273) describe as a 'holistic, harmonic and interactive world'. Thrift (2008: 12) cites Kwon's (2004) notion of 'site' as apposite here: the synchronous interaction happens at the surface of things, creating an 'active and always incomplete incarnation of events, and actualisation of times and spaces, that uses the fluctuating conditions to assemble itself'.

Much of the sensorium becomes available to us at the site. Interaction and connection with it is both facilitated and prohibited here. Tools and things can enable us to access and augment, prevent and reduce sensory engagements. For example, appropriate clothing allows us to experience otherwise difficult ambient conditions. I am reminded of researching outdoors in a north-facing English seaside town in winter: light, persistent rain tapping at my waterproof hood; a sharp, chill wind tightening my face while my body and hands remain warm; the tactile stability afforded by a good pair of walking boots. Adopting the use of things here allowed me the opportunity to further experience other sensescapes in real time: the salted spray from the sea whilst lumbering over wet sands; the shrieking immediacy of busy seagulls; the tang of smoking kippers sometimes on the wind; the omnipresent acridity of fish and chips and salt and vinegar filtering through grey drizzle. Awareness of how things permit us to engage with place at the site might improve our understanding of how experiences are encountered and participated, so that something of the elusive place essence might be captured.

Experimental

Non-representational theory is inevitably experimental. Practitioners hold an aversion to traditional social science's empirical tendencies, uncomfortable with positivist conventions and the conservatism that realism insists upon (Vannini, 2015), and the approach used tends to bend, blur, or break seemingly restrictive covenants.

Ingold (2015) describes the employment of non-representational theory as akin to an ongoing correspondence: the social researcher's inevitable contact with the subject is not retreated from; rather, as things happen around us, questions are answered with reflected and reciprocal interventions, responses, and further questions of our own. There is an experimental exchange around the subject: anticipation, response, and exploration are preferred to representation and prediction. Description, then, is favoured over diagnosis, and enquiry is typically developed through the use of core qualitative research techniques, particularly ethnographies, observations, interviews, and diaristic exercises (Cadman, 2009). Again, there is no defined method of how to do non-representational theory, rather the researcher is encouraged to experiment with the language, methods, and associated ontologies, adapting and creating advantage as situationally appropriate.

Thrift (2008: 12) enjoys the idea of conceptual exploration in the undertaking of research, and calls for the researcher 'to let the event sing' just 'to see what will happen'. We are to wholeheartedly 'leave room for values like messiness, and operators like the mistake, the stumble and the stutter' (Thrift, 2008: 12). Anything goes. Nothing is discarded without toying with it first. Thrift implores us to play with the methods, to enthusiastically employ unconventional means as a response to capturing the traces of the myriad of entities in the world, and to vigorously rummage through the seemingly limitless streams of enquiry hidden in the overgrowth (rather than the undergrowth). Non-representational work seeks 'to rupture, unsettle, animate, and reverberate rather than report', and a deliberately immature, wonderous, and restless approach can initiate this (Vannini, 2015: 5).

Affect, Sensation, and Atmosphere

Non-representational thought assigns significance to affect and sensation, as must be clear at this point. Thrift (2008) draws from feminist theorists, and positions affect as the way that each and every thing manifests itself in simply just being. Affect is the embodiment of the essence of things: how something acts, lives, and performs to maintain its existence is an affect by default.

The body itself becomes the subject of attention: we are to place interest in the driving forces of affect which pass between the body and other experiential things, those influences that cause change and push assemblages into motion (Hill et al., 2014). The body is seen as a vehicle for transmitting, receiving, and producing affective capacities; namely 'moods, passions, emotions, intensities, and feelings' (Vannini, 2015: 5) – supremely important in that 'how things seem is often more important than what they are' (Thrift, 2008: 13).

These forces are naturally on-flow, energetically accumulating and dissipating in anticipation and reaction to events and things. Comparable to the continuously melding notion of 'the site', the body is seen as having a porous boundary, where we are sensitive to our environment and to the sensitivities of others (Hill et al., 2014). Pre-cognitive mechanisms charge affects, often unconsciously changing our moods and our feelings. There is no personal volition. We intuitively sense, feel, and embody atmospheres rather than controlling and consciously managing our ambient positions. For Hill et al. (2014), sensed atmosphere is the accumulation of affect on different bodies and the spaces through which they flow, and as an explanatory concept is helpful in explaining how affects transfer between bodies without choice. Atmospheres are *contagious*.

The sensorium is extremely influential here, naturally, as our entire perceptual apparatus performs as an operational complex which interweaves us with our atmospheres (Bull et al., 2006). Sensory receptors are concomitant processors which connect us physically, socially, and emotionally to our surrounding environment (Rouby et al., 2016). We tangibly sense an atmosphere without the need for metaphor. Notably, atmospheres are central to the conceptual 'sense of place', and in turn, crucial if place brands are to develop prospective messages of uniqueness (Campelo, 2015). If branding efforts are to emulate the essence of place, then exploration of collected atmospheres, cultural meanings, and signifiers can assist with recognising aspects of imbedded habitus, enabling a more sincere connection with likely or established place users.

Experience and Ethics

Thrift (2008: 14) argues for an 'ethic of novelty' to be applied to non-representational consideration in order to promote an 'out of jointness' where 'every familiar is ultimately strange' (Santner, 2001: 6, cited in Thrift, 2008: 14). Thrift (2008: 14) looks to boost aliveness here: too often in everyday life we are closed off from much of what is happening to us and around us, 'clipping our own wings because we inhabit cringes which limit our field of action'. We are in the midst of life yet most of it does not register. We should be more attuned to the 'events, relations, practices and performances, affects, and backgrounds' of life lived (Vannini, 2015: 11). We are asked to be mindful of potentiality in the act, to hold an awareness of possibilities as life moves forwards in the slightest bracket of time and space, 'as it acts or exists in the interstices of interaction' (Thrift, 2008: 15).

Cadman (2009: 461) notes that the ethics needed 'are pulled away from judgement and universal [ontologies]' so that we can focus on witnessing as experience of the world unfolds. The outcomes of experimental non-representational approaches cannot be prescribed in advance and they are therefore risky, but something might happen – new forms of life might surface in the 'processual registers of experience' (Dewsbury et al., 2002).

Again, non-representational theory argues that some practices and associated materials assist and even generate a heightened awareness of the world around us, introducing new sensory experiences and granting their sustain. Thrift (2008) calls for an attempt to gather the ethics of craftsmanship so that a different model of 'homo faber' might be accomplished. Utilising tools can afford us the actuality of reaching and maintaining new experiences. Bodily practices can amplify passions and provide transcendent experiences, accentuating sensory appreciation and enhancing a harmonious relationship with the environment (Thorpe and Rinehart, 2010).

Conclusion

Dewsbury et al. (2002: 437) postulate that, as an open-ended, constantly unfolding entity, 'the world is more excessive than we can theorise'. Thrift's manifestation of non-representational theory acknowledges this with enthusiasm, and wholeheartedly expects methodological consideration to inspire open-ended responses to make room for excess in the research process. This will be a problem for those with firmly planted objectivist assumptions about the nature of social science. Hill et al. (2014) highlight the problem of a wandering research boundary if we are building accounts from the interrelations between people, the sensorium, materials, meanings, competences, affect – if we are to consider everything that occurs in life, where do we stop?

Further criticism is perfectly reasonable. The 'non-' prefix is a problem for some: suggestions that Thrift's work eschews representation altogether are perhaps precarious though not without objective concern, leading to Lorimer (2005) preferring the term 'more-than representational' to describe the concept. Representations are not dismissed by Thrift, more accurately they are regarded as happenings in their own right, 'as lively things in a world that is always becoming rather than achieved' (Cresswell, 2012: 100). Thrift (2008: 2) makes it clear immediately that he wants to promote a 'supplement to the ordinary, a sacrament for the everyday, a hymn to the superfluous'. The non-representational might be considered to be supporting addenda here, were it not for the glaring promise of potentialities brimming under the surface of research, almost within reach. Lorimer's modified nomenclature may well be more appropriate than Thrift's.

Canniford (2012) comments that the writings of non-representational theory authors tend to be dense, verbose, and notoriously challenging to fathom, perhaps unsurprisingly, as the content will likely be conceptually performative in the presentation of its discussion. Cresswell (2012: 100) adds the natural oxymoron of describing the 'world-as-it-is [with] reverential referencing [of] texts upon texts upon texts', and criticises that empirical conversation is lacking. Again, the reader is generally assumed to have read from the same texts as the author, and may well feel inadequately prepared if they have not.

Undoubtedly, non-representational thought can be daunting for an early career researcher. It is difficult to get into, hard to present, and requires some skilled deduction to practise it. It is truly heuristic to the point of forced autodidacticism. Cresswell (2012) goes as far as to say that it is entirely acceptable to ignore non-representational theory altogether. Yet a non-representational approach towards place branding practices might be worth persevering with for the possible rewards, not least for the opportunity to maximise a higher return from valuable and limited collected data. If non-representational theory is applied competently, then the chance of uncovering unexpected and beneficial insight can be improved, consequently offering new ways of how we think about thought and action in place. The potential of non-representational thinking might open up unexpected opportunities not just in the consideration of the senses and their interrelationship with place, but in all place-based research.

References

Adams, M. and S. Guy (2007), 'Senses and the city', *Senses and Society*, **2** (2), 133–6.

Adams, M., Moore, G., Cox, T., Croxford, B., Refaee, M., and S. Sharples (2007), 'The 24-hour city: Residents' sensorial experiences', *Senses and Society*, **2** (2), 201–15.

Amin, A. and N. Thrift (2002), *Cities: Reimagining the Urban*, Cambridge: Polity Press.

Anderson, B. and P. Harrison (2010), 'The promise of non-representational theories', in B. Anderson and P. Harrison (eds), *Taking Place: Non-Representational Theories and Geography*, Abingdon: Routledge, pp. 1–36.

Bourdieu, P. (1990), *The Logic of Practice*, London: Polity.

Boyd, C. (2017), *Non-Representational Geographies of Therapeutic Art Making: Thinking through Practice*, London: Palgrave Macmillan.

Boyd, C. and C. Edwardes (2019), 'Creative practice and the non-representational', in C. Boyd and C. Edwardes (eds), *Non-representational Theory and the Creative Arts*, London: Palgrave Macmillan, pp. 1–15.

Bull, M., Gilroy, P., Howes, D., and D. Kahn (2006), 'Introducing sensory studies', *Senses and Society*, **1** (1), 5–6.

Cadman, L. (2009), 'Nonrepresentational theory, nonrepresentational geographies', in R. Kitchen and N. Thrift (eds), *International Encyclopaedia of Human Geography*, 1st ed., Oxford: Elsevier, pp. 456–63.

Campelo, A. (2015), 'Rethinking sense of place: Sense of one and sense of many', in M. Kavaratzis, G. Warnaby, and G. J. Ashworth (eds), *Rethinking Place Branding: Comprehensive Brand Development for Cities and Regions*, Cham: Springer International Publishing, pp. 51–60.

Campelo, A. (2017), 'Smell it, taste it, hear it, touch it, and see it to make sense of this place', in A. Campelo (ed.), *Handbook on Place Branding and Marketing*, Cheltenham, UK and Northampton, MA, USA: Edward Elgar Publishing, pp. 124–44.

Canniford, R. (2012), 'Poetic witness: Marketplace research through poetic transcription and poetic translation', *Marketing Theory*, **12** (4), 391–409.

Canniford, R., Riach, K., and T. Hill (2018), 'Nosenography: How smell constitutes meaning, identity and temporal experience in spatial assemblages', *Marketing Theory*, **18** (2), 234–48.

Cresswell, T. (2012), 'Non-representational theory and me: Notes of an interested sceptic', *Environment and Planning D: Society and Space*, **30** (1), 96–105.

Daugstad, K. (2008), 'Negotiating landscape in rural tourism', *Annals of Tourism Research*, **32** (2), 402–26.

Degen, M. and G. Rose (2012), 'The sensory experiencing of urban design: The role of walking and perceptual memory', *Urban Studies*, **49** (15), 3271–87.

Dewsbury, J., Harrison, P., Rose, M., Wylie, J., and D. P. McCormack (2002), 'Enacting geographies', *Geoforum*, **33** (4), 437–40.

Donald, M. (2001), *A Mind So Rare: The Evolution of Human Consciousness*, New York: Norton.

Henshaw, V. and O. Mould (2013), 'Sensing designed space: An exploratory methodology for investigating human response to sensory environments', *Journal of Design Research*, **11** (1), 57–71.

Hill, T., Canniford, R., and J. Mol (2014), 'Non-representational marketing theory', *Marketing Theory*, **14** (4), 377–94.

Hitchings, R. (2011), 'People can talk about their practices', *Area*, **44** (1), 61–7.

Hulten, B. (2011), 'Sensory marketing: The multi-sensory brand-experience concept', *European Business Review*, **23** (3), 256–73.

Ingold, T. (2015), 'Foreword', in P. Vannini (ed.), *Non-Representational Methodologies: Re-envisioning Research*, New York: Routledge, pp. vii–x.

Jones, O. (2008), 'Stepping from the wreckage: Geography, pragmatism and anti-representational theory', *Geoforum*, **39**, 1600–612.

Kim, J. (2018), 'The impact of memorable tourism experiences on loyalty behaviours: The mediating effects of destination image and satisfaction', *Journal of Travel Research*, **57** (7), 856–70.

Kwon, M. (2004), *One Place after Another: Site-specific Art and Locational Identity*, Cambridge, MA: MIT Press.

Landry, C. (2007), *The Art of City Making*, London: Earthscan.

Le Corbusier (2000), *The City of Tomorrow and its Planning*, 8th ed., New York: Dover Publications.

Lorimer, H. (2005), 'Cultural geography: The busyness of being "more than representational"', *Progress in Human Geography*, **29** (1), 83–94.

Maller, C. (2015), 'Understanding health through social practices: Performance and materiality in everyday life', *Sociology of Health and Illness*, **37** (1), 52–66.

Medway, D. (2015), 'Rethinking place branding and the "other" senses', in M. Kavaratzis, G. Warnaby, and G. J. Ashworth (eds), *Rethinking Place Branding: Comprehensive Brand Development for Cities and Regions*, Cham: Springer International Publishing, pp. 191–209.

Medway, D. and G. Warnaby (2017), 'Multisensory place branding: A manifesto for research', in A. Campelo (ed.), *Handbook on Place Branding and Marketing*, Cheltenham, UK and Northampton, MA, USA: Edward Elgar Publishing, pp. 147–59.

Pink, S. (2015), *Doing Sensory Ethnography*, 2nd ed., London: Sage.

Porteous, D. (1990), *Landscapes of the Mind: Worlds of Sense and Metaphor*, Toronto: University of Toronto Press.

Reckwitz, A. (2002), 'Toward a theory of social practices: A development in culturalist theorising', *European Journal of Social Theory*, **5** (2), 243–63.

Rodaway, P. (1994), *Sensuous Geographies*, Abingdon: Routledge.

Rodrigues, C., Skinner, H., Dennis, C., and T. C. Melewar (2019), 'Towards a theoretical framework on sensorial place brand identity', *Journal of Place Management and Development*, **13** (3), 273–95.

Rouby, C., Fournel, A., and M. Bensafi (2016), 'The role of senses in emotion', in H. L. Meiselman (ed.), *Emotion Measurement*, Cambridge: Woodhead Publishing, pp. 65–81.

Santner, E. (2001), *On the Psychotheology of Everyday Life*, Chicago, IL: University of Chicago Press.

Schafer, R. (1977), *The Soundscape: Our Sonic Environment and the Tuning of the World*, Rochester, VT: Destiny Books.

Shove, E., Pantzar, M., and M. Watson (2012), *The Dynamics of Social Practice: Everyday Life and How It Changes*, London: Sage.

Thorpe, H. and R. Rinehart (2010), 'Alternative sport and affect: Non-representational theory examined', *Sport in Society*, **13** (7–8), 1268–91.

Thrift, N. (2008), *Non-Representational Theory: Space, Politics, Affect*, Abingdon: Routledge.

Tuan, Y.-F. (1977), *Space and Place: The Perspective of Experience*, Minneapolis, MN: University of Minnesota Press.

Vannini, P. (2015), 'Non-representational research methodologies: An introduction', in P. Vannini (ed.), *Non-Representational Methodologies: Re-envisioning Research*, New York: Routledge, pp. 1–18.

Ward, S. (1998), *Selling Places: The Marketing and Promotion of Towns and Cities 1850–2000*, London: E. & F. N. Spon.

Warde, A. (2005), 'Consumption and theories of practice', *Journal of Consumer Culture*, **5** (2), 131–53.

Wiedmann, K.-P., Labenz, F., Haase, J., and N. Hennigs (2017), 'The power of experiential marketing: Exploring the causal relationships among multisensory marketing, brand experience, customer perceived value and brand strength', *Journal of Brand Management*, **25** (2), 101–18.

PART IV

Creativity

17 Illuminating identity: The capacity of light festivals to enhance place?

Tim Edensor

Introduction

In an article by Elaine Yau in the *South China Morning Post* dated 23 July 2019, the author takes issue with how 'Chinese cities have been gripped by a craze for staging large-scale light extravaganzas', detailing the large economic revenues that accrue from these increasingly popular events. She draws attention to the excessive light deployed to illuminate landmarks and renowned buildings, typically identified in Hong Kong's famous nightly Symphony of Lights (identified as the largest permanent light and sound show in the world by Guinness World Records), which plays across the city's harbour, producing an ever changing panoply of light and colour across the imposing corporate skyscrapers that line the harbourside. Such events are often staged to mark national celebrations and, Yau alleges, are increasingly homogeneous, lacking innovative design and replicating those of elsewhere. Citing the critical views of light designer Qi Honghai, Yau also emphasises the baleful effects of illuminating the entire side of Hangzhou's Baoshi Mountain in 2000, a vast lighting design that drove birds away and killed millions of insects, a practice repeated at other scenic sites with equally malign ecological effects. The night sky is obliterated and the vast spectacles of light dominate the landscapes, while electric capacity is squandered. Yau's article does not call for a blanket ban on light festivals but insists that the illumination they deploy should become more inventive, subtler and place specific, less ecologically harmful, less wasteful and more modest in scale and style. Others, such as Chepesiuk (2009), point to the harmful effects of excessive light on human health. Her essay crystallises the key criticisms that increasingly accompany the proliferation of light festivals.

There is no doubt some salience to these critiques. The proliferation of large-scale light festivals is undoubtedly inspired by neoliberal policies whereby festivalisation is commonly deployed by local authorities to promote culture-led regeneration programmes often devised to replace local manufacturing industries that have declined. Events that range from art, music, sports and commemorative festivals to light festivals – along with increasing dining, shopping, gallery and entertainment space, as well as high-end shopping, upmarket accommodation and tourist provision – are designed to market cities and attract investment, visitors, shoppers and middle-class residents (Picard and Robinson, 2006). They seek to brand cities as lively, creative and eventful. These branding strategies chime with the rise of numerous culture-oriented festivals over the past four decades, signifying an extensive growth of 'eventification', and producing an abundance of occasions that, according to Doreen Jakob, provide an intensified 'emotional and aesthetic experience' (2012: 448) for residents and visitors alike.

Critics have directed their ire at such events, construed as exemplifying cynically instrumental, neoliberal strategies that seek to conceal ongoing disinvestment and increasing social inequality, neglecting the needs of poorer citizens while gentrifying space for privileged, middle-class residents (Fox Gotham, 2011). More critically, as far as festivals are concerned, others point to the ways in which in seeking to appeal to middle-class participants and satisfy key economic stakeholders, such eventification results in pallid occasions at which artists and designers are forced to compromise, producing bland installations, displays and performances that avoid any contentious political issues. As such, and resonating with Lau's critique, in the case of light festivals a serial homogeneity is the result. As Giordano and Ong (2017: 701–702) point out, 'international networks of experts and lighting professionals' organise the production of large light festivals. Generic festive light designs circulate between large-scale festivals and are curated and planned by these members of the international 'creative class', whose predilections are far removed from the tastes of the audiences to which they seek to cater. These light designs accord with what Guy Julier (2005: 874) refers to as a collection of 'brand design, architecture, urban planning, events and exhibitions' that articulate shared tastes and produce an 'aesthetic consent'. Accordingly, as with other large events successively staged across cities, placelessness ensues as 'cultural strategies fail to connect with the specificities of the places within which they are located' (Quinn, 2010: 271–2) and branding strategies that champion place uniqueness are instead advertising serial, homogeneous, placeless events.

For some, these large displays at light festivals at which projections and installations enthral onlookers are synonymous with Guy Debord's (1994) notion that we live in a 'society of the spectacle' in which spectators passively behold seductive shows organised by capital and the state that replace 'authentic' life. Such spectacles bedazzle individuals and limit their ability to perceive the 'real' conditions that underlie their enslavement as workers and consumers, diminishing capacities for critical thought and collective political action. With regard to light festivals, Heather Diack (2012: 11) contends that the popular *Nuit Blanche* or 'White Night' events are dominated by 'an extravaganza of electronic and digital media' that lures spectators 'towards machine-like states of attention, objectification, and endurance', feeding what she calls the 'attention economy', where creative leisure is supplanted by absorption in spectacle. Such critiques have also been levelled at Melbourne's (Australia) now discontinued White Night event, a single night in which a panoply of light displays, sculptures, illuminated mechanical forms and projections are supplemented by performances and music to cater for the estimated 300,000 people that throng the city's central streets.

For instance, Mercer and Mayfield (2015: 528) maintain that the festival is a 'top-down' event that 'promotes passive engagement with spectacle' rather than encouraging widespread, active participation in the arts and constitutes the 'wholesale commodification of Melbourne's creative and cultural practices'. They further contend that creative expression is constrained by commercial and promotional interests, and that there is a selective focus on iconic sites and buildings. Melbourne's White Night is similarly critiqued in an edited collection (Butt, 2015), where chapters draw attention to the exclusionary strategies of crowd control that channel the movements and discipline the bodies of spectators, and express an overriding concern with the tendency of spectators to consume the illuminated spectacles they behold via mobile devices, which they hold aloft to record the proceedings. These accounts conceive White Night, and presumably similar light festivals and showpiece events, as instrumental and construe onlookers as dupes, unable to gain any real pleasure, adopt critical positions or, possess any agency in the face of such visual extravaganzas.

While there is some salience in depictions of the ways in which such displays rely on modes of spectatorship and do not actively solicit interactivity, such claims conspicuously overlook scholarship in communication and media studies that conceives audiences as active (Livingstone, 2013). Indeed, it seems misplaced to assume that the still and captivated gaze of spectators provides evidence of passivity and refutes any idea that they may be thoughtfully considering the artistic installations that they behold. These assumptions about spectator passivity are as misplaced in accounts of large festivals such as White Night as they are for smaller festivals. For the vast crowds that move across the city are far from sedate, excitedly chatting in family or friendship groups, larking about and, crucially, many adorning themselves with car-nivalesque strings of lights, flashing headgear or, as in Figure 17.3, comical illuminated glasses. Crucially, spectators do not uncritically consume branding and promotional literature or staged events but interpret them in their own ways. Moreover, as Giordano and Ong (2017: 701–2) contend, 'simple serial reproduction' rarely occurs, with installations 'selectively acknowledged and appropriated by local actors'. However much the same installations may be circulated amongst cities that stage festivals, they are always contextualised by the distinctive material and social setting in which they are installed.

Having discussed negative assertions that light festivals are producing homo-geneity, passivity and placelessness, for the remainder of this chapter I contend that such assertions are overly pessimistic, misplaced and abstracted from place branding, the qualities of the light designs and artworks that are staged, the practices of attendees and the particular places in which they are held. As such, primarily attending to smaller community-oriented festivals but also large-scale events, I focus on four key attributes of light festivals: the potential for festive installations to enhance a sense of place, their paradoxical capacity to defamiliarise place, their contribution to the production of potent atmos-pheres and the ways in which they bring together different communities of expertise and thereby generate innovation and experimentation.

Placemaking

Above all, I suggest that light festivals of all scales, even those larger events that seem somewhat homogeneous, offer occasions where a sense of place may be deepened. Light installations, projections and parades that expand place enhancement take several forms.

First, light is especially able to highlight the architectural attributes of a build-ing, drawing attention to features that fade from prominence in the ambient wash of daylight which subsumes all in its glare. Carefully directed light can thus pick out specific elements of sills, pilasters, domes, architraves, finials and capitals. For instance, Melbourne's White Night formerly drew huge crowds to view the vast projection mapped onto the extensive 150 metre southern wing of the venerable Royal Exhibition Building in Carlton Gardens. Though the content of the projection changed annually, each work was aligned with the features of the building, amplifying awareness of its huge central arch and towers either side, Florentine dome, fanlight, numerous columns and symmetrical decorative stucco. Spectators were thus reminded of the architectural qualities of the building even as they gazed upon the fantastic forms that reconfigured everyday experience of the iconic structure. Buildings can also be illuminated to bring out a deep tactile sense of the materialities out of which they are composed. For example, the much smaller installation, Harmonic Portal by Chris Plant, placed on an ancient wall situated along a marginal street in an unprepossessing part of Durham, United Kingdom during that city's 2017 Lumiere festival, used saturated, ever changing colours inside and outside a circular frame to utterly transform the appearance of the stonework (Figure 17.1). A visual awareness of the rough lithic textures of the aged surface, irregular stone blocks and crumbling mortar was heightened, experienced with an attentional intensity that could not have been mobilised under other circumstances.

Source: Author's own image.

Figure 17.1   Enhancing the sensory experience of place

Second, certain light designs can draw out the overlooked or forgotten histories of place. Exemplary here are Australian light design collective, Illuminart, who deploy large-scale projection mapping to create what they term 'architectural storytelling'. For example, during the Port Festival of 2009 in Port Adelaide, South Australia, they created an animated audiovisual narrative that was mapped onto the architectural features of the façade of Hart's Mill (Illuminart, 2020). The narrative reimagined the building as a long-standing resident, a character that related some of the key historical moments of the port's history that it had witnessed, details that were gathered through consultation with local groups and residents. Similarly, I have discussed how at the enormous festival, Fête des Lumières 2009 in Lyons, the facade of the city's medieval Cathédrale St-Jean-Baptiste was the venue for a 10 minute projection, Les Bâtisseurs (The Builders), that through animated storytelling and the highlighting of distinctive architectural elements related the historical emergence of the building upon which the display was mapped (Edensor, 2017).

Third, besides disclosing historical tales that engender a sense of the temporal depth of place, light festivals can also draw attention to unheralded and neglected sites and structures. At Durham's 2013 Lumiere festival, illumination was deployed to reassess the reviled 1960s brutalist building Milburngate House, transforming its rectilinear form into a giant visual jukebox with coloured lights and music that pulsed through the night. In a different vein, the much ignored Creek in Bendigo, Victoria, Australia, was the site for a communal walk that was filmed and subsequently manipulated to form the subject matter for a projection on the town's library during the town's 2018 Enlighten Festival. Created in the nineteenth century to allow the sludge from surrounding goldfields to flow away from the town, the Creek, a wide, stone-lined channel that cuts through the centre of the town and affords fascinating views, a wildlife corridor and a route for walking and cycling, has nonetheless been shunned by the townsfolk. The projection of a throng of walkers sought to revalue the Creek as a recreational and historical element of Bendigo, to overcome its reputation as an abject, dangerous drain (Edensor and Andrews, 2019).

Fourth, this projection at Bendigo underlines how light festivals, especially small events, can offer opportunities for inhabitants to reclaim place and mark their presence on their environs, often through participating in lantern parades. These reterritorialising practices are exemplified by the participation of the inhabitants of west Yorkshire mill town, Slaithwaite, in their biannual Moonraking festival (Edensor, 2018). In a 400 strong, mile-long circumnavigation of their streets while carrying self-made lanterns, participants re-energise the usually quiet, dark streets of the small town. A similar effect is produced during the annual Lighting the Legend parade in the Ordsall area of Salford, Greater Manchester (Skelly and Edensor, 2020). This is particularly salient in the context of the extensive regeneration that has taken place in the area over the past 40 years, which is conceived by inhabitants as a threat to their continued residence, as well as reconfiguring Ordsall's place image for newer middle-class residents. The lantern parade allows them to reclaim possession of the surrounding streets, performing an expression of community pride as they hold their lanterns aloft accompanied by music from bands who join the procession and are part of this reterritorialisation. Ros Derrett (2003) contends that such community-based festivals can evolve over time to reflect shared values and foster a sense of community and place amongst local residents. Moreover, in staging a parade, as Katrina Brown (2012: 803) contends, 'the struggle for public space does not just take place through the pages of legislation or Codes but in the spaces of bodily encounter'. Such parades offer opportunities for groups to 'manifest their visions of the world and create meaningful frameworks of their being together', transmitting identities, cultural practices and values to locals and outsiders (Picard and Robinson, 2006: 12). Such visions typically veer away from those generated through place branding and reveal that deeper, more engaged, diverse and inclusive ways of expanding place image and a sense of belonging can be mobilised through the creative use of light.

Defamiliarisation

As well as affording the potential to undergird awareness of the material, historical and overlooked attributes of place, illumination – and darkness – also offers opportunities for experiencing place otherwise. Here, illumination can make the familiar look odd or uncanny. Indeed, since its emergence in the latter years of the nineteenth century, electric illumination has produced phantasmagorical scenes (McQuire, 2008) and extravagant nocturnal pleasure sites across urban landscapes. Gary Cross (2006: 635) describes how at New York's Coney Island, 'Luna Park and Dreamland created a dazzling architectural fantasy of towers, domes and minarets, outlined by electric lights, giving these strange oriental shapes an even more mysterious and magical air at night'. Illusory, distorting and subverting effects are commonly utilised at light festivals, often rendering familiar spaces and objects deeply peculiar. Bell, Blythe and Sengers (2005) draw out the political implications of revealing how everyday understandings about the nature of place are invariably culturally and historically specific, borne out of unreflexive habits of perception. Through defamiliarisation, they argue, we may consider the familiar world from a suddenly distant, critical perspective, undermining tenacious common-sense understandings. In considering how projection art can reveal unexpected, indeed unimagined flights of fancy in apparently mundane realms, Stephen Vilaseca (2014: 217) contends that far from encouraging passive spectatorship, this art practice can transform the meaning and affective impact of architecture into 'poetic space' that 'breaks with the imposed order of the original design to become something completely different'.

Anywhere that is re-enchanted by illumination can purvey such impressions of weirdness and disorientation, but certain installations and projections are particularly efficacious in rendering the familiar strange. I have written elsewhere about the extraordinary application of light to a Scottish wood-land during the annual Enchanted Forest event near Perth, where trees are bestowed with unusual colours while their forms are more lucidly exposed to the gaze of onlookers. I have also focused on Benedetto Bufalino and Benoit Deseille's Aquarium, a work installed at Durham's 2013 Lumiere festival in which a traditional red telephone box was transformed into a glowing, brilliant blue scene of live fishes and green plants that contrasted with the grey stony surroundings of an urban square that appeared especially gloomy in a cold November (Edensor, 2017).

At Melbourne's modestly staged Gertrude Street Projection festival, numer-ous fantastic scenes unfold on local walls, shop windows and facades, their commonplace exteriors bathed in animated dramas and dances, fluid shapes, science fiction dystopias, uncanny creatures and humans, images of other places, meditative and swirling colours, luminous geometric designs and ghostly architectural features. Weird monsters prowled across a portal in a shop window, a woman floated in calm blue water above a shop front and the textures of Berlin, New York and Amsterdam are transposed onto a Melbourne building (Edensor and Sumartojo, 2018). Durham's 2017 Lumiere festival fea-tured a particularly arresting vision of another time and place – Amsterdam – that hovered high above a view of the city. Drawn in Light by Ralf Westerhof was an installation made of thin steel wire shaped into a canalside building, a tree, two lampposts and car and cyclist (Figure 17.2). The piece magically rotated, shifting the configuration of its illuminated elements, illuminated against the dark sky and the urban scene below. These light works must be seen *in situ*, and cannot be managed through place branding exercises, which tend to fix rather than open up place identity. Their potency lies in their capacity to surprise, to generate unanticipated meanings and feelings, and so simultane-ously defamiliarise and thereby deepen a sense of place.

Source: Author's own image.

Figure 17.2   Defamiliarising place

Atmosphere

In recent years, with the turn towards the non-representational and affective in the social sciences and humanities, scholars have acknowledged the social forces of those numerous dimensions of experience that are neither symbolic nor cognitive, that shape the mood, feel and comfort of place. An important contribution here has been the surge in considerations about atmospheres that weave together the representational, the immaterial and the affective, as they signal shifts in feeling in particular settings. Atmospheres are typically characterised by their multiplicity, constituted by the diverse 'qualities, rhythms, forces, relations, and movements' (Stewart, 2011: 445) that coalesce in changing configurations. Bille and Sørensen (2016: 159) explore how 'less tangible phenomena such as light, sound and air, are part of the sensuous experience of buildings, and how manipulations of architectural form through the use of lighting technologies, heating and so forth influence the experience of built space'. Atmospheres are notably conjured by the distinctive, various qualities of illumination – 'texture, accent, spatial transition, visual cues, security and perception of security, moods, cerebral temperature and drama' (Cochrane, 2004: 12–13) that radiate diverse qualities of sparkle, glow, glare, highlighting and diffusion. Such immersive sensations and emotions can shape feelings about particular spatial and social settings and prompt us into action.

At light festivals of all kinds, the general 'buzz' of a special occasion is augmented by the qualities of light amidst the nocturnal darkness. As I have suggested in the case of the annual two month, five mile extravaganza that constitutes Blackpool Illuminations (Edensor, 2012), anticipation before arrival stokes the disposition of people upon arrival at the resort. They thereby contribute to a potent, festive atmosphere that ripples across space, their excitement melding with the animated lights, dark sea, smells of food and drink and noisy traffic. Though atmospheres cannot be designed to predetermine experience, light designs can intervene to enhance the emergence of particular atmospheres (Sumartojo and Pink, 2018). Thus, at large light festivals such as Melbourne's White Night, showpiece installations and projections can promote large gatherings and solicit a sense of communion with fellow spectators. These brief interludes in the nocturnal life of the city can be absorbing and inventive, and though there may be some projection fatigue with the typical format that many pieces adopt, such gatherings can be compared to crowds at firework displays from which sighs, applause and astonished ejaculations are emitted. This underpins that members of these assemblies are not passive spectators stunned by spectacle. This is also emphasised by the tendencies of groups and individuals to wear strings of light, illuminated headgear or absurd accoutrements, as Figure 17.3 demonstrates.

A sense of place can also be fomented at smaller festivals as intensified sensations and heightened affective experiences are stimulated and emotions expressed around festive installations. At Melbourne's 2018 Gertrude Street Projection Festival, such atmospheres swirled, collected and dispersed, continuously emerging out of an amalgam of forces that drew different spaces, objects and technologies within their orbit, while animated participants responded to their lure (Edensor and Sumartojo, 2018). Pools of atmosphere gathered and dispersed as large and small aggregations of neighbours, friends and families temporarily collected around displays. Somewhat differently, the lantern parades that constitute Ordsall's Lighting the Legend (Skelly and Edensor, 2020) and Slaithwaite's Moonraking (Edensor, 2018) festivals are characterised by the moving atmosphere conjured by lantern-carrying throngs winding their way through local streets, who along with the music produced by accompanying bands transform the atmosphere of their locales. Not only is the atmosphere produced by those in the processions but also by other residents

who emerge from their homes to shout encouragement and greet the participants, creating transient hubs of conviviality.

Source: Author's own image.

Figure 17.3   Audience participation in producing festive atmospheres

One element of light festival design that is integral to the production of lively
atmospheres is the creation of interactive attractions that lure participants to
play. This is exemplified by an installation Colour by Light, produced by light
design outfit Floating Pictures, that was staged at Durham's 2017 Lumiere
festival in a central city street. Here, festivalgoers could transform the street
upon which they walked through means of a USB camera, projector and computer that transformed light sources such as torches and mobile phones into
paintbrushes, affording a dynamic daubing of different colours, strokes and
patterns on the asphalt, the walls or bodies (Figure 17.4). As Quentin Stevens
asserts, festivals open up the city to ludic experiences in multiple ways and
provide a 'myriad of settings and props which can catalyse imaginative play'
(2007: 40). Light festivals in particular offer opportunities to engage in playful
activities that prioritise a non-instrumental and liberating being-in place that

contrasts with the often rationalised, regulated practices prioritised during the day (Woodyer, 2012). Once more, atmospheres can be alluded to in place branding, but given the contextual, unpredictable, mutable qualities of atmospheres, they can never be captured by such exercises.

Source: Author's own image.

Figure 17.4   Soliciting playful atmospheres

Collections of expertise

Finally, light festivals, like other festivals, draw together light designers, artists, event managers, local authority personnel, engineers and technicians in order to stage and manage the event. Accordingly, these temporary constellations of diverse experts work together and share ideas. In constituting occasions for the exchanging of ideas, artistic visions, techniques and know-how (Picard and Robinson, 2006), festivals can develop ways of staging, managing and designing with light, processes that can also be transmitted within the settings in which they occur. Shared improvisation and experimentation can foster networks of association that 'offer different social groups open access and a variety of opportunities to share experiences and encounter the new' (Schulte-Römer, 2013: 152). Working in a temporary community of practitioners inculcates novices into shared 'values, ethos and social persona, and the learning of related professional competencies' (Marchand, 2012: 261) through specialised training and work with fellow artisans.

This gathering of expertise in a local setting is exemplified by ways in which lantern-making skills have been developed over the more than 30 years of staging Slaithwaite's biannual Moonraking festival. The early involvement of artists in the festival in creating their own light designs to supplement the numerous community-made lanterns, and their participation in lantern-making workshops, has helped to develop skilled expertise amongst some of the town's residents over time. Indeed, participating in these making workshops over several years has engendered the acquisition of skills that have encouraged a handful of Slaithwaite's residents to become professional lantern makers, sharing their expertise and contributing works to light festivals elsewhere.

These ongoing creative processes have ensured that new light designs and installations continue to emerge, and in recent years, imperatives about sustainability have inspired the evolution of new expressions in light. Besides rebuking Lau's assumptions that homogeneity is becoming more widespread, these developments also respond to her concerns about the ecological imprint of festive illumination. Exemplary here is Madrid's anonymous art collective, Luzinterruptus, who create ephemeral outdoor light installations fabricated out of waste items such as empty water bottles, plastic containers and carrier bags. For a street art festival in Katowice, Poland, in 2014, they manufactured a huge labyrinth of 6000 discarded water bottles that were contained in transparent rubbish bags, hung on a metal framework and illuminated with neon blue LED lights. Such ecological intentions are also becoming more pervasive as characterised by the *i Light Singapore* annual festival, which seeks to provoke awareness about climate change and environmental sustainability. For this festival, light artists are selected for their use of energy-efficient LED lights and the incorporation of sustainable, recyclable materials into their designs. Some also reduce energy use by utilising solar, kinetic or wind energy to light their installations. I submit that these dynamic processes can be encouraged by local authorities and can form an ingredient in place branding strategies that can accurately represent place as inclusive and amenable to forms of creative collaboration and experimentation, rather than merely reiterating 'traditional' craft products and creative practices.

Conclusion

In this chapter, I have countered contentions that light festivals are increasingly producing homogeneous, placeless, empty spectacles that are unable to contribute to deepening a sense of place. I argue that such notions chime with broader academic critiques of festivals and eventification. While acknowledging that there is some salience in such objections, I consider that an alternative perspective reveals that light festivals can potentially contribute to what Fisher and Drobnick (2012: 36) term 'the nocturnal carnivalesque', or engender what Jane Bennett (2001: 5) calls 're-enchantment', through which we may become 'transfixed, spellbound' by being charmed and delighted and by experiencing the familiar space in new ways. In deepening the experience of place and defamiliarising familiar environments, festive light installations can destabilise the 'self-evident facts of perception based on the set of horizons and modalities of what is visible and audible as well as what can be said, thought, made, or done' (Rancière, 2004: 85). Light festivals can thus sidestep serial neoliberal cultural strategies that generate a bland, unstimulating sameness, and literally encourage us to see our communities in a different light and invigorate place after darkness falls.

Instead of reiterating tired tropes that refer blandly to an unspecific 'vibrancy' and staging serial forms of light display and other events, I suggest that place branding focuses more extensively on the multiplicities of place, on its less heralded and overlooked aspects, its capacity to contain surprises, unpredictable events and unimaginable sights, its potential to inclusively welcome creative experimentation and collaboration, and to manage settings in which potent atmospheres might emerge. As I have underlined, the creative use of festive illumination is a powerful tool in generating such exciting place potentialities.

References

Bell, G., Blythe, M. and P. Sengers (2005), 'Making by making strange: Defamiliarization and the design of domestic technologies', *ACM Transactions on Computer–Human Interaction*, **12** (2), 149–73.

Bennett, J. (2001), *The Enchantment of Modern Life: Attachments, Crossings and Ethics*, Princeton, NJ: Princeton University Press.

Bille, M. and T. Sørensen (2016), 'A sense of place', in M. Bille and T. Sørensen (eds), *Elements of Architecture: Assembling Archaeology, Atmosphere and the Performance of Building Spaces*, London: Routledge, pp. 159–62.

Brown, K. (2012), 'Sharing public space across difference: Attunement and the contested burdens of choreographing encounter', *Social and Cultural Geography*, **13** (7), 801–20.

Butt, D. (ed.) (2015), *White Night: City as Event: Researching Melbourne's Festival of Illumination*, Melbourne: University of Melbourne.

Chepesiuk, R. (2009), 'Missing the dark: Health effects of light pollution', *Environmental Health Perspectives*, **117** (1), 20–7.

Cochrane, A. (2004), 'Cities of light: Placemaking in the 24-hour city', *Urban Design Quarterly*, **89**, 12–14.

Cross, G. (2006), 'Crowds and leisure: Thinking comparatively across the 20th century', *Journal of Social History*, **39** (3), 631–50.

Debord, G. (1994), *The Society of the Spectacle*, New York: Zone Books.

Derrett, R. (2003), 'Making sense of how festivals demonstrate a community's sense of place', *Event Management*, **8** (1), 49–58.

Diack, H. (2012), 'Sleepless nights: Contemporary art and the culture of performance', *Public*, **23** (45), 9–22.

Edensor, T. (2012), 'Illuminated atmospheres: Anticipating and reproducing the flow of affective experience in Blackpool', *Environment and Planning D: Society and Space*, **30** (6), 1103–22.

Edensor, T. (2017), *From Light to Dark: Daylight, Illumination and Gloom*, Minneapolis, MN: Minnesota University Press.

Edensor, T. (2018), 'Moonraking: Making things, place and event', in L. Price and H. Hawkins (eds), *Geographies of Making, Craft and Creativity*, London: Routledge, pp. 60–75.

Edensor, T. and J. Andrews (2019), 'Walking the Creek: Reconnecting place through light projection', *Geographical Research*, **57** (3), 263–74.

Edensor, T. and S. Sumartojo (2018), 'Reconfiguring familiar worlds with light projection: The Gertrude Street Projection Festival, 2017', *GeoHumanities*, **4** (1), 112–31.

Fisher, J. and J. Drobnick (2012), 'Nightsense', *Public*, **23** (45), 35–63.

Fox Gotham, K. (2011), 'Resisting urban spectacle: The 1984 Louisiana World Exposition and the contradictions of mega events', *Urban Studies*, **48** (1), 197–214.

Giordano, E. and C.-E. Ong (2017), 'Light festivals, policy mobilities and urban tourism', *Tourism Geographies*, **19** (5), 699–716.

Illuminart (2020), *Hart's Mill Inhabited*, accessed 10 March 2020 at: https://illuminart .com.au/project/harts-mill-inhabited.

Jakob, I. (2012), 'The eventification of place: Urban development and experience consumption in Berlin and New York City', *European Urban and Regional Studies*, **20** (4), 447–59.

Julier, G. (2005), 'Urban designscapes and the production of aesthetic consent', *Urban Studies*, **42** (5/6), 869–87.

Livingstone, S. (2013), 'The participation paradigm in audience research', *Communication Review*, **16** (1–2), 21–30.

Marchand, T. (2012), 'Knowledge in hand: Explorations of brain, hand and tool', in R. Fardon, O. Harris, T. Marchand, C. Shore, V, Strang, R. Wilson and C. Nuttall (eds), *Handbook of Social Anthropology*, London: Sage, pp. 260–9.

McQuire, S. (2008), *The Media City: Media, Architecture and Urban Spaces*, London: Sage.

Mercer, D. and P. Mayfield (2015), 'City of the spectacle: White Night Melbourne and the politics of public space', *Australian Geographer*, **46** (4), 507–34.

Picard, D. and M. Robinson (2006), 'Remaking worlds: Festivals, tourism and change', in D. Picard and M. Robinson (eds), *Festivals, Tourism and Social Change: Remaking Worlds*, Clevedon: Channel View, pp. 1–31.

Quinn, B. (2010), 'Arts festivals and urban tourism and cultural policy', *Journal of Policy Research in Tourism, Leisure and Events*, **2** (3), 264–79.

Rancière, J. (2004), *The Politics of Aesthetics*, London: Continuum.

Schulte-Römer, N. (2013), 'Fair framings: Arts and culture festivals as sites for technical innovation', *Mind and Society*, **12** (1), 151–65.

Skelly, G. and T. Edensor (2020), 'Routing out place identity through the vernacular production practices of a community light festival', in C. Courage (ed.), *The Routledge Handbook of Placemaking*, London: Routledge, pp. 258–68.

Stevens, Q. (2007), *The Ludic City: Exploring the Potential of Public Spaces*, London: Routledge.

Stewart, K. (2011), 'Atmospheric attunements', *Environment and Planning D: Society and Space*, **29** (3), 445–53.

Sumartojo, S. and S. Pink (2018), *Atmospheres and the Experiential World: Theory and Methods*, London: Routledge.

Vilaseca, S. (2014), 'The projection on the wall: What audio-visual architectural mapping says about Catalan identity', *Journal of Urban Cultural Studies*, **1** (2), 215–34.

Woodyer, T. (2012), 'Ludic geographies: Not merely child's play', *Geography Compass*, **6** (6), 313–26.

Yau, E. (2019), 'Unsustainable living: How crazy light shows are damaging China in the name of tourism', *South China Morning Post*, 23 July, accessed 1 March 2020 at: www.scmp.com/lifestyle/travel-leisure/article/3019699/unsustainable-living-how-crazy-light-shows-are-damaging.

18 'The artist in you': Thinking differently about place branding research

Mihalis Kavaratzis and Gary Warnaby

Read this before reading the chapter…

> So what do you do?
> Place branding academic
> Is what I do.
> So tourism is what you do?
> No it's bigger than that.
> So International tourism
> is what you do?
> Evaluate the risk
> of punching you
> in the nose
> is what I do. (Ian Loughran, 'Place brander what do you do?', 2017)

The title of this poem, 'Place brander what do you do?', is perhaps a question that is asked of many who are responsible for the marketing and branding of places. The poem itself indicates some of the misconceptions that arise about place branding (Is it just about tourism?). Such misconceptions frequently exist in relation to place marketing/branding *research*: 'What do you actually *do*?' is a question often asked by our bemused families, and occasionally our – equally bemused – students (particularly when we're not teaching them).

In response, when trying to explain how the concepts of 'place' and 'brand' might possibly link together, we can sometimes get ourselves tied up in inter-disciplinary and conceptual knots about how such a complex phenomenon as place can be boiled down to a logo or slogan, without becoming trite or overly simplistic. So how do we explain – and communicate – what we do as place branding academics? The fruits of our labours can be read in (hopefully top quartile!) academic journals, or enjoyed/endured (delete as applicable) in conference presentations. Of course, as academics, we live and die by the pen rather than by the sword (publish or perish!), but in this chapter we want to ask whether there may be other, alternative ways for us to convey our understanding of how 'place', 'marketing' and 'branding' may sit together. In seeking to do this from the perspective of the place marketing academy (rather than the place branding 'industry'), we begin by 'starting with place', to consider what we mean by the 'place' in place branding research, highlighting the importance of more phenomenologically oriented aspects, such as place attachment. We then 'turn to the arts', to discuss how we represent places in our academic inquiry into place brands (given its inherent interdisciplinarity). We conclude by considering the potential for more creative, 'alternative' means for such expression through our attempts at creating work exhibited at the International Place Branding Association (IPBA) Art Gallery, held at the IPBA Conferences in 2017 and 2019 (from which the poem that prefaces this chapter is drawn).

Starting with place

When Gary teaches place marketing and branding, he begins by getting students to unpick their understanding of what 'place' actually is. In doing this, Agnew's (1987) discussion of the tripartite nature of places – incorporating *location, locale* and *sense of place* – is a useful theoretical starting point. To illustrate, we will take the example of St Ann's Square in Manchester.

Agnew defines *location* in terms of the point on the Earth's surface where the place exists (and indeed, locational advantage in relation to other, 'competing' places is a common trope of place marketing messages). So, if we find ourselves at Latitude 53.4817° N and Longitude 2.2458 W, we are outside St Ann's Church on the southern edge of St Ann's Square, which is a somewhat nondescript urban space. However, the space is occasionally animated by periodic specialist markets – notably the Manchester Christmas Market in November–December each year (see Warnaby, 2013) – or occasionally, music performances (e.g. open air concerts as part of the Manchester Jazz festival; see Oakes and Warnaby, 2011), with these events illustrating Agnew's second aspect of *locale*. Here, Agnew refers to the settings in which formal and institutional social relations are constituted. However, in late May 2017, St Ann's Square was covered in floral and other tributes to the victims of the Manchester Arena bombing, becoming an epicentre of remembrance. This demonstrates Agnew's notion of *sense of place*, which 'reinforces the social-spatial definition of place from the *inside*' (1987: 27, original emphasis), potentially creating an identification with – and feelings of attachment to – place. This complexity is suggested in Cresswell and Hoskins' (2008: 394) discussion of place and memory, where they suggest place, 'simultaneously evokes a certain material-ity (it has a tangible material form to it) and a less concrete realm of meaning', which come together in a particular location. Highlighting the importance of the *experience* of place, they also emphasise that place 'involves different levels of practice and performance', noting that place is a 'lived' concept.

In the context of place marketing/branding, when representing places as 'products' many practitioners (and academics) focus on *materiality*, devel-oping assemblages of facilities, attributes and resources located therein as 'contributory elements' of a 'nuclear' product (Sleipen, 1988) where marketers can 'shuffle the pack' to create different combinations of elements designed to appeal to different target audiences. In turn, researchers often seek to outline these elements and ascertain their relative importance in an attempt to increase the efficacy of place marketing/branding activities.

But what about Cresswell and Hoskins' notion of 'realm of meaning'? This relates to the more phenomenological approach to place outlined by Cresswell (2004: 51) that 'seeks to define the essence of human existence as one that is necessarily and importantly "in-place"'. This resonates with the concept of place *attachment*, defined in terms of 'an affective bond or link between people and specific places' (Hidalgo and Hernandez, 2001: 274). How, as researchers, do we capture and investigate this more affective and emotional attachment to place, especially with a greater emphasis on experience and co-creation in both place management (see Warnaby, 2009a) and marketing (Warnaby, 2009b)? Indeed, as human actors, we researchers would be unusual if we did not often feel a sense of connection to particular places, resonant with Tuan's (1974) notion of topophilia. So instead of being dispassionate academic observers of place(s), on a quest to analyse the most effective means by which they can be marketed and branded, can we instead celebrate these phenomenological associations with place(s) rather than downplay them, or worse, ignore them completely?

Such questions are particularly apposite when we consider the inherently interdisciplinary nature of place marketing/branding research inquiry, which 10 years ago was still described as being somewhat 'confused' in relation to its identity (Skinner, 2008), and subject to various 'unresolved issues' (Kavaratzis, 2007). More recently, some have articulated the need for a 'rethinking' to occur (see Kavaratzis, Warnaby and Ashworth, 2015). In her proposed research agenda for place branding, Fona (2019) places great emphasis on the issue of contested places and identities. As globalisation proceeds with the growing mobility of people and goods, but failing to fulfil the promise of a borderless world, the consequences are alienation and loss of sense of place. Therefore,

'Future investigations should reflect on this complexity by focusing on the nature of contested place identities and the conflict generated by the creation of multiple senses of the same place' (Fona, 2019: 331).

Turning to the arts

The tools that we use to build knowledge determine to a great extent what type of knowledge we consider worth building and the way in which we undertake research. At the same time, the available mechanisms of presentation and dissemination determine what form of knowledge can be sought. Currently, the dominant mechanisms of academic research presentation are based on journal articles and books, which fundamentally affect the way in which knowledge is sought and designed, as well as the type of data that are deemed relevant and appropriate. However, all vehicles of research dissemination legitimise certain types of knowledge while excluding others (Bettany, 2007), imposing limits within which we collect and interpret data, and possibly closing down new avenues for exploration and knowledge generation. One of the pioneers of arts-based research, Elliot Eisner (1997) notes that the topics we choose to research are bound to the available knowledge-building tools, and that our capacity to undertake research – and even to be curious – is linked to the methodologies and forms of representation with which we are familiar. In order to expand the array of knowledge-building tools, to investigate aspects of social life that traditional methodologies cannot capture and to represent data and findings in novel ways, many researchers across the social sciences have developed and used arts-based and other alternative methods and research practices. They redefine the way in which knowledge can be sought, explicitly challenging 'logical positivism and technical rationality as the only acceptable guides to explain human behaviour and understanding' (Cole and Knowles, 2008: 59).

Arts-based research is a mode of qualitative research that incorporates the arts or, as Savin-Baden and Wimpenny (2014: 1) define it, 'research that uses the arts, in the broadest sense, to explore, understand and represent the human action and experience'. Arts-based qualitative research uses a range of methodological tools (including the traditional qualitative tools of interviews, ethnographies, projective techniques and so on, but also more innovative, artistic tools) that are informed by creative and artistic processes (either of the research participants, the researcher or both) during all stages of research (i.e. data collection, analysis, interpretation and presentation). As Leavy states: 'These emerging tools adapt the tenets of the creative arts in order to address social research questions in holistic and engaged ways in which theory and practice are intertwined' (2009: ix). In other words, arts-based practices infuse scholarly inquiries with the languages, processes and forms of literary, visual or performing arts, with the main aim to deepen our understanding of the human condition and to reach wider audiences for scholarly research (Cole and Knowles, 2008). Leavy (2009) suggests that using the arts in scientific, academic research offers *resonance* (building on emotional bonds that are vital for human beings), *disruption* (e.g. challenging stereotypes and dominant ideologies and raising consciousness) and *diversification* (bringing academic scholarship to wider audiences for pedagogical and transformative purposes).

The arts have not always been regarded as a form or source of knowledge because, 'traditionally, the arts have been considered ornamental and emotional in character' (Eisner, 2008: 3). However, there are numerous examples of arts-based research within all social sciences, predominantly within educational research and psychology (for a useful review, including the four 'turns' in arts-based inquiries, see Visse, Hansen and Leget, 2019). Arts-based research approaches have been used within two of place marketing's main 'mother' disciplines, namely marketing/consumer research (e.g. Sherry and Schouten, 2002; Canniford, 2012; Canniford, Riach and Hill, 2018; Rokka, Hietanen and Brownlie, 2018) and human geography (e.g. Latham, 2003; Cloke et al., 2004; Jones, 2014). Cloke et al. note that there is a:

> growing acceptance among geographers of the legitimacy of using sources of information which are overtly products of human imagination and whose primary original purpose is not to make factual statements about the world but, instead, to entertain, provoke, inspire or move the reader, listener, viewer; in short to engage the emotions and, indeed, the imagination. (2004: 93)

The same authors also discuss the imaginative sources of data that geographers use: literature, travel writing, music and the performing arts, painting and the visual arts, photography, cinema and television, architecture, objects and material culture and electronic media.

While the use of such data sources and arts-based processes seems very promising for place marketing research, the accompanying methodological novelty is important, not simply for the sake of 'new' or 'more' methods, but rather for 'opening up new ways to think about knowledge-building: new ways to see' (Leavy, 2009: 254). However, this comes with significant challenges. Lafreniere and Cox (2012) describe these as questions of: 1) what level of expertise on the particular art form one should possess in order to utilise the arts effectively (something we will return to below); 2) whether all methods of art creation are appropriate; and 3) what criteria can be used to assess arts-based contributions. The issue of assessment criteria is particularly contentious. Traditional criteria to assess scientific work are clearly not usable as arts-based practices cannot be judged on the usual terms of reliability and validity. At the same time, artistic criteria are also inappropriate, as arts-based research is not pure artistic creation, but serves research purposes. Brearley and Darso (2008: 647) remind us that 'challenging the shape and appearance of research simultaneously opens doors and creates barriers. The complexities involve knowing the rules *and* challenging assumptions, being creative *and* maintaining rigor, and honouring content *and* exploring form.'

Despite these challenges, we believe that arts-based approaches are amongst the very few methodological approaches well placed to investigate and capture the phenomenological complexities of place outlined earlier. This has to do with the ability of the arts to get at multiple meanings and 'represent the multiple viewpoints made imperceptible by traditional research methods' (Leavy, 2009: 15). Furthermore, the production of imaginative works has a geography to it, in the sense that it is not only a product of geographical context, helping to understand that context, but also itself produces and embodies imaginary geographies and illuminates issues of interest to geographers such as human feelings for place (Cloke et al., 2004). As Leavy (2009) states, arts-based research practices are exciting in part because they have not yet reached their full potential, and this, we argue, is certainly the case within place marketing research.

The artists in us...

In this section, we will use the experience of our own attempts at using the arts for place branding-related explorations to illustrate the benefits and challenges of such endeavours. The works we discuss below were created for the IPBA Art Gallery. Initiated by Mihalis (the help of Massimo Giovanardi in curating the first edition of the Gallery is gratefully acknowledged), the aim of the Gallery was to 'encourage unconventional thinking around the topic of place branding and to engage IPBA members in creative dialogues that advance our understanding of this fascinating field' (from the IPBA Art Gallery Call for Artworks). Two editions of the Gallery have been successfully organised (in Swansea, 2017 and Volos, 2019), and the third is being organised at the time of writing (Barcelona, 2020) as the Gallery is now a standard feature of the annual IPBA conference.

Mihalis' Experience

At the first edition of the IPBA Art Gallery, I exhibited two artworks: a poem called *City Echoes* (Kavaratzis, 2017) that I wrote on my own (after more than 30 years of writing poems in Greek, this was only the second time I attempted a poem in English), and a collage called *No Mud – No Lotus* that was co-created with Andrea Szentgyörgyi (2017). Let me reflect on these experiences.

It was with trepidation that I decided to present the poem in the IPBA Art Gallery (and with excruciating nervousness that I actually recited it in Swansea). The initial enthusiasm over expressing ideas poetically turned into wondering whether it is a 'good poem' or simply a childish attempt; this turned into an anxiety that aesthetically it did not even qualify as poetry, and then into the certainty that all I would gain from the whole endeavour would be embarrassment. Then, I decided that this was not the point. First, the IPBA Art Gallery had been my initiation, I had worked hard to get it organised, I believed in it and I felt the obligation to expose myself in that way. In other words, 'backing out' was not an option. Second – and more related to the value of arts-based research approaches within place branding – at the end of the day what I was interested in was not aesthetic or artistic perfection. In arts-based research, if we insist on assessing the work on aesthetic quality and artistic excellence, we lose sight of its main purpose, which is to move forward our understanding of a particular topic. Jones (2014) asserts that social scientists should not worry about aesthetic inadequacies as this will stop them from following a powerful innovative methodology. Leggo (2008: 169) describes this position eloquently:

> as a poet and language educator, I am often asked, '*Is this a good poem?*' as if I carry some kind of standard measuring device for assessing the value of poems. But perhaps the important question is not '*Is this a good poem?*' but instead '*What is this poem good for?*'.

This resonates with Gadamer's view of aesthetics and the qualities and functions of art (see Arthos, 2013; Davey, 2013; Visse et al., 2019). For Gadamer, art is relational and dialogical. He sees the arts as an experience and event (Visse et al., 2019), which attends to movements of an artwork (Arthos, 2013; Davey 2013). An artwork's aesthetic qualities and properties are not interesting for Gadamer; what is important is the way in which 'art is a partner in conversation. This is about being phenomenologically involved in an artwork, resonating with it, receiving it and being transformed by it' (Visse et al., 2019: 9). Gadamer sees the event of art as unfinished, forever-going (Davey, 2013). The realisation of the ongoing, dialogical nature of the poem gave me the excuse I needed to simply go ahead. Writing the poem gave me the chance to 'talk' about places in a way that academic writing would not let me: from the heart. *City Echoes* does not reflect on any data collected and does not present research findings. In a sense, it is a conceptual piece about the difficulties of capturing place identity into a place brand that we know is there, but we don't know how to create it. Free from academic conventions, I was able to talk about the elusiveness of the place brand and that was a great relief. In this way, it helped me express long-standing beliefs about place brands that I had not been able to put down on paper in a conventional academic form of representation.

Gadamer's dialogical approach to the arts was even more prevalent in the other artwork presented at the Gallery, the *No Mud – No Lotus* collage that was created with Andrea (Figure 18.1). This is a piece conceptualising the complexity of place using photographs of urban instances arranged to form a lotus, a symbol common in Eastern philosophies. Co-creating it, I was able to feel and express several emotions that otherwise would have been kept silent. Perhaps the most important outcome of the 'Lotus', though, relates to the relational aspect of art and its creation. One of the main benefits of using arts-based research practices is that they 'promote dialogue, which is critical to cultivating understanding' and 'address diversified audiences' for research (Leavy, 2009: 14). Co-creating the 'Lotus' gave me the chance to engage in a dialogue about place and the place brand with someone who could enlarge my understanding by infusing ideas from Eastern philosophies and also their own artistic criteria. That was certainly an enriching and valuable experience. In terms of a diversified audience, it might sound trivial, but my 12-year-old son understood much about my work through this piece – he has never read any of my articles.

What writing the poem and creating the 'Lotus' did was – to quote Gablik (1991: 11) – bring my 'head and heart together'. Due to an inner need, I try to do that in my academic writing. However, the truth is that it is not easy, or always possible, to write an academic article like that, and a lot can be said about attempting to publish it in the contemporary academic publishing industry.

Gary's Experience

I submitted photo-essays for each edition of the IPBA Art Gallery (Warnaby, 2017, 2019a). The first comprised a series of pictures of 'ghost signs' (see Schutt, White and Roberts, 2017, for a detailed discussion of this topic) that are visible in a walk around Manchester. The second highlighted some of Manchester's historic and contemporary architecture featured for place branding purposes in banners located around the city centre, and how this was juxtaposed with

Source: Andrea Szentgyörgyi and Mihalis Kavaratzis.

Figure 18.1   *No Mud – No Lotus*

the surrounding buildings (Figure 18.2). These attempts at artistic expression reflect a long-standing interest in photography and a desire to incorporate it more fully into my academic work (the vast majority of illustrations in my published outputs are my own images; indeed, many years ago I would develop my own black and white images, but in this digital age my darkroom days are long past!).

Source: Gary Warnaby.

Figure 18.2   Photos from *The Stones of Manchester*

Why use photography to highlight place branding? One answer could be that place marketing/branding practice is inherently visual, which is perhaps not surprising given Porteous' (1990: 4) description of sight as 'the common sense, the dominant sensory mode; in humans, it yields more than 80 per cent of our knowledge of the external world'. However, Porteous suggests that vision 'is a cool, detached sense' (1990: 7), which 'distances us from the landscape'. It is therefore 'easy to be disengaged' (Porteous, 1990: 5). Having previously written about such issues in relation to how places are represented in general terms (Warnaby, 2012), what I wanted to do in these photo-essays was engage with the *detail* of the urban landscape, if one knows where to look for it.

Photographer Robert Adams (1994: 31) states that, 'Art is by nature self-explanatory. We call it art precisely because of its sufficiency', and in relation to his chosen medium, 'For photographers, the ideal book of photographs would contain just pictures – no text at all' (1994: 33). Here, I ideally wanted the photos to speak for themselves, but felt that there needed to be some explanatory detail to contextualise the images. Indeed, returning to an earlier discussion on the dominant mechanisms of academic research presentation, this was important when subsequently preparing the 2017 photo-essay for publication in an academic journal (Warnaby, 2019b). It seemed essential that the photos be accompanied by some commentary and theoretical contextualisation in order to get it through the review process. I've yet to decide what (if anything) to do with the images from the 2019 photo-essay. The images have been sitting on my hard drive for over 10 years now, waiting for an opportunity to be used in my academic endeavours. I wonder how many other images that might be relevant for place research remain lurking in similar obscurity, without an outlet for their wider dissemination?

Setting free the artist in you

Arts-based works can help explore many themes that are pertinent in place branding. Some of the works exhibited in the two editions of the IPBA Art Gallery provoked a lively and interesting discussion around theories and practices related to place marketing and place branding. For instance, the work of Giorgos Sfouggaras (Figure 18.3) deals with issues of place identity and how the personal history of an individual is intertwined with elements of the identity of places that have been important in this individual's life.

The work of Szilvia Gyimóthy (Figure 18.4) demonstrates the emotional response of the art creator to the routes followed by cruise passengers once they disembark for their half-a-day walking tour around Copenhagen.

The issue of overtourism, as well as being an ever present meme for place branding practice, is explored in Magdalena Florek's painting (Figure 18.5) that caused somewhat of a sensation at the 2019 Gallery.

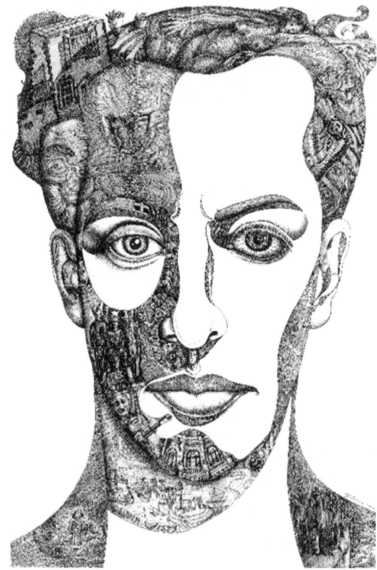

Source: Giorgos Sfouggaras.

Figure 18.3   *Personal Maps*

Routines of Langelinie

**One step at a time
we follow the traces
of the beaten mile.
Leaving our own piles
of sighs,
   sweat
      and smiles**

One step a time...

Source: Szilvia Gyimóthy.

Figure 18.4   *Routines of Langelinie* (detail)

In order to realise the potential offered by arts-based research practices for the advancement of place marketing and place branding, we suggest that certain conditions need to be met, which include:

1. A clear justification of the general approach to such modes of inquiry within the scholarly community. The IPBA Art Gallery might be a good start, and we hope that this chapter might stimulate more of this work and support the work of place branding scholars who are already undertaking such endeavours.
2. A research agenda of themes that will be interesting to study and clarify. These might possibly include the evaluation of studies where arts (and other alternative methods) have been used, the examination of whether and to what extent such work resonates with and stimulates further research and, importantly, whether and to what extent these methods are suitable for 'real-life', 'real-industry' projects with residents, visitors or policy makers.

Source: Magdalena Florek.

Figure 18.5   *Overcity*

3. Obviously, relevant methods need to be established and developed. These can be advancements of the imaginative sources of data and arts-based methods discussed in this chapter, such as photo-essays, videography, smellscape/soundscape methods or interactive narratives (where research participants choose between alternative plots, or where a conversation is developed through a reader's answers). The work we advocate here is not

limited to the arts but extends to other non-traditional expressions. In a field as 'spatial' as place marketing and branding, experiential methods such as walking tours might be a very reasonable way forward. With the popularity of gamification and the proliferation of mobile phone apps, this is another fascinating line of inquiry. In doing this, we should perhaps be open to collaborating with colleagues from other disciplines where arts/practice-based research inquiry is more commonplace and learn from them where appropriate.

In conclusion, this chapter is a call for alternative ways of thinking about, doing and presenting place marketing/branding research. We think it is time to embrace more innovative and pluralistic methods of research, and more artistic, creative expressions of research dissemination. Or, to look for knowledge made, as Cole and Knowles (2008: 59) put it, 'in the imaginative spaces created between the lines of a good book or an encounter with an evocative photograph, in an embodied response to a musical composition or interpretive dance'. We invite place branding researchers, scholars, artists, students, practitioners and anyone else interested to look for the knowledge that can be made using the arts – and to bring more arts-based and alternative research into the field of place branding and place marketing. In order not to finish the chapter but to start something new, we invite you to embrace what Norris (2000: 41) calls 'the magic of what if'...

Acknowledgment

We would like to thank the following artists (in alphabetical order): Magdalena Florek, Szilvia Gyimothy, Ian Loughran, George Sfouggaras, Andrea Szentgyörgyi, for kindly granting permission to reproduce their work in this chapter.

References

Adams, R. (1994), *Why People Photograph: Selected Essays and Reviews*, New York: Aperture.
Agnew, J. A. (1987), *Place and Politics: The Geographical Mediation of State and Society*, Boston, MA: Allen and Unwin.
Arthos, J. (2013), *Gadamer's Poetics: A Critique of Modern Aesthetics*, New York: Bloomsbury.

Bettany, S. (2007), 'The material semiotics of consumption or where (and what) are the objects of consumer culture theory?', in R. W. Belk and J. F. Sherry (eds), *Consumer Culture Theory: Research in Consumer Behavior*, Vol. 11, Oxford: JAI Press, pp. 41–56.

Brearley, L. and I. Darso (2008), 'Business studies: Vivifying data and experience through artful approaches', in J. G. Knowles and A. L. Cole (eds), *Handbook of the Arts in Qualitative Research*, Thousand Oaks, CA: Sage, pp. 639–52.

Canniford, R. (2012), 'Poetic witness: Marketplace research through poetic transcription and poetic translation', *Marketing Theory*, **12** (4), 391–409.

Canniford, R., Riach, H. and T. Hill (2018), 'Nosenography: How smell constitutes meaning, identity and temporal experience in spatial assemblages', *Marketing Theory*, **18** (2), 234–48.

Cloke, P., Cook, I., Crang, P., Goodwin, M., Painter, J. and C. Philo (2004), *Practising Human Geography*, London: Sage.

Cole, A. L. and J. G. Knowles (2008), 'Arts-informed research', in J. G. Knowles and A. L. Cole (eds), *Handbook of the Arts in Qualitative Research*, Thousand Oaks, CA: Sage, pp. 55–70.

Cresswell, T. (2004), *Place: A Short Introduction*, Oxford: Blackwell.

Cresswell, T. and G. Hoskins (2008), 'Place, persistence, and practice: Evaluating historical significance at Angel Island, San Francisco, and Maxwell Street, Chicago', *Annals of the Association of American Geographers*, **98** (2), 392–413.

Davey, N. (2013), *Unfinished Worlds: Hermeneutics, Aesthetics and Gadamer*, Edinburgh: Edinburgh University Press.

Eisner, E. (1997), 'The promise and perils of alternative forms of data representation', *Educational Researcher*, **26** (6), 4–10.

Eisner, E. (2008), 'Art and knowledge', in J. G. Knowles and A. L. Cole (eds), *Handbook of the Arts in Qualitative Research*, Thousand Oaks, CA: Sage, pp. 3–12.

Fona, C. (2019), 'Place branding in context: Current challenges, global changes and future trends', in P. Foroudi, C. Mauri, C. Dennis and T. C. Melewar (eds), *Place Branding: Connecting Tourist Experiences to Places*, London: Routledge, pp. 325–38.

Gablik, S. (1991), *The Reenchantment of Art*, London: Thames and Hudson.

Hidalgo, M. C. and B. Hernandez (2001), 'Place attachment: Conceptual and empirical questions', *Journal of Environmental Psychology*, **21** (3), 273–81.

Jones, P. I. (2014), 'Performing sustainable transport: An artistic RIDE across the city', *Cultural Geographies*, **21** (2), 287–92.

Kavaratzis, M. (2007), 'City marketing: The past, the present and some unresolved issues', *Geography Compass*, **1** (3), 695–712.

Kavaratzis, M. (2017), *City Echoes*, artwork presented at IPBA Art Gallery, 3–5 December, Swansea.

Kavaratzis, M., Warnaby, G. and G. Ashworth (eds) (2015), *Rethinking Place Branding: Comprehensive Brand Development for Cities and Regions*, Cham: Springer International Publishing.

Lafreniere, D. and S. M. Cox (2012), '"If you can call it a poem": Toward a framework for the assessment of arts-based works', *Qualitative Research*, **13** (3), 318–36.

Latham, A. (2003), 'Research, performance, and doing human geography: Some reflections on the diary-photograph, diary-interview method', *Environment and Planning A*, **35** (11), 1993–2017.

Leavy, P. (2009), *Method Meets Art: Arts-based Research Practice*, New York: Guilford Press.

Leggo, C. (2008), 'Astonishing silence: Knowing in poetry', in J. G. Knowles and A. L. Cole (eds), *Handbook of the Arts in Qualitative Research*, Thousand Oaks, CA: Sage, pp. 165–74.

Norris, J. (2000), 'Drama as research: Realizing the potential of drama in education as a research methodology', *Youth Theatre Journal*, **14** (1), 40–51.

Oakes, S. and G. Warnaby (2011), 'Conceptualising the management and consumption of live music in urban space', *Marketing Theory*, **11** (4), 405–18.

Porteous, J. D. (1990), *Landscapes of the Mind: Worlds of Sense and Metaphor*, Toronto: University of Toronto Press.

Rokka, J., Hietanen, J. and D. Brownlie (2018), 'Screening marketing: Videography and the expanding horizons of filmic research', *Journal of Marketing Management*, **34** (5–6), 421–31.

Savin-Baden, M. and K. Wimpenny (2014), *A Practical Guide to Arts-Related Research*, Rotterdam: Sense.

Schutt, S., White, L. and S. Roberts (eds) (2017), *Advertising and Public Memory: Historical, Social and Cultural Perspectives on Ghost Signs*, London: Routledge.

Sherry, J. and J. Schouten (2002), 'A role for poetry in consumer research', *Journal of Consumer Research*, **29** (2), 218–34.

Skinner, H. (2008), 'The emergence and development of place marketing's confused identity', *Journal of Marketing Management*, **24** (9–10), 915–28.

Sleipen, W. (1988), *Marketing van de Historische Omgeving*, Breda: Netherlands Research Institute for Tourism, cited in G. J. Ashworth and H. Voogd (1990), *Selling the City: Marketing Approaches in Public Sector Urban Planning*, London: Belhaven.

Szentgyörgyi, A. and M. Kavaratzis (2017), *No Mud – No Lotus*, artwork exhibited at the IPBA Art Gallery, 3–5 December, Swansea.

Tuan, Y.-F. (1974), *Topophilia: A Study of Environmental Perception, Attitudes and Values*, New York: Columbia University Press.

Visse, M., Hansen, F. and C. Leget (2019), 'The unsayable in arts-based research: On the praxis of life itself', *International Journal of Qualitative Methods*, **18** (1), 1–13.

Warnaby, G. (2009a), 'Viewpoint: Managing the urban consumption experience?', *Local Economy*, **24** (2), 105–10.

Warnaby, G. (2009b), 'Towards a service-dominant place marketing logic', *Marketing Theory*, **9** (4), 403–23.

Warnaby, G. (2012), '"Spatial stories": Maps and the marketing of the urban experience', in L. Roberts (ed.), *Mapping Cultures: Place, Practice, Performance*, Basingstoke: Palgrave Macmillan, pp. 201–15.

Warnaby, G. (2013), 'Synchronising retail and space: Using urban squares for competitive place differentiation', *Consumption Markets and Culture*, **16** (1), 25–44.

Warnaby, G. (2017), *'Place' Brand Revenants: A Walk around Manchester*, artwork presented at IPBA Art Gallery, 3–5 December, Swansea.

Warnaby, G. (2019a), *The Stones of Manchester: An Architectural History in Place Branding*, artwork presented at IPBA Art Gallery, 27–29 November, Volos.

Warnaby, G. (2019b), 'Of time and the city: Curating urban fragments for the purposes of place marketing?', *Journal of Place Management and Development*, **12** (2), 181–96.

19 Peak place marketing: My part in its downfall

Stephen Brown

Peak peak

Peak Pilates. Peak prosecco. Peak Pinterest. Peak parkour. Peak Primark. Peak pornography. Peak pandemic. Peak pulled pork. Peak *Peppa Pig*. Peak pumpkin seeds. Peak Pot Noodle. Peak paradigm shift. Peak post-truth. Peak *Peaky Blinders*. The word peak, in its adjectival form, is the buzzword du jour. It refers to people, objects, things, passing fads that have reached their zenith in the public's estimation or popular culture more generally. And simultaneously insinuates that the passing fad is past its best, that a falling off is imminent. So popular indeed has the 'peak' descriptor become that its own apogee can't be far away. Peak peak, presumably, is just around the corner.

The life cycle of buzzwords isn't a pressing issue for most marketing scholars, even though marketing scholarship is far from short of passing fads. Thus positivism peaked in the 1990s, after the paradigm wars of the mid-1980s. Postmodernism summitted at the start of the present millennium, when it offered an expressive alternative to pseudo-scientific academic endeavour. Service-dominant logic, once seen as the saviour of marketing thought, doesn't dominate the journals the way it did a decade ago. Actor-network and assemblage theories, meanwhile, are in their pomp at present, though if marketing history is anything to go by, peak pomp is short-lived.

Place branding, as the existence of this volume bears witness, is enjoying its moment in the sun. It is, if not quite the buzzword on everyone's lips, a topic that's attracting a lot of attention. So much so, some assume it's set to continue on an ever onward, ever upward trajectory. As a booming, blooming, blossoming subject, it'll generate ever more articles, ever more anthologies, ever more special issues, ever more textbooks, conferences, monographs, interest groups, doctoral students, research grants and all the rest. Even as I write, eager researchers of a bibliometric bent are no doubt proving through article counts, citation counts, download counts and the like that place branding is not only on the up and up, but that the only way is up, up, up. And in cumulative terms they might be right, since scholarship has its own momentum. But more than a few early career marketers – those who did their doctorates on service-dominant logic, for instance – must be wondering what just happened to the paradigm that promised everything and has largely fizzled out, qualitatively speaking.

Peak place

This reflective chapter, then, explores the extent to which place marketing has peaked.[1] It doesn't do so, however, through a review of the literature. That'll be more than adequately covered in the other learned contributions to *A Research Agenda for Place Branding*. I have nothing to add to what has already been said by better place marketing scholars than me. This chapter, rather, tackles the topic through an alternative lens, a lens that has itself risen to prominence in recent years and is itself on the point of peaking, perhaps. That lens is the past. Recent years have seen a 'nostalgia boom' of unprecedented magnitude, an outbreak of yestermania that is made manifest in everything from movie remakes and retro motor cars to kitsch kitchen equipment and the vinyl album revival.[2] It is an approach that is prevalent throughout place branding, where old towns, walled cities, festival marketplaces, repurposed buildings and heritage attractions of one sort or another are a key part of the package, the product, the proposition.

As Patterson points out in his analysis of Liverpool's lauded attractions:

> The tried and tested format of such a makeover, to a cynic at least, involves: scouring the history books for points of hometown distinction; celebrating a sense of place by making local landmarks more tourist friendly; erecting plinths in honour of famous locals from the past and present; renovating and renewing public architecture, shopping precincts; and generally polishing the town's jewels, whatever they might be for public display... The danger, of course, is that if everyone follows this trajectory then it becomes a zero-sum game, one culture-led regeneration project simply cancels out another.[3]

The point of departure for the present chapter is Morris Holbrook's, 'Loving and Hating New York'.[4] Although his seminal article is rarely, if ever, cited by place branding scholars, it is a wonderfully written account of living among

Gotham's granite canyons. It is an exercise in personal topophilia, love of place, which plays an important if sometimes unsung part in the place branding process. It was love of the Dear Green Place that underpinned Glasgow's Miles Better campaign. It was love of the Big Apple that inspired Milton Glaser, a native New Yorker, to come up with the I Heart NY campaign that changed perceptions of the city and has been copied by self-promoting places the world over. It is love of Rome, Paris, Barcelona et al. that has led to the recent spate of anti-tourist protests by concerned citizens who see their home town overrun by hordes of mini-breakers, bucket listers and selfie snappers who're destroying the precious fabric of the place.[5]

My own story is rather different. However, it is illustrative in its own way because it tells the tale of someone who got involved in place branding by accident, who became a place marketer before place marketing was formally conceptualised and who was a pioneer of dark tourism for good measure. Well, that's what I tell myself. Whether you believe it or not is entirely up to you…

Peak past

Like more than a few marketing academics, I am a defrocked geographer. For my sins, which are manifold and various, I studied the subject at university. Sadly, the subject I studied bore no relation to the stuff I'd learned at school. The discipline back then was in the throes of a short-lived but very impactful 'quantitative revolution'. It was a time when statistical analysis rather than spatial awareness was the order of the day. And, having been brought up in the chaps-with-maps tradition, where oxbow lakes and occluded depressions dominated the grammar school syllabus, I found it difficult to transfer my affections to multivariate analyses of farmsteads in Iowa and hexagonal central places in southern Germany.[6] Although I did okay in the end-of-year examinations, I cared little for the ongoing assignments and workshops and field trips and such like. I failed to submit so many of them that I was in danger of defenestration, rustication, being sent down (or whatever getting the boot was called back then).

My Damascene moment occurred three years in, when the principal item on the pedagogic agenda was 'doing a dissertation'. Mooching around in the library stacks, as was my wont, I stumbled upon *Consumer Behaviour* by Engel, Kollat and Blackwell. And, as I'd always been fascinated by shops and shopping, I experienced what can only be described as an academic epiphany. Up until that point, you must understand, I hadn't the faintest inkling that shops and shopping and shopper behaviour and so on could be – and had been – studied by researchers.[7] Yet I knew, then and there, that consumer behaviour was something I wanted to investigate. For the rest of my life.

Enraptured for once, I not only immersed myself in the brave new world of 'marketing geography', but immediately made up my mind to do a doctorate in it.[8] Unfortunately, the supervisor who drew the short straw that was me, was enraptured by David Harvey's brave new world of anti-capitalism. We never really saw eye to eye and I was pretty much left to my own devices.[9] Unencumbered by taught modules in research methods, I blundered around for a few years, getting nowhere slowly. And when my maintenance grant ran out, I had to find a source of funding, fast. It was then that place branding's benison burst forth.

The centrepiece of my PhD was a questionnaire survey of every retailer in the centre of Belfast. In order to incentivise my respondents, I included a few open-ended queries about the future (i.e. how best the city centre could be revitalised). And in order to further incentivise my 1,000-plus interviewees, I approached the City Council and asked for its support (since the imprimatur of the Lord Mayor could only improve response rates).[10] Any help was welcome to shop owners back then because the sad reality was that Belfast city centre was dead on its feet. A decade of car bombs, fire bombs and drive-by shootings, coupled with security countermeasures – a ring of steel around the central shopping district, where everyone was frisked on entry – had precipitated a headlong flight from the city. Suburban shopping development was booming metaphorically while the stores that remained in the centre boomed literally.

Grasping at any passing straw, the City Council not only backed my questionnaire survey, they embraced it by employing me for the duration. I worked in the council's marketing/PR department and, when my research was complete, *A Brighter Belfast* was published under the council's official auspices. Despite a decidedly ill-timed launch, which coincided with the absolute nadir of the infamous Hunger Strikes, my study struck a chord.[11] A one-day conference was subsequently organised to build on *A Brighter Belfast* and, although the City Council rightly received all the credit, I piped up with an impassioned plea – predicated on Yi-Fu Tuan's peerless *Topophilia* – about the symbolic significance of places in general and city centres in particular. Unbeknown to me, an Undersecretary of State for Northern Ireland, one Chris Patten, was in attendance and was sufficiently impressed by my ludicrously lachrymose lament to make Belfast's revitalisation the centrepiece of his time in office. Government money was channelled into the place brand, town planners' priorities were rearranged and steps were taken to improve car parking, the physical environment, all-round beautification and what have you. A non-sectarian scheme at a time when the city's sectarian divisions were considered unbridgeable, it helped change the Northern Ireland narrative and provided a modicum of common ground that every political faction could stand on, without falling over.[12]

Although *A Brighter Belfast* was far from the first work of place branding – cities, as Ashworth shows, have been selling themselves successfully since the late nineteenth century[13] – it was one of the first such attempts in my home town. Not that it did me much good professionally. My PhD supervisor was appalled by the literary flourishes and unashamed hyperbole of *A Brighter Belfast*, deeming it a work of junk journalism rather than serious scholarship (which is what it was, in fairness to him). However, I'd earned just about enough to fund the remainder of my doctorate and, more importantly in the long term, attract the attention of the marketing department at the then Ulster Polytechnic. I was invited to give a guest lecture and, on arrival, knew right away that this was the place for a prolapsed geographer like me.

What I'm saying, in short, is that I owe my academic career to place branding, though I didn't know so at the time.

Peak present

The best part of 40 years has passed since I dipped my toe in the roiling waters of place branding. In that time, Belfast has been transformed. Although it has not escaped the travails that assail many British high streets – the long arms of Amazon, Asos, eBay, etc. stretch across the Irish Sea – nowadays it is near enough indistinguishable from analogous regional cities like Liverpool, Cardiff, Glasgow and Newcastle-upon-Tyne. Grandiose shopping malls, gleaming office blocks and glamorous international hotels are two a penny, as are the seemingly obligatory sports stadiums, concert halls, indoor arenas, convention centres, multiplex cinemas, dockland redevelopments, inner-city apartment complexes, renovated and spec built both. The rubble-strewn streets of yore have been pedestrianised, plantered, paviored, prettified; public transportation has been transformed thanks to Belfast's bright purple 'bendy buses', aka Gliders; and, bicycles for hire are everywhere, though most seem to be drawn, like spawning salmon, to the lower reaches of the River Lagan, where they are dumped by disgruntled riders and dredged up by downcast council workers wearing waders.

Belfast, in effect, has pursued the three-part place branding process spelled out by Ashworth. Hardly a week goes by without an *event occasion* of sorts, be it parade, performance or protest march (the city is particularly adept at the latter). Urban *design statements* are ubiquitous – every roundabout's a plinth, every bollard's a billboard, every gable end's an oil painting (near enough). And *personal associations* are celebrated with bombastic immodesty, most notably the C. S. Lewis Square in east Belfast, not far from the childhood home of Narnia's renowned nurturer (his walk-in 'wardrobe', by the way, is in the library at nearby Queen's University).

In promotional terms, too, Belfast hasn't been backward about coming forward. Expensive advertising campaigns tout the city's inestimable attractions, especially around Christmastime. Extravagant claims are made about Belfast's incomparable ability to attract conferences, conventions, cruise ships and city-breakers. Euphoric headlines are guaranteed when the city appears on one of the many top-ten, must-see, hidden-gem lists, inventories, rankings and the like that infest the hospitality industry every January, February, March and monthly thereafter. Every so often, moreover, the city is rebranded at enormous expense and with sufficient edginess to set social media alight about the risible slogan, ludicrous logo and lavish launch events that waste public money when bins aren't being emptied and roads are full of potholes. Never mind the quality of commentary, feel the width of column inches:

> Belfast has been named one of the top places to visit in Europe. The city is fourth in a new list compiled by leading review site TripAdvisor. Belfast beat Edinburgh, which was ranked ninth, and Dublin, which came in at number 10 on the list. The top-ranked city was Tromso in Norway, with St Petersburg in Russia second and Santorini in Greece third. Belfast came next with Funchal in Portugal ranked fifth for travel experiences.[14]

Place race notwithstanding, there's more than a little grit in my home town's urban oyster. Perhaps the most striking thing about the Belfast brand is that it is deeply steeped in darkness. Although there is a 'don't mention the war' mentality among the city's place marketing master planners – Belfast is bright, buzzing, bouncy, beautiful, bedazzling, don't you know! – its urban selling proposition is ultimately predicated on the menacing image that the town acquired during the Troubles and is periodically re-enforced by intermittent upticks in inter-tribal hostilities.[15] A punishment beating here, a score settled there, a rent-a-mob riot during the so-called 'marching season'. All is grist to the dark marketing mill. As is Belfast's seemingly ineradicable soft spot for home-grown 'bad boys' like George Best, Alex Higgins and Gary Moore, the hard-rockin' hedonist of Thin Lizzy fame.

Unsurprisingly, perhaps, the city's foremost tourist attractions include the ill-named Peace Lines, gigantic Berlin Wall-esque barricades between scores of rival communities; the equally monumental Murals, open-air art galleries that primarily depict scenes of paramilitary intent and serve as territorial markers in a still segregated city; a decommissioned Victorian gaol which offers guided tours of its manifold morbid attractions, death cell and trap door included; and, needless to say, a veritable flotilla of open-top double-decker buses, which not only circumnavigate the former hotspots where sectarian factions fought themselves to a standstill back in the day, but also allow *plein air* passengers to partake of the town's signature climatic conditions, black sheets of stair-rod rainfall, with thunder and lightning thrown in for free.

As if that weren't enough, the jewel in Belfast's crown of thorns is a £100 million visitors' centre devoted to RMS *Titanic*, the legendary ocean liner that was built in the city, sank in less than three hours on its maiden voyage and lies entombed, spread-eagled, rusticle-ridden beneath the bitterly cold waters of the north Atlantic. Opened in 2012 to commemorate the centenary of the catastrophe, Titanic Belfast attracts approximately 1 million paying visitors per year. Thanks to its striking, iceberg-shaped architecture, moreover, the building serves as a symbol of the unsinkable city that sustains it, much as the Opera House and Armadillo do for Sydney and Glasgow, respectively. Although the term Dark Tourism is avoided like the Black Death by Belfast's brand managers, few would deny that the ghost of the *Titanic* is the city's genius loci.

Peak future

As you've probably gathered, I'm a modest man who has much to be modest about.[16] But when it comes to the Belfast place brand, I was on the money in one important respect. Forty years ago, when I was working on *A Brighter Belfast*, I concluded that the ring of steel around the city centre had tourist-attracting potential, as did many of the other Troubles-era artefacts. These scandalous suggestions, needless to say, were dismissed out of hand at the time. Ditto the seriously sick puppy who suggested them. But when it comes to dark tourism, I was well ahead of the game. Modestly, admittedly.

In my proven capacity as a soothsayer of sorts, it therefore falls to me to forecast the future of place branding. And, in that regard, a trio of preliminary points is worth noting. The first of these is that, far from being a fast-growing, forging-ahead, bright-future field of marketing endeavour, place marketing has peaked. North Korea possibly excepted, there can't be a nation, region, city, town, village, hamlet or hole in the hedge that doesn't have a place marketing policy in place. These place marketing policies, what's more, suffer from the Same Difference Syndrome where 'much of a muchness meets seen one seen 'em all'.[17] And while these me-too place marketing policies can be and doubtless will be refreshed, reinvigorated, reimagined on a regular basis, there are next to no fresh fields to conquer (unless of course they start branding individual fields, hedgerows, drainage ditches and so forth).[18]

Set against this, second, is the simple fact that the growing shortfall of physical places in need of marketing's ministrations is not an impediment to future development or further growth. Thanks to the incredible, and incessant, creativity of the culture industries – movie makers, novel writers, television producers, video games designers, Netflix fixers and so forth – there is an ever expanding archipelago of fictional, fanciful, phantasmagorical places that can be and are being colonised by the conceptual conquistadors of marketing. New Zealand's embrace of 100 per cent Middle Earth is testament to the truism that, when it comes to space invaders, Kotler is Cortes, Cook and Columbus combined.

Third, and perhaps most importantly, there is ample scope for 'solving the problems' of place marketing. Not unlike the pharmaceutical industry, which creates ills to sell pills and, in due course, develops money-spinning antidotes to the addictions its analgesics accelerate,[19] so too place marketing consultants can capitalise on the unconscionable outcomes of over-eager place race profiteering. Place marketing may or may not be a spatial Ponzi scheme but it's not a million miles from three card monte, where places are patsies, scholars are shills and capitalism's the calculating con artist.

Consider the case of 'overtourism'. Recently anointed an *Oxford English Dictionary* word of the year, overtourism refers to an excessive number of visitors at celebrated locations who damage the environment and adversely affect residents' wellbeing. Barcelona, Venice, Rome, Bath, Edinburgh, Amsterdam, Paris, Oxford and many other iconic destinations are suffering from a surfeit of popularity, as are must-see sites such as the Taj Mahal, Machu Picchu, Angkor Wat, the Great Wall of China, Istanbul's Blue Mosque, Bavaria's Neuschwanstein Castle, one of the inspirations for Disneyland's centrepiece, and Hallstatt in the Austrian Alps, widely believed to be the model for Arendelle in *Frozen*.[20]

Even the ends of the earth aren't immune. Apart from the growing popularity of package tours to polar regions, which are adversely affecting their delicate ecosystems, few sights are more shocking than that captured by photographer Nirmal Purja in May 2019, when a queue of 320 crampon-clad, Goretex-swaddled, oxygen tank-akimbo climbers stood in line at the Hillary Step, waiting for their turn to conquer Mount Everest and capture the moment with an Instagrammable commemorative photograph. Hesitant as I am to use the words peak peak, I did predict their appearance at the outset…

Be that as it may, the causes of this crush rush condition are copious.[21] Purported culprits include overpopulation, Airbnb, bucket-list compilers, mini-break barkers, low-cost airline operators, selfie stick-wielding social media manes and, in a seemingly unseemly outbreak of gross national stereotyping, the irrepressible wanderlust of China's itchy-footed, increasingly affluent middle classes.

Although the scapegoating of China's happy wanderers is unconscionable, and although the proselytes of place marketing must surely be held accountable for a situation that they are partially responsible for, overtourism is an opportunity as well as an indictment. One of marketing's most imperishable rules of thumb involves turning negatives into positives, threats into triumphs, perils into pearls.

And in classic 'here's one we prepared earlier' fashion, marketing has a concept up its sleeve that can be tailored to suit the overtourism situation. That concept is demarketing, yes, demarketing. Written 50 years ago by the Crick and Watson of marketing scholarship, Kotler and Levy's construct deals with conditions where demand exceeds supply and how managers can best discourage consumers without disaffecting them. Taking Bali as an example, they reveal how the island sought to avoid overtourism by pricing middle-class consumers out of its market. Affordable accommodation was expressly eschewed in favour of luxury hotels, swanky restaurants and advertising in high-end magazines and, by doing so, Bali kept the undesirables at bay.[22]

Kotler and Levy's lessons have not been lost on today's top-tier attractions. Many are going down the demarketing route, whether it be Bath demanding £100 from every tourist bus that trundles through its Grade 1 Georgian thoroughfares, or Edinburgh's £2 per person per diem tax on overnight stays in its hotels, hostels and Airbnbs, or Florence's €300 fine for visitors who eat takeaway food in the streets – how dare they, the barbarians! – or, for that matter, Santorini's cap on the number of cruise ships its deep-water caldera can accommodate, which aims to reduce the number of daily visitors from 10,000 to 8,000 on average.

Place marketing may have peaked, my friends, but destination demarketing is just getting started! Doubtless dozens of dedicated destination demarketing consultancies are being established as I write. Breakdown With Brown is awaiting your call.

Peak off

Such endeavours are all fine and dandy. And will prove profitable, presumably. The only problem, as the luxury goods industry bears witness, is that such impositions can increase rather than decrease demand. Just as there is a waiting list for the waiting list for Hermès Birkin handbags, so too denying tourists access to Australia's incomparable Uluru or Thailand's exquisite Maya Bay, where *The Beach* was filmed, or New Zealand's Mount Ngauruhoe, the active volcano that played Mount Doom in *Lord of the Rings*, makes them more desirable not less and, in so doing, provides ample opportunities for unscrupulous tour operators and shady activity more generally.

Nor, for that matter, should scholars overlook the appeal of consumer scrimmaging. There is a widespread assumption that consumers can't and won't tolerate the overcrowding on, say, Barcelona's Las Ramblas or Rome's Spanish Steps or at the entrances to Dubrovnik's old town. Yet the mobs of bargain seekers in Primark on a Saturday afternoon, or in Asda on Black Friday, or outside H&M when the store releases its annual capsule collection by big name fashion designers, are testament to the love-to-hate mentality – the madness of the crowd – that denial marketing can and does engender.[23]

So where do we go from here? Well, Belfast for starters, since my home town's in that happy-clappy state where visitors are still very welcome. The more the merrier. Overtourism is not something Belfast frets about. But if that doesn't tickle your fancy, look no further than photoshopping, virtual reality and deep fake video technology. Taken together, these can convey the impression of visiting must-see places without the expense and inconvenience of going there. If, as Bucks reports, more than 40 per cent of Brits gild the lily about their globetrotting, by claiming that they've been to all sorts of glamorous destinations when they've done nothing of the kind, then there's an opportunity there for faux place marketers like me.[24]

In this respect, phoney place marketers might be advised to consider the contentions of French literary theorist Pierre Boyard, who argues that most places are best not visited.[25] In *How to Talk about Places You've Never Been*, he notes that quite a few of the world's most renowned explorers – Marco Polo and Chateaubriand among them – never actually made it to the places they wrote about so eloquently and, if they had actually done so, their influential works of travel writing would have been less impressive, less imperishable, less impactful than they proved to be. Flights of fictional fantasy, he observes from his swaddling armchair, are infinitely better than those that involve close encounters with back-breaking, exhaustion-inducing, mosquito-assailed reality.

And I for one agree with him. Have I been to Dubrovnik? Hell no. Have I visited the Great Barrier Reef? Get a grip. Have mine eyes seen the glory of the Taj Mahal at eventide? In Belfast's Indian restaurant of that name, yes, yes, and thrice yes. You should try it sometime.

The place race is best pursued sitting down. Ideally with a good book to hand. A book like *A Research Agenda for Place Branding*. You read it here first.

Notes

1. For the purposes of this chapter, I'm using the terms 'brand' and 'marketing' interchangeably. Yes, I know there are differences between them, but they are near enough synonymous. Indulge me.
2. Retro, I reckon, has pretty much peaked, though many marketing scholars appear to think otherwise. History shows that nostalgia comes and goes in waves and, with an unavoidable lag, academic interest is sure to follow suit.
3. Patterson, A. (2010), 'Extreme cultural and marketing makeover: Liverpool home edition', in D. O'Reilly and F. Kerrigan (eds), *Marketing the Arts: A Fresh Approach*, London: Routledge, p. 241.
4. Holbrook, M. B. (1993), 'Loving and hating New York: Some reflections on the Big Apple', *International Journal of Research in Marketing*, **11** (4), 381–5. Morris has written a lot about places, albeit his brilliant contributions often go unacknowledged.
5. See, for example: *The Economist* (2016), 'Nothing to see here', 13 August, p. 53; Bleach, S. (2019), 'Hell is other people', *Sunday Times Magazine*, 8 August, pp. 30–9.
6. Okay, I eventually warmed up to central places and once wrote a paper on the subject. Its title, if I say so myself, was brilliant. But is 'Christaller Knew My Father' worth reading? Of course not!
7. The school I attended was very traditional in its subject offerings. Business was way, way beyond the pale. Even economics was deeply suspect. I studied geography because I was good at it. But shopping was something I'd loved since childhood. The environment more than the experience, admittedly.
8. Enraptured by my Engel, Kollat and Blackwell encounter, I soon discovered that there was a small group of United Kingdom geographers, dominated at the time

by John Dawson and Ross Davies, who toiled away in the retailing trenches. Their research students went on to great things.

9. I don't want to give the wrong impression. My supervisor was an outstanding scholar. And a very decent man to boot. But we weren't right for each other.

10. My grand plans backfired abysmally, needless to say. The Lord Mayor's seal of approval – I wrote the covering letter, with his signature attached – adversely affected response rates. It transpired that he had only gone and cut the annual Christmas promotional budget! Many city centre retailers were miffed, to put it politely, by his decision to play Scrooge rather than Santa with the council's coffers. I paid the price. Hey-ho-ho-ho. You live and learn.

11. Our findings, believe it or not, were released on the day of Bobby Sands' funeral. Headlines were few, unsurprisingly.

12. I was subsequently conscripted by the strategic arm of the town planning service. Hey, I needed the money to finish my thesis! Suffice it to say, I didn't fit in. Round peg, square hole. You know how it goes.

13. Ashworth, G. J. (2009), 'The instruments of place branding: How is it done?', *European Spatial Research and Policy*, **16** (1), 9–22.

14. Campbell, B. (2018), 'Troubles tours help Belfast to top four spot on tourism list', *The Belfast Telegraph*, 24 August, p. 3.

15. Brown, S., McDonagh, P. and C. J. Shultz (2013), 'A brand so bad it's good: The paradoxical place marketing of Belfast', *Journal of Marketing Management*, **29** (11/12), 1251–76.

16. Apart from failing to impress my PhD supervisor, I made the elementary error of studying qualitative matters with quantitative methods. In my day, there were no taught components on doctoral programmes. I learned by trial and error. Error mostly.

17. See Dinnie, K. (2007), *Nation Branding: Concepts, Issues, Practice*, Oxford: Butterworth-Heinemann.

18. Don't laugh, it is already happening in my neck of the woods, where the 'Dark Hedges', a local beauty spot which featured in *Game of Thrones*, is not only on the brandwagon but suffering from overtourism.

19. The shocking marketing shenanigans of the pharmaceutical industry are brilliantly exposed by Ben Goldacre (2012) in his frightening book *Bad Pharma: How Medicine Is Broken and How We Can Fix It*, London: Fourth Estate.

20. Humphries, W. (2019), 'Bath goes cold on coach party tourists', *The Times*, 24 December, p. 3; Hutton, A. (2020), 'Fairytale alpine village gets the shivers and begs Frozen tourists to stay away', *The Sunday Times*, 5 January, p. 18.

21. Turner, J. (2019), 'Bucket lists are killing the places we love', *The Times*, 17 August, p. 31.

22. Kotler, P. and S. J. Levy (1971), 'Demarketing, yes, demarketing', *Harvard Business Review*, **49** (6), 74–80.

23. On denial marketing, see my *Free Gift Inside* or, better yet, R. B. Cialdini's (2001), *Influence: Science and Practice*, Boston, MA: Allyn and Bacon.

24. Bucks, J. (2020), 'Forty per cent of Britons fib about fake holidays', *Mail on Sunday*, 5 January, p. 27.

25. Boyard, P. (2016), *How to Talk about Places You've Never Been: On the Importance of Armchair Travel*, London: Bloomsbury.

Index